STEALING
HISTORY

STEALING HISTORY

Tomb Raiders, Smugglers, and
the Looting of the Ancient World

Roger Atwood

ST. MARTIN'S PRESS   NEW YORK

www.stmartins.com

Frontispiece: The looted Sipán backflap (photograph courtesy of the Museo Tumbas Reales de Sipán)

Book design by Phil Mazzone

Map by Paul J. Pugliese

Library of Congress Cataloging-in-Publication Data

Atwood, Roger.
    Stealing history : tomb raiders, smugglers, and the looting of the ancient world/ Roger Atwood.—1st U.S. ed.
        p.   cm.
    Includes bibliographical references (p. 315) and index (p. 323).
    ISBN 0-312-32406-5
    EAN 978-0312-32406-3
    1. Archaeological thefts.   2. Art thefts.   3. Cultural property—Protection. I. Title.

CC135.A85 2004
364.16'2—dc22

2004050862

First Edition: December 2004

10 9 8 7 6 5 4 3 2 1

For my mother

How can we live without our lives?
How will we know it's us without our past?

JOHN STEINBECK, The Grapes of Wrath

CONTENTS

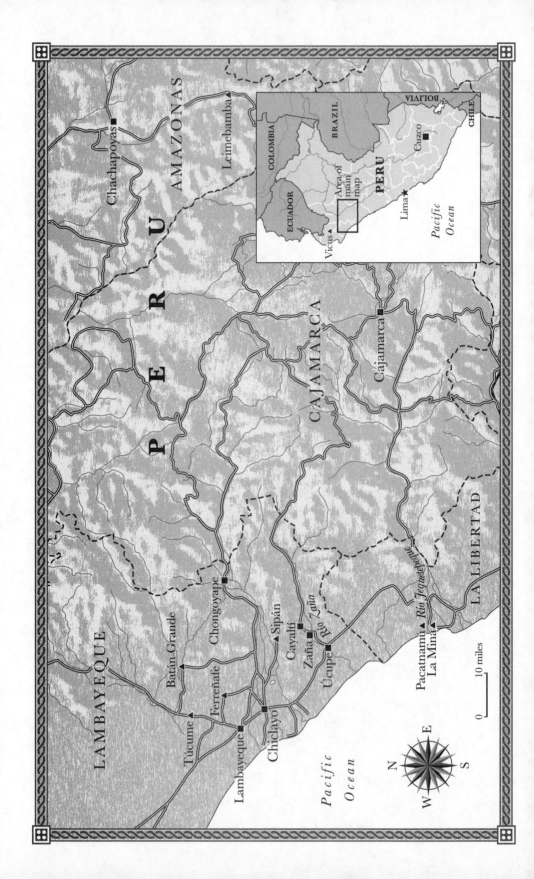

STEALING
HISTORY

Introduction

LOOTERS IN THE TEMPLE

THE FIRST SIGN we were approaching the ruins of Isin in southern Iraq was the motorcycles that came buzzing down the dirt road in the opposite direction. Each one carried a driver, a passenger, and a bulging saddlebag draped over the back fender. A few bicycles came along, each with a rider, his head wrapped in a scarf, and more saddlebags. Then a big cattle truck trundled by, carrying a pack of men in the flatbed in soiled white robes and holding more bulging sacks that swayed as the truck bumped along.

It was one month after the fall of Saddam Hussein. In Baghdad, American tanks rumbled down the crowded streets, bombed-out government buildings lined the Tigris like charred skeletons, and merchants sat languorously by their shop doors with assault rifles to guard against thieves. At night a curfew kept the streets empty, and at dawn they filled again with Iraqis starting their day in the sour, chemical odor of smoldering pools of oil torched by Saddam's forces outside the city to send up curtains of smoke and foil American aerial bombers. The National Museum of Antiquities, facing an intersection that had been one of the city's worst battlefields between Saddam loyalists and the Americans, was in shambles. Thieves had swept in during the last days of fighting and stolen about 13,000 objects, nothing like the 170,000 reported in the first, overheated stories but still a huge loss that included icons of ancient Mesopotamian art—the Warka vase, the hauntingly placid image of a woman in marble known as the Lady of Warka, the lower torso of a man in cast copper known as the Basetki statue that thieves dragged down a marble staircase, breaking each stair along the way. The most famous pieces, including those three, were of course impossible to sell and were abandoned or quietly returned to the museum within months, but thousands of smaller and less famous objects were gone. Thieves had ransacked the administrative offices, rifled through storerooms, crowbarred open steel safes.

An odd, only-in-wartime mix of people had since been gathering at the ruined museum: buzz-cut American soldiers, shy Iraqi curators, reporters and television crews of a dozen nationalities, and a stream of international cultural eminences, including the director of the British Museum and sunburnt archaeologists, all coming to assess the damage, prevent more looting, and start piecing back together one of the Middle East's great museums.[1]

In those dazed, nervous weeks after Saddam's fall, the first, quite unbelievable reports about the looting of archaeological sites began reaching us at the museum. Rumors held that all over Iraq, and especially at Sumerian sites in the south, the guards appointed by Saddam's government had fled in the first days of the U.S. and British bombardment and hundreds of looters had rampaged in, digging up the sites for artifacts, destroying the work done by archaeologists over decades, ripping out sackfuls of treasures. This was not at one or two sites, but at dozens of them. Few people had actually seen it. The looters were armed with assault rifles and prepared to kill intruders, the American military told me and others. They advised us not to go.

"They'll have no compunctions about throwing you into one of their holes and burying you alive," an American army officer, Captain William Sumner, told me.

It all sounded too automatic, a bit too on-cue to be real: the guards leave, looters enter en masse, they start digging up everything. The theft at the National Museum had proved to be an embarrassing exaggeration, one that would wreck the credibility of more than a few self-appointed culture saviors, so I could not help being skeptical about the next breathless chapter in the supposed rape of Iraq's priceless heritage.

More motor scooters buzzed past, with more sacks.

"Looters, every one of them. Look at all they're carrying out," said Susanne Osthoff, an archaeologist. There was alarm in her voice.

Four millennia ago, Isin was a Babylonian Lourdes, a place for the sick to come to be healed. It attracted the lame, the arthritic, and the chronically ill who came to pray to the city's patron goddess, Gula, to deliver them from pain. Archaeologists found bones all over the site with signs of deformity, trauma, and disease. Now Isin was little more than a set of eroded, sandy mounds, a city betrayed by the Euphrates that used to flow nearby but shifted course over the centuries and left it high and dry in the desert.

In 1990 Osthoff was a graduate student in archaeology at the Ludwig-Maximilians Universität in Munich and worked with a team of German researchers to answer the mysteries of Isin. Iraq was then a lively locus of research, with the Americans at Nippur, the British at Abu Salabikh, the Germans at Isin, and distinguished Iraqi archaeologists at all sites working to broaden the knowledge we have today about how Mesopotamians invented writing and agriculture, tamed wild animals and put them to the service of man as livestock, and created the first classical images of women. It was some of the most important work in the history of archaeology. The end of that era came in 1990, the last year of major excavations in Iraq under the old rules, when Saddam Hussein invaded Kuwait and the United Nations imposed on Iraq the international sanctions that threw the country into total isolation, cutting it off from virtually all foreign financing and cultural exchange. The research ceased, the archaeologists stopped coming, and all through the 1990s, looters started creeping down the carefully excavated shafts, shoveling out the soil to find treasures, digging new holes, ransacking ancient graves, temples, and dwellings by night. They sold what they found to middlemen who took the pieces to the world's great clearinghouses for looted antiquities in Switzerland and Britain, and eventually to the United States. Iraqi antiquities, once a rarity on the market, began finding their way to European and American galleries, collections, and online auction sites. In May 2003, Susanne Osthoff, a tall, elegant woman whom I had first noticed in the Baghdad museum chatting in beautiful Arabic with the employees, had returned to Iraq to deliver medical supplies on behalf of a German humanitarian agency and to check out reports that her old study site was being systematically destroyed by looters.

When the men who had worked as security guards for the Germans saw Susanne in the Shiite town of Afak that morning for the first time in fourteen years, they could barely believe their eyes and embraced her with speechless affection, as if her presence meant that Saddam was really gone. With that ceremoniousness of rural Iraqis, they invited us to a traditional meal with their families: tabouleh, eggplant, and freshly slaughtered chicken on platters spread out on a mat. Yes, they told us, looters had taken over the site. There were hundreds of them, working without fear. Now and then people with big cars and satellite phones came from Baghdad to buy what the looters had found. American troops had taken over the district mayor's palace in Afak and made it their headquarters for the area, ringed the building with tanks and armored personnel carriers, and sent armed patrols through the town. But they had made no effort to stop the destruction of Isin.

The Iraqi guards took their Kalashnikov submachine guns and escorted us to the site. Within a few hours, we were all approaching the ruined Sumerian city in a white Hilux pickup. Pits dug and abandoned by looters started appearing by the roadside. Then more pits until finally, when we reached the mound that marked where the Temple of Gula used to stand, the land was pockmarked with holes. We parked and saw the heads of young men popping out of some of the nearest holes.

Susanne charged up the mound, her veil trailing in the wind behind her, and let out a short scream.

"They are destroying the site, destroying it! Twenty-five years of work is being ruined," she said. My interpreter, Azher Taher, and I looked at each other incredulously and ran up behind her, and then came the bodyguards with their rifles.

Looters were swarming all over the temple. They crawled up out of their holes, emerged from behind mounds of backfill, came running toward us from every direction in robes and turbans, shouting with excitement and carrying knives and shovels. Atop other mounds off in the distance, more bands of looters stood stark against the horizon, waving their arms at us. There were no guards or police of any kind, and the nearest American troops were twenty miles away in Afak.

We followed Susanne and found ourselves walking along parapets between giant pits. We counted about two hundred holes, some of them twenty or thirty feet deep, but gave up counting after a while and contemplated the riddled landscape stretching for a mile or so in every direction. Some pits seemed to branch off into tunnels, some curved, and some were too deep to see the bottom. A few pits looked so meticulously cut on their sides that they could only be the remnants of archaeological work.

We looked down into one hole that trailed off into a rough, stone bottom.

"This was where I worked. This was the temple floor," said Susanne, pointing down.

On the far side of the mound, maybe two hundred feet away, a white pickup was parked. A man got out and stood there with an assault rifle, as if to let us know who was in charge. We tried to ignore him and walked along the narrow ridges running between the pits. The looters seemed to think we were buyers, for they approached us to offer us things they had found that day: a clay tablet bearing an inscription in cuneiform, the world's oldest form of writing ($100), an exquisite little cylinder seal made of black hematite stone ($200), a clay votive plaque with an image of the goddess Ishtar ($500). Each would bring thousands of dollars in New York or London. Cylinder seals like the black hematite one, about the size of a wine cork, could sell for $30,000.

"When did all this looting start?" I asked one looter, a young man with a tired look and several days' beard growth. He had not stopped digging long enough to sleep.

"When Saddam Hussein fell," he said, with Azher interpreting.

"Did this ever happen when Saddam was in power?"

"Only at night, and only a few people. Now we can dig all day. Many people are coming to do it."

"Were friends of yours ever caught looting in Saddam's day?"

"Yes."

"What happened to them?"

"They were executed."

Another looter who looked to be no more than fifteen years old told me he had been digging every day for a week.

"I heard everyone was coming here, so I came," he said. He had found a small tablet, he said, making a square on his palm about the size of a matchbox, and sold it for $50 to a rich man who came in his car, but the other looters said he should have demanded more.

There was a giddy, ecstatic feeling in the air, the feeling of young men digging for their fortune and expecting to find it any minute. "Saddam is gone! Saddam is gone!" a few shouted spontaneously in Arabic, as if the news were still sinking in. The house nearby where archaeologists and their staff once lived was itself a looted, abandoned shell, its roof, plumbing, and fixtures all ripped out.[2]

While he ruled, Saddam Hussein took pains in his own homicidal way to protect his country's ancient sites from antiquities hunters, according to many archaeologists. He had his own reasons, of course. Saddam cast himself as a modern-day Nebuchadnezzar, heir to the glories of Mesopotamia, a man so blinded by his own megalomaniacal folly that, at the reconstructed ruins of Babylon, he inscribed bricks with his name, just as successive rulers did at the real Babylon in antiquity. In billboards all over Baghdad, he stood smiling in front of the Dome of the Rock in a doctored photograph meant to evoke Nebuchadnezzar's own biblical siege of Jerusalem and the expulsion of its Jews in 587 B.C. Along the roof of his main palace, at the center of a complex of parks and buildings entered through a sandstone arch known as Assassin's Gate, and which later became the U.S. occupation force headquarters, Saddam erected four gargantuan metal busts of himself dressed in fantasy garb of a headdress and shirt meant to make him look like the scourge of the Crusaders, Saladin.[3] It was historical memory put to the service of a fascist political agenda, and anything that archaeologists could dig up to lend legitimacy to that agenda was welcome. In 1998 vandals decapitated the stone statue of a winged bull with the head of a king, complete with crown, at the ruins of Khorsabad in northern Iraq. They intended to sell the head, but soon Interpol learned of the theft and published photographs of the head on its Web site. The piece became unmarketable. Saddam's police tracked down the head, now in thirteen pieces, in a house in Mosul and arrested ten of the supposed looters. All were executed.

"He who chops off the head of a king shall lose his own head," Saddam was reported to have said in official Iraqi media. The only Iraqis I met who seemed sad to see him go were archaeologists. "He supported the museum adequately, this is true. It has to be said," Donny George, research director of the Baghdad museum, told me. "We got almost everything we wanted. When people would present [archaeological] things to him as gifts, he would return them to the museum."[4]

All over Iraq, looters took Saddam's disappearance as a signal to descend on ancient sites and turn them inside out to find artifacts. The speed of the destruction was stunning. At the ruins of the Sumerian city of Umma, looters overran the site as soon as American and British air raids began, and three hundred were still there a few weeks later when University of Chicago archaeologist McGuire Gibson arrived on a U.S. military helicopter to inspect the site.[5] Hundreds of men were sinking holes into the remains of the ancient city of Adab.[6] At the ruins of Nippur, Susanne Osthoff and I climbed the eroded, mud-brick platform known as a ziggurat, the once-mighty Babylonian tower that Hebrew exiles thought an impious attempt to reach heaven and inspired the story of the Tower of Babel. Looters had dug at least three deep pits nearby, not bad compared to the hundreds elsewhere but ominously the first ever to appear at Nippur in more than forty years of scientific excavation at the remote site,[7] which, when we visited, was guarded by one frightened old man in a kaffiyeh with an assault rifle dating from the war with Iran twenty years before. At the ruins of the Roman-era city of Hatra, north of Baghdad, looters with good stonecutting equipment hoisted a ladder to the apex of an arch and carved out a sculpture of a man's face. It has disappeared, presumably sold.

Everywhere I went in Iraq that month, the trickle of plunder that began after the Gulf War in 1991 had become a flood. I visited six sites, and all were under some kind of attack by looters, some dismantled in a spasmodic wave of destruction as at Isin, others under piecemeal assault.

A week after seeing the pillage in the south, Azher and I drove straight north from Baghdad, past Saddam's hometown of Tikrit and the gracefully spiraling minaret of Samarra, to the city of Mosul. Chinooks and Black Hawks rattled overhead all day, and grimly businesslike American soldiers in beige fatigues stopped lines of cars to search for weapons and fleeing Baathist diehards. The occupation felt raw here, more in-your-face than in Baghdad.

A short drive south of Mosul, the ruins of the legendary, 3,500-year-old city of Nimrud stood amid gently rolling hills overlooking the Tigris valley. Enormous winged sphinxes carved in stone mark the entrance to the palace of Assurnasirpal II, its walls formed by massive slabs of polished stone bearing images in low relief of kings and deities and cuneiform inscriptions recounting centuries of conquests and heroic exploits. The Old Testament calls it "the principal city" of the Assyrian empire that ravaged neighboring kingdoms from Persia to Egypt.[8] For a few centuries, Nimrud was the center of power and wealth for much of southwest Asia.

And then, as empires have a way of doing, it collapsed. Nimrud was sacked by the Babylonians in 612 B.C., and the Assyrian realm disappeared forever. Some of the city's loveliest artifacts, including an enigmatic carving of a smiling woman known as the Mona Lisa of Nimrud, date from this era and were found at the bottom of a well inside the palace. Archaeologists speculated that residents threw their prize possessions down the pit rather than see them grabbed by the invaders.

No one was going to sack Nimrud now. Half a platoon of U.S. soldiers guarded the roofless and overgrown site with M-4 rifles firing 50-caliber armor-piercing incendiary rounds, two Humvees equipped with antitank gunner positions, seven shoulder-fired antipersonnel missiles, 40mm grenade launchers, and thermal imaging devices that could spot a person, night or day, within ten kilometers.

"We've got so much armament in here, it's unreal," said the commanding officer at Nimrud, Lieutenant Cory Roberts, a serious, compact Texan who sounded at times like he had just emerged from a Pentagon briefing. "Our orders are to protect key resources, whether it's oil or medical shipments or the cultural treasures that belong to the Iraqi people like this one, and that's what we're doing."

I could say for sure that Nimrud was, at that moment, the best-guarded archaeological site in the world. Problem was, the posse arrived a bit late. Looters first entered the site on April 11, two days after the fall of Saddam Hussein, and hacked out a chunk of a stone frieze showing a winged man carrying a sponge and a holy plant. It's a distinctively Nimrud image, one that a buyer anywhere in the world would have to know was looted from this site, and yet the piece has disappeared.

"They knew just what they wanted. They ignored everything else, went right to that frieze, and took it," said Muzahim Mahmud, the Iraqi director of the site.

The attack had all the markings of customized looting, a band of well-equipped stonecutters venturing into the ruins to remove a specific piece on orders of a buyer who had put in his request in advance. Mahmud, an archaeologist of about sixty with a thatch of white hair and a polite, courtly air, brought in two armed guards, but over the next three weeks the looters kept returning to threaten them. The Americans were too thin on the ground to help.

"The thieves would come at night and shoot at us. We heard them shouting, 'Go away, leave this place,'" said Moufak Mohammed, a guard, who stayed day and night in a dilapidated trailer at the site.

On the night of May 3, Mohammed and the other guard awoke to the sound of hammers inside the palace. Looters had broken in. The guards fired in the air to scare them away, but the looters blasted the guards' station with Kalashnikov assault rifles—Mohammed showed me the thirty bullet holes in the trailer's metal siding. Outnumbered and outgunned, the guards retreated. For three hours, the looters had the run of the place, carving out pieces of two more stone friezes and damaging others that they apparently started to cut but gave up on, maybe realizing their equipment wasn't sufficient for the job. Again, they bypassed galleries of stone reliefs and went deep inside the complex, as if they knew precisely what they wanted and where it was.

The next day, after urgent pleas from the director of the well-respected Antiquities Museum in Mosul, the Americans arrived with a full infantry battalion. Hyped or not, the looting of the National Museum had proved to be a huge international embarrassment for the Americans, and they wanted to show they could prevent more disasters like it.

When I visited Nimrud, two weeks after the American troops arrived, Mahmud gave me a lecture-tour of the site like a professor giving a master class on Assyrian history as Roberts, in fatigues and a Kevlar vest, hovered around us and corrected Mahmud on dates or details of the looting. Mahmud graciously ignored him. I sensed that Roberts and Mahmud didn't entirely trust each other but had formed an uneasy alliance to keep the looters at bay. When I asked Mahmud if he was concerned about having so much military hardware next to such a fragile and irreplaceable cultural asset, he seemed surprised at the question.

"No, I am not worried," he said. "If the Americans leave, then the robbers will come and steal everything. Then I will worry."

I was impressed by the earnestness of Roberts and his men in protecting Nimrud. One had embarked on a project to photograph the entire site and had so far filled nine compact discs. I asked Roberts, What will happen when the American troops leave? Won't the looters all come back? "Well, that's the concern," he said. His strategy was to embolden the Iraqi security guards by withdrawing his troops to about thirty yards inside the site, so that if an intruder tried to enter, the first line of defense would be the security guards, not the Americans. I wasn't sure it would work, but Roberts didn't seem to have any other ideas for battling a foe that could easily afford to wait and outlast his platoon in this isolated place.

"The guards are from villages around here," said Roberts. "They're scared to shoot at looters. The looters come here and tell the guards, 'If you shoot us, we'll kill you,' and they will. That's what we're up against."

Facing enough American artillery to stop a tank column, the agents of the antiquities trade had not given up. Early one morning, Roberts caught a young man whom he assumed was an antiquities hunter hanging around the entrance to the palace, as if testing the troops. The man left without incident. Often the guard Mohammed still heard strange voices outside the site at night.

"They'll be back, you can be sure," said Roberts.

Looting robs a country of its heritage, but, even worse, it destroys everyone's ability to know about the past. When ancient sites are excavated carefully and methodically by trained archaeologists, all of humanity can gain an understanding into how those societies lived, how they worshiped, how they raised their children, what they valued. Most of what we know about ancient life has been gained in this way. Through modern archaeology we know that Iraqis invented the wheel about 3000 B.C., that Vikings reached America five centuries before Columbus, that humans first crossed from Asia to Alaska about fourteen thousand years ago and filled the American continent within a few centuries, that the Incas practiced a form of brain surgery, that plagues of European diseases like smallpox swept through Indian settlements in Florida a few years before any Europeans arrived there, that early Mexicans took a weed and cultivated it over centuries to turn it into corn. None of this knowledge was handed down orally from generation to generation; nor, in most cases, was it written in ancient texts. We know it because scientists were able to spend years descending through minute layers of sediment with toothbrushes, trowels, and picks at undisturbed sites. How do we know about the origins of corn, for example? Because archaeologists near Mexico City discovered *grains of pollen* from corn plants dating from thousands of years back at 150 feet below ground.[9]

When those sites are ransacked by looters, all that knowledge is lost. All we are left with are random objects that may be beautiful or valuable but which tell us very little about the people who made them. Looting obliterates the memory of the ancient world and turns its highest artistic creations into decorations, adornments on a shelf, divorced from historical context and ultimately from all meaning. In the course of writing this book I've met many collectors who gave me no reason to doubt their love, appreciation, and sincere connoisseurship for the antiquities they own. Yet as long as collectors buy objects on the open market, with no documentation showing they were excavated in an archaeological context or removed from the ground before international codes against the trade in looted goods were signed in 1970, then they are contributing to the destruction and depriving themselves and all of us of the full breadth of understanding that might be gained if the pieces had been properly excavated. As one archaeologist has said, looted objects are pretty but dumb.

We can never know how many pieces were looted, or how much information was lost, from Iraqi sites after Saddam's demise. Gibson, who has worked in Iraq since 1964 and knows as much as anyone about the volume of artifacts at risk, said it was more than the thirteen thousand stolen from the National Museum of Antiquities in Baghdad and probably much more. The only sites getting temporary reprieves were those like Nimrud and Ur that the U.S. military had decided, for whatever reason, were worth protecting. "Anything that the U.S. military isn't sitting on is being destroyed," said Gibson, a man with a cane and an air of old-school erudition whose dry wit in both English and Arabic lifted everyone's spirits at the trashed museum. "There are going to be a lot of happy collectors."

Thousands more objects were destroyed because looters deemed them too damaged or unlovely to be sold to middlemen. At Isin worthless pottery shards littered the ground in places. Most of the valuable plunder will be untraceable once it reaches that border-busting shell game known as the antiquities market because, barring a few pieces with enough cuneiform to identify the origin, only the looter knows where the pieces originated.

In May 2003, a few days before I saw the devastation at Isin, the United Nations passed Resolution 1483 that called on all member states to ban the trade in Iraqi cultural property without a verifiable provenance. The governments of the main buyer countries all supported the resolution, and many established antiquities dealers have insisted that they will not knowingly buy or sell recently pillaged Iraqi antiquities. Yet no matter how much central governments, police, and customs officers everywhere promise to stop and confiscate Iraqi loot, and no matter how many dealers promise not to touch it, they all know that once those pieces are past border and airport controls, it is extremely difficult to detect them. It is riskier to buy and sell pieces hacked off standing monuments because there will be records and photographs of what those pieces looked like and where they stood originally. The same is true of pieces stolen from museums: in most cases, there will be records and accession numbers showing where they came from. The thoroughly studied and catalogued ruins of the ancient biblical city of Nineveh, just across the Tigris from Mosul, were severely damaged by looters after the first Gulf War, and chunks of the site's elaborately carved walls soon made their way to the back rooms of European and American antiquities galleries and warehouses, as archaeologist John Malcolm Russell has documented.[10] So even famous ruins are not immune to the looters' saw. Antiquities pulled from the ground, however, have no such records, no catalogue numbers or schematic drawings, and so it is that much more difficult to detect them as they move through the market and, if seized, to prove that they were plundered.

As the Iraqi experience showed, the modern antiquities industry has acquired speed and flexibility. Within hours of Saddam's downfall on April 9, 2003 (or even before, as at Umma), looters were overrunning archaeological sites as well as museums in Baghdad and Mosul.[11] Within weeks, artifacts pilfered from Iraqi sites or museums started turning up at border stations and airports in Europe and the United States. About four hundred objects, most of them stolen from the Baghdad museum, were seized by Iraqi paramilitary forces when, by chance, they stopped a car headed for the Iranian border in May 2003. Thousands more treasures made it out. By June 2004, U.S. Customs inspectors, police, and other authorities in the United States had seized some six hundred artifacts stolen from the Baghdad museum. That figure included three, 4,300-year-old Akkadian cylinder seals confiscated at Kennedy airport in New York from an American writer, Joseph Braude, who bought them on a sidewalk in Baghdad and who, in August 2004, pleaded guilty to smuggling charges in federal court in Brooklyn. In Italy, three hundred pieces had been seized, and authorities in Jordan, which almost alone among Iraq's neighbors made a serious bid to prevent itself from being used as a transshipment point, had confiscated an extraordinary 1,054 pieces. A further two hundred had been seized in Syria and thirty-five in Kuwait. All of these pieces were relatively easy to identify because they were stolen from the museum. There were records and photographs of every one of them, and many, including Braude's pieces, still bore the museum's distinctive "I.M." (for Iraqi Museum) accession tag painted on them.

If authorities were seizing this many provably, identifiably stolen Iraqi antiquities, and only in those few countries that were making serious recovery efforts, it did not take much imagination to suppose that thousands more were getting through. At least sixty Iraqi cylinder seals that were *not* in the Baghdad museum collection had been seized at airports in the United States alone by June 2004; those pieces had probably been looted from archaeological sites. Pieces like them will be rippling through the global antiquities market for decades to come.[12]

The demand for antiquities is drilling the life out of the last undiscovered remains of the ancient world. Collectors, museums, auction houses, and dealers are snuffing out any chance of expanding humanity's knowledge about the ancient world by buying looted artifacts with a speed and rapacity that calls into question whether there will be anything left to excavate in a few generations, save for the best-known sites on tourist circuits. Grave robbing is an old phenomenon, some will argue. The Romans looted the tombs and temples of the Greeks, the Vandals looted Rome, and then European colonialists looted nearly everyone. Most of the tombs in Egypt's

Valley of the Kings were robbed within one hundred years of their sealing, and even the famously pristine tomb of Tutankhamen had been penetrated at least twice in antiquity before Howard Carter found it in 1922. Mexicans before the arrival of the Spaniards were known to appropriate items from the tombs of their forebears the Olmecs. The modern antiquities market dates from as far back as the eighteenth century, when European travelers started returning home from Greece and the Levant with classical carvings, sculpture, and relics.

Today's antiquities trade bears no more relation to those historical examples than modern weapons of war to muskets and pistols. Nor does it much resemble the world of eccentric dealers and moonlighting graveyard scavengers described in 1973 in Karl Meyer's landmark reportage *The Plundered Past*. With sharp increases in the frequency and reliability of daily air links from the most remote provinces of the world, in container shipping volumes, and in movements of people and information in the last twenty years of the twentieth century, looted artifacts can reach buyers far more quickly than they did even a generation ago. Improvements in hand-held metal detectors, which can now detect man-made objects as deep as twenty feet beneath the surface, have expanded the downward frontiers of looting. Better roads and communication technology have transformed the antiquities business, allowed it to become as nimble, efficient, and sensitive to market demands as any other export-driven industry. These advances have also put retailers in closer contact than ever before with antiquities suppliers, the looters.

The streamlining of this industry over the last few decades has allowed traders to bring looted goods to market with once-unimaginable speed. A Mayan ceramic pot looted from a tomb in Belize can be in a gallery in Atlanta the next day; those cylinder seals they offered us in Isin could be in Europe a few days later, and very possibly were. In 2002 a man with a French passport was detained at an airport in northern Peru with twenty-one carefully wrapped ancient ceramic pots, all of them allegedly purchased from grave robbers, in his bags. The traveler carried an onward ticket to Paris for that evening. This happened in a city that thirty years before did not even have an airport. Multiply that case by a hundred times in a few dozen countries, and it is not difficult to see why there has never in human history been such a wide variety of artifacts on sale at one time. Never has the marketplace for the ancient world's treasures been so large and so diverse. Take a stroll through central London, as I did in December 2002, and find galleries displaying Roman-era vases, Chimú ceramics, Nepali temple torana, West African terra-cotta funerary pieces, ancient Chinese ironwork, a head-spinning gamut of objects with no listed provenance or sign whatsoever that they came from anything other than a looter's sack. Whole cultures are swallowed up by this business. A Peruvian archaeologist told me how the polychromatic pottery and artifacts of an entirely unknown culture, a nameless Andean civilization that lived centuries before the arrival of Spaniards near the modern town of Bagua Grande, turned up one year in galleries in Europe. Nothing like them had ever been excavated, and none made it to Peruvian museums.

"We know nothing about this culture, and its finest known creations are turning up in Germany and Switzerland." He shook his head with that expression of sadness and desperation common these days to archaeologists everywhere. "It's as if I went to Europe and stole their royal families' jewels and brought them back to Peru to sell."

Most countries with a vigorous looting industry have some date that kicked off the destruction, some event that catalyzed it. The business may have been simmering along for years, as in Iraq after its defeat in the Gulf War of 1990–91. But just as April 2003 brought looting to a new and catastrophic level in Iraq, most places have a date at which a kind of tipping point is reached, the modern antiquities industry makes its move, and the gradual obliteration of a nation's archaeological endowment begins.

In Peru, that date was February 6, 1987, after which the modern antiquities trade—lean, customer-focused, occasionally violent—settled on Peru like a vulture. That evening, a group of five grave robbers working at a burial mound known as Huaca Rajada, near the village of Sipán, discovered a mausoleum where, over two centuries, a dynasty of Moche rulers and their wives and attendants were buried, starting around the year A.D. 100. Addled on cane liquor and sucking coca leaves, the looters laughed and gasped in amazement as they pulled out gold and silver artifacts and filled up sacks with them. Within days they were selling the artifacts to middlemen, who began offering them to a select group of exporters and collectors. Word swept through the international antiquities market from London to Los Angeles that Peruvian looters had stumbled upon a major site. Buyers had to move fast because the police were sure to bust the whole looting operation soon. Three weeks after the tomb's discovery, Peruvian police got wind of the pillage, chased away the looters and villagers who had flocked to the site, and notified archaeologists. They then began a four-year excavation of the site that uncovered a dozen more tombs, two of them nearly as rich as the looted one, and brought unprecedented insights into how people lived, worshiped, and died in the Americas before the arrival of Europeans.

Meanwhile the looted artifacts had already hit the market, whetting the appetite of collectors and helping turn Peruvian artifacts, once an exotic niche product, into one of the hottest segments of the global antiquities trade. Up and down the Peruvian coast, looters began digging into burial pyramids looking for the next Sipán. They found one site that came close, but mostly what they succeeded in doing was to demolish thousands of tombs. Peru's underground universe had suffered big hits before from waves of grave robbing, most recently in the mid-1960s, but never like this.

"After Sipán, it was a gold rush. It was something no one could stop," said Walter Alva, chief archaeologist at Sipán, whose lonely campaigns against tomb raiders in his native northern Peru began drawing international attention.

The effects of Sipán, its looting and later its excavation, were felt in various fields: archaeology, anthropology, collecting, and, perhaps most intensely, the law. It galvanized efforts in the United States to use police powers to rein in the trade in plundered artifacts and led directly to the toughest U.S. code written up to that time against antiquities smuggling. It was the catalyst for a series of U.S. Customs raids, undercover FBI probes, and court cases that exposed the contours of the illicit trade and pointed the way to how it might be stopped. After Sipán, no museum or dealer in the United States could plead ignorance about the damage done by looting or how the antiquities business relied on smuggling. In Peru, and to some extent in all of Latin America, it brought a sharper understanding of how commercial pillage exploited the poor and marginalized, who lived on top of these riches, and how the value of preserving them rested not in filling museum shelves in Lima, Baghdad, or Rome, but in restoring a long-alienated part of a people's identity.

Like few other countries, Peru brings together within its borders all the characteristics of the antiquities trade—its past, its present, and, as I hope to show, possibly a better future for stopping its destructive influence. It is for that reason that I focused on Peru to write this book, rather than gathering short vignettes from many different countries that may all be under attack from the antiquities trade just as surely and quickly. Although I refer often to other countries with great underground riches to be pillaged, I have chosen to let Peru, and the Peruvians, tell this story in the hopes that it will serve as a kind of case history for other peoples.

As we left Isin that day, a barefoot looter came running toward us. He carried a dark, oval-shaped object that at first I thought was an unexploded hand grenade but turned out to be a Sumerian cylinder seal, completely covered in cuneiform text. To write on soft clay is one thing, Susanne told me, but to carve cuneiform into stone took skill and tools that only an important person would have had, an artisan working for a king or high priest. She examined it, turned it over and over with a look of fascination and despair.

"This is top-level stuff. It's worth thousands of dollars," she whispered.

Using her black head veil as a backdrop, she asked me to photograph the stone from every side so that her colleagues in Munich might read the inscriptions. I snapped a few pictures, but then it seemed so pointless. The piece had been wrenched from its context, reduced to the status of *objet d'art*. Most of the tales it might tell had been lost.

The looter eyed us greedily.

"This will sell fast. I won't have it for even five days," he said. Now and then a buyer came from Baghdad who claimed to represent an American client, he said. He could sell it to the buyer for $5,000 but he would give it to us for $1,000 because one of our bodyguards was his friend. By then we had gathered that some of the bodyguards, the men the archaeologists once relied on to protect the site, were now in cahoots with the looters. They were selling parcels of the site to looters, like prospectors in the California gold rush.

The looter drew closer to me. He had a big knife.

"If you buy this one, I'll show you others."

PART ONE

Chapter 1

LOOKING FOR A TOMB

WE SAT UNDER a tree in the moonlight chewing coca leaves, a heap of shovels and metal poles resting on the ground next to us. We chased down the coca's weedy taste with cane liquor known as *llonque* and talked in whispers so as not to awaken dogs at the adobe farmhouses across these fields on the south coast of Peru, where workers slept after a day harvesting cotton. Waves washing onto the beach a few miles away sounded like a distant sigh. A stone's throw in front of us, lying in the moonlight like a huge, slumbering animal, rose the pale burial pyramid built by the Incas five centuries ago which these three men were about to assault.

"La coca está dulce," said one. The coca is sweet. They will have luck tonight.

They were *huaqueros,* a uniquely Peruvian word for a global phenomenon, professional grave robbers. The leader of the group was known to everyone as Robin, a nickname he took from the Batman comics he liked as a boy and which stuck through his young, successful career digging up the remains of three millennia of history along the cool, arid coast of Peru. Robin did not know if it was luck or natural gift or a combination of the two, but he had developed a knack for finding the gorgeous textiles that ancient Peruvians wove, wore, and took to their graves. He had a sharp instinct for which of the thousands of eroded mud-brick burial pyramids, known as *huacas* in the indigenous language Quechua, would yield marketable artifacts and which only bones, worthless bits of ceramics, and tattered rags. Dealers and collectors contacted him because he found the good stuff: delicate, exquisitely designed weavings in a galaxy of colors that, centuries ago, were considered beautiful enough to accompany the dead to the underworld and today, for the very best ones, could fetch more than a Renoir or a Matisse.

Wearing dark sweatpants and T-shirts, Robin and his buddies talked about strange and beautiful things they had found over the years—perfectly preserved pots, color-spangled weavings, piles of bones and skulls. Robin told of jars in the shape of animals, a clown, a corncob. Looting a tomb, the three of them once found an Inca weaving that bore a design of a condor with outstretched wings, directly facing the viewer with penetrating, human eyes. But when they picked it up, the weaving was so delicate it fell apart.[1]

They talked about the fickle spirits of the dead that can bring them luck or frustration. The talked of the *huaca* as a living force with jealousies and resentments, moments of generosity and fits of spite.

"If you act greedy, the *huaca* won't give you anything. You take too much, and it will close up and never give you anything again," said Robin.

"Sometimes it helps you out, sometimes it won't give you anything. But it warns you. It speaks to you," said his friend Remi, a tall, narrow man with a grave air.

At twenty-three, Robin had been digging up tombs almost every night since his early teens. He earned a little money on the side driving a taxi. He looked a lot like the boxer Oscar De La Hoya and had the body to go with it; looting kept him in great shape, he said.

"We're going to walk up the middle of the *huaca*, start at the top and work our way down. And keep your voice down," Robin whispered to me, as if discussing a military attack. I wore dark clothes, as instructed, and I knew the rules: pictures were allowed but no flash, and if you must talk, whisper. He had had some close calls but was never arrested, and he didn't want to start tonight.

I met Robin through a veteran grave robber named Rigoberto, whom in turn I met through a friend of mine who collected antiquities in Lima. Robin and Rigoberto were neighbors in Pampa Libre, a village of a few hundred people north of Lima where the local economy had been based for generations on the looting of ancient burial grounds in the hills nearby. Those cemeteries, never rich to begin with, were yielding fewer and fewer treasures and so, having exhausted the community's principal source of revenue, its young men were forced to range further and further afield to meet the demands of their buyers. Carrying knapsacks and cell phones, they took buses up and down the coast and built up contacts with looters in other villages to form digging teams and split the proceeds. The *huaqueros* of Pampa Libre were known as businesslike, honest, and adaptable to any

place and digging environment. Chimbote, Ica, Casma, Nazca, Arequipa—
they had worked everywhere. Rigoberto, now in his early forties, had developed strange lung ailments that no one could explain and his bones felt
weak, so, at the urging of his teenaged son, he had given up grave robbing.
He was reduced to selling ceramic pots to tourists in the streets of Lima.

Robin, on the other hand, was still strong and enthusiastic, and he
loved his job. "I dig whenever I get the chance," he told me. In four years in
Peru, I couldn't remember meeting anyone so happy about his work. It
took some persuading, but he agreed to let me come along with him and his
buddies that evening.

To tell others about how the antiquities trade works at its source, you first
have to see grave robbers in action. You must look deeply and unflinch-
ingly down their holes, watch the violent and nauseating act of the living
evicting the dead from their graves. You have to become a witness to a
crime, and you have to risk arrest.

Robin and I met that day on Jirón Leticia, a street in the center of
Lima with a reputation for muggings and assaults. I walked past grimy mechanic shops, street vendors selling stolen radios and mirrors, taxis pushed
up against the sidewalk with their hoods open, a man with his head in the
engine and another on his back underneath. Robin stood on the corner
waiting for me, a knapsack over his shoulders.

"So the pickpockets didn't get you. Good. Let's go," he said. We
walked around a corner to a cavernous garage and boarded a bus whose
engines chugged to life, and the bus drove out into the morning sun and
headed south.

The Pan-American Highway makes its way past tidy, middle-class
neighborhoods and shopping centers, ramshackle districts of street stalls
and half-finished cinderblock structures and shantytowns climbing the
hillsides, before winding out into a landscape of sand dunes, billboards,
and green irrigated fields, a jagged knife of mountains on the left and ocean
on the right. The contrasts that define Peru are all around you, wealth jux-
taposed with poverty, mountains with ocean, desert with farm.

As we headed south, the ruins of the ancient shrine of Pachacamac appeared, a complex of mud-brick walls, terraces, and enclosures rising on a
hillside above the coastal plain, a few tour buses parked nearby. Pachacamac was to pre-Conquest Peru what Delphi was to Greece or Santiago de
Compostela to medieval Europe, a sacred shrine that drew pilgrims from
all over the realm and the site of an idol whose oracular utterances were re-
layed to the crouching faithful by the altar's priests. The Incas told the first
Spanish chroniclers in the 1500s that before being allowed to climb the
shrine to its uppermost sanctuary and hear the idol speak, pilgrims were

supposed to have fasted for a year. No one can survive a year without eating, of course, but the point was that people endured a once-in-a-lifetime regime of privation and sacrifice before the oracle would deign to speak to them. What was so extraordinary about the Pachacamac cult was how long it lasted: some 1,300 years, through the rise and fall of successive indigenous Andean cultures and civilizations until the last of them, the Incas. Pilgrims were still fasting and trekking to Pachacamac from across the Andes when, in Tumbes in the far north of the Inca realm, the Spanish conquistador Francisco Pizarro landed on May 16, 1532, with a few hundred men and written permission from Queen Isabella of Spain to conquer the empire they knew lay to the south. Neither Pachacamac nor the Incas could survive the Spanish onslaught. The conquistador's brother, Hernando Pizarro, and his men marched into the sanctuary in January 1533, evicted the priests, threw the wooden idol to the ground, and spent a month ransacking the shrine's rooms and platforms in a fruitless search for gold.[2]

"With greed and yearning they reached Pachacamac, where they had heard news that there would be great treasures," wrote the Spanish priest Fray Martín de Murúa in about 1590. After the conquerors left, "this memorable temple was deserted and uninhabited."[3]

Robin pointed.

"No one has ever found anything at Pachacamac. All the *huaqueros* try, but there is nothing to find or it's so deep underground that we can't reach it," he said. "The first time we tried, the guards came over right away and chased us out. The second time it was at night, and we entered around the back side over by the *pueblo joven* (shantytown), and we started to sink our poles into the ground. We sank one, two, maybe three poles into the ground, and then the night guards came over and chased us away. Some of the guys went back and sank more poles into the ruins, but they never found a thing.

"Some *huacas* are bad. They don't give you anything."

"What kinds of things are you looking for when you loot?" I asked.

"We don't look for ceramics anymore because they're hard to sell, except for the very best pieces. A really good pot can sell for $500 or so. But we don't get many orders for ceramics, I guess because too much of it entered the market at once," he said. "What people want these days is textiles and more textiles, or metalwork, although there isn't much metalwork in the places I work. So we look for textiles."

His assessment of the market astonished me. It was almost identical to the one I heard from art dealers and collectors in pre-Columbian art in the United States: textiles currently drove the pre-Columbian antiquities market, fine metalwork also had a niche, and ceramics were definitely out after experiencing a long glut, though top-quality pottery still sold well. This looter, who had never finished high school, never set foot outside Peru or used a computer, was completely in tune with the demand side of the looting industry.

We got off at Chilca, a sad, deracinated town of truckstops and half-finished houses jumbled out along the highway, a place best known to Peruvians as the frequent epicenter of earthquakes, built as it is on a geological pressure point that keeps the town in constant danger of being wiped from the earth at a single stroke. Robin led me through dusty lots and alleys to a small house that looked recently constructed of Eternit cinderblocks and corrugated-metal roofing. Inside were a few mismatched chairs on a dirt floor, a tattered poster with a calendar and a beer ad, a version of *The Last Supper* in dark velvet hanging over an uneven table. This was the home of Remi, Robin's best buddy in looting and a lanky man who, at twenty-one, still had an adolescent awkwardness. As he greeted us and tended a few chickens in the yard, I could tell Remi was nervous about meeting me. His uncle, a lifelong looter, had been arrested one night recently along with six others at an old Inca graveyard across the highway, where they had found many small weavings over the years. The police had come with a television crew, and under a harsh white TV spotlight, the police handcuffed and took them all to jail in the provincial capital of Cañete, where they languished for a few days until one of their buyers hired a lawyer to persuade (or perhaps bribe) a judge to release them. The buyer's motive was clear: he was losing his suppliers. Robin had been with Remi's uncle in the graveyard that night, but he and another looter managed to evade the police and walked all night to Pucusana, a village on the southern outskirts of Lima, one of the unlikely escapes that gave Robin his reputation as a master grave robber with a Houdini-like ability to dodge arrest. Remi was apprehensive about meeting another journalist. His uncle stayed in his little room off the chicken coop, refusing to emerge or let me see him.

Soon the third looter came around, a deeply tanned man of twenty-five with a shy smile whose name was Luis, but everyone called him Harry after the Clint Eastwood character that he liked. Harry was born high in the Andes in the city of Huaraz. He ran away from home in his early teens because his father beat him and came to the coast where he fell in with the Pampa Libre people and had been busting into tombs every night since. That afternoon the four of us walked for miles out of town, past brick kilns the size of houses, soccer pitches, fig groves, and poultry barns, out to a desolate hill overlooking a wide, scallop-shaped bay dotted with fishing boats.

People had once lived on this hill. As the *huaqueros* led me up, I could make out a network of mortarless stone walls with narrow lanes running between them, a kind of rough grid running over the crest. These walls had stood mostly undisturbed until about 1990, said Remi, who had lived in the area all his life.

"Then the *huaqueros* came," he said with a grin. Now the walls were in ruins. Jawbones, pelvises, and skulls bleached by the sun lay everywhere, and gaping holes showed where the looters had scraped out tombs like backroom dentists pulling teeth. From the simple objects and ordinary textiles that they pulled from this hill, they deduced that it had been inhabited by Inca commoners. But if it had been a graveyard, a village, or something else, we would never know because this place, perhaps overlooked by archaeologists, looked like a tornado had come through. Looters did not return to the place now because there was nothing left. The tombs were all dug up, the place tapped out. It all happened very fast and very recently, in the last two decades of the twentieth century, a period that will be remembered as one in which more Andean historical heritage was lost than in the previous four centuries, a time when looting reached a fury never before seen in this country's long history of plunder.

A few black vultures soared overhead, looking suddenly very close.

Just before nine o'clock that evening, we flagged down a bus on the highway and clambered on. We drew a lot of stares, these three Peruvian workers and me, a thirty-nine-year-old foreigner, all carrying knapsacks and loads of shovels and poles, but no one said anything before we alighted at an empty stretch of highway a few miles north of Cañete and began walking silently through fields of corn and cotton. A dog barked somewhere in the darkness, but we encountered no one as we walked along and came finally to the big tree. For three hours we sat on its gnarled roots, sucking and spitting out quids of coca and sending rivers of cane liquor roaring down our throats. There are some five thousand known *huacas* on the coast of Peru, some as tall as ten-story buildings and holding the tombs of monarchs, others merely a hump in the landscape where commoners were buried. These looters had gone after hundreds of them. But this *huaca* they preferred above all others in the area because its tombs were close to the surface, there were few houses in the immediate vicinity, and not many other looters had discovered it yet. They had heard that good textiles could be found here.

It was after midnight when they packed the plastic bottles, gathered the tools, and walked along a line of scrubby bushes toward the treeless mound of the *huaca* that towered over the fields and stretched a quarter of a mile wide. There was no fence of any kind around it, not even a sign.

It was risky work. The police could come and arrest them, the holes they dig could cave in and bury them alive, they could be set upon by local farmers' dogs. But the rewards were great. Made with skill and attention to detail unmatched in the ancient Americas, Peruvian textiles were used to spread ideas and information in the Andes before the Spaniards brought paper and written language. Even simple weavings could carry colorful, complex designs mixing abstract and realistic elements. Like ancient scrolls in the Middle East, textiles were crucial historical documents about life in Peru before the Conquest.

There was also the remote possibility they could find Paracas-era textiles. Named for the peninsula where some of its finest remains were found, the Paracas culture predated the Incas on the south coast of Peru by about 2,000 years, and the weavings with which the Paracas people swaddled their dead are at present some of the most coveted ancient artifacts in the world. A large, top-quality Paracas weaving can sell for half a million dollars. They are heartbreakingly beautiful mantles with semi-abstract designs of deities flying among pelicans, sharks, and hummingbirds, "some of the most magnificent cloths that the world has ever seen," as one specialist wrote in 1957.[4] If the looters found any Paracas textiles at this burial mound and couldn't keep it a secret, the site would instantly become a magnet for looters from all over Peru. Paracas textiles are old, sometimes 2,500 years old, a fact that increases their value and cachet and that also means very few have survived in good condition. It also means they are very deep in the ground, requiring looters to rip through centuries of Peruvian civilization before hitting them, sometimes just above bedrock. Retrieving south-coast textiles often requires earth-moving equipment or else gangs of a dozen or more looters working for days to excavate a bowl in the ground as deep and wide as the foundation for an office building. Sometimes in remote valleys near Nazca and Ica one comes across these enormous pits in the desert, a clutch of discarded bones and shards at the bottom.

I followed Robin, Remi, and Harry up the *huaca* and sat on the bare, chalky surface of dried mud bricks as they got down to business. For the first hour, all they did was prospect for tombs by driving in their slender, six-foot-long steel poles, the kind used in construction to reinforce load-bearing columns, with a short, perpendicular handle welded to one end. If they hit nothing, they moved on. If the pole suddenly met no resistance, that meant it had pierced an empty pot that probably accompanied a tomb. And if the pole made a certain muffled crack, that meant it had hit a body. I began to recognize that excruciating crack of metal hitting bone, a sound that first made me recoil and soon made me feel physically sick.

After sinking their poles and making mental notes of where they hit bodies, they began to dig—fast. The speed with which they dug astounded me. In fifteen minutes, they could excavate a hole six feet deep; in half an hour, they had broken into tombs ten feet down. The tombs belonged to ordinary Inca folk, simple graves of farmers and artisans with gourds containing peanuts or bird bones, woven bags containing coca leaves, and coils of string. There were knitting instruments, broken ceramics, a small woven bag containing a clutch of pointy bones that I found out later were deer antlers, a child's tiny llama-bone flute with a string attached. I looked at this all in the moonlight, fascinated, disgusted, and saddened. They couldn't sell this stuff, and they were throwing it all away into heaps of debris.

"We know what people are buying and what they don't want. We have to leave these things because we can't sell them," said Robin.

A car drove slowly down a dirt road at the bottom of the *huaca*, headlights ablaze. We ducked into the emptied graves, cowering among skulls and bones until it passed.

At about 2 A.M. Harry's pole made a promising noise. The other two came over and began digging furiously. In no more than ten minutes they had dug about three feet down and shined their flashlight on a row of partly disintegrated adobe bricks. It was the outer wall of a tomb, they believed. Ten more minutes and they had dug underneath the line of bricks and up into the tomb, into which Robin could reach with his arm. He then took his shovel and scraped out everything inside: bones, tattered bits of weavings, dried corncobs and lima beans, a skull. It was a tomb all right, but he could tell it had been looted before and that there was nothing of value. When? They couldn't be sure.

"Maybe the Spaniards, in the colonial era," said Robin.

They moved on, prospecting now higher up the mound and emptying half a dozen graves. They grasped human skulls by their tufts of hair and chucked them out. They shoveled out bones, some with what looked like bits of desiccated human tissue still attached to them. I jotted in my notebook: "1,200 years ago they buried their dead here and tonight they are unburied one by one."

Remi clutched more bones and dumped them out. "Find someone who wants to buy bones and we'll be rich," he said. I liked his lack of guile, the way he used no euphemism. "We violate tombs. That's what we do for a living," he told me once.

By 4 A.M., as the moon began sinking into the hills, they finally struck something good. Robin's pole had made that crunching noise of a corpse and the soil did not seem to have been disturbed, suggesting that looters had not struck here before. He and Harry dug about nine feet straight down for half an hour. Finally they found it: a body wrapped in a weaving of red and yellow.

"Look at those colors! We've got a good one," said Robin. "Now I'm going to dig around the sides carefully so as not to damage the weaving. If you rip it out, you'll destroy it. You have to remove it very carefully or it's worthless," he said. He enjoyed telling me how they worked with clinical detail, like a mechanic describing step by step how to fix a transmission. They tossed out bones and lesser objects lying around—gourds, bits of gauze, polished stones. With the pit nearly twice his height, Robin dug anxiously and threw the dirt halfway out to where Harry and Remi shoveled it out the rest of the way. Another half hour of digging with the shovel and his hands, and Robin finally pulled the weaving free and clambered out. He held up the fabric to the flashlight and gave it to Remi, who shook it, releasing a cloud of dust.

It was indeed a lovely piece, a perfectly intact tunic in terra-cotta red, olive green, yellow, beige, and sky blue. It had probably belonged to a boy or young man who wore it in life and whose naked bones now lay at the bottom of the pit: a femur, a spine, a skull gazing up at the stars.

"*Mierda*, this is the best thing we've found in two weeks," said Robin.

The roosters were crowing but the sun had not yet lifted as they gathered their tools and put the weaving in a knapsack. We walked back across the fields, all of us dirty as pigs. They bathed in an irrigation ditch and dickered over how much money they might receive. Eight hundred dollars, a thousand maybe. They wouldn't call Alex, the dealer who had bailed Remi's uncle out of jail, because he was known to be cheap and probably wouldn't give them more than three hundred. No matter what, they had to sell the piece fast because the longer it was in their hands, the more danger there was that the police could come and take it from them. The risk multiplied with each hour. And if they waited until the afternoon to sell it, any buyer would think that other dealers had seen it and turned it down, that it had been "handled." That perception would automatically reduce its value.

As the sun rose behind the Andes, we flagged down a bus making the all-night trip from Cuzco to Lima and rode back to Remi's house, where the men spread the weaving on the dirt floor. They were tired but excited as they made calls with Robin's cell phone to find a buyer. By 9 A.M., they had one, a smuggler they knew only as Lucho, and asked him to come see it. Lucho received lots of calls at this time of morning from grave robbers with fresh merchandise, Robin said, and they would have to promise him that their piece would be worth the drive because he would be giving up others.

"Believe me, it's a good piece, *una belleza*," I heard Robin telling Lucho. "We're not going to bring you all the way down here for something that's not worth it."

That was when I had to leave. The looters told me I could not be present at the deal because Lucho might not like it. Would he be armed? I asked. No, he does not carry a weapon, but he is an important buyer and might feel uncomfortable having a stranger present, Robin explained.

They told me later that Lucho arrived before lunch in his Nissan station wagon. He loved the piece. The looters asked for $1,500 but he bargained them down to $1,000. Lucho was known for smuggling out suitcases of ancient textiles to Europe and North America in violation of Peruvian and—for artifacts bound for the United States—American law. Robin learned that the weaving, their little *belleza* from the pyramid that night, was on a plane to Chile within a few days. Peruvian antiquities bound for the United States usually go via Chile these days, while those bound for the European market typically go via Ecuador, according to smugglers. That weaving plucked from a grave in Peru likely reached the United States a few days later.

Fifty years ago, offerings at the major international antiquities-trading centers such as London, Paris, and New York were mostly limited to goods from countries in the Mediterranean basin, with a smattering of Latin American and Southeast Asian objects for the specialists. Collecting, like culture at large, was more Eurocentric than it is today.

Now the supply side in the antiquities market has gone wide. In Mali, dealers have been known to hire whole villages of two hundred or more people, arm them with hoes and shovels, and organize them in gangs to level burial mounds wholesale and take everything.[5] Such plunder is to supply a taste for West African terra-cotta figures that began to develop in the West only in the late 1960s.[6] In Central America, where the Maya devised writing and a sophisticated knowledge of astronomy six centuries before Galileo, looters are gradually obliterating all traces of that civilization, save two dozen or so sites under active archaeological excavation, to supply the market for gold, jade, and stone artifacts. According to two scholars researching Belize, "the overall scale of looting has, at least in the area we know best, risen dramatically" since the first major international treaty aimed at combating looting in 1970. They estimated that there were two hundred looters for every archaeologist working in that country alone, and the problem was, if anything, worse in neighboring Guatemala.[7]

Thomas Killion, an archaeologist at Smithsonian's National Museum of Natural History, has seen evidence that looters use bulldozers, backhoes, and chain saws at Mayan sites. In one case they used a chain saw to strip off the carved front of a Mayan limestone monument known as a stele, leaving the mangled rest of the stone standing. It would have been too heavy to haul out whole.

"They know enough about archaeology and ancient custom to identify the potentially rich deposits, and then they crack into them," said Killion, an affable, energetic man who spoke with more resignation than anger about his efforts to stay one step ahead of those who would ransack his study sites. Lately he had been working in the Mexican state of Veracruz, at an Olmec area that he knew had been picked through by looters. "There's a hot little market going for small, portable Olmec objects," he said with a defeated shrug.[8]

Cambodia ended thirty years of civil conflict with a peace agreement

in 1991 and almost immediately came under unprecedented assault by
the antiquities trade. Rival factions in the fighting, even the genocidal
Khmer Rouge, were reported to have respected the monuments of
Angkor and, despite damage from mortar shells in a few places, left them
essentially intact. But not so the looters, who have been chiseling out wall
carvings, hacking off limbs and heads from stone sculptures, dismantling
the artistic elements from whole sections of temples, largely to feed antiquities dealers based next door in Thailand.[9] When I visited ten years after
the peace agreement, most of the 540 huge, stone figures lining the five
causeways into the mysterious ruined city of Angkor Thom had been decapitated, their heads lopped off and carried away by smugglers who
knew that heads are easy to hide, easy to transport, and easy to sell.
(Some of the heads had been replaced with copies, which somehow
added to the sense of loss.) In Angkor Wat, the ethereal temple in the
center of the sprawling complex, barely a single free-standing statue retained its head. Cambodians told me that most of the damage had been
done since the peace agreement. A complex of stone temples, cities, and
canals covering seventy-five square miles, Angkor is one of the best-
known ancient sites in the world, a place lavished with conservation
grants and depicted on the Cambodian flag. Yet more damage was done
by looters to this fascinating, captivating place in the last quarter of the
twentieth century than in the previous eight centuries.[10] In another eight
hundred years, as historians study how the heads of Angkor ended up in
Paris and Chicago, they might well conclude that people cleared the site's
jungle and soil in our time for the sole purpose of chopping it up and
shipping its contents around the globe.

If you want to see a few of Angkor's decapitated heads or sawed-off
carvings, a good place to start is the art galleries at the River City complex
along the banks of the Chao Phraya river in Bangkok. There I found a couple of heads in a softly lit room with air-conditioning, a plush carpet, and a
honey-voiced salesman. He smiled as I walked in and asked, "So, what culture are you interested in? Khmer?"

Cambodia has, within its limited resources, significantly stepped up enforcement efforts and border controls, and looting is said to have eased in
the last few years around the best-known monuments. I detect some embarrassment from antiquities dealers, at least in the United States, over the
speed and rapacity with which looting swept through Angkor in the 1990s.
One told me that he will no longer sell anything taken from a standing
Khmer monument unless he is sure the provenance dates from before the
usual cutoff date, 1970 (thus implying that he will continue to take pieces
from elsewhere). But once pillage has been introduced into a local economy, it is, like other illicit industries, difficult to extirpate. Looting has

taken hold so thoroughly in Angkor that even concrete copies replacing previously looted statues have been stolen.

Dealers and other apologists for the antiquities trade often maintain that their goods were brought to the market years ago, that they stayed in private collections and then recirculated through the market. Time and again the facts on the ground contradict the old "grandmother's attic" argument. Colin Renfrew, head of the University of Cambridge's archaeological institute, writing about China, said: "Nothing could be more telling, for instance, than the extraordinary flow of Chinese antiquities in recent years, most of them passing through Hong Kong. Few British or American grandmothers had access to Chinese antiquities prior to 1970. And those that did were more likely to be collecting porcelain—Ming vases and the like—than figures and ceramics of the Han and Tang dynasties. These could only have been preserved complete if buried in tombs, from which they have subsequently been removed."[11] In other words, you can be sure that almost any stone or ceramic Chinese artifact more than a few centuries old on the market today has been recently looted.

On Hollywood Road in Hong Kong, center of China's bustling antiquities industry, shop after shop sells artifacts so recently dug up that they still have dirt in their cracks. Letting people assume that I was an antiquities buyer (one of only two times I did that in the course of researching this book), I poked through a few shops and asked dealers where they got artifacts: looters or "farmers," they replied, without reserve and without exception. A shop owner named Thomas told me how trucks jammed with pillaged artifacts came over the border from China proper into Hong Kong every few nights (no doubt with a good number of fakes mixed in), "so come around often because you never know what will turn up." A plump, cheerful Hong Kong native who seemed well practiced in ensuring that no customer felt the slightest remorse about buying antiquities, Thomas was selling a slightly larger-than-life, five hundred-year-old headless Buddha for $20,000. He said it had drawn the interest of a major museum in the American Midwest.

"Recently arrived," he told me with a conspiratorial nudge.

He showed me a cabinet full of about fifty terra-cotta statuettes from the Han dynasty, more than two thousand years old. At $200 each, they were attractive pieces, sweet-faced women standing in shy poses and smiling coyly through pursed lips.

"A single tomb will have 150 or 200 of these. They're not exactly scarce," he said helpfully. "Of course it's illegal to dig up these things in China. You know what they do with looters in China? They kill them. But once they're in Hong Kong, you can buy and sell them freely. You could fill your suitcase with them and take them home and nothing would happen."

What is punishable by death in China proper is evidently legal, or at least tolerated, in Hong Kong's freewheeling capitalist system.

Yet some pieces are too hot to handle.

"If somebody offered me a Xi'an marching soldier in terra-cotta, I couldn't sell it," Thomas said, referring to the armies of life-size soldiers found by Chinese archaeologists. "It's too famous. I'd be arrested!" he said, laughing.

Dealers, he told me, adore the recently created fifteen-hour nonstop flights from Hong Kong to New York. It allows them to bring looted Chinese antiquities to the best American galleries quickly and easily without the two-day ordeal of stopovers and connections they used to endure, with all the risk of seizure, delay, or breakage that entailed. Artifacts can go from tomb to dealer to plane in a matter of hours.

"The direct flights have made things so much easier," he said.[12]

Many art dealers freely admit that the antiquities they're selling might be freshly looted. They're not in a position to run an exhaustive provenance study to ensure that a given piece was not recently taken from a tomb, they say. And anyway, a collector who has paid for a piece has more reasons to cherish and take care of it than an underfunded museum in an underdeveloped country where it will only gather dust.

Torkom Demirjian runs the Ariadne Galleries on New York's Madison Avenue, where he sells high-quality Greek, Turkish, and occasionally pre-Columbian and other artifacts. No matter how you feel about the trade, it is impossible to enter this gallery and not be struck by the grace and ingenuity of the objects he sells. Armenian by birth, Demirjian is an unabashed spokesman for the sale of antiquities that most people would agree bear the telltale signs of looting—no record of having been in any other collection, no record of having been excavated in an archaeological context, no record of having been legally exported from the country of origin.

"I don't care what the provenance of an object is. It's like a baby. The piece is out there, someone has got to take care of it, and it's much better off with someone who loves it than an archaeologist who sees it as just the subject of his dissertation," he said. "That is the difference between the archaeologists and us. To them, it is simply a document. To me, it is a work of art. It *moves* me."

In the late 1990s he sold a collection of about two hundred Colombian, Peruvian, and Costa Rican gold artifacts in separate deals for about $3.5 million. He admitted it might all have been looted, though he couldn't say when.

"It's against human nature to tell people not to buy beautiful objects. It's like telling them not to have sex," said Demirjian. "We can't stop purposeful plunder from here because it has to do with each country's reality.

So the argument is that we should restrict the flow of objects to stop plundering, but that will not work because people who collect know that they are not harming a piece but protecting it."

A slight, severe-looking man with black-rimmed glasses and a close beard, dressed casually in New York blacks, he has a booming, raspy voice that seems too big for his body when he rails against the elitist archaeologists who try to demonize collecting. "Archaeologists destroy, too. To get to the layer below, they have to destroy the layer above so they can say this object was leaning against that object or something, and they take five pages to say it. Then you go to their conferences and they all talk so pompously about ideas that have no application in the real world, or they come up with slogans like 'the power of money versus the power of culture.' Sounds good, doesn't it? But they don't even know what culture is."

Demirjian told me that he had "stringent purchasing practices" that involved requiring people who sold him artifacts to sign a form saying they had good title to the object, a common practice in modern art dealing. Nevertheless, he said, if he is not satisfied that the source is legal, "we don't buy it. And contrary to popular belief, we won't buy just anything that comes along."

As the U.S. government signs more treaties with source countries restricting the import of antiquities (discussed in Chapter 8), American dealers have been losing business to their competitors in Europe for the best, fresh-from-the-ground artifacts. "My government is working to put me at a severe disadvantage to European art dealers. But is that going to stop someone in Peru from digging up tombs? Of course not. These pieces go to Europe now," said Demirjian. "They will find their market."[13]

Before I took the bus back to Lima that morning, and before Lucho arrived, I took Robin, Remi, and Harry out to breakfast at a truck stop on the highway. In the photos I took at that breakfast, we're all sitting at a table looking exhausted but pleased. Robin put my camera around his neck and walked over to flirt with women at the other tables.

Digging up bodies did not strike me as a very satisfying way to make a living, no matter how much it paid. I asked them if it didn't bother them.

"When you first start doing this, it makes you nervous," Remi said. "Digging up bones, you think you're going to incur a curse. But after a while it becomes easy. You don't even think about it."

"But doesn't it bother you personally? I mean, how would you like it if someone dug up your grave and stole everything your family had put in it?"

They didn't have an answer for that. They looked at each other nervously and then at me as if suddenly they wished I wasn't there. Then Remi said, "Around here there is no other kind of work. I used to work at the dairy factory but it closed. There is no work but looting."

Chapter 2

TWENTY-THREE FEET DOWN

THE ROAD TO Sipán winds for miles through fields of radiant green sug-arcane rustling in the breeze, past irrigation ditches, tiny roadside chapels, a sugar mill belching smoke and an odor of burnt molasses. Now and then the road bends around small, barren hills that rise up from the fields. At one of those rocky outcrops, shamans gather during Holy Week to speak in tongues and draw ancient pottery out of the ground in a hybrid of Christian and pagan ritual. During Holy Week, people say, ancient in-digenous ceramics respond to the shamans' incantations by magically ris-ing to the surface so that people can dig them up and take them home. Whole families come with pots of food, bottles of sweet corn liquor, and trowels to dig up a few trinkets left centuries ago by their ancestors.[1]

This is northern Peru, where the ancient past is never far from the surface.

As one approaches Sipán, the *huaca* appears above the forests of sug-arcane, standing as tall as a twelve-story building. It looks like a treeless hill but it is entirely man-made, constructed in stages starting two thou-sand years ago with millions of mud-and-gravel bricks laid in rows by armies of builders during the early stages of the Moche culture, which dominated the north Peruvian coast in the first six centuries of the Chris-tian era. Little was known about the Moche until modern archaeology came to Peru in the first half of the twentieth century, and not until the 1950s was it fully recognized as a distinct civilization. Its arts, crafts, and

technologies in agriculture, hydraulics, and metallurgy are now understood to be among the most advanced in the ancient world, a culture
whose accomplishments were so varied and extraordinary as to make people who have spent a lifetime studying it still shake their heads and wonder how they did it.

The Moche built networks of irrigation canals and sluices that watered
an area of northern Peru not exceeded until the 1960s,[2] and thus they
raised beans, squash, corn, peanuts, and avocados. They were the first in
the Americas to reach industrial proportions in their production of ceramics, employing molds and pit kilns to make hundreds of pots at a time. Yet
many of those pots are works of art of striking grace and realism, particularly the well-known Moche portrait vessels, which depict real individuals
in three-dimensional sculpture and give tantalizing clues about the lives
they led—the first true portraits ever created in the Americas. The Moche
adorned their pots and bowls with paintings depicting a wide variety of
scenes from home life and ritual, everything from deer hunting to sex to
warfare to cooking. These paintings reached an artistic refinement utterly
unmatched in the Americas and comparable to the best Greek vase painting.[3] Unlike their contemporaries the Maya, the Moche never devised
writing, but in these paintings one senses a narrative impulse pushing
through, a visual language of life's horrors, comedies, delights, and dramas
all fighting to be heard.

One of the great innovating cultures of the Americas, the Moche per-
fected metallurgical industries, which allowed them to make elegant and
durable gold and silver artifacts in large quantities. They devised a way to
gild copper pieces—that is, to coat copper with gold to make it look like
solid gold—using a complex salt-and-potassium-nitrate solution not
matched anywhere in terms of technological sophistication and quality until the nineteenth century.[4] It was shortly after their decline, about A.D.
800, that basic copper-based metallurgy suddenly and strikingly appeared
in Mexico.[5] Andean prowess in forging gold and silver jewelry so exempli-
fied by the Moche had evidently spread north via Panama, in much the
same way that old-world metalworking was first developed in ancient Iraq
and later spread across Europe and Asia.

Much of the art of the Moche depicts battles in which elaborately
dressed fighters whack each other with clubs and maces. The nature and
purpose of Moche warfare is the subject of much scholarly debate, but
armed conflict does not seem to have been driven by a wish for territorial
expansion; rather, the aim appears to have been to capture prisoners for
human sacrifice. Prisoners were taken bruised and bleeding before an en-
throned Moche lord, their throats cut, and their blood drunk from a golden
goblet. Such sacrifices happened on the *huaca* in Sipán, as archaeological
discoveries were to show, and on other key Moche pyramids.

Sometime around A.D. 600, the Moche disappeared. Archaeologists are still piecing together why, but erosion and sediment point to a series of climatic disasters after about 550. Severe drought was followed by a catastrophic El Niño event in which eighteen months of rain assaulted the Moche cities. Human sacrifices to the gods came to no avail as floodwaters washed through the alleys and *huacas*, stripping away whole sections of towns, destroying their cane and adobe homes and potable water and sanitation systems, washing away several yards of soil.[6] The Moche civilization was in ruins. It had a brief revival in the next century, when the old deities, perhaps blamed for the cataclysm, were replaced by new gods with a more maritime character, but high Moche culture was gone forever. Other cultures and civilizations followed over the next nine hundred years and built atop the Moche structure at Sipán, adding their bricks and tombs over the glorious old regime, borrowing deities and artistic styles from it, until the last major Peruvian coastal culture, the Chimú, were subdued by the Incas in about 1470. It was a short-lived conquest: within seventy years the Incas were themselves vanquished by the Spaniards.

The word *huaca*, derived from the indigenous language Quechua, can mean any sacred or venerated object, but most often it denotes the mudbrick burial pyramids that punctuate the Peruvian coastal landscape. Centuries of wind and rain have eroded the *huaca* at Sipán known as Huaca Rajada so much that it looks like an old man's weathered face. Its sides show wrinkles, grooves, and ravines. Yet so many bricks were added on top, and so well-made were the Moche foundations, that in the two thousand years since its construction began, the *huaca* has lost no more than twelve feet of its original elevation.[7] Standing on its summit, you can see twenty-eight other, smaller *huacas* within a few miles.

In the shadow of the *huaca* lies the modern village of Sipán. The mudbrick skyscraper rising up behind the village's modest adobe homes and chicken coops has been both its blessing and its curse. Blessing, because the 1987 discovery of the tomb of a Moche lord bedecked with gold and silver deep inside the *huaca* made a few looters here very rich and then brought an influx of archaeologists and tourists and made the area famous. And curse, because all that fame and treasure brought almost nothing of value to Sipán. Its name has been proclaimed on banners at the American Museum of Natural History in New York and at the Smithsonian Institution. Sipán has been the subject of glossy catalogues, coffee-table books, symposia, and conferences. But Sipán, population two thousand and site of one of the most important archaeological discoveries of the twentieth century, has almost nothing to show for it: no running water, no paved roads, no medical care to speak of, and no hope.

After years of broken promises, the people of Sipán scowl and glare mistrustfully at visitors. Hotel owners now warn tourists not to visit, and archaeologists cannot come without armed protection. The villagers are poor, forgotten, and angry.

"They take those treasures all around the world, and what happens to us? We have to bathe in the irrigation ditches. First the horses, then the cows, then the goats, then us," a stout old woman named Isabel Rodríguez told me, her thin cotton dress waving in the dry afternoon breeze. "The archaeologists come here and dig up all the gold and silver and leave us with nothing. And they call us the looters."

Go to the hinterlands of Cambodia, Egypt, or Guatemala and you'll find places not too different from Sipán or a hundred other villages all over northern Peru, places where millions of dollars in antiquities have been yanked from the ground and all that remains are neglected, embittered communities. Commercial looters descended on the town or hired locals to do the digging for them, took all they could from the ancient burial sites, and now there is nothing to show for it except tales of a few looters who struck it rich, bought a fancy pickup truck, and moved out of town. This is where the antiquities business walks naked, revealing itself as the extractive industry it is, like mining or oil drilling, except that those activities operate legally and are subject to taxes and regulations, whereas the antiquities trade is regulated only by the market and the muscle power of men who ransack tombs. As an industry, it depends on poverty and weak policing at its source. It has become another route by which the wealthy of the world exploit the poor, with the loss of not a renewable resource like timber or water but the history and heritage of whole peoples.

Looting is not a new phenomenon in Sipán. People had been looting Huaca Rajada for at least fifty years before Ernil Bernal and his brothers struck a tomb in 1987. But Sipán differs from other looting communities in one crucial respect: archaeologists later chased away the looters, took over the site, and saved at least part of its rich historical record from destruction. Like few places in the world, Sipán offers a side-by-side, moment-by-moment comparison between what the antiquities trade does and what archaeology does, showing with unprecedented clarity how the one treats ancient art as a resource to be consumed and the other as an object of scientific retrieval to broaden our knowledge of the past. It is a measure of how deeply embedded looting had become in this community's fabric, and how deep its poverty and despair run, that people here consider archaeologists to be their enemies.

The first time I went to Sipán, in December 2001, the villagers had shut the steel gate across the main road into town and covered it with bedsheets printed with angry slogans. The banners denounced the Sipán site's lead archaeologist, Walter Alva, whose work excavating the site earned him an international reputation as a field researcher. "Alva! Thanks for keeping us in the most extreme poverty," said one. "Walter Alva is a wolf in sheep's clothing—beware!" and "Walter Alva, give us back the jewels," said others. Walter Alva wasn't around to read the banners. He had not come to the town in about four years out of fear for his safety. There was in fact no one to read the banners except for the villagers themselves. They gathered around me as I walked down the main street, a rutted dirt road bordered by a fetid ditch on one side and a few shacks and avocado trees on the other. People looked at me suspiciously, examining me for the telltale tools of the hated archaeologists, asking each other in whispers if I might be a spy sent by Alva.

"Alva comes here, brings all the foreigners around, shows them the *huaca*," said one old man standing by his crumbling adobe home. "And we never got a dollar. Look at this place—we have nothing."

Gabino Chero, a young farmworker with a face that could have been a model for a Moche portrait vessel, drew close to me and spat on the ground. "Do they think we're a bunch of sheep? They want us to shut our mouths while they come in and take the treasures out of the *huaca*. But we're the real heirs of the Moche, not Alva and his pals."

"The archaeologists wait around to see what the looters will find, then they go in and take everything," said Isabel López Delgado, standing in a T-shirt and shaking her finger in anger. "Would that Alva came back here someday so we could push him in his ditch and bury him alive."

I wandered over to the *huaca*, recognizable from photographs in *National Geographic* and PBS documentaries, and up to the archaeological site where I found three policemen sitting on a bench in the shade and one barking dog. A bit beyond them, the excavation site consisted of a series of deep, wide pits carved neatly into the dried mud brick. At the bottom of the pits lay reproductions of human bones where the Lord of Sipán and his various wives and attendants had rested, along with painted metal-and-plastic copies of some of his royal garb and hundreds of ceramic pots like those he was buried with. The pits dug by the looters had long since been filled, and there was no sign of where they had been.

For a long time I had the site completely to myself. Then a clean-cut man in his thirties came running up the *huaca* in khakis and introduced himself as José Bonilla, archaeologist. He was looking after a tiny exhibition hall down the hill, with a few mock-ups of the tomb. His eager solicitousness suggested that he did not get many visitors.

"Doctor Alva told me you might be coming," said Bonilla. He gave me a brief tour, at the end of which he had a little request. He wanted to leave town that afternoon. Could I please carry him out in the trunk of my rented car, he asked, so he could avoid the villagers? He could not ride as a passenger because they would stone the car.

"They used to throw things at me," he said. "They don't do that much anymore because they know they'll be arrested. So they shout obscenities, things like, 'Watch out, there goes the thief.' Very unpleasant."[8]

The *huaca* in Sipán has been known since the 1950s as Huaca Rajada, or "split huaca," because a dirt road runs over the pyramid and splices it in two, according to villagers. On the north side of the road, two adjacent pyramids tower 130 feet above the sugar fields. One of those pyramids was built in the original Moche construction, and the other was built several centuries later, around A.D. 700.[9] On the south side of the road stands a much lower, Moche-era platform about the size of a football field, overlooking farm plots and adobe houses. In 1987 a group of looters—led by thirty-six-year-old Ernil Bernal; his two brothers, Samuel and Emilio; and two of their friends—struck a tomb in this lower end of the structure.

The Bernal brothers knew plenty about looting. For generations robbing graves had been a seasonal trade on the north coast, a way to make some money between sugar harvests or a weekend diversion in which men would go off into the hills with shovels and poles and return with a ceramic pot, some copper artifacts, a textile fragment they might be able to sell for the equivalent of a few dollars an hour away in bustling Chiclayo, the largest city in the Department of Lambayeque. (Peru is divided into twenty-four departments, similar to provinces, of which Lambayeque is one of the smallest.) Or they might keep the artifacts as household mementos, decorations on a shelf next to the Virgin Mary or family pictures.

Grave robbing had powerful ritual properties, with traditions of shamanism and incantations that involve asking permission of the dead to remove their offerings.[10] A *curandero*, or shaman, would accompany the looters to a pyramid and make a *pago*, or payment, of coca leaves, tobacco, alcohol, or food to the spirits of the *huaca* before the men would start digging, and they would always be men, as women were thought to incite the ire of the *huaca*'s spirits. The shaman would ask the spirits to protect the looters from landslides and guide them to the treasure. He would never himself dig; that would be sacrilegious and might cost him his channeling powers.

"I always respect the dead. Even today, when I walk past a *huaca*, I make a small offering so that their spirits won't damage me or my family. They are powerful, and I am a small man," said a retired *huaquero*, aged 105, interviewed by anthropologist Réna Gündüz.[11]

The Bernal brothers were a new kind of looter. They didn't care about *pagos* or incantations or shamans. Once they found a good tomb, they cared only about getting the priciest stuff out, selling it to their dealers as quickly as possible, and dumping the rest. They were quite literally the shape of things to come. Instead of the fragile, aged bodies of the traditional *huaqueros*, the Bernal brothers were blocky, powerfully built men who could dig a ten-foot pit, wiggle their way into a half-buried tomb, and empty it in minutes. They organized themselves and their diggers into efficient looting teams, developed good contacts with Peru's top dealers and collectors, and had no qualms about bullying other looters off the most promising sites or stealing objects from them at gunpoint. Police in the area knew the Bernal brothers both for their brazen grave robbing and for their reputation as small-time thugs.[12] Their aggressive, brute-force style of looting brought them a reputation for results with dealers. Sometime around 1984, Ernil Bernal cracked into a pre-Columbian tomb in the sandy hills above the village cemetery and found a silver figurine of a man that he sold for $2,700.[13] When people in Sipán heard about this fabulous sum, they descended on the area with shovels and poles and pockmarked the area with hundreds of holes. They found nothing to rival Ernil's idol, only increasing his aura as looter extraordinaire, and twenty years later the area remains a lunar landscape of pits and craters.[14]

The Bernal brothers' depredations ranged all over Lambayeque, and occasionally they dug holes into Huaca Rajada. It stood only a fifteen-minute walk from their parents' rambling, adobe-and-stucco house in the sugarcane fields beyond the village's edge. From their house they could see the mound rising above the canebrakes, and they watched it to prevent other grave robbers from prospecting. In 1986 the Bernal brothers began finding simple copper objects and bundles of human and animal bones, nothing to brag about at first but enough to make villagers believe that, somewhere in the *huaca,* there was treasure to be found.

Archaeologists had done preliminary excavations at the site some years before, found little of interest, and moved on. Researchers assumed that Huaca Rajada had been built by the Chimú civilization that dominated northern Peru about eight hundred years after the Moche. They thought this because of the kind of bricks used to build the *huaca*—rough and narrowly rectangular.[15] Until the Bernal brothers sunk their pits into the structure, no one realized that beneath those Chimú bricks were layers of smoother, broader Moche-style bricks encasing the tombs of an entire Moche dynasty.[16]

One of the enduring mysteries of Sipán is how the *huaca* could have been such an important center of Moche ritual and pageant, with fabulous wealth interred there, and then be forgotten. The Spaniards established a major settlement barely seven miles away, at Zaña, but evidently knew nothing of what the strange, two-headed burial mound contained. There is strong evidence that nine centuries after the demise of the Moche, their legends, mythology, and romantic histories were still recounted orally by native Peruvians when the Spaniards arrived in 1532.[17] Many other Moche burial *huacas* were betrayed by natives to the Spaniards. So why not Sipán?

Spanish settlers writing in the sixteenth century often called such structures "mosques" and organized mining teams to level them in search of gold and silver, which the Spaniards then melted down to convert to bullion. The Spaniards were well aware that the Indians buried their dead with booty. A visitor to Peru wrote before 1587:

> So, the Indians of this realm were accustomed to bury, with the bodies of the caciques and great lords, gold and silver drinking vessels, and much other silver and gold, and precious stones, and valuable clothes, and they even buried alive the women they loved the most, and their servants, because they thought that they would revive and those who were buried with the dead would serve them with the gourds and vessels that they put there . . . and these burials they called in Quechua *chulpa* or *aya*, although the populace commonly called them *huaca*.[18]

At a huge Moche pyramid known as Huaca del Sol, the Spaniards diverted the course of the Moche River to wash away the structure and leach out its treasures. They destroyed about two-thirds of the huaca and extracted over six thousand pounds of precious metals with this hydraulic looting and yet, at 130 feet tall, the structure remains today one of the largest pre-Columbian monuments in South America and an active archaeological site.[19] The amount of treasure in the *huacas* was staggering. At one, the Huaca Yomayoguan, a team of ninety Indian laborers and African slaves in 1559 extracted 642 gold and silver "bars," two silver pitchers described as the size of Spanish wine jugs, a silver trumpet, silver spoons and ladles, and hundreds of other precious objects—and this was only what their Spanish masters recorded and reported to tax authorities.[20]

Deeply disturbed by the vandalism of their temples and the malignant forces they thought it might unleash, the north-coast peoples were known to keep silent about burial sites to save them from depredation. The Spaniards suspected as much and often complained about the reticence of the Indians. Perhaps Sipán's status as an old seat of power had been forgotten. It is entirely possible, however, that Sipán, like the Inca ruins of Machu Picchu, was overlooked by the Spaniards in part because of the passive resistance of the conquered subjects. One can well imagine them keeping silent about the site as its memory slipped away in the cataclysm of conquest.

Four centuries after the Spanish conquest, the *huaca* still occupied a central place in the lives of the people who lived near it. Sometime in the early 1980s Ernil Bernal, with a nasty reputation in his hometown, moved to the Amazonian town of Rioja and worked at odd jobs. He returned in late 1986 because his mother had fallen ill, according to the version his father told people, but in fact his brothers had told him they were on to something at the *huaca*. A man who lived at the foot of the pyramid, Ricardo Zapata, had found some golden necklace beads in the *huaca*. Although they were squatters, Zapata and his family considered themselves to be the "owners" of the pyramid, and since so few visitors came to the site and the Zapatas lived alongside the pyramid and not on top of it, authorities had let them stay there for over twenty years. When the Bernal brothers heard that Ricardo Zapata had found gold beads, they ordered him and his digging partners to clear off, reportedly threatening to kill him and his mother if they told the police.[21] By the time Ernil returned home from the Amazon, now married with two children, the Bernal brothers had taken over the *huaca* and had been sinking holes into it for a few months.[22]

"I would hear them digging there all night. In the morning people would come around to see what they had found, but they [the Bernals] always shouted at them to go away. So people started coming later with buckets and bits of window screen to sift the earth and find those little gold balls. And then at night *los huaqueros* would come back to work," said Narda Montalvo, an elderly woman who lived near the foot of the pyramid.[23] Maybe the villagers were intimidated by the Bernals' violent reputation, or maybe they thought there would be some tidbits left over for them, but no one told the police. The villagers found more gold beads in the backfill left by the Bernal gang and sold them on the sidewalks in Chiclayo.

Ernil long dabbled in hallucinogenic mushrooms and a mind-bending substance made from the sap of a cactus known in Peru as the San Pedro plant (*Trichocereus pachanoi*), similar to mescaline and long associated with ritual grave robbing. When he returned from the Amazon, his habit became much worse. Although San Pedro was thought to enable communication with the spirits of the dead, it was the shaman, not the looters themselves, who was supposed to ingest it to facilitate contact.[24] Ernil's family knew he was overdoing it with the San Pedro. He was interested in paranormal phenomena, and he claimed it would put him in contact with extraterrestrial beings. He would slip into ecstatic trances to try to make contact with aliens and talked about building a platform behind the house that would be a landing pad for spaceships.[25]

"He was a strange guy," said a friend. "He would talk to you all the time about flying saucers, shamanism, occult forces, that stuff. He took San Pedro every night. And then he would sink into these terrible depressions."[26]

Upon his return from the jungle he immediately took up looting the *huaca* with a varying cast of characters that included his brothers Samuel, Juan, and Emilio; their friends Eulogio "Pipa" Galvez and Teófilo Villanueva; and a few other local men.[27] They found more canine and human bones, copper objects, and gold beads. After a night of digging, they would return home exhausted and filthy, sleep all day, and return to the *huaca* in the evening. High on San Pedro, Ernil rattled on to his increasingly skeptical mates about his visions of unimaginable treasures awaiting them.[28]

On February 6, 1987, at about 10:30 P.M., Ernil Bernal was digging in the toe of a boot-shaped pit about twenty-three feet below the surface of the platform. He heard a hollow, muffled sound. He punched the roof of the tunnel with his shovel, and an avalanche of crumbled mud bricks and debris fell onto him, cutting off the tunnel into which he had crawled. He could easily have been buried alive if Samuel and the other looters, who were inside the pit but in different "toes," had not begun frantically digging on their side of the tunnel toward him. They realized what had happened before Ernil did, for they saw that, mixed in among all the dust and debris, were metal objects. After freeing Ernil, they took a few of these objects in their hands, crawled up the bamboo ladder out of the hole, and looked in the moonlight at some of the most extraordinary pre-Columbian objects ever found.[29]

"After that night, no one said Ernil was crazy anymore," said his brother Samuel.

For the next three or four nights, Ernil and his gang carried out the valuable-looking things in rice sacks, smashing or discarding whatever they thought they couldn't sell. They salvaged about three hundred objects. Hundreds, perhaps thousands, more were lost or destroyed, most of them ceramic pots that would have contained offerings to the Moche lord interred there. They had enough treasure, said one of the *huaqueros*, to "turn the poorest man among them into the richest hacienda owner on the coastal plains."[30]

Samuel Bernal described to me in 2002 how they extracted the goods. Without realizing it, Ernil had dug up into the tomb from beneath. He crawled out, and then the whole gang widened and broadened the shaft so that it exposed the top of the tomb, finding a layer of about two hundred pottery jars. Underneath the pots they found a layer of eighty or so copper artifacts, very few of which survive, for the Bernal brothers knew that where the Moche left copper, they also left gold. The looters tossed the copper pieces away and kept digging. Next they found a trove of delicate silver artifacts, not as many as the copper but enough to start filling those rice sacks with objects. When morning came, they took a few precautions to prevent other *huaqueros* or the villagers from climbing into their honeycomb of shafts and tunnels, filling in part of the pits with backfill and posting an armed guard.

That night or the next, they hit gold.

First they found a delicate gold layer, like foil. "It was thin as paper. Ernil tugged at it but it wouldn't come free. So he dug and dug some more around its sides, and pulled some more, and finally it came out." After that everything was pure gold, "like a hallucination," said Samuel.

The gold sheet, probably made of many small panels, could not stand up to their shovels and boots, and none of it is known to have survived. Beneath it they found the tomb's main chamber. Its wooden support beams had long since rotted and collapsed, filling the chamber with earth and loose debris in which the golden artifacts were liberally mixed. As they shoveled the dirt, they picked out gold artifacts from their shovelfuls or found them embedded in the earth. The looters marveled at the strange and whimsical objects they found, unlike anything they had seen in all their lives in looting: tiny standing men with turquoise and lapis adornments, feline masks of hammered gold, a golden jaguar head hung with a string of beads of tiny owl heads. They found a set of about ten hollow beads of gold, hammered and sculpted into the shape of peanuts.

And there was a set of semicircular rattles, each made of a single sheet of folded and hammered gold, with tiny metal pellets inside that made a ringing noise. The looters called these *depiladores*, tweezers, because they could be squeezed shut like large tweezers. There were ten of them, according to Samuel's recollection, each measuring about five inches across. Sculpted into each was a spiderlike being with a man's face; he held a ceremonial knife known as a *tumi* in one hand and a severed head in the other. They passed these strange objects from looter to looter up to the top of the pit, where the men above admired them in the moonlight. They dropped them into the nylon sacks.

As they filled each bag, one looter would bring it down to the base of the mound where a light blue Toyota sedan was waiting. The car belonged to Ernil's brother Segundo Carlos Bernal, an officer in the Peruvian air force who lived at a base a day's drive north, in the town of Talara. They put the sacks into the trunk and then drove a few minutes to the family's house, where their parents slept. Carlos Bernal Vargas, their father, was a fairly prosperous man of about sixty and the closest thing Sipán had to a distinguished citizen: a shareholder in the local sugar cooperative, he owned a small herd of livestock and that great status symbol in rural Peru, a tractor.

It was close to midnight when the edge of a large metal object caught Ernil's eye. It was so large it took the team several minutes to dig it out. Inch by inch, it emerged: an enormous gold blade with wide, flaring edges that gave it the shape of a half-moon. It was by far the biggest object they had found in the tomb, in fact, the biggest artifact any of them had ever seen. It was stained and faded and bits of textile were stuck to it, but the looters could tell by its weight and shine that this object was pure gold. Attached to the top of the blade was what appeared to be a handle, which, on closer inspection, proved to be another one of those strange tweezers with the same image of the snarling spider-man grasping the severed head. Made of a single sheet of gold, the piece was no thicker than a sheet of cardboard. Yet it felt sturdy and substantial in their hands.

It was "immense, it weighed a ton," Samuel recalled, searching for words to describe its size, so big in fact that it wouldn't fit into a rice sack. They wrapped the piece in dirty T-shirts and brought it down to the Toyota, stashed it in the trunk, and Ernil and Samuel made a special trip back to the house.

On their treasure runs back to the house, the Bernal brothers had been placing the objects in a tall wooden sideboard in a hallway. This object was much too large to fit in any of the sideboard's drawers, so the brothers carried it out back to the chicken coop, where they kept their fighting cocks. The Bernal brothers were known as breeders of roosters used in cockfights at festivals and fighting rings, sometimes attaching bits of sharp metal to the hind claws of the birds to make their kick more lethal. One bird would kill another in an orgy of blood, flesh, and flying feathers. They had a few dozen cocks, each tied to a post or kept in a cage so they wouldn't tear each other apart. The Bernals buried their new golden colossus in the soil under their pen, with the fighting cocks acting as watchdogs ready to attack intruders.

What the Bernal brothers had found was the backflap, a piece of ritual armor created in a Moche furnace around the year A.D. 250 and worn at royal ceremonies by the lord whose tomb they had just ransacked. It was as much a part of the regal garb as the scepter or ermine robe of a European monarch. That night on the *huaca* was the backflap's first stop on a long journey that would take it through three countries, the hands of dozens of people, and many more car trunks.

They returned to the *huaca* and retrieved more treasures. It was like "pulling potatoes out of a fire, one after the other," said Samuel. They put down their shovels and watched speechlessly as Ernil climbed up the ladder from the bottom of the pit with more gold in his hands and his pockets. They found more of those strange peanuts, both in gold and silver. They found another backflap, the same size as the other but made of silver, too tarnished and deteriorated to sell. It had a bad odor, that oddly flatulent smell of rancid silver, and they tossed it away as garbage.

Three or four more trips back to the house that evening, and the whole place was bursting with booty. After filling the sideboard's drawers and cabinets with artifacts, they hollowed out a stereo speaker and filled it with gold, and they stashed more pieces in boxes behind the fighting cocks' pen. They put the golden peanuts into a manila envelope and shoved it in a drawer. Recollections differ on how many sacks they brought back — eleven, fifteen, twenty-five, they lost count after a while. When they finished, they filled part of the hole with backfill, drove home one last time, gave the key to the sideboard to their mother, and slept.[31]

The objects found by the Bernal brothers were unlike anything ever seen: delicate figurines of silver and turquoise, intricate nose and ear ornaments, gold masks of faces that were part feline and part human. Some of the artifacts vaguely resembled ones from other famous plundered Moche tombs, but even the looters could see theirs were superior, the product of a more refined aesthetic sensibility. This was the discovery that a looter made once in a lifetime, at best, and they knew it.

Yet they were apprehensive. Ernil was scared that thieves would break into their house to steal everything, and he kept watchdogs around in case. Word had spread through the village that the looters had found treasure, and villagers started poking around the house, asking for objects or permission to join them in the digging, until the Bernals barked at them to go away. The brothers felt they had dug enough for now. The spirits that Ernil saw in his San Pedro trances told him there were more tombs to find, but his brothers and parents told him to stop.[32]

Over the next few weeks, Samuel was in charge of selling the objects. The first few he brought to the homes of well-known buyers in Chiclayo and Trujillo, but pretty soon buyers were coming straight to their home. The Bernal brothers' main agent was a former policeman known to everyone simply as Pereda. Described by people who knew him as a tough-talking, intimidating man, Pereda was known to small-time and professional looters all over northern Peru as the man with the right connections with buyers. He wasn't interested in third-rate trinkets; he dealt in the good stuff, taking on consignment, for example, the artifacts from a site known as Balsar, found by looters a few years before and considered to have contained some of the finest examples of Moche metallurgy yet seen. He would bargain only on his own turf, in the shaded courtyard of his villa in the center of the colonial city of Trujillo, a few hours' drive south of Sipán. Samuel and his brothers had dealt with Pereda before, and this time they had the kind of top-quality merchandise they knew would interest him. Within days of receiving the Sipán treasures from the Bernal brothers, Pereda had top collectors and smugglers knocking on his door in Trujillo.

One was Fred Drew, an American living in Lima who had become attracted to ancient Andean art while stationed as a diplomat at the U.S. Embassy. He began small-scale dealing and gradually moved into the business more seriously, retiring from diplomatic service in the 1970s to work as a full-time antiquities exporter. A discreet, elderly man, he was, as Sidney Kirkpatrick wrote in his early account of the Sipán case, "unknown to the general public, had no gallery, never advertised, and sold only to a select clientele. For the right price he could obtain practically anything, from a two-thousand-year-old ceramic burial urn for a London collector to a rare Peruvian blue-green hawk-headed parrot for a Japanese businessman."[33] Drew was well aware of laws barring the export of pre-Columbian artifacts. But, as he told associates, he believed he was rescuing Peru's ancient art from being damaged, lost, or unappreciated in pitifully underfunded museums by exporting it to foreign collectors.[34] Even if he had to work outside the law, Drew was determined to save Peruvian art from the Peruvians and to make a profit doing it. The 1970s and early 1980s saw a rush of very high quality Andean ceramics and metalwork into American museums and private collections, and no doubt many pieces came through Drew's hands.

Drew worked closely with north-coast *huaqueros*, traveling with them to their most prolific sites to see what they were finding and to ensure he got right of first refusal for the best objects. On one of those trips he fell into a looter's shaft near Trujillo, injuring his legs; from then on he was forced to walk with the aid of crutches. By the time of the Sipán discovery, Drew had a well-established network of looters and runners who sold him merchandise from ransacked graves and monuments all over Peru. Few serious, professional grave robbers in Peru had not worked at some point with Drew, who had well-greased systems for exporting the goods. Large shipments would go via truck to Bolivia, where customs controls were far less stringent than in Peru, and from there on long-haul flights to North America or Europe. For smaller-scale deliveries, he had contacts in airlines and courier services who could carry items on flights direct from Lima.

He was, in short, the ideal person for obtaining the foreign clients who could pay the right price for these magnificent artifacts. Drew's role in the illegal export of Sipán artifacts has been well documented.[35] Within a couple of weeks of Ernil Bernal's discovery, he was at Pereda's house in Trujillo, negotiating for the purchase of the Sipán stash. Photographs of the pieces soon began buzzing through the elite of the international antiquities market.

Drew's first rival for the Sipán cache was Enrico Poli, an imperious Italian immigrant to Peru and former hotel manager whose rather ordinary-looking house in a wealthy suburb of Lima contained one of the best private collections of Peruvian antiquities anywhere. He had gotten into the pre-Columbian market in the 1960s, when it was still cheap, buying up gold and ceramic pieces directly from looters or providers like Pereda, who had sold Poli the glittering highlight of his collection, a set of four slender gold trumpets from Balsar, each about a yard long. Poli was never ashamed of telling visitors that he bought directly from looters, once revealing to a television interviewer that he liked to dig up tombs himself. He compared himself to arts patrons of the Italian Renaissance, but instead of sponsoring artists, he sponsored looters, taking them under his wing, paying and encouraging them, whetting their ambitions to roam up and down the coast ransacking tombs and bring him back the best items. Once he bought artifacts, he rarely sold them, and he took pride in the fact that he kept his collection in Peru, shunning the smuggling life of Drew and his ilk. Poli had a discerning eye, and he never bargained. Looters knew not to bring him fakes or ask exorbitant prices for inferior pieces if they wished to do business with him.

"My looters are my angels. They bring me anything I want. They would go to the moon if I told them to," he told me. "It was the looters who found Sipán, the world must know this. And who are the archaeologists? Parasites, all of them!"[36]

Poli had amassed a collection that was the envy of every museum in Peru. Alva and other researchers might decry looting in public, but they often visited Poli's collection of brazenly looted goods for the chance to see and photograph them and keep tabs on what *huaqueros* were finding. When Alva's article on Sipán appeared in *National Geographic*, with its denunciations of treasure scavengers and the collectors who paid them, it was accompanied by pictures of pieces from Poli's collection, an irony that incensed Alva but which he knew he could do nothing about. Poli had some of the finest Moche ceramics anywhere, and Alva knew it. In Poli's view, all the archaeologists—and particularly Alva—were worse than just high-class looters. They were hypocrites, attacking him for buying plundered goods while begging him to let them visit his collection. He showed his collection to paying visitors on appointment-only tours that attracted a stream of visiting dignitaries, including United Nations secretary-general Javier Pérez de Cuéllar and opera tenor Luciano Pavarotti, who was so impressed that he stood in Poli's garden and burst into song.

Poli had been arrested three times over the years on suspicion of buying illegally excavated antiquities. Each time he was released "because they couldn't prove a thing," he said, with a self-satisfied smirk and his distinctively high-pitched piercing laugh. He regarded his run-ins with the law as so many feathers in his cap. His enemies claimed he got off through bribes or Italian Mafia connections.

But what his enemies cannot deny is that, under Peruvian law, Poli's collection is perfectly legal. Although it is technically illegal to buy looted artifacts, a collector need only "register" his pieces with the government's Instituto Nacional de Cultura (INC) in order to gain legal title to them, as Poli has scrupulously done. A pot held by a looter and considered stolen property under Peruvian law today can be legal tomorrow, once the buyer obtains INC registration. Thousands of such registrations, with a grainy photograph and a technical fiche for each piece, fill gray-metal file cabinets at the INC headquarters in Lima. It's a charade of a conservation system, a poor imitation of France's comprehensive inventory of nonexportable cultural property, and it protects wealthy investor-collectors while punishing the looters who supply them.

The only restriction is that collectors may not legally export ancient pieces, and that, to its defenders, is the registration system's chief virtue. By offering local collectors the chance to gain legal title to looted art, but threatening to strip that legal title the minute they try to export it, the system effectively keeps at least some antiquities inside Peru, instead of dispersed around the world. It's a system based on the assumption that the main market for Peruvian antiquities is overseas and that, with five thousand known major archaeological sites in the country and few resources to protect them, the state's only realistic possibility of stopping the trade is to stop the export.[37]

"In this country there are only three ways to get rich: from drug trafficking, from the state, or from *el arqueo-tráfico*," says Ruth Shady Solís, head of archaeology at Lima's prestigious Universidad Nacional Mayor de San Marcos. A handsome, intense woman, she has a face that reminds people of Frida Kahlo, and her eyes burn with passion and sadness when she speaks of the damage done by looters to Peru's most precious sites and of the registration system that sanctions it. "Every single day the history of this country and the objects of our study are being extinguished so that the rich and powerful can have a few more trophies in their living room. We are approaching a situation in which our heritage may be wiped out, simply nothing left." Ironically, she is one of the few archaeologists who need not worry about looting at her own study site. Caral, the 4,700-year-old city north of Lima whose excavation she directs, is so old that it predates the invention of ceramics. Looters have sunk pits around this sprawling site of mounds, walls, and stone circles over the years and left empty-handed, never suspecting that the reason they found no ancient pots or metalwork was because they had not been invented when this site was created. Shady's biggest problem comes from the theft of bricks. Local villagers enter the site and walk off with four-thousand-year-old bricks to make house repairs or additions.[38]

Within days of the Bernals' discovery, runners from Trujillo brought some of the first Sipán pieces to Poli. He bought them on the spot. They were six trapezoid-shaped panels of solid gold, each about eight inches long and three inches wide, which Poli recognized as part of a sumptuous necklace. That very day, Poli got in his car, withdrew $40,000 from the bank in small bills, and drove straight to Pereda's home to score as much of the Sipán cache as he could. He arrived at almost the exact same time as Drew, and over the next few days the two of them courted Pereda like assiduous suitors, wheedling and cajoling him to show them the best he had to offer. Now and then one of the Bernal brothers would come with more fresh loot to top off the consignment.[39]

A few stragglers bought some of the Sipán pieces later, grabbing what Poli and Drew had missed or what the brothers had not yet sold. The most important in this second wave was Raúl Apesteguía, a Lima collector who had been involved in the antiquities trade for twenty years.

Apesteguía was nothing like the arrogant, eccentric Poli or the businessman Drew. He was a connoisseur, or at least fancied himself one, a bohemian favorite in Lima's cultural and artistic circles who could be seen at gallery openings, museum benefits, and philanthropic events to raise money for good causes like the Lima choir in which he sang. When President Alan García took office in 1985, Apesteguía lent the incoming first lady, Pilar Nores de García, one of his prize pieces, a five-hundred-year-old authentic Inca jewel necklace, to wear at the inaugural festivities. He was a diplomat of sorts, too, able to play host to all sides in the contentious world of Peruvian antiquities. Archaeologists came to his penthouse to study and photograph his most interesting pieces, knowing all of them were looted, and buyers and collectors came to do deals. He had a reputation as a master authenticator and appraiser, an oracle to whom museum curators, diplomats, and collectors could bring an artifact and receive, for a fee, his wisdom on what culture created it, roughly when, and what it would be worth on the open market. His own collection was particularly strong on the Chancay culture that once flourished in the sandy hills north of Lima and whose tombs were filled with large, earth-colored storage pots that had contained victuals the dead would take to the underworld. Because these tombs are close to the surface and because the Chancay people had the misfortune to live in an area that one thousand years later would lie near the voracious Lima art market, evidence of the Chancay society has been largely wiped out. Little archaeological study has been done on them, for traces of this culture had been almost obliterated by the antiquities trade. Apesteguía had some of the finest Chancay pots to emerge from those tombs, the cream of the culture.

Despite these strengths, Apesteguía was more of a dealer and market-maker than a collector. A photograph of one of Apesteguía's star Sipán acquisitions, a delicate gold bracelet, found its way into the October 1988 issue of *National Geographic* magazine. Poli was furious at Apesteguía when he later sold the bracelet to a well-known Peruvian bank president, according to a friend of Apesteguía. Poli had wanted it for himself.

"Raúl was a referee in the market. If you were buying or selling, you could take things to Raúl and he would appraise them," the friend said. "Everyone respected him."

Not all his friends knew that Apesteguía had another talent: smuggling, in which he had dabbled since the 1960s, shipping out his own or his clients' antiquities to Europe or the United States. About a dozen successive Peruvian statutes, starting with a presidential decree in 1921, prohibited the export of any artifacts that dated from before the Spanish Conquest.[40] Although contradictory, overlapping, and erratically enforced, all those laws were intended to preserve the country's cultural treasures as a national asset whose value to Peruvian society would be diminished if they were spread around the world. Like most Latin American countries with export bans on certain classes of cultural property, Peru often turned a blind eye over the years to antiquities smuggling or let artifacts out of the country with payoffs to border or airport authorities. It was fertile ground for corruption. But the export ban did force antiquities exporters to operate in secrecy, or at least with some discretion, as Apesteguía knew.

In 1968, when he was still new to the business, Apesteguía and several other figures in Lima's antiquities trade were implicated in a scandalous case of smuggling. Police found crates of freshly looted artifacts, reportedly some twenty thousand pieces in all, awaiting export at Lima's international airport. A left-wing military government under President Juan Velasco Alvarado had recently taken power, and the heavily publicized seizure was seen as its way of putting the antiquities-consuming elite on notice that the old ways of doing business—paying Indians a few coins to dig up pots and then shipping them out to hungry buyers abroad—would no longer be tolerated, at least not so openly. The resulting publicity stung Apesteguía, owner of a reputable antiquities gallery in downtown Lima, and he began working more carefully with a select group of clients.

He went for about five years before being caught again, but this time he didn't get off so easily. He was sent to Lima's notorious Lurigancho prison, where inmates were condemned to a diet of dogs and rats and lived among open sewers, bleak concrete prison yards, and knife-wielding gangs. For a man accustomed to being waited on, life in prison must have been traumatic indeed. No one remembers for sure how long he stayed there; some associates remember it as a matter of weeks or months, others, over a year. He was never tried, and, given how much Peru's leftist rulers at the time despised the Lima oligarchy, one wonders if he wasn't the victim of a vendetta or even a frame. When he was finally released and went home to his apartment, where some of his finest artifacts had been confiscated by authorities, Apesteguía vowed to get completely out of the smuggling business. He would sell, authenticate, and curate antiquities for local collectors and institutions, but he promised friends he would never again sell overseas.

He kept that promise to himself until Sipán. As the hottest items to hit the market in years began to emerge, with huge potential for foreign buyers, Apesteguía found himself drawn back into the trade that had gotten him into so much trouble. He was not doing well financially, "not very solvent," as one friend described him. Here was his opportunity to make one big killing and get out of the smuggling business forever.

Back in Sipán, villagers had overrun the burial mound and were sifting the backfill left by the looters for scraps of metal or anything else that looked valuable. "Holy Week came early that year," one resident told me, smiling as he remembered it.

People from nearby villages had come, too, all hoping to strike it rich. The brothers tipped them with scraps of gold or tiny beads that they had found in abundance, not enough to reduce the looters' take but enough to keep the villagers happy and their mouths shut. They allowed the villagers to climb down into the shafts in groups of ten to look for any objects the professionals might have left behind. The Bernals knew there was nothing left; they believed they had cleaned out everything of any value save for the odd bead or shard. Each group had fifteen minutes. If they didn't come out, Ernil and his enforcers would threaten to throw in earth and bury them all alive.[41]

Several days after they emptied the tomb, Ernil gathered with Villanueva and Pipa in the sugarcane fields behind the house. Ernil placed the treasures on the ground and, one by one, he and his mates divided them up. Since he was representing his brothers and himself, Ernil thought he should get the lion's share of the treasures. The others disagreed, and, what was more, they accused Ernil and his kin of not bringing forth some of the pieces they had stashed in their house and already sold. Tempers flared. No two versions of the story are alike, but the dispute soon turned violent, and a day or two later at the *huaca,* a looter was shot and wounded. One of the diggers had had enough. Peru's national police had Sipán and nearby villages well infiltrated with informers, to keep tabs not on the *huaqueros* but on left-wing guerrillas.[42] That looter told his contact in the police, and his revelation set in motion the dismantling of the looting operation. If he had not alerted the police, the remaining tombs in the pyramid would have been emptied within days.[43]

Walter Alva was sound asleep before midnight on February 25, 1987, in the cottage where he lived behind the museum of which he was director, in the town of Lambayeque. His wife, Susana Meneses, and their two young sons were visiting her parents in Trujillo. He was awoken by a loud knock on the door. The museum's night watchman had received a phone call for Alva from the deputy chief of police for the department of Lambayeque, Colonel Edilberto Temoche. Alva was to come immediately to the police station. Two of Temoche's men, acting on a tip, had raided the home of some looters in the village of Sipán, a place with a reputation for grave robbing and petty crime. The officers had confiscated a rice sack containing twenty-three artifacts that they believed to be of excellent quality, so good that Temoche believed Alva should see them right away and confirm their authenticity.

When he walked into the police station that night and unwrapped the artifacts, Alva was stunned by what he saw. The first object was a gold mask, a bit bigger than a tea saucer, with a man's face and eyes of silver and lapis lazuli. There was a golden goblet and handfuls of golden beads that must have been parts of opulent necklaces. There were gold peanuts and strange gold discs with checkerboard patterns lightly incised on them. They superficially resembled Moche artifacts from other sites, but these were of vastly finer workmanship. Some, like the peanuts, were completely new. Nothing remotely like them existed in any museum or private collection anywhere in the world. Because they had been wrenched out of context by the looters, Alva could say little about the purpose of the objects, but he had no doubt they had come from the tomb of a Moche figure of the first order. In a judicial affidavit he later estimated the value of the pieces at $50,000, but he knew they were truly priceless and unique. Alva congratulated the police on the find. Though he agreed to accompany them the next morning to inspect the damage at Huaca Rajada, Alva didn't expect to find much beyond the usual detritus of looting: backfill, bits of broken ceramics, and bones.

In 1987 Walter Alva was the thirty-five-year-old director of the Brüning National Archaeological Museum, a public institution named for a German immigrant to Peru who donated his ceramics collection to the state. Alva had turned the institution from a dusty, disorganized collection into a well-respected museum on north Peruvian indigenous cultures. He was also inspector general of archaeology for Lambayeque department, which meant that the museum in his charge would receive all pre-Columbian objects that archaeologists unearthed or that police seized from looters in the area. The museum's basement and warehouse contained some twelve thousand objects, mostly ceramics, from all over the region.

As a "dirt archaeologist," he would often collaborate with visiting American or European researchers who were excavating ancient sites near Lambayeque, and sometimes he would work with his own team at out-of-the-way sites. Born and raised in the town of Contumazá in the Andes, he had been a star student at the Universidad de Trujillo and had written two well-regarded books on formative north-coast cultures. He might have spent a lifetime in semiobscurity, digging up tombs, filling museum shelves with pots and shards, publishing an article now and then, until Sipán came along.

To the general Peruvian public, Alva was well known for his tireless campaigns to stop looting and protect the ancient sites under his supervision. He would lecture schoolchildren about the damage grave robbing did to the common heritage of Peruvians, rail against it in the media and at academic symposia. Like all Peruvians, he knew that poverty, rural isolation, and lack of opportunities in legal industries contributed to the destruction of ancient sites. But he added a more subtle, psychological twist. Looting was also the product of Peruvians' lack of pride in their past. Young men were willing to dig up the tombs of their ancestors and sell their contents to fatten private collections because they had been conditioned by centuries of indifference or disdain toward Peru's indigenous heritage, an attitude inherited from the colonial Spaniards. To Alva, the fight against looting was not only about saving the information lost when tombs were ransacked, although that was a very important reason. It was to prevent the objects that gave life to Peru's cultural identity from being swallowed up by the antiquities trade and to preserve them so that they could instead give pride and a sense of identity to Peruvians, a people in bad need of national self-respect.

"The antiquities trade treats us like a colony. It extracts our cultural heritage for the consumption of a few," Alva told me in February 2000. It was our first meeting, and Alva was sitting behind a desk at the modern Museum of the Nation in Lima, looking so out of place with his suntan, unkempt beard, and many-pocketed shirt that it made me want to hurry through the interview so he could get back to the *huaca*. Everything about him bespoke a man born to be an archaeologist—the careful consideration of each question; the measured, patient way of speaking; the enormous, rough hands with each finger the size and color of a potato. Like only a handful of archaeologists in the world, he was unafraid of taking a vocal, political stand against the antiquities trade.

"If you have objects looted from a tomb," he said, "it's as if you have the mutilated parts of a body—the hands, the feet—but no idea what the body was like. This is what the antiquities trade does to us. It mutilates us. I would make buying antiquities like wearing fur, but instead of 'If you love animals, don't wear fur' the slogan should be, 'If you love culture, don't buy antiquities.' Of course animals can always be raised and reproduced, but not culture. Once the history of humanity is gone, it's gone forever."

There isn't a single archaeological site on the north coast of Peru that has not been damaged by looters "to one degree or another," he said. "At this rate, pretty soon there will be nothing left." Yet there are areas on the south coast under even worse assault due to the international demand for ancient textiles, he said. The days of small-scale looting for a few local collectors were long gone. "What we have seen in the last twenty years is the development of true criminal organizations dedicated to looting and contraband. They have created a well-defined tactic of shipping pieces to Europe and from there to other markets. It's a triangle trade."[44]

The morning after seeing those first artifacts in the police station in Chiclayo, Alva, his twenty-six-year-old deputy at the museum, Luis Chero, and a police team went to see the Bernals. The brothers were not there, their father told the visitors. He didn't tell them the brothers had gone to Trujillo the day before to sell artifacts. Only the brothers knew why they hadn't taken the pieces seized by police, but most likely they were selling the valuable ones piecemeal to give the impression that treasures were still emerging fresh from the tomb.

Bernal allowed the police to search his home. They found nothing in the house, not thinking to look in the cock pen. Before they left, Alva happened to look down into the irrigation canal that ran alongside the home. At the bottom of a steep ditch about six feet deep he saw pieces of broken pottery, and then more broken shards, and more and more—hundreds of pots in all, in various states of destruction and decay. The Bernal brothers had chucked the pieces that they could not sell into the ditch. As Alva and Chero clambered down into the ditch to gather a few of the pieces, they noticed that there were also mangled and broken pieces of copper artifacts. Alva was starting to get an idea of the volume of the tomb's contents.

Nothing could prepare Alva and Chero for what they saw next at the *huaca*. As the police approached in their car, followed by Alva and Chero in the museum van, the archaeologists saw that the low end of the structure, where the Bernal brothers had dug up the tomb, was covered with hundreds of villagers digging holes and sifting dirt. Looters' holes pockmarked the site. Desperately poor women, children, and men were scavenging all over the mound, hoping to find tidbits missed by the looters, sifting the dirt, and digging new holes. The villagers shouted obscenities and threw stones at them. Police told the villagers by megaphone to clear the site, and, when that failed to bring a response, they fired shots in the air. The villagers scattered, some running into the trees, others running farther up the mound, a few clambering down into the holes. There was complete chaos for about half an hour before police succeeded in clearing the site. Once they did, it took Alva and Chero a few more hours to locate which of the thirty-some pits in the huaca was the one where the Bernals had struck the tomb. When Alva thought he found it, he crawled into the tunnel with a flashlight and found a burial chamber about seven feet square and nine feet high. Merely from the size of the chamber, he could tell it must have been the tomb of an important personage, probably a whole family group. It was completely wrecked. All that was left was the dust of bones and ceramics pulverized by the looters' sneakers.

Shots in the air, police guards, barbed wire—this was how the excavation of Sipán began. Within a couple of weeks, Alva and a small team of assistants, graduate students, and dirt haulers, including one repentant looter from the village, were living under police guard directly on the *huaca*. Getting police protection wasn't easy. Alva had to plead over the phone with the director of the INC in Lima to keep the pressure on the chief of the national police to maintain a twenty-four-hour armed guard at the site, lest it be overrun again by the villagers. Most other archaeologists he talked to did not think it was worth the effort. They were convinced the looters had cleaned out the site after weeks of digging and, surveying the desolation that day, Alva had no obvious reason to disagree. Yet with a knowledge that was part instinct and part empirical, gathered over years of trying to stay one step ahead of looters and usually failing, Alva sensed that Huaca Rajada had more stories to tell.

As he and his team began to haul dirt and clear the mountains of backfill left by the looters, they endured the daily taunts of the Sipán townspeople. He and his assistants often slept inside in the looters' tunnels so they would not be pelted by stones, Alva with his hand on a Mauser revolver. Now and then they would be woken by gunfire from police scaring off would-be looters. Alva, to the surprise and dismay of his colleagues, was going to excavate the site where the looters had left off.

Out in the sugar fields at the family homestead, the elder Bernals thought their son Ernil was coming unhinged. He would go into delirious trances, tremble uncontrollably, and scream that he was being persecuted by men or swarms of insects visible only to him. He stumbled home one night, his clothes soiled, telling his family he had been chased down the highway by a band of unrecognizable people and that he had thrown himself into the canebrakes to escape them. He was terrified that the police would come again, terrified that thieves would break in and steal all the gold. But most of all, he was terrified that spirits of the tombs were coming to exact revenge.

"Mother thought he was really going crazy," said Samuel Bernal, who shared a bedroom with Ernil to try to calm his fits. "He was getting worse every day." Eloísa Bernal, their mother, recognized that Ernil's suffering was not caused by the *huaca* spirits but by a severe and undiagnosed mental illness of which he had shown symptoms for years and which was surely intensified by cane liquor and drugs. She wanted him to see a doctor in Chiclayo, but Ernil was too terrified to leave the house. As he holed up in his room, a shivering, tortured man in the throes of what was probably full-scale psychotic break, his brothers went out to sell the loot.[45]

By April 1987 it was clear to Alva that the February raid had netted only a small portion of the treasures the looters had dug up. Pieces were still being pumped onto the market, via Samuel. One of his clients was a Lima collector and dealer named Carlos Gallardo, who, early that month, tried to launder a group of eighteen Sipán pieces by offering them for sale to the museum of the Central Reserve Bank, whose vaults in downtown Lima housed an impressive artifacts collection. Gallardo's Sipán stash included a golden belt ornament similar to the distinctive "tweezers" found by the Bernal brothers but slightly larger and made of gilded copper, not gold, and therefore much less valuable, and a single ear ornament similar to two that had found their way into Poli's collection. The bank was about to buy the pieces when an alert employee recognized them from news reports as distinctively Sipán. The employee called Alva, who informed a judge. Such was Alva's credibility and authority that the judge ordered the police to seize the pieces (which, after litigation that dragged on until 1993, were surrendered to the Brüning Museum).[46]

Beginning excavations on one hand and working fast to salvage what had already been looted on the other, Alva pressed a local prosecutor to order police to raid the Bernal house again. Alva came along on the raid and brought a portable metal detector to search for gold the Bernal brothers might have buried. The police had also arranged to bring a television crew from a Lima news program called *Panorama*. With the TV crew and Alva waiting a few steps behind them in the Brüning Museum van, police surrounded the Bernal house before dawn on April 11 and surprised the brothers' father, Carlos Bernal Vargas, as he was milking his cows. He shouted, and Ernil dashed out in a panic. A policeman fired and hit Ernil, who staggered a few more steps before collapsing under an avocado tree. The police surrounded him and, pointing their guns, demanded to know where he had buried the loot. Before he could mumble anything about the cock pen, where the backflap was still buried, he lost consciousness. Police carried him out to the van, and in a Chiclayo hospital, he died later that morning. A bullet had perforated his liver.[47]

Ernil Bernal's killing was front-page news in Peru and forever poisoned the relationship between Alva and the people of Sipán. Alva was, according to associates, deeply shaken and saddened by the killing and knew that it would greatly complicate any excavations he undertook at Sipán.

"Walter has struggled all his life against looting. He knows that we have a choice, that we can sit locked in our museums while everything outside is destroyed, or we can try to combat this problem. But this is not a war. It's not about killing looters," said archaeologist Carlos Wester, who later became Alva's successor at the Brüning.[48]

Ernil was buried after a long funeral cortege through the village and past the *huaca*, where people wept and shouted curses against Alva and the police. The grave was an opulent slab of slick black marble etched with Ernil's name in gold, a sharp contrast to the simple wooden crosses, plastic flowers, and weathered cement monuments around it. Ernil Bernal had made a lot of money in life but could spend it only in death.

If the find might have been a godsend for the village of Sipán, it has been almost cosmically unlucky in the years since. Peru's government, sensitive to charges it was neglecting Sipán, built a new steel bridge over the Reque river into town in 1998. It collapsed the day it opened. In November 2001, officials spruced up the place for a visit by the king and queen of Spain, who were to see the tombs. Workers came to lay a fresh layer of dirt on the roads; rumors spread that they were finally going to be paved. In the end, the monarchs never came. The road remained unpaved, and in the clouds of dust that rose every time a car pulled into town, the people of Sipán tasted their own bitterness and disillusion.[49]

Alva knew that the villagers regarded him and his colleagues as simply a higher class of thieves, who had gained from excavating the site but left nothing in return.[50] Alva and the stream of other archaeologists who have worked in Sipán say they sympathize with Sipán's plight but that open sewers, bad roads, and unemployment are not their problem. Looting is.

"If anyone wants to know the damage that looting does, look at Sipán," Alva said. "In one night they destroyed a tomb that would have taken us a year to excavate. In a few more nights they would have gotten the rest of it, and all this knowledge would have been lost." The village's current population is descended mostly from people who migrated to the area from farther north over the past century to work on the sugar plantations, so they have little or no blood connection to the Moche lords buried in the *huaca*, he said. Their claims of ancestry are a romantic fantasy. "The great majority of the people in Sipán are from elsewhere. They don't have a connection with the land there, and unlike some of the other villages in the area, they don't respect the past."

Fifteen years after his son found that tomb, I found Carlos Bernal Vargas sitting alone at his sparsely furnished home out in the sugar fields, chickens wandering in and out and a breeze flowing through the open windows. As he recounted the misfortunes that descended on his family, he seemed more exhausted than angry.

"I wish my son had never found that damn tomb. It brought me nothing but curses," he said.

Bernal, a lanky, hale man of European features, was still cultivating farm plots and tending his animals well into his seventies. Nothing has gone well for him since Ernil died. Juan, another son involved in the looting, fell off his father's prize tractor and was crushed to death by its wheel. Segundo Carlos, owner of the Toyota, was expelled from the air force and ruined financially after he, too, was accused of trafficking in looted Sipán pieces. Samuel only recently emerged from twenty years of alcoholism, which he feels was worsened by the events unleashed by the discovery of the tomb. Eloísa Bernal, holder of the key to the sideboard that contained the treasures and the glue holding the family together, died of cancer a few years ago. Then one by one, Carlos Bernal Vargas's seven cows were stolen.

Small comfort that the villagers repeat his son's name reverentially like an outlaw saint. Even the local soccer team is named Ernil Bernal.

"My son is lying on the ground dying, and there's Alva with his metal detector looking for who knows what," said Carlos Bernal, recalling that day in 1987. He recently married a much younger local woman and built a new house a stone's throw from the one where he lived with his sons. "Too many ghosts in the old place," he said. It's now in ruins, roofless and overgrown. Behind it, the avocado tree where his son lay mortally wounded still grows. For a time the tree became an informal shrine for townspeople, who prayed or left little offerings to Ernil's martyred spirit, but over the years they stopped coming.

Compared to the row houses and farm huts that most people in Sipán call home, Bernal's new house is strikingly large, a mansion of brick and concrete with a stately wooden front door, a Spanish-style roof, a brick patio, and a few rosebushes in bloom. His new wife, an attractive, dark-haired woman of about thirty-five, worked in the kitchen and emerged now and then to shoo out the chickens. A faded, poster-sized photograph of Ernil was tacked to the living-room wall, in a place where, in another house, you might see the pope or a crucifix. Beneath it, in a tattered armchair, his father sat lamenting the bitter destiny of a man who buries his children and then lives off the money they earned.

"I always said to Ernil, 'Don't go to the *huaca*, it will swallow you up. Let those spirits be.' I prohibited him from going there. But he went anyway, and who knows what bad spirits he released from that tomb? It cost me everything," he said. "But you know what they say, *no hay bien que por mal no venga.*"[51]

Which means, good things have a way of turning bad. Every silver cloud has a dark lining. He was the first in a long line of people, Peruvian and American, who felt that their lives were destroyed by the gold of Sipán.

Chapter 3

THE EXCAVATORS

THE EXCAVATION OF Sipán began as an emergency salvage operation. "We were trying to salvage what the looters had left behind," recalled Alva.[1] Born in blood and chaos, the project had no money, no supporters, and no one who believed it would yield anything but pottery shards, bone fragments, and discarded cigarette butts. It was a mop-up operation that couldn't afford a mop. And Alva, its lead archaeologist, was surrounded day and night on the *huaca* by people who wanted to kill him.

The one thing the dig had going for it was Alva's belief that where there was one royal Moche tomb, there would be others. It seemed like a hunch, but people who knew Alva and the archaeological process knew that his intuitive feeling was honed by years of excavating a wider variety of sites than anyone else then working in Peru. Like other archaeologists, he knew the attention paid to the site by looters over the years could indicate the importance of the site and the wealth and variety of deposits beneath its parched, chalky surface. It had been ransacked for much longer than he or anyone else had realized. As he descended into the Bernals' pits, he saw that the network of tunnels and galleries that riddled the burial platform was more extensive than the brothers could have dug in only weeks or months: it was the work of looters over years. There were no fewer than eight major vertical shafts and twice that many smaller ones.[2] Most had innumerable tunnels and holes branching out like boughs of an inverted tree.

Ever since the advent of modern archaeology in Peru, commercial looting had long existed alongside it like an evil twin. For many decades, the
distinction between the two was a bit blurry. One of Peru's best ethnographic collections, that of the Museo Arqueológico Rafael Larco Herrera
in Lima, was gathered in the first half of the twentieth century by methods
that today might be considered more ransacking than research, with men
using spades and picks to dig up graves on the Larco family's personal estate. The father of Peruvian archaeology, Julio C. Tello, a man of humble
mestizo background who devised a basic sequence of the evolution of Andean cultures that is still used today, told an associate in 1946, "I'm neither
a professor nor a writer, but merely a man of the country, a *huaquero*."[3] Archaeologists rightly deplore the damage caused by looters, yet most will ac-
knowledge a perverse debt of gratitude to looters, who often show them
where to dig and what they will find.

"You might hear some archaeologists take the high road, but the truth
is that we all use what looters find. I think it is rare, if ever, that an archaeologist finds a site in this area without looters finding it first," said Izumi
Shimada, an archaeologist from Southern Illinois University and one of the
most respected figures in Moche scholarship, who excavated a site known
as Batán Grande in northern Lambayeque. A vast complex of ancient
mounds and settlements that postdate Sipán by about seven hundred years,
Batán Grande had been pillaged for decades before Shimada began excavating the site in 1978. As he began his research, he surveyed the site by air
and horseback and counted the pits left by looters. He stopped at 100,000.
When Shimada told me that figure, I assumed it was an estimate. Yet it was
neither estimate nor hyperbole, explained Shimada, a shy, intense man
with wire-rimmed glasses who, while we spoke in his museum laboratory,
continually consulted pages of neatly written old notes. He had photographed most of the terrain owned by the Aurich family from the air in
the 1970s and spent weeks hunched over the grainy, black-and-white images with a magnifying glass, counting the pits. He gave up at 100,000,
although there were unquestionably thousands more, the physical evidence of more than forty years of pillage. Most of those pits are still
there—shallow, sandy craters that make walking over the estate's
scrubby lands a slow and tiring task.

"Every archaeologist routinely examines what the looters have dug out,
what they discarded, what they missed. You could almost say that looters
are testing a site for us," said Shimada. A serious, soft-spoken man whose
family moved to the United States from Japan when he was a teenager,
Shimada took a break from laboratory work to greet me in sandals one
morning at the sleekly modern archaeological museum, the Museo Nacional Sicán, he created, with Peruvian and foreign funding, in the town of
Ferreñafe, outside Chiclayo. He and Carlos Elera, its Canadian-trained

director, have created a museum that, almost unique in the world, does not display a single looted item. Every single piece has been excavated by archaeologists.

"We do in some way—I don't know if I want to use the word—benefit from what looters have found as an indication of what we can expect to find below the surface," said Shimada.[4] Usually the best that archaeologists can do is try to stop the looting before it destroys a site entirely and hope something is left to excavate. In Sipán's case, it was Alva's own intuition, persistence, and good contacts among the police that allowed him to achieve that aim.

Alva and Chero were astonished to find that the Sipán grave robbers had missed some objects in their own shaft. Clearing one side of the ruined burial chamber, they found a piece of a crown made of gilded copper festooned with metal discs hanging from wires. This was the first object retrieved in situ from Sipán by archaeologists, and it was quickly followed by more: four complete ceramic jars in the shape of human forms, a life-size copper mask with inlaid turquoise eyes, two beads from a necklace in the form of owl heads made of gilded copper, and round ear ornaments made of gilded copper and similar to the ear ornaments seized by the police in their first raid on the Bernal homestead.

Next out of the dirt of the plundered tomb came the clearest evidence yet of its regal status: a heavy, three-foot-long scepter made of copper, the sort of object that only a person of exceptionally high status could hold. One end the scepter tapered to a point, and the other bore a miniature model of a kind of lodge, three sides of which opened onto a balustrade bordered by rows of tiny mace heads. The fourth side of the lodge was formed by a wall, and on that wall was a barely distinguishable scene that, on closer inspection, revealed a creature, half reptile and half feline, pinning a woman to a crescent moon while driving its penis into her.[5]

Alva's mind raced. Could the structure be a model of a building used by the monarch buried here, perhaps a kind of throne room? And what did the scene of the copulating Moche chimera and woman mean? Was it some kind of creation myth? From this plundered space, answers would be hard to come by. The objects inspired all kinds of ideas, whetting the enthusiasm of his corps of colleagues, archaeology students, and diggers, but, as far as Alva was concerned, they remained little more than that: objects, fascinating and tantalizing, but shorn of their meaning. The context in which their creators had left these pieces had been irretrievably lost, and for this reason Alva couldn't be completely sure of what he was looking at.

Squatting amid the broken debris and crushed bone splinters left by the waves of looters, the archaeologists began making notes about the tomb's shape and structure. They were able to establish that it once had wooden beams for a roof, although the wood had long since rotted away into a light gray powder, and that the tomb had been set meticulously on an east-west axis. Alva made one more curious find: a piece of a tooth. Examinations later revealed it to be a molar of an elderly man, but more than that, and whether it belonged to the ruler buried there, the sample was too small to say.[6]

At the same time, research by Alva's wife, Susana Meneses, was shedding light on the history and design of the burial platform itself, the lowest of three main parts of the *huaca*. Analyzing the style, patterns, and composition of the bricks, Meneses drew up schematic plans showing six distinct building phases stretching over three hundred years. The exact age of the platform could not be determined, but it appeared to date from the dawn of Moche society in the first century A.D. and grew until about the year 300.[7] With each building phase, the structure expanded toward the north and grew taller until it acquired roughly its present height.

Meneses's research offered more signs that the looters' tomb was no fluke. It lay at the matrix of a site that generations of Moche builders made wider and taller during precisely the years of greatest expansion of Moche power on the north coast. As a symbol and seat of power, this long-neglected pyramid was plainly much more important than anyone had realized.

The diggers sifted through the scraps left by the looters. The site was guarded all the time by uniformed police and now surrounded by a low, barbed-wire fence that was so rickety it could barely keep out a dog, much less the angry villagers who daily surrounded the excavators and hurled abuse at them. The project had little more than Alva's meager savings and the goodwill of some prominent citizens on which to work. A pasta manufacturer in Chiclayo pledged support for the project and supplied it in the form of noodles. Alva had to pay his workers in a mix of money and macaroni. At night the diggers slept under makeshift tents of sheet plastic or woven reeds, or they clambered down into the looters' tunnels to sleep in safety against flying rocks, bottles, and rotten fruit. Now and then they would be woken by a policeman firing warning shots to frighten away looters. By day, police sometimes had to fire tear gas to keep looters at bay.

"We had descended to a very primitive level of life," said Meneses a few years later. "There were four or six precarious reed tents, erected only through the goodwill of some workers. That was all we had to protect us from the sun and the wind. . . . You better like what you're doing very much if you're going to put up with it and keep working."[8]

Alva and his group of five to ten assistants persisted in the belief that there was more to find. By early June the excavation was on sounder financial footing. Christopher Donnan, a UCLA professor known as the world's foremost expert on Moche iconography, visited the site and gave Alva about $900 as an emergency down payment to keep the excavation going and later arranged financing from the National Geographic Society.

Donnan also gave Alva the excavation's first camera, a Nikon, and more than sixty rolls of film.[9] Alva was able to hire a team of twenty-four workers, six of them students from his alma mater, the Universidad de Trujillo, to step up the pace of excavation. Alva had wanted to keep the staff of diggers entirely Peruvian, if possible, and so far he was achieving that goal, even though most of the financing was foreign.[10]

On June 14, Alva and his excavators were working a few yards from the looters' main shaft in a study area measuring thirty by thirty feet. Like the Bernal brothers, the archaeologists could see that a cut had been made in the *huaca,* the bricks removed, and then refilled with gravel and loose bricks. This was the first clear sign they were in the presence of another large tomb. As Alva's crew slowly brushed away the earth, they found the remnants of wooden beams indicating the top of a large burial chamber. Then, using toothbrushes, teaspoons, and trowels, they found the rim of a brick red ceramic pot. Excitement rippled through the camp as yet another pot emerged, then another and another, then whole clusters of ceramic pots until, after twelve hours of digging, they had found a total of 1,137 ceramic bowls, pots, and jars. Most were modeled in the form of standing or sitting men in various activities. There were pots with prisoners, naked and tethered around the neck, facing an authority figure. There were groups of musicians, figures standing together or alone, some next to seashells, llama bones, or small copper ornaments. Slowly a tableau of Moche ceremony was emerging.[11] The fact that there were so many models of prisoners and musicians suggested that it was a kind of reenactment in ceramic of a part of the "sacrifice ceremony" depicted in elaborate line paintings on Moche pottery. Those paintings showed prisoners of war being dragged up the *huaca* platform, where ruling personages awaited, dressed in the elaborate, feathered costumes of Moche deities. The rulers would draw the blood of their captives, toast each other, and drink it down.[12] Police had seized from the Bernal family's sideboard a goblet similar to that depicted in the line drawings.[13] Alva knew that another such Sipán goblet, made of solid gold, had wound up in Poli's collection in Lima. Behind the barbed-wired fences and police sandbags at Sipán, a picture was emerging of the *huaca* as a center of human sacrifice and ritual cannibalism.

Produced in two-sided molds, the pots had rough, unadorned surfaces and little sign of wear or use, suggesting they had been manufactured not long before their burial in the *huaca*. To an archaeologist, they were full of meaning. Their style and technique offered clues to the age of the site, about A.D. 300, and their arrangement offered an intriguing image of Moche society.

To the antiquities trade, however, they were practically useless. They had no unusual scenes or designs on them beyond the rather inexpressive faces on their tops, and anyway the pre-Columbian antiquities market was glutted with ceramics. To collectors like Enrico Poli, such pots would have been as interesting as so many coffee mugs. The Bernal brothers knew not to bother with such pieces. When they found a similar trove of ceramics embedded in the *huaca*, they smashed through them with their shovels to get to the merchandise underneath.[14]

Nine feet away from the looted tomb, and almost adjacent to the crowds of ceramic men, the archaeologists found another area of loose soil, marking the spot where bricks had been removed and later refilled. Slowly and methodically over the next few weeks they dug to a depth of about twelve feet below the surface and found the skeleton of a man, lying prone with his feet amputated, though whether they had been cut in life or in death, they had no way of knowing. He was wearing what seemed like military garb—a gilded copper helmet and a round copper shield—suggesting he was a guard, and in his left hand and mouth were ingots of copper. Tests later showed that he was about twenty years old, but the body was too decomposed to offer any details as to how he died.[15]

The archaeologists dug further and came again upon traces of wooden beams, now a mere gray powder, followed by a discovery that set their hearts racing. Arranged in a rectangle about seven by four feet, they found eight clusters of copper straps that had corroded to a livid green. Further digging revealed that the straps had been used to bind together wooden beams, also now decomposed to dust. They had discovered a coffin.

Descending inch by inch, they found two largely decomposed textile shrouds sewn with small, delicate panels of gilded copper, followed by a solid gold ingot and three long copper spear points. The wooden shafts of the spears had rotted away over the centuries.

After painstakingly retrieving those pieces, photographing and recording everything about them, the archaeologists found two rectangular banners, each about two feet wide, made of copper platelets and decorated with forms of men with outstretched arms. Next came "a large sheet of gilded copper," as Alva and Donnan described it in their account of the excavation, again made of small platelets arranged in the form of a man's torso like a mail coat. This might have been a counterpart to the gold sheet that the Bernal brothers described seeing as they descended into the other royal tomb nearby. A series of sixteen small cones that looked like candle snuffers hung from the bottom of the torso-shaped sheet in a decorative fringe. Similar fringes hung from the two banners. Police had seized one such cone from the Bernal brothers during the first raid in February, and Alva had scrutinized it that night in the police station and wondered what it was. Now he knew.[16]

From then on, the archaeologists were met with a dazzling procession of artifacts made of gold, silver, gilded copper, and precious stones, all lying amid thousands of white, pink, and green shell beads from hanging pectoral ornaments. There could be no doubt that the looters had found one royal tomb and that here was another. Like the British royals who interred their dead under the floor of Westminster Abbey, the people of the Moche potentate at Sipán buried their lords in the ground beneath their most important religious and ceremonial shrine.

Descending millimeter by millimeter with their most delicate camel-hair brushes, the excavators next found three sets of ear ornaments known as ear spools, made of gold with turquoise and shell inlay. A distinctive part of the high ceremonial garb of the Moche and of some later Andean cultures, the ear spool consisted of a metal cylinder that would fit through large holes in the earlobes, with a disc-shaped, ornamental panel on the front of the ear and sometimes a counterbalancing spool or wooden block on the back. Years of using ear ornaments gave their wearers huge, drooping lobes; hence the Spaniards called the Inca pooh-bahs they encountered *los orejones*, or the big-eared people. Two sets of ear spool now before Alva showed animals in naturalistic poses. One bore an image of a leaping, panting deer in an exquisite mosaic of gold, turquoise, and white shell, and the other depicted a duck standing in profile in a flawless arrangement of gold wire, turquoise, and blue-green stone.

The third set of ear spools bore a striking, three-dimensional image. Each spool depicted a man carrying a mace in one hand and a shield in the other and bedecked in some of the ceremonial garb that the wearer of the ear spools must have worn. No larger than Alva's thumb, each tiny figure wore golden rattles, a nose ornament, an elaborate headdress of gold and turquoise, and a necklace of minute, golden owl heads—miniature versions of the owl heads confiscated from the Bernal brothers. The mace he carried in his right hand was removable, and parts of his royal garb were suspended with tiny gold wires so that, when worn, they would have shaken with the slightest movement. The man's anatomy was depicted with masterful detail. His face, fingers, thighs, calves, even his kneecaps were all crafted in gold. Two other figures in turquoise and gold inlay stood on either side of the central warrior. Only under a magnifying glass were Alva and his team able to appreciate the full virtuosity of these pieces, which, together with the deer and duck spools, "are certainly among the finest pieces of ancient jewelry ever found."[17]

The pieces that followed were just as magnificent, yet disturbingly similar to artifacts confiscated from the looters. How many masterpieces like the ear spools had been lost in the ransacking of that tomb? Alva could only guess and continue the painstaking excavation. He found a set of twenty beads shaped like peanuts, ten in gold repoussé and ten in silver, identical to the four peanut beads seized from the Bernals and possibly created by the same artists. The cotton threads that had strung the beads together in a necklace had disintegrated, so it never occurred to the Bernals that these curious peanuts were part of a single piece. They had sold them separately, and the beads wound up in at least three different private collections.

The peanut necklace excavated by Alva, by contrast, has been recognized as a masterpiece of craftsmanship and design, a tour de force of style and elegance that has shown millions of people how societies divided by seventeen centuries of history can be united by the aesthetic principles of harmony and refinement. The peanut necklace later became one of the most recognizable pieces of the Sipán traveling exhibition and one of the best-known objects of pre-Hispanic art anywhere.

Next came a necklace of golden discs, each nearly two inches in diameter and again similar to a silver piece seized from the looters, except that the discs excavated by Alva showed wear in their holes, suggesting frequent use. Perhaps it was one of the deceased's preferred pieces.[18]

The right hand of the Lord of Sipán, as Alva had dubbed him, grasped a gold-and-silver scepter, eerily similar to one the looters plundered and sold to Poli. The bottom end of the scepter had a sharp, flattened blade, and the other end carried a boxlike chamber bearing a scene with a characteristically Moche mix of beauty and brutality. A warrior in feathered garb was subduing a naked, cross-legged prisoner, bashing his face with a mace, while another figure stood behind the prisoner grasping his arm and hair. Hummingbirds flitted about in the background, accompanying and narrating the action like a Greek chorus.

As they stripped away the pounds of jewelry and accoutrements that the Lord of Sipán took to his grave, the excavators knew they were approaching his actual remains. They cleared the soil over his head and began finding pieces of sheet gold molded to resemble the deceased's facial features. Due to the absence of perforations, Alva deduced they were not used in life and must have been placed on the man's face after death. Nothing like them had ever been found in Peruvian archaeology.[19] There were five pieces of paper-thin, hammered gold. One covered his chin, mouth, and jaw; another covered his nose; two others covered the eyes and were incised with impressions of his eyeballs and lashes. The fifth apparently went inside his mouth because it would have covered his gums and was incised with a detailed reproduction *of his teeth*.

The man was practically embalmed in gold. Decked out in so much metal at his burial that his skin could barely be seen, he probably looked more like a reclining golden statue than a human being. The soles of his feet were covered in sandals made of solid silver. Two tweezers made of silver and then bathed in gold rested at his waist, as if for plucking whiskers. For even the most mundane tasks, this was a man of gold.

Finally they came to the bones. With great care and reverence they lifted out the remnants of the man's frame, splinter by tiny splinter, first with their hands and then with a layer of liquid acrylic, thick enough to gather the three-hundred-some pieces into which the body had decomposed, yet thin enough not to damage the artifacts that might lie below. As the wooden roof beams and coffin had collapsed over the centuries, tons of earth had fallen into the chamber and crushed his bones into little more than dust in some places. But enough of his frame and his skull were left for a forensic anthropologist, John Verano of Tulane University, to determine later that the Lord of Sipán had died between the ages of thirty-five and forty-five and had stood about five feet five inches — tall by Moche standards. He had very early signs of arthritis, probably not enough to cause him discomfort, but the cause of death could not be determined. He showed no signs of long-term wasting disease, physical trauma, or fractures, and he had a full set of teeth that showed no decay except for one small cavity in a lower left molar. The back of his skull showed pronounced flattening, suggesting he had been cradleboarded as a child. Moche remains at other sites had shown that such occipital flattening of the skull was common, in roughly equal proportions between men and women. Because the flattening was uneven and varied widely from person to person, Verano concluded it was most likely an unintentional deformation caused by the practice of carrying children in cradles made of wooden slats. Even today, Peruvian women can be seen carrying children over their backs while they work with their hands. The Sipán find suggested that the high-status individual buried there, wrote Verano later, "was bound to a cradleboard as an infant like any common Moche child."[20]

Although the average lifespan for Moche men was only about thirty-five, the death at that age of a man who lived in such privilege remains another of the enigmas of Sipán. He may have died quite suddenly from epidemic or intestinal disease, not an unlikely outcome for one who habitually drank warm human blood. That he died unexpectedly was already suggested by the lack of wear on the ceramics populating the upper reaches of his tomb.[21]

To Alva, identifying the Lord of Sipán and ascertaining some of the basic facts of his life suddenly gave the excavation a transcendental importance. Here on a table in the laboratory of the Brüning Museum lay the remains of the first identifiable leader of Peru. Radiocarbon tests on the remains of the timbers dated the tomb to A.D. 290, give or take half a century. Alva believed that no archaeological source had ever produced evidence of an actual, individual leader with real biographical data this early in Peru or anywhere else in the Americas, with the arguable exception of the Maya of northern Guatemala, whose earliest recorded dynasties were roughly contemporaneous. At Sipán, archaeology was offering the Peruvian people an unprecedented personal connection to their past, not through books or research papers but through the remains of a flesh-and-blood ancestor who, during his short life, commanded the allegiance and respect of the people who walked this same land. From then on, Alva insisted that Peruvian authorities, politicians, and his own staff treat the remains of the Lord of Sipán like the remains of a head of state, deserving the respect and ceremony accorded to the nation's former presidents.

Underneath the remains, archaeologists found still more gold. A huge golden headdress shaped like a crescent moon appeared, glistening in the desert sun as Alva and his students brushed and blew away the dirt. Plumes of decomposed feathers atop the headdress hinted at the lavishness that must have attended the man's burial. Subsequent analysis showed that the feathers belonged to the Chilean flamingo, a pink wading bird that inhabits the marshy lagoons and salt pans of the Andean plateaus. Alva also found shells of a type of mollusk known as the spondylus; it was venerated for its meat and its shell was used to make jewelry. The nearest the spondylus lived to Sipán was the coast of modern-day Ecuador, suggesting that Sipán people developed trade ties with distant regions.

One layer lower, Alva found another counterpart to the looted tomb. It was a semicircular rattle, similar to the one sold by the Bernal brothers to Gallardo and, like that one, made of copper bathed in gold. It was in better condition than the looted rattle: its original inlays of turquoise and spondylus shell were still in place in the decapitator's eyes, mouth, and cheeks, giving the figure a stern, fearsome appearance. Its eyes glared out at the excavators from the bottom of the grave where it lay. There were two such rattles, and next to them lay twin backflaps of polished gold and silver. The silver one had corroded to a dull green, but the gold backflap gleamed as if had been buried the day before.

Backflaps were a uniquely Moche object worn only by male warriors of high social rank, an artifact that held tremendous symbolic importance. They seem to have gone out of fashion as the Moche declined, and they never reappeared. Much of what we know about how backflaps were used comes from their depiction in combat scenes in paintings on Moche pottery. The backflap hung from a waist cord at the small of the back, shielding the warrior's lower back and buttocks. The name in Spanish for this artifact is *protector coxal,* or coccyx protector. Judging from those pottery paintings, high-ranking warriors wore backflaps in actual combat, although the ones buried in the tomb would presumably have been too heavy to wear in war and had only ceremonial uses. In this tomb (and the looted tomb, as Alva was to find out), the backflap was the largest single artifact.[22]

With so many parallels to what he knew about the looted tomb, Alva might have suspected that the looters had found a gold backflap in the tomb they looted. But Ernil Bernal was dead, the surviving looters weren't talking, and anyway Alva was preoccupied with interpreting the objects he had found. By the time he had finished excavating Tomb One, as the Lord of Sipan's grave became known, he had retrieved 451 objects that would change everything that scholars thought they knew about the artistic achievements and social organization of cultures before the Incas. Sipán "would revolutionize thinking about the ancient Moche, their rulers, their artisans, their metalwork, and countless other aspects of the Moche life and history," wrote one scholar.[23]

The remains of seven more people of humbler rank—attendants and wives whom the Lord of Sipán brought with him to the next world—lay arranged around his body inside the burial chamber. There were three adult men, a child whose sex could not be determined, and three females between the ages of fifteen and twenty, one of whom was wearing a large copper headdress. The men and the child seemed to have been sacrificed at the time of the royal burial. But not the young women. Their bones were jumbled so haphazardly in their simple cane coffins that they could not possibly have decomposed undisturbed in their final graves. They had been dead for a long time, maybe years, possibly even before the central figure was born, before their bodies were lowered into the tomb of their lord.[24]

What did this mean? What did it say about that society's idea of the death of the flesh and the life of the spirit? The mysteries of Sipán were endless, and a few random objects plied by looters weren't going to supply many answers. Only through careful excavation and interpretation of the remains and objects in their original surroundings could insights be gleaned.

As Alva and his team finished excavation of the tomb in March 1988, they found on the south side of the platform loose dirt that could only mean another tomb. Alva wasn't sure how the looters missed this spot, but when he began excavating he found the tomb of the "bird priest" depicted in the blood-and-sacrifice rituals on Moche pot paintings. Part bird and part man, the bird priest joined the ruler figure, or warrior priest, in drinking the blood of captured prisoners of war. In his grave, the bird priest's body came complete with a massive, three-tiered headdress decorated with 170 hanging platelets of gilded copper that must have shaken and glistened in the sun. Archaeologists had seen pictures of such headdress on pottery but had no idea, until now, what it was made of or how it was constructed.[25] As it settled some questions, Sipán opened many others.

At a news conference at the National Geographic Society in Washington, D.C., on September 13, 1988, Alva and Donnan announced to the world the details of the work done so far at Sipán. Alva had tried to keep it secret as much as possible, partly to avoid further provoking the looters, but reports of the quality and quantity of the artifacts had been circulating in the media for well over a year. What the excavators had found so far, Alva and Donnan told the news conference, exceeded even the most excited rumors and reports. It was the richest unlooted funerary complex ever found in the Americas, and they believed that still more tombs awaited excavation.

"The quality of the gold work is stunning. It puts our understanding of New World metallurgy on a different plane," Donnan said. Images of the artifacts appeared on front pages of newspapers in the United States and around the world, with inevitable comparisons to the discovery of Tutankhamen's tomb, the Dead Sea Scrolls, the temples of Ur, and the terracotta soldiers of Xi'an. But the discoverers of those sensations didn't have the antiquities trade breathing down their shafts to the degree that Alva and his Sipán team did in Peru's chaotic atmosphere.[26] Alva finally had the financing to build more comfortable living quarters and outhouses for his staff. He had endeavored to keep the digging staff composed entirely of Peruvians, but he knew there was no hope of getting much financing at this stage from Peruvian sources. Inflation was running in four digits, the national government was bankrupt, with international currency reserves at literally less than zero, and public services like electricity and running water had practically collapsed. In the city of Chiclayo, tap water was a cloudy, brownish liquid that dribbled out the faucet. A Maoist insurgency called the Shining Path had brought much of the Andean highlands under its control, and, although the north coast did not see major violence, police forces all over the country suffered frequent guerrilla attacks and were stretched thin. The sandbag emplacements on the *huaca* were not just to keep looters at bay but were used by police as a routine precaution against guerrilla attack (which never came).

In the middle of this contrast between brilliant work at the dig and national crisis all around, the *huaca* yielded yet another great discovery. In August 1989, at the lowest level of the platform, some sixteen feet below its surface, Alva's team struck the tomb of another member of the Moche elite who, judging from the objects around him, enjoyed in life the same ruler status as the Lord of Sipán. From its position at the bottom of the platform, the tomb, named Tomb Three, was clearly older than either Tomb One or the looted tomb. Excavation of the tomb over the following eight months offered more evidence of a Sipán monarchy and the platform as a family mausoleum. The burial was more modest than at Tomb One, with the deceased buried in a simple pit instead of a grand funerary chamber. Instead of a retinue of murdered or reburied attendants, the man interred here had only one attendant, a girl between sixteen and eighteen years old, buried facedown and with arms splayed away from her body, as if she were trying to break her fall as she was pushed in and buried alive. A llama had been thrown on top of her.[27]

This tomb yielded one of the most intriguing objects to emerge from Sipán. Around the chest of the man, whom Alva dubbed the Old Lord of Sipán, lay a necklace of ten oval golden beads, each about three inches in diameter. The bottom of the bead was a gold cup, and the top bore a complex, latticework design of a spiderweb, with a spider in the middle of it, and on the thorax of each spider was depicted, in low relief, a realistic face of a man. Thus man was depicted as spider, not caught in a web as victim, but astride it, as if waiting for prey. Made of evenly wrought gold wire, the spiderweb on each bead had been flawlessly soldered together at 140 tiny points.

Even more than in the first grave, Alva found echoes of the looted tomb. There was a necklace of fanged cat's faces that looked like miniature replicas of the gold-and-inlay feline heads seized in the first raid on the Bernal house. The resemblance was perfect, but the meaning was not so clear. Did these feline faces represent the jaguar, supreme predator of the Andes and lowlands, or some other wildcat? Or could they be meant to represent something entirely different—the faces of sea lions, as some scholars later suggested? Sea lions, plentiful today along the cold Peruvian coast, had mystical attributes for the Moche because they straddled the border between sea and earth, fish and furred animal, and by extension between life and death. The pebbles found inside the stomachs of slaughtered sea lions were believed to have mystical properties.[28] With each new discovery, Alva's work at Sipán was opening new interpretive frontiers and new controversies that would boil through pre-Columbian scholarship for years to come.

In another parallel, a collection of ten golden rattles lay draped over the shoulders of the buried man. They looked nearly identical in design to the one seized from Gallardo and bore only a few minor stylistic differences from the two gilded copper rattles excavated in Tomb One. Two or three rattles would have been worn on a waist cord that would also hold a gold or silver backflap—those were also found in the tomb, somewhat smaller and less ornate than the two excavated from the other tomb. Forensic tests later showed that the man stood five feet three inches tall, and his teeth, although heavily worn, showed no cavities. A large gold ingot had been placed inside his mouth. He was longer lived than the Lord of Sipán, having died between the ages of forty-five and fifty-five.[29]

Some years after the excavation of the Old Lord of Sipán's tomb, Alva sent a sample of bone tissue from the deceased man's grave to a Japanese laboratory. The results have yet to be published, but preliminary findings show that the principal figures in Tombs One and Three were blood relatives divided by no more than three generations.[30] Most likely they were grandfather and grandson, with the figure in the looted tomb the generation in between, the father of the Lord of Sipán. Bone material in the looted tomb was too pulverized and contaminated for DNA testing, but Alva felt certain the Bernals had cracked into the middle generation of three lords of this dynasty. Judging from the size of the looted backflap and the purity of the artifacts' goldwork, it was during that middle generation that the sumptuous Sipán style reached its zenith. Only further scientific excavation might reveal what happened to this dynasty, the first known hereditary monarchy in the Americas whose existence could be proven with actual human remains. Either it stopped burying its dead in Huaca Rajada or died out with the ruler buried in Tomb One. Or more tombs remained undiscovered.

Ernil Bernal and his men came within three feet of finding the Lord of Sipán's burial chamber. One more night of digging and they would have discovered it.

As Alva excavated the Old Man of Sipán's tomb in late 1989, he knew that news of the fabulous treasures that had escaped the looters' grasp was attracting *huaqueros* to the area from all over Peru, every one of them dreaming of finding the next Sipán. Some were experienced tomb raiders, others were simply unemployed. The story of how the Bernal brothers had found the glittering tomb by luck and wiles had become a folk tale among the Peruvian underclass, retold, repeated, and embellished in dusty cantinas, farmhouses, and shantytowns. A gold rush was on. At *huacas* and cemeteries up and down the Peruvian coast, grave robbers worked day and night, ripping into tombs at a rate not seen in the lifetimes of most of the people who witnessed it. Looting is always difficult to quantify, but the depredation of Peru's archaeological heritage in the late 1980s and 1990s was, at least in some areas, probably the heaviest since the Spanish Conquest. Alva could only speculate about how many of the tombs destroyed in this wave of looting belonged to high-status individuals. But there was at least one.

Forty miles south of Sipán, the Jequetepeque Valley traverses the desert from the Andes to the sea in a green ribbon of farms and thickets. A Moche state ruled the area at the same time that others held court in Sipán and nearby valleys up and down the coast. They coexisted as a loose confederation, with similar artistic styles and marriages between the children of their elites, much like the modern royal families of Europe. In 1988, a farmer in the Jequetepeque Valley discovered a Moche burial chamber beneath the floor of a long-abandoned gold mine known as La Mina, on a hillside above the valley. In quantity, the artifacts were fewer than at Sipán, but the quality was equally fine. There were golden ear spools, owl heads, and a necklace made of exquisite golden monkey heads, among other treasures. For a time the farmer managed to keep the find to himself, using the tomb, in Kirkpatrick's memorable words, "as a type of savings account, making withdrawals only when he needed cash" and selling them to a dealer in Trujillo.[31] But as treasures began trickling onto the market, organized looters found the site, pushed out the farmer, and quickly emptied at least one Moche elite tomb at La Mina and possibly others.

Alva and other archaeologists heard rumors that looters had discovered another major Moche tomb in the valley but could not pinpoint the lo-

cation. Christopher Donnan, who had worked at a nearby site called
Pacatnamú and knew the valley well, surveyed it from the air to look for
the telltale piles of dirt but found nothing. The looting continued until the
supposedly guilt-stricken Trujillo dealer called Alva at the Brüning Museum. The dealer had heard about Alva's success in excavating Sipán and
keeping the looters at bay and wanted him to do the same thing for La
Mina. Unfortunately, the dealer had waited until the flow of artifacts dried
up before his pangs of conscience led him to call the famous archaeologist.
Alva and Meneses rushed to the site the next day, but by the time they arrived, the place had been thoroughly emptied. The looters got everything.
When a group of archaeologists ventured to the site to begin salvage excavation in May 1989, they frightened off ten looters who were busily widen-
ing the main shaft into the tomb. Once the place had been secured,
excavations revealed traces of colorful abstract designs painted on the
tomb's side walls of plastered mud brick, six high-quality ceramic urns, and
the crushed and splintered remains of five people, including those of a
woman in her fifties. Yet the salvage operation was a rather tedious job,
and the ruined site yielded little of interest.[32]

Artifacts from La Mina circulating through the antiquities market over
the years suggest that it was, as Alva and Donnan wrote, "every bit as rich
as the royal tombs at Sipán and Loma Negra, and had contained many objects of nearly identical size, form and iconography."[33] Adding to the parallel with Sipán was the fact that analysis of the artifacts and the tomb
structure at La Mina suggested that the two sites were almost contemporaneous, both dating from about A.D. 300, a time that must have been a kind
of golden era for north-coast art and metallurgy.

Artifacts from La Mina have occasionally been confused with those
from Sipán, passed off as them, or even amalgamated with them. From the
looted tomb at Sipán Poli has a gold headdress with, in its center, the face
of an owl peering through a hole that probably once contained a medallion
or amulet of some kind. Alva believes the owl head is actually from La
Mina. The owl head rests incongruously above a pair of open human hands
etched into the headdress's gleaming sheet of gold.[34]

In 1990 Alva and his team returned to the looted Sipán tomb to investigate
more fully its dimensions and contents before refilling it. After the thrill of
excavating the other tombs, going back to Ernil Bernal's bare pit was a sad
and dispiriting task that Alva had been avoiding. He found that Bernal had
been even luckier than he realized. When the master looter burrowed up
into the burial room from below, he entered directly under the body of the
principal figure buried there, as Alva could tell from the remains in the soil
of the wooden slats of the casketlike box that had contained the body. A

few feet to the left or right, and Ernil would have hit the body of one of the ruler's concubines or attendants and would not have felt that avalanche of golden artifacts that set in motion the emptying of the tomb. Excavating around the sides of the ruined chamber, Alva and his team found a dozen or so artifacts, mostly gilded copper or ceramic, and the remains of four people buried with the lord, although Alva had no doubt that the bodies of many more were destroyed by the looters. One man, presumably a guardian, had had his left foot amputated. There were two women, and most of the body of one had been inadvertently smashed by the looters. Finally there was a young man buried with a huge war club, a weapon measuring nearly five feet long and made of copper and hardwood now mostly decomposed. A spearhead, its wooden rod long since rotted away, lay on his left leg. With this small arsenal, Alva deduced that he was a soldier belonging to the royal house and sacrificed to act as the lord's bodyguard in the underworld.[35]

After retrieving the last of the objects and the bones for forensic anthropologists to examine in the laboratory, he refilled the tomb with the backfill left from years of looting and archaeology. The looted space had given up all its secrets.

Judging from what he knew about the artifacts that flowed onto the world market over the next few years, Alva was fairly sure the looters had in fact hacked into two major tombs, not one. Ernil might even have realized it himself. One tomb was certainly that of a ruler of the stature of the one buried in Tomb One, and the other was probably that of an elite religious figure like the bird priest whose tomb had cast so much light on the nature of Moche worship.[36] Two major tombs would also account for the large number of artifacts that had made their way into private collections.

The French received their first look at the Sipán find with a show in 1988 at the Grand Palais in Paris: it featured eighty pieces from Enrico Poli's stash, every one of which he freely admitted he bought from grave robbers or their agents. Entitled "Gold and Its Myths," the sprawling, extravagant show at one of Europe's most prestigious art venues included a total of 359 pieces from Poli's collection. It was all legal because Poli had registered his looted purchases with the Instituto Nacional de Cultura and received temporary export permits, granted on the condition that he bring all the artifacts back to Peru, which he did. The introduction to the show's catalogue was written by Jacques Chirac, at the time mayor of Paris. In the city that fancied itself the capital of culture, loot had been elevated to the status of high art. Poli was delighted. Years later, he still gave his wicked cackle every time he talked about it.

Peruvian cultural figures and some politicians were outraged. Alan

García, the country's populist president, told Alva that he had no idea the INC had allowed the temporary export of Poli's treasures and that he was considering asking French authorities to seize the whole collection. In the end García did nothing and the whole incident served only to increase Poli's aura of invincibility.

"It was a perfect play by Poli," said Alva.[37] More Sipán loot would soon turn up abroad, under much less prestigious circumstances.

Chapter 4

BACKFLAP

E RNIL BERNAL AND his gang destroyed hundreds, perhaps thousands, of copper and ceramic objects that they thought they couldn't sell, plus a good number of smaller gold and silver objects that didn't make the cut. Like grave robbers everywhere, they went straight for the best merchandise and trashed everything else along the way.

Judging from what he later excavated, Alva felt sure they lost or destroyed much more than they managed to salvage. The piles of smashed pottery, copper artifacts, and tiny metal panels found in the irrigation ditch outside the Bernal homestead were likely only a small portion of the rejects.

Of all the pieces the looters managed to pull intact from the tomb, the biggest and heaviest of them all was the backflap. At 2.9 pounds of gold, alloyed in a Moche furnace with trace amounts of copper and silver to give it form and durability, the backflap was so large that it intimidated buyers.[1] It was the largest gold object found in Sipán, the largest, in fact, that anyone in the long history of the Peruvian antiquities trade ever remembered seeing. And it could not find a buyer.

This is how Alva and Donnan described the fantastic bulk of the backflap in 1993: "It is the largest and heaviest Moche gold object known today. It must have been an extremely impressive, and probably famous, object to these ancient people."[2] But they were not talking about this backflap. They were referring to the stylistically very similar but *smaller* one excavated in Tomb One, back when the archaeologists had heard only vague rumors about the looted backflap. The backflap in Tomb One weighed two pounds and stood 17.5 inches high. The Bernal brothers' piece weighed nearly three pounds and had a height of 25.6 inches—a massive piece of metallurgical prowess the likes of which had never been seen in Peruvian archaeology or anywhere in the Americas. Although no exhaustive surveys exist, it is widely believed to be the largest extant pre-Columbian gold artifact of any kind.

Three years after Ernil pulled it from the tomb and lugged it up the bamboo ladder, their backflap remained buried under the Bernal family's rooster pen while photographs of the piece circulated from collector to collector. In contrast to the delicate workmanship of the figurines and intricate design of necklaces and ear ornaments found at Sipán, the backflap had a blunt, almost functional look. It was made from a single sheet of hammered gold that included the half-moon-shaped rattle attachment, the "tweezer" with which it hung from the waist cord. It was impressive but, to most collectors' eyes, a bit flashy. To Enrico Poli, the Lima patron of pillagers, it bordered on vulgar.

"They brought me this tablecloth, this towel of gold. It was enormous. I didn't like it," he recalled. "And it had been handled by too many people. Those are the pieces that always bring you problems, the ones that have gone through too many hands."[3]

Poli first saw the backflap in 1987 at the home of Pereda, the dealer with whom the Bernals worked, and turned it down, and then he saw it again a few years later, still unsold. Poli claims not to remember who offered it to him the second time but said the dealer wanted $60,000, a bargain-basement price which, if Poli's recollection is correct, reflects how much trouble the Bernals had in selling it. By the time of Poli's second viewing, someone had bent back the two-sided rattle attachment so far that it had snapped off. The backflap was now in two pieces. Whoever did this, perhaps Ernil Bernal himself, must have been trying to make the piece look bigger. Instead, he mutilated and permanently damaged it. For an artifact that had been grabbed from a monarch's tomb, stuffed into a car trunk, and passed around like a pawned wedding ring, this was the ultimate indignity.

The president of one of Peru's largest banks had seen the backflap, legions of the rich or merely curious had seen it, and none of them wanted it. The wife of a prominent Peruvian textile industrialist saw the backflap still for sale in Chiclayo in 1988 when the piece had already achieved a certain underground notoriety.

"It was spectacular but it was too well known by then. It wasn't the sort of piece you could put in your dining room and show your friends," she said. "By the time we saw it, half of Chiclayo had seen it."[4]

It would have been impossible to register it with the Instituto Nacional de Cultura and legalize it in the normal way because the Sipán style was so distinctive and had become practically synonymous with looting. Carlos Gallardo had registered his Sipán stash with the INC only to see it seized anyway and the registration annulled. Thus Peru's judicial system, arbitrary and prone to pressures from the powerful though it was, had set a precedent for confiscating items looted from a well-known site under active archaeological excavation. It had effectively granted a unique status to Sipán artifacts, and every collector who saw the backflap knew it.

"No one wanted it. It was a hot potato," said Alva, who heard the rumors of a gigantic piece of gold making the rounds in the high-end antiquities market. "It was vox populi that there were Sipán pieces still circulating despite the police operations in 1987."[5]

The backflap should have commanded hundreds of thousands of dollars, but it seemed that, for Peruvian collectors at least, the Sipán craze had run its course. Ernil Bernal had pumped so much treasure onto the market that he had single-handedly created a glut. Now and then the surviving Bernal brothers would dig up the backflap from the rooster's pen and show it to a potential buyer or take fresh pictures of it when the original Polaroids became too frayed to pass around. Eventually they gave up trying to sell it themselves and left it on consignment with a shifting cast of dealers and providers.

In 1992 one of those dealers sold it to a Chiclayo hotel owner named Manuel Bacigalupo for what was rumored to be $80,000. There is some ambiguity about the price because the surviving Bernal brothers won't tell, perhaps embarrassed by how small it was, and Bacigalupo died suddenly a few months later, a death from natural causes that nonetheless convinced still more people that Sipán was cursed. He probably hadn't been planning to keep the backflap for long. Friends in Chiclayo knew him as an experienced loot buyer and reseller, and dusty grave robbers continually made their way to his hotel, the Costa de Oro, on the city's busiest thoroughfare, Avenida Balta, to offer him fresh merchandise for purchase. Like many businessmen in Chiclayo, Bacigalupo had bought and sold looted antiquities for years without really considering it a career. He was close friends with Edmundo Aurich, whose family's 200,000-acre cattle ranch about two hours north of Chiclayo included the complex of pyramids known as Batán Grande, built around A.D. 1,000. The Batán Grande people were consummate metallurgists; they stuffed the tombs of their elite with gold and silver buckets, trumpets, masks, necklaces, and other artifacts to a degree that made the Moche seem stingy by comparison. One thousand years later, the Auriches used plows and well-organized teams of ranch hands equipped with shovels and pickaxes to extract tons of treasures from the fifty *huacas* dotting their vast fiefdom. By the 1960s the Auriches had brought in bulldozers and heavy earth-moving equipment to dig out the gold, flattening burial mounds and employing teams of hundreds of peons to sift their contents in what was probably the largest and most systematic destruction of a single ancient site in Peruvian history since the Conquest. Much, perhaps even most, of the Peruvian gold in the permanent collections of American museums today was excavated by the Auriches' looting squads at Batán Grande.[6]

And then the Aurich family lost everything. In 1972 the left-wing military government under Juan Velasco Alvarado began an ambitious land-reform project aimed at breaking the back of Peru's semifeudal oligarchy, which it blamed for the country's poverty and backwardness. The government confiscated the Aurich lands, along with those of the other coastal sugar barons, and the family was ruined. Their land became a giant peasant cooperative. Edmundo Aurich and his brothers remained active in the antiquities trade, however, advising and appraising and occasionally dealing to friends and collectors, including Bacigalupo. According to a family friend, Aurich advised Bacigalupo on the quality and value of the backflap before he purchased it. Bacigalupo was not just stumbling into the deal. Already an experienced dealer himself, he was getting advice on the backflap from one of Peru's best authorities on the acquisition and resale of pre-Columbian gold artifacts.

Before he died, Bacigalupo gave the backflap to his brother and sometime business partner, Luis Bacigalupo, who kept it hidden in a suitcase in a liquor-bottling plant he owned in the dingy, working-class Lima neighborhood of Rímac. The plant went bankrupt in 1993, but Luis held on to the building and the backflap, employing an old woman named Petronila Cabezudo to act as guardian. There it sat as the rumors of its circulation dried up and collectors who had turned it down lost all trace of it.[7] For a long time, the backflap disappeared.

The Moche monarch buried at Sipán would have worn the backflap at important ceremonies and rituals. Too heavy to wear in actual hand-to-hand combat and showing little of the damage or wear associated with frequent use, the backflap would have been viewed by the Moche as a glamorously stylized rendition of military body armor. Presiding over pageants and arraignments of doomed prisoners, the Sipán lord would have worn the backflap slung over a waist cord made of rope that circled his torso, an indispensable symbol of his power and authority understood by everyone around him.

At the same time, he would have worn two or three half-moon-shaped bell ornaments, or rattles, of folded and repoussé gold, draped over the waist cord.[8] These were the pieces the Bernal brothers called tweezers, the pieces that made a curious, scratchy, ringing noise every time someone moved them. The sound emanated from eight spherical chambers along the edges of the rattles like pea pods, each with metal pellets inside. When the Lord of Sipán walked while wearing the waist ornaments, the pellets would have made a sound of metal hitting metal, a sound that the Moche believed would summon supernatural forces.[9] Dressed with the aid of attendants, the Lord of Sipán must have been a magnificent sight to behold in his full ceremonial regalia—the gold of the backflap, the rattles, the headdress, and the ear spools gleaming in the equatorial sun. Unfortunately, no one today can know what that full royal panoply looked like because its constituent pieces are spread out in private collections all over the world.

The fate of the golden rattles in the looted tomb offers an intriguing case of how the lord's royal artifacts rippled through the global antiquities market in the years following their extraction. Delicate, portable, and full of meaning and symbols, the rattles were far more popular than the backflap and captivated the imagination of everyone who saw them. The Bernal brothers sold all of them within weeks of finding them. Poli and perhaps other better-informed buyers knew that rattles had profound importance for the Moche, that ones of this quality could be worn only by royalty, and that rattles of various shapes and sizes were still used in modern times by the descendants of the Moche in folk healing.[10]

The rattles, both those looted by the Bernals and those excavated later by Alva, remain today a prominent public symbol of Sipán and all of northern Peru. Images of them appear on a vast array of advertisements for everything from hotels and cellular phones to beer and shampoo, anything to which an advertiser wants to give a distinctly north Peruvian flavor. The central image on each rattle is a compelling mix of cruelty and beauty. A snarling, fanged deity that was half man and half spider clutches a knife in one hand and a decapitated head in the other, its mouth still agape in horror and pain. This figure was known to art historians as Ai-apaec, or the Decapitator, depicted in Moche murals and pottery paintings and often cited as the supreme deity in the Moche pantheon.

The total number of looted rattles has never been ascertained. Samuel Bernal, witness to the pillage from beginning to end, said there were about ten, and comparative evidence from the other tombs would support that estimate. The Old Lord of Sipán's tomb, excavated by Alva, had the most stylistic parallels to the looted one, containing ten gold rattles and ten identical silver ones. The presence of gold-and-silver mirror images reflected the Moches' dualistic view of the universe, gold associated with the sun and man, silver with the moon and woman.

If in fact there were ten golden rattles, as Alva believed, they must have been all identical and hammered on the same mold, and very likely by the same Moche artisans, as individual parts of an indivisible whole, like beads in a necklace.[11] Three were immediately snapped up by Poli in 1987 and registered with the INC before almost anyone else had heard of Sipán. They remain in his private collection today. Apesteguía was believed to have bought another one, and a fifth rattle wound up in the private collection of Chilean millionaire arms dealer Carlos Cardoen.

A sixth Sipán gold rattle found its way into the home of American art collector and conservator Ben Johnson in August 1987 in the first major shipment of Sipán treasures to reach the United States. Johnson was a prominent figure in the elite heights of American art dealing, selling to some of the richest collectors in the country, including such luminaries as Norton Simon and Armand Hammer. His clients knew they were buying goods that had been looted and illegally exported from their country of origin and they bought them anyway. In a famous exchange with a reporter, Simon was asked whether a bronze Shiva idol that disappeared from a temple in India in 1969 and wound up in his Los Angeles collection had been smuggled. "Hell, yes, it was smuggled," he replied. "I spent between $15 million and $16 million over the last two years on Asian art, and most of it was smuggled."[12] Johnson's clients were usually more circumspect than that, but in private they shared a conviction that there were few ancient treasures in poor countries which they were not entitled to have dismantled, shipped to America, and placed in their living room.

Johnson dressed his dealing in the clothes of scholarly inquiry, stressing his background as a curator at the Smithsonian Institution's Freer Gallery and as head of the conservation department at the Los Angeles County Museum of Art until 1978. In the 1970s, Johnson moved heavily into dealing in ancient Andean and Meso-American art, working with his sometime business associate David Swetnam to import and sell top-of-the-line ancient Peruvian pottery and textiles. Swetnam built up enough inventory to open a gallery in Santa Barbara, while Johnson worked from his home in a quiet neighborhood of Santa Monica. Johnson couldn't partake fully in Swetnam's glamorous life of cocktails and parties with millionaire clients, however, because he was wheelchair-bound. Childhood diabetes had forced the amputation of both his legs, multiple surgical operations, and a weekly hookup to a dialysis machine.[13]

Their contact in Lima was Fred Drew, the former U.S. embassy officer turned dealer. According to court testimony by one of their business associates, Michael Kelly, Drew would send packets of photographs of fresh Peruvian loot by DHL courier to Johnson, who would order the ones he liked, either for his own collection or for sale to his customers. "They knew as I did, and all dealers do, that it's illegal to bring pre-Columbian art from Peru to this country without the authorization of the Peruvian government," Kelly said.[14]

Drew or Swetnam could arrange for airline employees to bring in smaller pieces on flights directly from Lima to the United States, with payment of a bribe to Peruvian customs authorities, but that route was impractical for shipments of one hundred or more pieces. In such cases, Drew took the ceramics that Johnson had indicated he liked and sent them to a workshop in Lima, where craftsmen used mud and latex to add a false bottom to each pot, stamping it with the words *Hecho en Bolivia* (Made in Bolivia). The ancient pots thus looked like modern pots. Then Drew would arrange to have the pieces shipped overland to Bolivia, where customs controls were more lenient than in Peru, and from there he sent them by plane to Vancouver, where he and his associates thought they could count on Canadian customs authorities to let the pots go through as ethnic trinkets, if they checked at all. Swetnam would then arrange to bring them over the border into the United States, wash off the worthless mud bottoms, and, as Kelly said, "it was now pre-Columbian art."[15] He saw Swetnam washing off the false bottoms in his bathtub in Santa Barbara. Other pots, including some dating from the earliest stages of Andean ceramic development, 1,800 B.C. to 1,400 B.C., were wrapped entirely in a thin ceramic slip, hiding cracks or abrasions that might reveal their true age.

Swetnam brought in at least two shipments this way and would have brought a third if a Canadian customs agent had not checked eight crates of Peruvian artifacts in Vancouver in 1985 as part of a narcotics inspection and found ancient textiles and pottery. An archaeologist brought in to check the pieces found the textiles authentic; they were confiscated and later returned to Peruvian authorities. But some of the ceramics with the phony slips were good enough to fool the archaeologist, and they were released.[16]

Wrapping ancient ceramics in mud or ceramic slip to make them look like five-dollar tchotchkes is a time-honored smuggling technique. There are workshops in Lima that do it today. Still, Swetnam was frightened enough to look for a new modus operandi.

"The routes that we had previously used were no longer viable because he had been busted in Canada. . . . He also wanted to bring larger quantities of pieces so he couldn't use his normal courier system, which included airline staff and diplomatic staff," Kelly recalled later. They still needed to give everything they shipped from Peru a "false provenance," a document attesting to a phony but plausible origin or chain of ownership of the piece to dispel suspicions among customs agents that the pieces had been looted or stolen. After talks with Johnson at his Santa Monica house, Swetnam decided to try London. He asked Kelly for his help.[17]

Michael Kelly was a British expatriate in Southern California who in his youth had studied archaeology, worked at the famous National Museum of Anthropology in Mexico City and at the British Museum, and after 1977 had set himself up as what he called "an independent art broker and consultant." Things had not gone well for him. His Santa Barbara–based company, Art Collections Conservation Network, was close to bankruptcy, his plans to create a museum of pre-Hispanic art in Southern California had foundered, and he had grown more and more dependent on Swetnam.[18] He saw the pre-Columbian loot trade growing tremendously in the 1980s, and everyone seemed to be getting rich off it but him.

Kelly's plight really hit home in 1986: his father became gravely ill in London, his mother begged him to come home, and Kelly could not afford the air ticket. Swetnam offered to pay his roundtrip ticket if Kelly would agree to clear a shipment of freshly looted artifacts just in from Lima and waiting at a London warehouse and then put his name on the shipping documents with which Swetnam could send the load on to Los Angeles. Kelly would assume all the risk and Swetnam, who had already paid $3,000 in bribes to Peruvian airport customs officials to get the shipment out, would get the artifacts for his new gallery. Kelly agreed, and the two of them flew to London in June 1986. Kelly alone cleared the goods from an airport warehouse and took them to his family home, where he and Swetnam removed the Peruvian newspaper wrapping in which the artifacts had been shipped and rewrapped them in British newspaper so that they would appear to be from a British collection. This was part of the false-provenance ruse. Johnson had insisted that the provenance look convincing, so, at his suggestion, Kelly drew up a specious letter to potential buyers or customs agents claiming the Peruvian artifacts had belonged to his just-deceased father since the late 1920s, and he appended his father's real death certificate.[19] After the Canadian bust, they were taking no chances.

The first load of Peruvian artifacts under this new arrangement arrived in Los Angeles in November 1986. The next arrived in March 1987, with no hitches. Each shipment contained about a dozen Inca and pre-Inca weavings and ceramics, and each time, Kelly put his name on the customs paperwork and claimed the shipment as "personal effects," which, by U.S. law, meant that they entered the country duty-free. If caught, he could be subject to prosecution for fraud and smuggling, but Kelly needed the money. For the two shipments so far he had been paid about $3,700.

So when Sipán erupted onto the antiquities market that month, this group of smugglers ranging from the distinguished to the desperate— Drew in Lima, Johnson in Los Angeles, Swetnam and the front man Kelly shuttling between them—could hardly have been in a better position to exploit it.

Thanks to the first press reports about Alva's discoveries, the whole world knew about Sipán now, and Johnson was thrilled to receive a packet of photographs of the artifacts from Drew. Johnson wanted them, and no one else had anything like his network in place to ensure they would arrive safely at his door in Santa Monica. When Swetnam and Kelly brought them to his house in a footlocker straight from Los Angeles airport in August 1987, Johnson's face flushed with joy and satisfaction. He and Swetnam unwrapped them. Here was the culmination of Johnson's career in connoisseurship. There were between seventy and one hundred pieces in glorious gold forms—animals, warrior figures, necklaces, masks, and that golden rattle. Johnson had already called ten or so of his top clients to let them know that he, and he alone, had the treasures of Sipán and was taking advance orders. Now was the collectors' only chance to get a piece of the site that was causing the biggest sensation in archaeology in years.[20]

The only one not happy was Kelly. Swetnam and Johnson had paid him $2,500, instructed him to call the shipment another load of "personal effects," and led him to believe he was bringing in more ceramics when in fact Kelly had imported, under his own name, a shipment worth easily $1 million. They had cut him out of the deal, making him assume all the risk while they reaped the benefit. After using Kelly as a mule, they had even unpacked the artifacts in front of him, a move that was both cruel and unbelievably foolish.

Johnson was too preoccupied with dealing the artifacts to worry about hurt feelings. One of his clients was John Bourne, a sixty-one-year-old collector who had pursued adventures across Latin America in his youth and lived in a $3 million house in a leafy, exclusive neighborhood of West Hollywood. When Johnson called to tell him about the Moche artifacts, Bourne was intrigued. Send your people over with the pieces, he told Johnson, according to Bourne's later statements to the FBI. A few days later two men showed up at Bourne's door with one of the ten gold rattles. Bourne bought it on the spot, along with a pair of superb Moche ear spools. Each was made of gold and depicted a characteristically Sipán scene of a warrior holding a war club and shield in a mosaic of turquoise and shell. Bourne paid for them all in cash, no receipts. Eleven years later, in a loan agreement to a museum, he listed the value of the rattle at $80,000 and the twin ear spools at $40,000, presumably close or identical to the prices he paid.[21]

They must have liked doing business together, for sometime later Johnson had another dazzler to sell Bourne: a golden pendant in the shape of a monkey's head with its mouth opened in a scream. It was about the size of a tennis ball. Tiny pieces of turquoise and spondylus shell adorned its eyes, its nose was capped with lapis lazuli, and inside its open mouth were hints of more turquoise. About ten such monkey heads were circulating on the antiquities market, and collectors and archaeologists in Peruvian antiquities knew they were among the finest and most distinctive pieces to emerge from La Mina, the Moche tomb emptied by grave robbers in the gold rush after Sipán.

Bourne now had star artifacts from two of the most important Moche sites ever pillaged.

Chapter 5

GOLD MAN

LIKE THE LOOTERS, Swetnam and Johnson succeeded in getting the goods to market only to be betrayed by one of their own. Used and humiliated, Michael Kelly called the regional headquarters of U.S. Customs outside Los Angeles in September 1987 and offered himself as an undercover informant in exchange for immunity from prosecution. Customs agents initially reacted skeptically to Kelly's story, but it held together. And besides, Kelly had some proof to back it up: two ancient Peruvian gold-and-amethyst necklaces that he had slipped into his pocket after he and Swetnam brought them in one of their shipments.[1]

For the next few months, Kelly acted as a government mole, informant S-3 OX, in Southern California's art-smuggling underground. His account, taped in fifteen hours of conversations with customs agents, led to a series of raids on March 30, 1988, on the homes of Swetnam, Johnson, and their clients identified by Kelly. In what was called the largest U.S. Customs raid up to that time, the agents carted out 1,391 identifiably pre-Columbian objects ranging from the priceless to the plain. There were hundreds of expensive ceramics from the Moche and Chimú cultures, textiles and metal objects, and a vast array of smaller, less valuable knickknacks amassed by collectors who apparently bought anything offered to them. The collectors included the Nobel Prize–winning physicist Murray Gell-Mann and Charles Craig, whose four hundred choicest pieces had gone on display only two months before in a sprawling exhibition at the Santa Barbara Museum of Art.[2] The same museum was about to mount another show two days later—including at least seven pieces that the informant Kelly had identified as among those smuggled in by Swetnam. But the raids netted few objects from the famous Peruvian site. Johnson had already sold the cream of his Sipán treasures to clients unknown to Kelly.

Customs amassed what it thought was a rich trove of evidence, but the case never went to trial. Prosecutors decided that the case rested too heavily on Kelly's statements, easily dismissed in court as hearsay, and that a jury would take pity on the crippled, infirm Johnson, who had fainted and was rushed to hospital when he learned that Kelly was an informant. Under intense pressure and endless pretrial motions from lawyers hired by collectors and the antiquities lobby, prosecutors in the end indicted only Swetnam and his wife, Jacqueline, on charges of conspiracy, smuggling, and related customs offenses. In exchange for dismissal of the charges against his wife, Swetnam pleaded guilty and was sentenced to six months at federal prison in Boron, California, becoming the first person to be convicted in connection with the smuggling of Sipán treasures. The sentence was less than exemplary punishment. He served only four months in jail and, more important, was allowed to keep all but 8 of the roughly 360 ancient treasures seized from his house. He even paid his lawyer with one of the most celebrated pieces of the Sipán plunder, a golden jaguar head.[3] All the other treasures seized in the customs raids were returned to their American owners.

Shocked by the leniency of the sentence and by the U.S. government's failure to secure the return of more pieces, the government of Peru filed civil lawsuits against Johnson, the Swetnams, and four others. With its counsel paid for by a wealthy and mercurial American physicist named George Roberts, the Peruvian government aimed to have the pieces again seized and repatriated. The gist of its case was that because Peruvian law since 1929, if not before, had designated the state as the owner of all archaeological resources, Johnson and the others had actually received stolen property. It sounded a bit shaky, given Peru's own uneven enforcement on the ground, and one of Peru's litigators bowed out of the case early on in disagreement with that tack. There was, however, a precedent of sorts for it. In 1977 a Texas dealer named Patty McClain and three others sold a collection of Mexican antiquities which, to add notoriety to what were quite ordinary pieces, they boasted had been smuggled out of Mexico by a man they claimed was the chief of the Mexican secret service. The actual shipper was a California engineer who liked to travel south of the border now and then. The buyers of the antiquities turned out to be undercover FBI agents and Mexican government officials, and McClain and the other sellers were arrested and charged in a criminal suit with conspiracy and interstate commerce in stolen property because, under Mexican law enacted in 1897 and reaffirmed in 1972, ownership of pre-Hispanic remains had been vested in the Mexican state. The case see-sawed through the courts for years, but McClain and cohorts were convicted under the U.S. National Stolen Property Act, with their own statements to buyers used against them.[4] The judge in the case specifically said that export restrictions would not by themselves be sufficient to show the Mexican state's ownership of the pieces, but that Mexico's assertion of ownership was clear and consistent enough to be enforceable in U.S. court.

The defendants in the Peruvian case would need to show, therefore, that Peru did not in fact exercise effective ownership over its archaeological heritage. Johnson's defense attorney, Ronald Nessim, called experts including Stanford University professor and cultural-property-law expert John Merryman, a prominent defender of the interests of antiquities collectors, who said that Peru rarely enforced its provisions asserting state ownership of archaeological resources and did so now only because the case involved foreigners.[5] Pre-Hispanic art specialist Alan Sawyer also punched holes in Peru's record of stewardship of its own ancient riches and testified that, for all he could tell, Johnson's artifacts could have been exported from Peru before the 1929 law.

Peru's lawyer, Noel Keyes, a retired Pepperdine University law professor with little trial experience, repeatedly shot himself in the foot by calling unprepared witnesses to the stand, according to accounts of the trial. One was an INC official with an archaeology degree but little background in field research, Francisco Iriarte, who viewed the artifacts for an hour before his testimony and then admitted under cross-examination that he could not say for sure if they were from Peru at all. Actually, he said, some of them resembled artifacts from Ecuador, Mexico, or even Polynesia, an unfortunate statement that undermined the point of his testimony which was to establish that the artifacts originated in Peru. Nessim pounced on Iriarte's testimony as proof that the artifacts might not have come from Peru at all and that Peru could not claim to "own" the artifacts in question because it had no record of actually possessing them. Of course there was no record: the pieces were looted from underground sites and smuggled out of the country before anyone in authority even knew of their existence. The trial transcript does not show that Keyes successfully made this point.[6]

The surviving Bernal brothers would surely have remembered some of the more important Sipán pieces that wound up in Ben Johnson's living room. Could they have been asked to testify or give sworn affidavits? They might have welcomed the chance to clear their names, but nobody asked them. When I showed Samuel Bernal pictures of Sipán pieces in 2002, he remembered several of them, including the feline head with which David Swetnam paid his lawyer.[7]

Judge Edward Gray dismissed the suit and ordered the pieces returned to Johnson and the other defendants, saying he was "not satisfied that Mr. Johnson received any of the items here concerned with the knowledge that they were illegally removed from Peru."[8] All of Kelly's testimony as to the country of origin was strictly hearsay, he said, and anyway Iriarte had said some of the objects "may have come from Ecuador or Colombia or Mexico or even Polynesia." Gray did manage some sympathy for Peru's position: "The plaintiff [Peru] is entitled to the support of the courts of the United States in its determination to prevent further looting of its patrimony."[9]

The victory was costly and short-lived for Johnson and the antiquities racket, however. His reputation was tarnished forever by his association with the convicted smuggler Swetnam and by Kelly's damning testimony. The murky dealings of the antiquities trade had been exposed, and this time it was not small-time merchants like McClain but dealers in top-of-the-market treasures. To opponents of the antiquities trade, it was clearer than ever that the business exploited poor countries' historical heritage at the source, throwing up legal smoke screens and technicalities on the buyers' end. The role of the Santa Barbara Museum of Art also hinted at how prestigious museums were benefiting from, if not encouraging, the trade.

Kelly's testimony in particular offered an unsavory X ray of the antiquities trade. Out came the stories of the false bottoms, the wraparound slips, the fake letter from his dead father, the British newspaper packaging, the tricks and techniques to disguise the origin of looted goods.

"False provenance is a history of the piece," Michael Kelly said in court testimony on March 7, 1989, when asked to define what the term meant.

> Its authenticity, its value, its history of who has owned it, where it came from, which is a lie, which is a false provenance. It's been made up. . . . In my experience very few pre-Columbian artifacts have a genuine provenance. Most provenances are, false unless [the dealer] finds collections that have been made in the '20s or '30s. Most of the pieces that have been dealt and circulating in the '60s, '70s and '80s have false provenance if they have a provenance at all.
>
> KEYES: Why is this a peculiarity at all of pre-Columbian artifacts?
>
> KELLY: Because the market in pre-Columbian art has grown tremendously in the last ten years and to supply that demand pre-Columbian art is constantly having to be smuggled out of South America, so you have to create a false provenance for it.[10]

Johnson died in September 1990, and his heirs sold his collection of some five hundred pre-Hispanic artifacts at Sotheby's auction house over the next few years. As with most looted antiquities, no one could say exactly where the pieces in his collection came from. In its catalogues, Sotheby's listed their provenance as "Ben Johnson Collection." His civil trial remains today a conspicuous failure in source countries' efforts in U.S. court to stop the flow of looted goods. But it aroused a strong political reaction and brought about the U.S. government's first real efforts to restrain the antiquities trade, whose days as one of the last unregulated industries in America were numbered.

The Swetnam and Johnson trials made it clearer than ever that looted antiquities were flowing unhindered into the United States, despite the McClain ruling and despite passage in 1982 of legislation by the U.S. Congress giving the government stronger authority to curb the loot trade. Peru's feeble showing at trial against the powerful American antiquities lobby had convinced officials in Lima and at the country's embassy in Washington that American courts were a dead end, and that a more successful strategy would be to apply diplomatic pressure on the federal government to enforce border controls more stringently and allow easy repatriation of seized pre-Columbian goods.[11]

The 1982 legislation, signed into law by President Ronald Reagan on January 12, 1983, and known as the Cultural Property Implementation Act, or CPIA, granted the president the power to impose import restrictions on clearly designated types of archaeological or ethnographic material on a country-by-country basis. For a country to obtain those restrictions, it had to make a specific request to the U.S. government. There would be no general, blanket prohibitions on import of antiquities from a particular country, even if they were known to be illegally excavated. So far, only one country, El Salvador, had taken the White House at its word and requested import restrictions, in that case for artifacts from an early Mayan site known as Cara Sucia that had been devastated by looting teams starting in the 1970s. The destruction at Cara Sucia and at a group of nearby Mayan sites had resulted in a flood of Salvadoran artifacts reaching the U.S. market, where incurious dealers assumed the pieces were from neighboring Guatemala. Cara Sucia never caused anything remotely like the sensation caused by Sipán. By the time El Salvador requested import restrictions in 1987, the market was so awash in artifacts from the site that a dealer named Alfred Stendahl, member of the State Department's Cultural Property Advisory Committee, said he did not think collectors or museums would object strongly to the restrictions because the artifacts were not bringing high prices on the market anyway.[12] Most dealers had never heard of the site until the federal government banned the import of artifacts from a hastily demarcated Cara Sucia Archaeological Region in November 1987. The site had been "disastrously looted," noted the State Department, but protection of it "will still preserve invaluable archaeological information and clues to the prehistory of . . . ancient Mesoamerica."[13]

The State Department increasingly looked at antiquities smuggling as a place of both danger and opportunity for U.S. diplomacy: danger, because the existence of a big market for looted goods was harming America's relations with source countries, some of them important allies; and opportunity because cultural property could be an area for gaining favor with foreign governments and public opinion worldwide. In El Salvador, for example, the Reagan administration was pouring in military aid at the time to prop up the government against a left-wing guerrilla insurgency, and it did not help the U.S. effort that looters were hacking apart Mayan stone ruins to sell them piece-by-piece in New York and Miami. By issuing the ban on the import of such artifacts, the United States sent a signal of support to a client government while softening its image a bit in Central America.

When Peru filed its request for import restrictions in 1989, the U.S. administration had one clear priority in its policy toward Peru: drugs. At the time, the Bush administration, starting with the president himself, was pressing Peru hard to allow the Drug Enforcement Administration and the U.S. military to take a higher profile on Peruvian territory to curb the cocaine trade at its source. The DEA had begun crop eradication and drug interdiction in Peru, Bolivia, and Ecuador in a 1987 operation known as Operation Snowcap, and two years later it sent U.S. Army Green Berets to establish a counternarcotics base in the Upper Huallaga Valley, site of the world's most productive coca leaf plantations, with the reluctant acquiescence of Peru's government. In February 1990, at a summit meeting in Colombia, President George Bush and his Peruvian counterpart, Alan García, along with the presidents of Colombia and Bolivia, agreed on a huge increase in U.S. involvement in Peru; total U.S. aid increased from $8.7 million in fiscal year 1989 to $168.8 million in fiscal year 1992. Peru thus leaped onto the list of the top ten American aid recipients in the world.[14] About half the increased aid would consist of military and police aid and the other half of economic assistance, which Peru would receive only if it continued to accept the military aid.[15]

It was in this context of U.S. policymakers suddenly paying much more attention to Peru, that the Bush administration, responding to an official Peruvian request, issued on May 7, 1990, the toughest U.S. code against antiquities smuggling on record. Issued unobtrusively as a Treasury Department regulatory notice entitled "Import Restrictions Imposed on Significant Archaeological Artifacts from Peru," the order explicitly authorized U.S. Customs agents to seize any archaeological artifacts that might originate from a "Sipan Archaeological Region," whose precise boundaries were not made public if they existed at all, and shipped without express authorization of the Peruvian government. The regulation covered sixty-two kinds of artifacts in a list that a team of archaeologists hurriedly drew up at the State Department's request. Some categories were characteristically Sipán ("peanut-effigy beads," "rattles, semicircular or trapezoidal, usually with scenes") and constituted a virtual wish list of pieces looted from the tomb and presumed to be circulating on the black market. Others were broader and could come from almost anywhere in Peru, including stirrup-spout ceramic vessels, open-spout vessels, and copper masks. Supposedly only Moche artifacts were covered but, again, the wording of the regulation and the artifacts list meant it could apply to almost any pre-Columbian object in Peru. The intent was plainly to give U.S. Customs plenty of leeway to stop suspect antiquities at airports and borders and put the burden on the importer to show either that the pieces had a Peruvian export license (these were virtually impossible to obtain except for temporary, noncommercial reasons such as special exhibitions, scholarly study, or conservation work) or that they could not have come from anywhere near Sipán. The appearance of smuggled artifacts in the United States had "strained our foreign and cultural relations," the regulation said, and such artifacts "often constitute the very essence of a society and convey important information concerning a people's origin, history, and traditional setting."[16]

Most important, the regulation passed no judgment on whether or not Peru "owned" its undiscovered archaeological resources, the issue that had tied the California court in knots. Instead, it committed the federal government to apprehend and return to Peru a wide range of valuable and desirable artifacts that had a strong track record of market appeal, and in that sense it was unprecedented. For the first time, the federal government was getting in the way of something that antiquities collectors wanted.[17]

The regulation was not retroactive. Sipán items that had entered the United States before May 7, 1990, no matter how incriminating, were not affected. But as of that date, almost any authentic Peruvian pre-Columbian artifact carried into the United States by a collector, dealer, or tourist was subject to inspection, seizure, and possibly forfeiture. Customs offices at airports and sea terminals all over the country were notified.

On October 19, 1990, a museum in downtown Santiago, the Museo Chileno de Arte Precolombino, opened an exhibit entitled "Moche: The Lords of Death" featuring several prize pieces from the collection of Carlos Cardoen. At least three originated from the looted Sipán tomb. Something of a lord of death himself as arms dealer to some of the world's nastiest dictators, Cardoen had made a fortune building armored personnel carriers for use by his country's police forces during the Pinochet government. He was indicted in

Miami in April 1992 for allegedly illegally exporting from the United States 120 tons of weapons-grade zirconium used to manufacture cluster bombs, which he sold to Saddam Hussein's Iraq.[18] The museum show included one of the ten golden rattles, four of which were now publicly accounted for with the set of three owned by Poli. There was also a feline head similar to the one Swetnam had owned but in much worse condition.

The show also included a Sipán deer's head made of gilded copper, although visitors might have been confused about what they were looking at because the exhibition catalogue identified it as a *dog's* head, which is what the Bernal brothers thought it was. The piece was most likely set on a turbanlike headdress that had decomposed or been destroyed in the looting, although the catalogue's writers made no mention of this and presumably did not know it.[19] Modeled after the animals that once abounded in the hilly scrublands around Sipán and that were depicted in hunting scenes in Moche pottery painting, the deer's head closely resembled a piece that Alva excavated from the Old Lord's tomb, featuring a clever little kicker: its tongue, suspended on a wire inside the sculpture, moved side to side inside its open mouth, as if the animal were panting. Laboratory workers at the Brüning discovered this delightful touch as they restored the piece. If the Cardoen relic ever had such a feature, and if it survived the shipping and handling to Santiago, the catalogue made no mention of it.[20]

Alva, who supplied photographs of the tombs for the show with no knowledge it would include actual Sipán artifacts, assumed that Cardoen had bought the pieces from Apesteguía or Poli. They had been looted three years before and now were on display in a public museum. There were no legal avenues for regaining the pieces; Chile had not even signed the 1970 UNESCO treaty against the trade in illicit antiquities, and still has not.[21]

The Cardoen show suggested Sipán pieces were still shuttling through the global shell game of collectors and dealers, but in the United States the seizures of looted Peruvian antiquities tapered off for a while. The new customs regulations, the raids in California, and Ben Johnson's disgrace all had a chilling effect on pre-Columbian loot smuggling. The head of the State Department's Cultural Property Advisory Committee, Jack Josephson, could state with some accuracy that the 1990 order had "virtually stopped [Sipán artifacts'] illegal importation into this country."[22]

It took a few years for the market to find its feet again. But when it did, it came roaring back.

In early September 1993, U.S. Customs agents at Dallas–Fort Worth International Airport found a crate flown in from Italy holding twenty-nine Peruvian and Mexican artifacts, including what seemed to be ancient Peruvian metalwork and some absolutely top-of-the-line Moche and Mexican Colima ceramics. The agents immediately suspected Sipán. They called in archaeologist David Wilson, of Southern Methodist University in

Dallas, who had excavated Moche settlements in the lower Santa valley, a day's drive south of Sipán, and had grown accustomed to receiving calls to come out to the airport to inspect detained artifacts and give his professional advice on whether they were authentic, where they might be from, and what they might be worth. The year before, he had inspected a shipment of seized Ecuadoran artifacts dating from about A.D. 500, several of them broken because of faulty packing. Wilson determined they were authentic, and the artifacts were eventually turned over to the embassy of Ecuador in a ceremony in Washington. Customs never told Wilson the name of the shipper, but whoever it was, he lost everything. No wonder antiquities dealers hated archaeologists.

This time, the agents had seen the metalwork in the crate and had "some expectation that they might be Sipán," said Wilson. The shippers had thrown in a few Roman or medieval coins, probably to give the Italian provenance some credence. Wilson had no doubt the pieces were robbed from graves, laundered through Europe, and given a new, phony provenance, then resent to the United States. But all the customs agents wanted to know was if the pieces were authentic and where they were from. They were definitely authentic, Wilson told them, but the metalwork was not Sipán and did not appear to be Moche.

Wilson and his wife were walking through Dallas's posh Knox-Henderson district a few weeks later and saw in an art gallery one of the ceramic pieces he had inspected. It was a Moche portrait vessel that Wilson thought one of the finest he had ever seen.

"That was when I knew they had given them back," he said. For whoever was importing the pieces, it was a close call indeed.[23]

The next year, a necklace made of turquoise beads and three large gold discs, each with a characteristically Sipán pattern of abstract swirls and avian heads, appeared in a Sotheby's catalogue of pre-Columbian art. Valued at $4,000 to $6,000 and with no listed provenance, the piece was to be auctioned on November 15, 1994. The design on each gold disc was nearly identical to the design on the obverse of the ten spider beads that Alva had excavated at the Old Lord of Sipán tomb.

Officials at the Peruvian embassy in Washington, who had taken to poring over auction house and gallery catalogues for pieces that could be covered by the emergency order, notified Alva about the necklace. There was another one, too, that struck them as potentially Sipán, this one with turquoise-and-gold triangular plaquettes bearing the shape of a Moche war club, a image that was common at Sipán but not unique to it. Described erroneously (in Alva's opinion) as "late Chavín ca. 700–400 B.C." and again with no listed provenance, it was valued at $5,000 to $7,000. Two other catalogue items bore traits of the Sipán style: a magnificent ear ornament in gold repoussé and turquoise depicting the angry face of the Ai-apaec deity riding on the back of a marine stingray, valued at $20,000 to $30,000, and an effigy of a cat with outspread limbs and a face similar to that on Cardoen's piece, also in gold and valued by the auction house at $1,200 to $1,800 and featured on the catalogue's back cover. But the two necklaces seemed like the most obvious candidates. The embassy asked Sotheby's to withdraw all four pieces from sale. It refused. The Peruvians contacted Attorney General Janet Reno, and the auction house relented. By the time U.S. Customs served a seizure warrant on Sotheby's and brought all four pieces to a Manhattan warehouse, in mid-December, Alva happened to be in New York to give a talk at the Sipán show at the American Museum of Natural History. Customs officials brought the four pieces to his hotel room for his inspection. The gold gleamed in his hands. He believed they were from Sipán and that all or most had passed through Apesteguía's collection, but he had no stomach for another protracted legal battle in which the antiquities lobby would fight to exhaust the patience and resources of the Peruvian side.[24]

This time, he was surprised. The auction house and unidentified consignor of the pieces gave up the two necklaces without a struggle, and U.S. officials turned them over to President Alberto Fujimori when he visited Washington in May 1996. The stingray piece and the feline effigy were returned to Sotheby's and sold. Alva placed the necklaces on display in the Brüning Museum in Lambayeque, the first items confiscated and returned to the Peruvian people under the Bush administration's 1990 order.

Two months after Alva saw those glittering necklaces in his hotel room, U.S. Customs agents in Miami made one of the largest and strangest antiquities busts ever on American soil. It happened entirely by accident, took months for almost anyone to realize its importance, and three years more for the rest of the world to find out about it.

Before dawn on February 24, 1995, customs inspectors at a Lufthansa warehouse at Miami International Airport came across a three-by-five-foot wooden crate marked "Peruvian handicrafts." The manifest said the crate had arrived on a flight from Lima and was bound for Zurich, Switzerland. Customs agents ordinarily inspected only about 3 percent of cargo coming through the airport, and there was little about this crate that would prevent it from following the other 97 percent on its way.

But the stated value of the contents seemed rather low for such a large crate: $2,764. Its Peruvian origin also raised suspicions. Cocaine shipments from Peru to Europe were known to come through Miami, but of course so did hundreds of other crates containing legal and legitimate Peruvian exports every week.

When agents finally opened the crate on a hunch and shined their flashlights inside, they found stacks of smaller boxes containing clay pots, weavings, and—alarmingly—bones. It was the bones that led them to pull the crate aside and flag it for more thorough inspection. When art historian Carol Damian from Florida International University looked at the shipment at customs' request four days later, she found tunics and headdresses of brilliant parrot feathers from the Nazca culture; forty-three Chancay pots, bowls, and wooden idols; piles of Inca caps, bags, and shawls; and top-quality Paracas and Wari textiles dating from as far back as 200 B.C.

And there were human remains—lots of human remains. The market for ancient body parts is a particularly macabre segment of the artifacts market, and here was enough to satisfy a connoisseur. Damian and the agents pulled out the heads of two women who died on the south Peruvian coast about 200 B.C. and were wrapped mummylike in textiles. There was a man's desiccated forearm, complete with hands, fingers, and a blue tattoo; a wooden mask with a feathered turban and human hair; and two stuffed wool dolls with human hair, all from the Chancay era. There were prehistoric animal bones, fossilized shark teeth, clam shells, and bird claws, and a piece of a mastodon's jaw with teeth still in it.

Someone had crammed this grab bag of objects from 100,000 years of Andean history and prehistory into a space the size of a refrigerator. They were well packed, though. Only a few had broken. A dozen or so were from museums, as Damian could see from the tiny accession numbers painted on them.[25]

At the bottom of the crate, in small boxes, lay the biggest treasures of all: ten objects from the looted tomb of Sipán, including one of the ten golden rattles. Damian immediately recognized them as Sipán. Her rough estimate of the value of the whole package was $500,000, a figure later raised to $1 million, then $2 million, and then replaced by a simple "priceless" in the investigations and court proceedings that followed.[26]

It took them two days to inspect the whole shipment, and when they were finished they counted 208 objects in all. Aside from the museum pieces, all probably stolen by employees, the shipment was likely the product of months of work by looters up and down the Peruvian coast.

Damian resided only ten minutes from the airport and received calls from U.S. Customs agents almost monthly to come down to inspect shipments suspected of containing loot. The airport cargo zone was a labyrinth of warehouses, barbed wire, and forklift trucks zipping down corridors between wooden crates stacked five-stories high, teams of agents in blue jumpsuits with drug-sniffing beagles moving from crate to crate twenty-four hours a day. It was a place of nonstop activity. In its cramped, fluorescent-lit inspection rooms, Damian had seen plenty of junk over the years but also some extraordinary objects—polychrome ceramics, stone lintels carved with Mayan iconography. Once she had been called to a Miami mail-sorting facility to look over a collection of about thirty padded envelopes mailed over several months from Peru to a West Coast address and pulled aside by postal inspectors. When opened on suspicion of containing narcotics, they proved to contain Paracas weavings, Chancay gauze textiles, and an Inca crown with beads and braided human hair. That was an unusual case of loot through the mail. Yet in terms of variety and quality, she had never seen anything quite like that shipment before her eyes those two days at the Lufthansa warehouse.

"It got more and more amazing as we went through it," she said. "And when we found the gold pieces in these small crates, that's when I said, 'We've got to get the consulate.' It was Sipán."

Customs turned the case over to an ambitious young lawyer in its chief counsel's office named Maria Capo. Born in Cuba and raised in southern Florida, Capo was a recent graduate of the University of Miami Law School, and she was happy to take a case that involved something other than her office's usual crop of gold-chained, gun-toting drug traffickers and the forced forfeiture of their glitzy cars and cabin cruisers. She began investigating the case with a determination that surprised her colleagues, who saw little opportunity for arrests, headlines, or forfeiture money. This was about a box of Indian curios, as far as they could see. Their skepticism was quickly justified as Capo's investigation bumped into one dead end after another.

The stated recipient of the crate, or the consignee, was a company in Zurich spelt variously as Transrover or Trans Rover. Antiquities traders frequently used Switzerland as a transshipment point because its network of seventeen "free ports," most notably at the Zurich and Geneva airports, allowed them to store merchandise indefinitely without paying Swiss import duties. Merchants could bring in goods, anything from machinery to wine to art, and keep them in the free port's storage lockers and warehouses and then ship the goods out again to another country (or sell them directly in the free zone) without paying Swiss duties. The merchandise would physically enter European space, but not fiscally. Steeped in the Swiss tradition of discretion, the free-zone system carried an added bonus for purveyors of illicit antiquities because it allowed them to slap a European-looking provenance on artifacts that could in fact have originated anywhere in the world, since the artifacts would arrive at their ultimate destination with documentation stating they were from Switzerland.

Maria Capo tried to contact Transrover in writing and by telephone but drew no response until April 1995, when she received a short letter from Transrover's New York attorney, Carl Soller, asking customs "to clarify the legal basis for this seizure." Customs replied that it had been detained pending criminal investigation. A few months later Soller stiffened his tone, demanding specifics and insisting "that you immediately inform us as to the grounds for the seizure."

He certainly had a point. The shipment could be considered smuggled under U.S. law because the true value was so much greater than the declared value. But it was not being introduced into the United States. It was merely in transit between Peru and Switzerland, and the fact that Switzerland was a notorious laundering point for looted artifacts bound for the rest of Europe and the United States was, legally speaking, irrelevant. Still, the crate was on U.S. soil, it contained Sipán artifacts, and for that reason customs lawyers felt they had a clear-cut violation of the 1990 order and were ready to separate the Sipán items and return them to Peru.

What Soller, Transrover, and some of Capo's own colleagues in Miami did not know was that she was determined to get the rest returned to Peru as well. She played for time, hoping to wear down the Swiss company's patience as she gathered evidence for smuggling charges to force the return of the whole crate. She was helped greatly by tough laws on asset seizures that were enacted in the zero-tolerance climate that developed in the late 1980s in drug transshipment points like Miami. Judges gave U.S. Customs wide leeway to enforce forfeiture laws. On the slightest whiff of suspicion of involvement in drugs, people could, and did, have their cars, vacation homes, and possessions embargoed for months or years while authorities sifted through their records and documents, looking for a case good enough for a prosecutor to take to a grand jury. It was a guilty-until-proven-innocent system ripe for injustice and excess, and a series of negative press reports later resulted in federal laws requiring customs to start proceedings within ninety days of a seizure like the one at Miami International Airport. But in 1995, there was no such deadline. Capo could take as long as she needed.[27]

"There was no question that customs was dragging its feet. They were looking for evidence, looking for a case," said Ana Barnett, at the time head of the forfeiture division at U.S. Customs in Miami and now a lawyer in private practice.[28]

The problem for Capo was that she could not find a prosecutor. None thought the case was promising or attractive, and if she didn't find one, sooner or later the whole crate, probably minus the Sipán material but even that was no sure thing, would resume its journey to Switzerland. There were hotter cases occupying prosecutors at the U.S. attorney's office. Coincidentally one of them was the cluster bomb case involving Sipán collector Carlos Cardoen, which in August 1995 again made headlines when a Miami judge sentenced a salesman for Teledyne Industries to forty-one months in jail for the zirconium export scheme. Cardoen remained indicted and his U.S. assets seized, although the government made no formal effort to have him brought from Chile for trial.[29] Soller wrote again on January 23, 1996, to complain about the "tortuous" process to which his client was being subjected.

Capo heard once more from Soller in March, this time in a telegraphic note to announce he no longer represented the company. Transrover was never heard from again. It "simply dropped off the face of the earth," said Capo, who by then suspected it had been formed purely for the purpose of importing that shipment. Not only did she lack a prosecutor, now she lacked anyone to investigate.

"Whoever was in Zurich didn't want to take the risk of coming to U.S. court to claim the property. It seemed to be nothing more than a front company, a curtain, and behind that curtain were the dealers, waiting," said Capo.

With Transrover out of the way, and with word from the Peruvian government that the artifacts had no export license, Capo assumed the return of the pieces could proceed. Customs supervisor John Atwood recommended in an internal memo that proceedings begin for forfeiture and repatriation of the entire package.[30] But the judge to whom the case was filed at random, Lenore Nesbitt, insisted that Capo and Barnett, who had now taken the case, try harder to track down the Swiss consignees to give them a chance to reclaim what was still legally their property. Nesbitt was herself an antiques collector and was intrigued by the case. Capo and Barnett published notices of the impending forfeiture in papers and trade magazines, stating essentially that the owner of the shipment should come forward to claim it. Perhaps fearing some kind of trap, the owners of Transrover never emerged. The crate, with all its 208 pieces, languished in a north Miami storage center known as the Fortress alongside the embargoed belongings of drug runners and gang leaders.

Even more enigmatic was what happened on the Peruvian side. Capo had sent word of the seizure to the Peruvian embassy in Washington, along with requests for Peruvian investigators to track down the man named on the export form as the shipper, one Rolando Rivas Rivadeneyra. They responded that he could not be located, and it was unclear if he was even a real person. She heard nothing more from the Peruvians.[31]

What the Miami case showed, worrisomely for the antiquities business, was that the bundle of new laws enacted since 1983 were starting to engender an ethic of passionate advocacy for cultural property within the U.S. government itself. The trade's enemy was no longer just the usual claques of archaeologists and tiresome third-world government officials. While the antiquities lobby focused on litigation and lobbying Congress to weaken laws, people like Maria Capo and Ana Barnett in the drab middle levels of the federal government were enforcing those laws to the full extent of their discretion—investigating violations, searching out criminal connections, keeping pressure on prosecutors, giving antiquities shippers real headaches on the ground. Their efforts slowly eroded the sustainability of the illegal antiquities trade in the United States. Accustomed to operating with a wide berth of impunity, dealers and shippers had underestimated the willingness of authorities to enforce the law. It was a trend that, in the late 1990s, would strengthen, accelerate, and spread to many more areas of U.S. government and law enforcement.

Back in Lima, in the world of Peruvian antiquities smuggling, plenty of people knew who was behind the shipment. It was Raúl Apesteguía, the collector, authenticator, and man of refinement who had been jailed before and whose bad luck had struck again. That golden rattle from Sipán had belonged to him. Alva, who did not find out about the Miami seizure until early in 1998, had visited Apesteguía's collection before the seizure as part of his effort to keep tabs on what was circulating in the market and had seen there some of the pieces later detained in Miami. Visiting Apesteguía's trove was part of the delicate dance in which archaeologists and collectors engaged. On the one hand, collectors like Apesteguía were responsible for the looting that was tapping out Peru's ancient heritage. On the other, Alva knew that if he denounced them or tried to initiate legal proceedings against them, they would close their doors to him. Never again would he be able to examine the latest treasure that looters had uprooted from ancient sites before archaeologists had even heard of them. An entire society, the Vicús, had come to light this way. The Vicús people lived in the Piura Valley in far northern Peru some two thousand years ago, contemporaneously with the Moche, with whom they shared many cultural traits. The memory and identity of the Vicús were lost to history until 1953, when looters found a group of their buried settlements near a mountain known as Cerro Vicús and ripped into them. For the next twenty years or so, looters systematically obliterated the remains of the Vicús, a society with a whole universe of culture, art, and worship as rich as any other in human history, but about which we know little because its memory was blasted out of the ground by the antiquities trade. What we have are mute objects, hundreds of Vicús artworks sitting in museums and collections all over the world, including a large group in the Metropolitan Museum of Art in New York.[32] Many others were owned by private collectors, including Apesteguía, and if archaeologists wanted to see the artifacts, they had to keep on good terms with the owners.

Through this uneasy alliance of convenience, Alva and Apesteguía had become friends, two men who shared a love for their country's pre-Columbian heritage but from completely different ethical standpoints. They disagreed on many things but they understood each other. Alva liked the collector's seriousness and erudition, in contrast to the vulgarity and greed he put up with from most collectors, and Apesteguía liked Alva's air of serene expertise, his humility, and his insights into the nature of the Moche derived from a lifetime in the field.

After the Miami bust, Apesteguía rarely left his high-rise apartment, sitting among his shelves of Chancay pots in his living room overlooking the Pacific. Acquaintances said he had a cocaine habit. He was seen so little that some of his old friends thought he had left the country.

The Miami shipment was never investigated in depth by police in any country, and few details about it are known. Its contents were shipped back to Peru in early 1998, after Alva came to Miami and inspected them at the fortress with Capo, exclaiming as he went through them, "This is a treasure! This is a treasure!"[33] At the time of the seizure, the rumor in the Lima antiquities underground was that there were actually two shipments bound for Switzerland; the second one reached its destination. True or not, Apesteguía was likely not the only dealer involved. Such elaborate planning and logistics, right down to the creation of a ghost receiver in Zurich, required an organization of many people.

Across town from Apesteguía's penthouse, the backflap sat in its suitcase in Luis Bacigalupo's bankrupt liquor factory. Times had certainly changed in Lima. It was suddenly South America's hottest boomtown, with new shopping malls, restaurants with New York prices, and neon casinos filled with tourists and foreign businessmen. Outside one casino stood a mock-up of the Statue of Liberty as tall as a four-story building, but instead of a torch, she was holding a multicolored roulette board that spun and glittered in the night. In the wealthier neighborhoods, old houses with verandas and gardens were being demolished to make way for boxy apartment towers, mirrored-glass hotels, and parking lots where the nouveau riche could park their Hondas and Mercedeses. Fujimori, savior of the nation, had crushed those stubborn guerrilla groups and was privatizing one chunk of the government after another, bringing a rush of foreign investment and business that gave Peru, in 1994, the world's fastest-growing economy.[34] Never mind that most limeños languished in poverty and apathy, living out their days in a dreary routine of shantytowns, rickety old buses, and miserable wages. At least some people were getting rich.

Luis Bacigalupo wasn't one of them. Living off the largesse of his three children, he had transferred his 25 percent share of the ownership of the hotel in Chiclayo to his son in 1992 and he was still drowning in debt. He liked to bet on horses at the Lima Jockey Club, and friends often saw him in the fourth-floor members' lounge. His ace in the hole was that hunk of gold his brother had left him. Before he died, Manuel had suggested that Luis offer the backflap to a close family friend named Jorge Ramos Ronceros to settle the brothers' business debts totaling about $120,000.[35]

Rotund and well-dressed as befits a man who has enjoyed a comfortable life, Ramos Ronceros was owner of a successful insurance brokerage firm, former president of the state-owned power utility Electroperú, and a distant relative of the man who had been Peru's president from 1985 to 1990, Alan García. He liked to be known by both his paternal and maternal surnames, Ramos Ronceros, instead of the customary Ramos, because Ronceros was the maternal surname of Alan García's father and that served to underscore his connection to the ex-president's family.[36] Ramos Ronceros called himself the president's uncle, and he was often referred to that way in the Peruvian media, where his name appeared often in association with petty corruption scandals left over from the García presidency. One such scandal involved the theft of gasoline from state-owned filling stations during Ramos Ronceros's tenure as president of Electroperú, and another focused on help he allegedly offered his "nephew" Alan García in the purchase of a house that became the subject of a judicial investigation.[37] Ramos Ronceros had a sporting side, too, as owner of the professional soccer club Defensor Lima.

The deal was that Bacigalupo would give Ramos Ronceros the backflap to settle the debt and also connect him through a business associate with a buyer, a Cuban-American businessman and old friend of Manuel Bacigalupo named Denis Garcia.[38] He and Ramos Ronceros would be free to work out whatever deal they wanted. One day in 1994, Bacigalupo put the backflap in a cardboard box, drove it to Ramos Ronceros's office in the wealthy district of San Isidro, and showed it to him. Ramos Ronceros liked it, and the two agreed to forget all about their debt.[39]

Ramos Ronceros was not known to be a player in the antiquities market, but he was smart enough to know it would be impossible to sell the backflap in Peru for anything like its market value. It had been seen by too many people, passed around a bit too much. It was damaged goods, as far as the Lima art market was concerned. He must have been glad the piece came complete with a dealer who could take it off his hands quickly. He put the backflap in a glass case in his living room, where only his wife, Liliana, and a few close friends saw it, and he bided his time, waiting for his new business partner, Denis Garcia, to come up with the money. The price, at least for the time being, was $100,000.[40]

Everyone who made Denis Garcia's acquaintance knew him as a warm, uncomplicated man who made friends easily, one who could move to a strange city in a strange country and establish himself quickly in its best social circles, which is just what he did in Chiclayo. Born in Cuba in 1940, he left the island for Miami as a young man and shuffled through various business enterprises. He became a U.S. citizen but never really took to life in the United States. He and his wife, Haydee (pronounced eye-DEH), moved to Peru around 1967 and headed for Chiclayo, a brash, fast-growing place with a reputation for raciness and none of the colonial cobwebs of other Peruvian cities. There, they joined a local rice grower in buying a company called Hurefran S.A., which sold farm machinery.

Chiclayo and the Garcias were a perfect fit. There was a popular song about Chiclayo in those days that could have been written for Denis. It went:

> *Let's hear it for Chiclayo,*
> *Generous land,*
> *Where everyone has a good time, pal,*
> *With not much to your name.*[41]

His business prospered and he and Haydee made contacts easily, becoming friends with Edmundo and Oswaldo Aurich, scions of the family whose very name, which was of German origin, coincidentally evoked gold with its first two letters, "Au", the symbol for gold. They owned that underground Louvre of inexhaustible tombs known as Batán Grande, two hours' drive north of Chiclayo. The Garcias visited the Auriches constantly, riding horseback with them all over their vast estate of rivers, forests, and ancient burial mounds, where hired digging teams were conducting industrial-scale gold extraction with bulldozers, shovels, and sieves. These outings were followed by dinner with the Auriches in their rambling old mansion with courtyards, porches, and servants in white aprons. In the back of the house was the locked and windowless "treasure room," where the family stored its looted gold and silver artifacts, sometimes hundreds at a time. The Auriches found so much wealth in their huacas, they scarcely knew what to do with it all. They were famous for inviting their most distinguished guests into the treasure room after dinner to choose an artifact, any artifact, and take it home with them as a token of friendship. Thousands of gold and silver objects passed through the Auriches' treasure room before being sold into the global antiquities market. Some of them sit today in the Dallas Museum of Art and the Birmingham Museum of Art in Alabama, among other American institutions.[42]

Life in the Peruvian countryside in those days was characterized by untouchable land barons and illiterate Indian serfs, carefree fun for the rich and white, hard labor for everyone else. It was a life not too different from that of pre-revolutionary rural Cuba, which Garcia knew in his youth. Now and then he and Haydee would themselves go *huaqueando*,

digging up tombs, just for the fun of it. It was like fishing; you might catch
nothing or you might catch a big one. There were no archaeologists scold-
ing people about the damage of looting in those days, and one of their digging partners was in fact Alva's predecessor as director of the Brüning
Museum. Pretty soon Denis and Haydee sent word back to friends in Miami that they wouldn't be moving back, for they loved Peru.[43]

The Garcias had arrived in northern Peru's world of treasure rooms
and feudal decadence in its last years, however. They watched, saddened
and horrified, as the military regime that took power in 1968 began to confiscate lands in the early 1970s and distribute it to the campesinos. The
president, General Juan Velasco, certainly looked the part of the traditional Latin American dictator with his natty uniform, mustache, and grim
expressions, but his views, like those of a whole generation of junior officers in the Peruvian military, were inspired more by the Cuban revolution
and the idea of state-driven economic development then in vogue everywhere in the region. Velasco set out to break the back of the landowning
aristocracy. "Peasant, the Master will no longer feed off your poverty!" he
proclaimed when he announced the land reform program to a stunned and
mostly supportive nation in June 1969.[44] The Auriches were ruined. They
lost their land in the reforms, as did the rest of Peru's rural elite, and their
wealth and status were shattered forever. The looting of Batán Grande finally stopped.

"We used to go to Batán Grande all the time, out to the hacienda where
the Auriches had all the treasures. They were like my family," Haydee Garcia recalled wistfully. She found Peruvians greedy and corrupt but has never
forgotten how welcome they made her feel. "The things they would pull from
the ground, you would drop dead if you saw them. But then they lost everything, except for small parcels of land here and there that they were allowed
to keep. Poor Oswaldo, he's got just a little piece of land now."[45]

The Garcias had amassed a respectable pre-Columbian collection of
their own in Chiclayo and now and then brought things back to the States
during their visits, as gifts, merchandise, or goods to sell on behalf of
friends in Peru.[46] As long as a few basic precautions were taken, it was a
low-risk way to earn money. The farm machinery business, however,
wasn't doing so well. Denis had a business dispute with his partner, Luis
Peralta, also an inveterate loot buyer and trader and co-owner, with
Manuel Bacigalupo, of the Costa de Oro hotel. For all three of them, buying and selling looted artifacts was just one more business venture, and by
the early 1980s almost the only one that was prospering.[47] They weren't
alone in their misfortune; the area around Chiclayo had been devastated by
floods caused by El Niño in 1983–84, and the national economy was in
shambles.

Around that time, Garcia told friends that he had sold his shares in the company and some of his antiquities. Finally he and Haydee moved back to Miami, though they dreamed about someday returning to Peru.[48] Chiclayo missed them, too, and that certain joie de vivre that their friends assumed just came with being Cuban. "Uncle Denis," as Peralta's sons called him, maintained his friendships in Chiclayo, and associates believed he had good contacts in the world of Peruvian antiquities collecting.[49]

By the time Denis Garcia heard about the backflap, around 1994, the loot market was nothing like the one he knew back in the 1960s. It was no upper-class lark anymore. In the post-Sipán era, the goods were found by cadres of professional grave robbers, working not on the orders of sclerotic landowners but as independent small businessmen themselves and Ernil Bernal wanna-bes who roved up and down the coast, muscling their way onto the choicest *huacas*. They brought the merchandise straight to dealers who received specific orders from foreign collectors. The bribes required to get the artifacts past Peruvian customs authorities were no longer a few twenty-dollar bills, but thousands of dollars. Most crucially, the supply end was becoming riskier every day as U.S. law-enforcement officers took notice, stopped crates, and brought in consulting archaeologists to call the bluff when the shipping manifest said "arts and crafts." Other factors made it a more attractive industry, though. There were dozens of direct flights to Europe or the United States every week, with no stopovers, and the market was bigger and pricier for those with the right connections. With greater risk had come much greater rewards. It was an underground racket that aped a lot of the tricks and techniques of the cocaine trade, with which it shared a certain geographical overlap. It was no place for a fun, unsophisticated, rather obtuse man like Denis Garcia.

Back in Miami, Garcia hooked up with a loose syndicate dealing in fake and smuggled art out of a warehouse near the Miami airport, led by a Colombian man who also operated a legitimate import-export business. Some men in this group had records for firearm violations, but they weren't known as criminal heavy hitters. They had the money and the weapons, and Garcia had the contacts in Peru to bring fine pre-Columbian artifacts to market.

In 1994 Garcia obtained some Polaroid photographs of the backflap, and he and the warehouse gang started circulating them among an extremely select group of potential buyers. They soon had an interested party, a man with a Midwestern accent and a gruff manner named Robert Bazin, who said he was a dealer for an important American collector. Bazin told the Miami group that he had learned of the backflap through Bill Becker, a sixty-two-year-old career criminal and down-on-his-luck con man whose record included more than fifty arrests, twenty convictions, and substantial spells in federal prisons across the country. Auto theft rackets, interstate gambling rings, fraud—Becker had done it all, including a fifteen-year term at federal prison in Terre Haute, Indiana, for counterfeiting U.S. Treasury bonds, from which he had been released on parole in 1991. There was one thing Becker could be proud of, though: he had never been convicted of any violent crimes. "I never hurt nobody," he once said. "And I never took money from the poor or from working guys. I robbed from the rich, kind of like Robin Hood, except I kept it."[50] Bazin had fourteen years' experience in art dealing and knew all about the fringe characters it occasionally attracted, and he would have had plenty of reason to doubt the authenticity of anything associated with Becker. Nonetheless, he was intrigued by the photographs of the backflap.[51]

Garcia and the warehouse gang had to clear a few things in their inventory first, however. They wanted to do a few get-acquainted deals, establish some rapport, and build a relationship with the buyer before doing the big sale. Of course, they couldn't show Bazin the backflap right away, even if they wanted to. It was still sitting in Lima, in Ramos Ronceros's living room, and no one was sure how to get such a large piece of metal past Peruvian airport controls and into the United States without being detected. They were offering merchandise they didn't yet have and might not ever have.

At a restaurant outside Miami, Garcia gave his pitch to Bazin and an associate, a clean-cut, Spanish-speaking young man whom Bazin brought along to put Garcia at ease. Garcia, who spoke broken English, bore a letter from somebody in Peru attesting to the authenticity and importance of the backflap and giving its measurements, weight, and condition, describing it "like a piece of furniture," Bazin remembered. The letter was in Spanish, with an English translation, and Bazin read the English letter aloud and his associate read aloud the Spanish version. Garcia looked a bit confused as to why they were doing this, but nothing seemed amiss.

A few weeks later, they made Bazin their first offer: a two-thousand-year-old headdress of hammered Peruvian gold. One of Garcia's contacts, a pilot, had smuggled the piece into the United States in the cockpit of a jetliner.[52] A single sheet of metal that, when rolled out flat, was about the size of a place mat, the headdress bore an embossed design of abstract lines and stylized feline heads with their teeth bared in a snarl. It dated from the Chavín culture that dominated northern Peru for a few centuries until about 100 B.C., and it closely resembled artifacts excavated by Japanese archaeologists at a site called Kuntur Wasi in the Andes near Cajamarca, about 150 miles east of Chiclayo. The headdress was older than the backflap but nowhere near as impressive. It was nice but, by the standards of top collectors, not the absolute best.

"We were thinking, we've got the crown, so let's get rid of that, and then we'll see about the body armor [the backflap], if Denis can ever find a way to get it into the country," said Becker. "It was all about this gold thing. You know, gold just does something to people. They want it. Everyone wanted to see the thing, and all we had was a couple of little photographs."[53]

Bazin flew to Miami and, with planes booming overhead, drove to the warehouse, where he was ushered in by five or six armed men. Becker was there. Unarmed and unfamiliar with the surroundings, Bazin was momentarily alarmed when someone walked in with a large, black submachine gun case. The man opened it to reveal the Chavín crown in polished and resplendent gold. A relieved Bazin handed the men $175,000 in cashier's checks, impressing the sellers with his good faith and deep pockets. Wary of police sting operations, they had checked out his art brokerage and found it was all legitimate, backstopped, and registered, with an 800 number and a real address. He had won their confidence, and now he wanted the backflap. It would cost $1 million.

Bazin didn't flinch at the price. "When are you going to get it for me?" he asked them, according to his recollection. They didn't have an answer but said they'd be in touch. He walked out of the warehouse, loaded the crown into his rented, air-conditioned Lincoln Continental, and waited to hear from them.

While Garcia dithered over how to move the backflap from Peru, the warehouse gang went back to Bazin with other, lesser things. They offered him some wood carvings from Benin, and then a small painting of a woman on a beach that they claimed was painted by the Impressionist master Claude Monet. Bazin spurned them all; the carvings were reproductions, and the Monet, which he showed in photographs to appraisers at New York's prestigious Wildenstein and Co. Gallery, was a ghastly fake.

"Look, you're still yanking my chain. It's not a Monet and I'm getting sick of this shit. I want the backflap," Bazin told them.[54]

And then, without warning, the warehouse gang stopped calling. Bazin assumed they had given up on ever getting the backflap out of Peru, or maybe they had sold it to somebody else. He was resigned to never seeing the backflap until one day, in the summer of 1997, three years after the Chavín crown deal, Denis Garcia finally called. Sounding excited, Garcia said he wasn't working with the warehouse gang anymore. He had his own team, and he could get him the backflap at last.

Bazin was furious. "I waited three years for this, you never came through, and now you call me? You are not a man of your word, and I should ignore you because you have not honored your commitments," he said. Garcia apologized profusely, promising never to string him along again. Besides, Bazin thundered, he was about to undergo triple bypass surgery and needed rest and was in no position to do a deal now, particularly not with a joker like Garcia.

"I will do one thing, though," Bazin said, relenting. "I shouldn't even do this, but I will tell my partner about you. I will advise him not to do business with you because you are not a man of your word, but I will give him your name."[55] Garcia thanked Bazin, apologized some more, and said, yes, please do pass my name on to your partner.

Bazin's business partner was a completely different sort of dealer and, as far as Garcia was concerned, a welcome change. Whereas Bazin was a blunt, impatient man from the prairies, the sort of American who grates on Latin American business sensibilities, with their premium on tact and discretion, the new broker had a smoother, more urbane touch. He was honey to Bazin's vinegar. He called himself Bob. He knew about the Chavín headdress deal and had seen the snapshots of the backflap. He was willing to forget about all that unfortunate business before and get things off on the right footing. Let's meet soon, he suggested in a voice that came over the phone in a cool, leathery whisper. Garcia took to him right away.

Along with a different style, the new broker brought a different boss. He was buying for an important collector in Philadelphia who, like Bazin's patron, could not be identified because he was a tempting target for thieves. We call him "el Hombre de Oro," the Gold Man, Bob explained jokingly, because he had such a discerning eye for gold artifacts.

Garcia was delighted that things had gotten back on track. A few days later he sent the broker a new set of snapshots and two editions of the *National Geographic* with Walter Alva's stories about the Sipán excavation, along with his compliments to el Hombre de Oro. Garcia had just one surprise for the broker. Bringing such a large piece of metal into the United States would involve great risk and expense, he said, and the price rose accordingly. He was now asking $1.6 million.[56]

What Garcia did not know was that Bob Wittman, the new "broker," and Bazin, the man Garcia and the warehouse gang had dealt with for three years, were undercover FBI agents. And el Hombre de Oro was in fact U.S. Assistant District Attorney Robert Goldman in Philadelphia. Garcia was walking straight into a sting operation.

Chapter 6

LORD OF SIPÁN

A S THE MARKET for looted Sipán artifacts went deeper underground, Alva's excavations at the *huaca* were bringing more enigmatic findings. The tombs he was unearthing were not as sumptuous as the earlier ones, but the people buried there were still connected to the elite, supporting cast members in the blood-soaked rituals of sacrifice and cannibalism in which the Moche rulers appeased the elements, courted immortality, and made sense of a random and violent universe.[1]

Some of the burials pointed to a military theme — soldiers, weapons, body armor — while others seemed more associated with religion and ritual. Taken together, the burials were leading Alva and scholars everywhere to a fuller understanding of the degree to which war and worship were intertwined in Moche society. The *huaca* was no elite dwelling or town square. It had evidently functioned as a dreaded altar of human sacrifice, where victorious soldiers hustled naked prisoners of war up the platform, slashed their throats, and collected their gushing blood in a golden goblet to feed to the lord of Sipán. The ritual known as the "sacrifice ceremony" lay at the heart of Moche notions of life and death, birth and regeneration. Since the early 1970s archaeologists led by Christopher Donnan had recognized the existence of this central ritual of Moche society from fine-line paintings and low relief on pottery and murals, which depicted the ceremony in detail, down to the blood dripping from the prisoners' faces. The most frequently cited depiction of the sacrifice ceremony appeared on a Moche pottery vessel at the Staatliches Museum für Völkerkunde in Munich, a masterfully expressive and detailed work that brings the ceremony alive. A man with a feline head and claws for feet draws blood from the prisoners' throats with a knife, while a priestess stands nearby, her long braids ending in serpent heads. The bird priest passes the goblet to the grimacing warrior-priest, who leans forward eagerly to grasp it, wearing a crown identical to the one Alva excavated in Tomb One. A backflap dangles from the warrior-priest's lower back, and at his feet a growling dog stands on its hind legs. In another depiction, this one on a pot at the American Museum of Natural History in New York, the stripped and bruised prisoners are being carried up the *huaca*, some dragged with a rope held by a soldier, some carried in a litter, and others running of their own volition with big, crazed eyes. The different ways in which they are being taken to their executioner suggest to some analysts a social hierarchy among the prisoners.

Then the prisoners were hacked apart and their limbs hoisted on the *huaca* as trophies. Contrary to romantic notions about peace and egalitarianism before the arrival of Europeans, the Moche created a violent and stratified society in which elite families waged war on each other, drank the blood of each others' young males, had little contact with their own subjects, and relied on armies of craftsmen to keep the furnaces fired and producing golden splendors to adorn their rulers in life and death. Since successive rulers took their greatest artistic treasures to the grave, more and more resources had to be invested with each generation to make new ones, fostering the development of an elite class of artisans. In this way, the string of feuding Moche ministates along the north coast developed such sophisticated standards of art and design.

The excavations at Sipán were showing more and more convincingly that the sacrifice ceremony was no legend. Before Sipán, scholars thought it was a mythological narrative or some kind of elaborate theater. Alva's work showed, with more clarity as each tomb was excavated, that the ceremony was a real and repeated event, with real blood and real people dressed as supernatural beings, including the bird priest, whose remains were found in Tomb Two, near the Lord of Sipán's own chamber. One by one the tombs revealed the ceremony's participants and their props, right down to the golden goblets, the growling dog, and the severed limbs.

On the south-central side of the platform Alva found the remains of a young man with the accoutrements of ritualized combat, as depicted in Moche painting. He wore a copper mask with an embossed face, a metal headdress, and nose ornaments, and next to him lay sheaths of combat weapons and an unusual wooden spear-throwing device inlaid with turquoise and shell. The weapons were similar to those in pottery drawings that had intrigued researchers but were rarely found because they were invariably destroyed by looters. Lying at the bottom of his unearthed funerary pit was the man's ceramic panpipe, another object that surely would otherwise have been smashed by looters. This last discovery led Alva to speculate that the soldier was also one of the lord's favorite musicians. After playing for the lord in life, the soldier was sacrificed to entertain him in the next world.[2] It was this bracing sense of identity, the feeling that Alva and his diggers were revealing pieces of the life stories of a cast of real people, associated with each other in life and yet each with a distinct self, that made the Sipán excavation unique in the history of Peruvian archaeology.

After the young musician-soldier, Alva and his team returned to the northern side of the platform and excavated the remains of two people in their late teens, one female and one male, buried with a rich assortment of ceramics, shell-bead necklaces, copper jewelry, and decapitated llamas. The young man's feet were missing and replaced with pieces of metal discs, as if he had endured ritual amputation to prevent him from running from his job as the lord's guard. The woman wore a headdress similar to that found with the principal woman accompanying the Lord of Sipán in Tomb One.

The next tomb posed some of the most intriguing questions of the whole excavation. It was a large chamber, twenty feet by fourteen, bigger than that of the Lord of Sipán himself, yet the artifacts inside were much more modest. Tomb size evidently was "not a faithful reflection of the rank of the individuals," Alva wrote later.[3] The remains of four people were found inside, one of whom, a young man, was so disarticulated that he must have been first buried somewhere else, disinterred, and then reburied with this group. Combat paraphernalia had been carefully placed around his corpse, including a war club, military emblems, a headdress, and a copper scepter of the same trapezoidal shape as those found in the looted tomb and the Lord of Sipán tomb. Alva believed such scepters were linked to military command, yet right next to the scepter bearer rested another man, also in a simple cane coffin, with an even more fearsome array of weapons. There were spear points, war clubs, shields, and pectorals, as well as a copper headdress with the embossed likeness of a man bordered by two mythological creatures. Alva believed they may have been military comrades, perhaps two favorite guards of a Sipán lord who died at separate times.

Alongside the second man's body rested a large image of hammered copper, nearly two feet wide, that looked like a scene from one of Ernil Bernal's nightmares. A winged dragon grasped a man in its talons, pulling his hair or some kind of headdress with its teeth and yanking a rope around his neck, while the man screamed and looked away in agony. It was like an image of death itself feasting on the live prisoner.

After excavating the remains of thirty-five people, twelve tombs, and thousands of objects, Alva had a problem. The Brüning Museum, a two-story building opened in 1966 on a quiet street in the center of Lambayeque, was ill equipped to hold such treasures. Although the Brüning had gained an international reputation under Alva as a solid museum of regional ethnic history, the Sipán treasures were so impressive and famous that they would overwhelm the rest of its collection of pre-Columbian artifacts and turn it into the *de facto* Sipán museum. With small gallery rooms arranged around a central atrium, the Brüning might be barely large enough to show the most important objects to the public, but it could not give any sense of the archaeological process involved in the excavation or its evolution over six years of work. No matter how well designed, the exhibit, inside the Brüning, would look like those at nearly every other archaeological museum in Peru: a cramped concatenation of random objects, displayed flat against a wall, devoid of context or explanation.

Thus was born the idea of a new museum, a permanent home for the Sipán treasures. A decade of debate on where to build the museum, in Lima, Lambayeque, or Sipán itself, would follow, but in the early 1990s, as the Brüning laboratory filled with artifacts brought from the *huaca* for the delicate and painstaking work of restoration, the biggest worry was where the money would come from. Alva and Meneses were determined to build an institution worthy of the treasures, one that would be sufficiently modern and visually geared to attract the young while focusing not on the objects themselves but on the cultural context that produced them and on the legacies of the Moche to present-day Peruvians. It would be a museum as much about the present as about the past. Corporate sponsors and foreign governments would help, but the best route for raising the kind of money needed to build such an institution was from a traveling museum show, from which the Sipán project would derive revenue from ticket sales and residual sales of catalogues, calendars, coffee mugs, and the like.

Entitled with elegant simplicity "Royal Tombs of Sipán," the show began its two-year American road show at the Fowler Museum of Cultural History in Los Angeles in September 1993, cocurated by Alva and Donnan. It later traveled to museums in Houston, New York, and Detroit, with a final stop in the United States at the Smithsonian's National Museum of Natural History in Washington. From there, the exhibition went to Mainz, Germany, where Alva had sent many of the most important pieces for restoration. At the insistence of President Fujimori, a somewhat smaller show followed in Japan, though Alva never thought the Japanese came up with enough money to justify sending the artifacts to Tokyo and declined to attend the opening.

Alva's reputation was riding high. In Peru, his own prestige was so intertwined with that of the Lord of Sipán that he had succeeded in persuading the government to treat the remains of "the first ruler of Peru," as he called the Lord of Sipán, like those of a deceased president. In March 1993, when the remains were flown back from restoration in Mainz, Alva wanted airport honors befitting a returning head of state, complete with a twenty-one gun salute. The foreign ministry's protocol office thought the idea a bit loopy and balked, but Alva insisted and managed to get the idea onto the desk of Fujimori, who liked it. The remains were received with full pomp and circumstance, and even the German ambassador got into the act, telling Peruvian news media, "We have had an illustrious figure visiting our country."[4]

In New York, the Sipán exhibit opened in June 1994 with a banner on Central Park West and the biggest buzz for an archaeological show in the city since Tutankhamen in 1978. Alva, fêted at its opening, gave a personal guided tour to Henry Kissinger, who apparently had no idea this unassuming, bearded Peruvian was the excavator himself until the end of the exhibit, when they came to a photograph of Alva standing at the bottom of the tomb.[5] Critics seemed a bit overwhelmed, as much by the beauty of the objects as by the idea that a civilization that had produced such incredible art could have escaped the general public's attention for so long. "Dazzling Jewelry from Peru's Mystery People," read a headline in *The New York Times*. "In their glorious metalwork, the Moche hammered paper-thin sheets of gold, silver and copper," its reporter wrote, enraptured by the "glowing images" and "mysteriousness of the Moche."[6] Indeed, the Moche were little known. Until the early 1950s they were lumped together with the north-coast Chimú people, whose culture was was still alive when the Spaniards arrived. Moche objects had simply been called proto-Chimú.[7] Other writers were interested in how the Moche developed sophisticated metallurgical techniques once thought to be exclusive to the Old World, such as chemical plating techniques for gilding copper. It was one of the rare times when the advance billing of a new archaeological discovery actually lived up to reality.

The Sipán show greatly strengthened the museum-going public's appreciation of pre-Hispanic civilization and its grasp of the cultural depth and complexity of the Peruvian nation. The show was followed by the discovery in 1995 of the perfectly preserved, five-hundred-year-old frozen remains of a young Inca woman who had been sacrificed on a volcano in southern Peru. The exhibit of the remains of the Lady of Ampato, as she was nicknamed, later in Washington and Japan aroused protests from Peruvian archaeologists and cultural figures, who compared it to a freak show. But the two events combined to give Peru's ancient civilizations a prominence in American museums and media not seen since the discovery of Machu Picchu in 1911.

In Peru, too, Sipán had changed everything—archaeology, looting, collecting, the way an entire nation studied and thought about its past. Among collectors, the irruption of Sipán artifacts added an excitement and a sense of discovery not seen in years. Everyone knew there would be no more Sipán treasures coming onto the market (although there was a steady stream of fakes made to look like them) yet the discovery gave dealers, connoisseurs, and the looters who supplied them a newfound and palpable sense of anticipation about what remained to be discovered. When treasures from La Mina hit the market after 1988, the excitement became even more feverish. A giddiness spread through the market as Peruvian antiquities, formerly of purely specialist interest, were viewed by dealers as an area of tremendous potential and profit. They were the motor of the market. It was the time when Robin, Remi, and thousands of looters like them got their start.

In his sprawling triplex flat overlooking the San Isidro golf course, collector Aldo Valerga reached over to a lighted vitrine and gently picked up a golden cup. It looked substantial but when he handed it to me, it was as light and delicate as paper.

"Sipán," he said.

Another, smaller gold cup and two ear spools on the same shelf were also from the famous site, he said. They had that soft, opaque luster of real gold. None of them jumped out at me as Sipán style, but then again Aldo is a first-class collector, the kind archaeologists come to see because they know he inhabits that small circle that buy the rare and the best. I took his word for it.

A smartly dressed man of about forty with the studied insouciance of the Peruvian nouveau riche, Aldo started collecting around the time Sipán burst onto the market and now his cache of about six hundred pre-Columbian objects would put many museums to shame. A mutual friend introduced us and, after explaining to him that I was writing about the antiquities trade, I asked if I might see his collection. I expected a long courtship, but he was surprisingly willing and invited me into his home that very evening, allowing me to return a few days later with a photographer for *Archaeology* magazine. The stars of his collection were a dozen or so textiles, including some of the finest Chimú and Inca weavings I had ever seen, framed and gorgeously displayed all over the apartment. In the living room hung a red Inca funerary wrap the size of a dining-room table, from Chuquibamba province in southern Peru. It was smelly, filthy, and wadded up in a ball when a looter first showed it to him in Arequipa, but Aldo cited its poor condition to leverage the price down to $3,500.

"What a steal," he said. Aldo knew how to drive a hard bargain. Not for nothing did two well-known U.S. retail clothing companies make him their chief representative in Peru.

He showed me his other favorites. There was a Wari feathered tunic, an erotic Moche pot showing two men engaged in anal intercourse ("This demonstrates that homosexuality was not unknown amongst the Moche," he intoned professorially), a small Paracas shirt and matching headband, and, most charming of all, a boy's cap knitted in vibrant bands of red, pink, and green with the distinctive four-pointed crown of the Wari culture that dominated the south Peruvian coast from about A.D. 500 to 1000. Knitting was women's work in ancient Peru, and in every stitch of that simple cap was a mother's love for her son.

"You like that one? There's an even better one at the Boston Museum of Fine Arts," he noted, with a touch of envy.

Next he showed me what he believed was the largest ceramic vessel in Peru, a beige-and-brown Chancay amphora the size of a hot-water heater, resting on a steel brace in its own alcove at the bottom of a staircase.

"I keep it down here away from the other stuff so the kids won't break it," he said. "You know kids, they play in the living room, they throw things, they break pots. Why, they've broken about fifty already!"

Now and then he would excuse himself to take a call on his cell phone. "Another provider," he said, with a bored roll of his chestnut eyes. "Wants to come around tomorrow with some new things." He had ancient ceramics hanging over the bar near bottles of Johnny Walker, a framed red-and-black Nazca banner hanging by the barbecue on the deck, and more Chancay amphorae alongside the rooftop swimming pool, so that it looked like a Tuscan villa. Yet there was no feeling of clutter or hoarding. Aldo and his wife, Patricia, had taken the pilfered treasures of two thousand years of Andean culture and used them to decorate their home with excellent taste and harmony.

Like most serious collectors of pre-Columbian art in the world, he said, he never bought from other collectors. "*Solo directo de la fuente*," he said. Fresh material, straight from the *huacas*. When he first started collecting he had to buy many pieces that he knew to be inferior to establish confidence with providers. He has kept some of those early pieces for sentimental reasons and sold others to more casual collectors. Now, with his reputation made, he can afford to pass up everything but the best-quality stuff and rejects all but one or two of every hundred objects offered to him.

The great majority of Peruvian relics are sent abroad, he said, particularly textiles. Smugglers (he was not one of them) can export textiles in large quantities because, unlike metal or ceramics, they won't show up in luggage or container X rays. "The best material goes abroad because obviously that's where the real purchasing power is," he said. Paracas and Inca textiles have become all the rage in comfortable living rooms in Chile, where they sell for three to four times their price locally, he said.

Aldo believed that certain ancient Peruvian cultures, Chancay for example, were essentially finished. There were no more sites left to excavate, looters had rifled through the last of them, and many more coastal civilization, including the Moche, were headed in the same direction. That was a familiar bleat from archaeologists, but it surprised me to hear it from a man like Aldo who had a businessman's dispassionate sensibility and a deep, genuine knowledge of the market's supply side.

"I would say that eighty to ninety percent of the total is now outside Peru."

"You mean eighty to ninety percent of what is currently on the market?" I asked.

"No, no. Ninety percent of all valuable, pre-Columbian Peruvian art ever created." Ninety percent of *everything*. "You can go for two or three years now without seeing anything new that's top-quality. That is because no more than ten percent still remains in the ground. All over the country, it's all running out. *Se está terminando todo.*"

And then, for the first time of the whole evening, he smiled.

"And when that happens, all of this will become much, much more valuable."

As director of the archaeological museum founded by his grandfather, Andrés Álvarez-Calderón Larco knows what's going on in the antiquities market. Collectors and dealers regularly show up at his museum's door with ceramic vessels known as *huacos* in their hands; they come to ask curators for professional advice on whether the pieces are real.

"If anybody were finding the next Sipán, I'd know about it," he said.

Housed in a stately, whitewashed house that looks as if were transported from a hilltown in Andalucia to a busy avenue leading out of Lima, the Museo Arqueológico Rafael Larco Herrera holds some forty thousand ancient Peruvian pots, jars, and decorative vessels, stacked to the ceiling in shelves that rise like canyons through the galleries. You can get lost for hours wandering down corridors, surrounded by Moche, Nazca, Chimú, and Inca pots in every conceivable form and style. It has been called more a warehouse than a museum, but nowhere else does a visitor get a better sense of the sheer volume of ceramic production in ancient Peru. Most of these pots were humdrum, household objects that were slapped together in molds and fired in batches in pit kilns. Some were used in rituals or adorned with paintings and sculptural details, but for most, their identity as artistic objects was a modern invention.

Unlike every other private museum in Peru, the Larco Herrera is not a collector's ego trip. It is a serious institution and center of scholarly study that claims not to have added a single piece to its shelves since 1966. This collection began with the private holdings of the Larco family, whose patriarch, Rafael Larco Herrera, was a north-coast landowner and pioneering connoisseur of pre-Columbian art in the early twentieth century. He left the bulk of the collection to his son, Rafael Larco Hoyle, a farmer-businessman who studied at Cornell, later became the mayor of Trujillo, and added thousands more pots to the collection by traveling all over Peru, buying up the collections of other landowners for prices that would seem laughable today. To call him an amateur archaeologist does not quite do justice to Larco Hoyle's contribution. He spent years studying his armies of ceramic vessels, working himself into ecstatic lathers about the genius of the Moche and noting subtle shifts in the style and form of their objects. In 1946 the Smithsonian Institution published an article of his called "A Cultural Sequence for the North Coast of Peru," which used pottery styles and motifs to devise a chronology of the region's civilizations that, with some adjustments, is still used today.

Most of the art on which Larco Hoyle based his sequence was looted or, in the best of cases, excavated under conditions that would seem less-than-scientific today. Little attention was paid to the context in which objects were found. Focusing almost exclusively on what the objects themselves could tell, which was often not very much, excavators did not take note of what other items lay nearby objects or what the soil indicated about the activities of the people who lived there.

It was somewhat like writing a history of the United States based solely on kitchen objects. What you would come up with would be a rough progression from ceramics to cast iron to stainless steel to Tupperware and beyond. It's not as silly as it sounds. With some good analysis and comparative evidence, you might detect broad social trends—the spread of mass production, urbanization, the rise of consumer culture. But it would probably obscure as much as it would illuminate, and you would miss a lot.

Brilliant and original though it was, Larco Hoyle's timetable of the sweep of Peruvian civilization through its objects required the work of modern archaeologists to fill it out and broaden our grasp of how societies evolved. Relying on great care at ancient sites and a sophisticated range of chemical and forensic techniques in the laboratory, scholars like Alva, Donnan, Shimada, Ruth Shady, and Santiago Uceda give us a better understanding every year of how people lived, worked, worshiped, and died before the arrival of Europeans.

Yet commercial grave robbing is finishing off our ability to add to that knowledge. And the current director of the Larco Herrera is seeing it happen before his eyes.

"There is very little left, and what there is, is going straight to the foreign markets," said Álvarez-Calderón. "As long as you have poverty in this country, you're going to have *huaqueros* looking for tombs, but you've got more and more *huaqueros* going after fewer and fewer places that hold anything valuable."

Part of the decrease in the flow of looted objects, he said, can be attributed to better protection of sites in Lambayeque. But, I asked, is it possible that ancient sites are simply being exhausted?

"Yes, I think something like that is happening. Certain cultures, certain areas, yes."[8]

A well-mannered, unpretentious man in his thirties whom you might confuse with the American graduate students who come to study pottery at the museum, Álvarez-Calderón is no enemy of the antiquities trade. On the contrary, he criticizes those who "demonize the collector," supports the legal and regulated purchase of antiquities within the borders of Peru and the INC registration system, and points out that many great art museums around the world began as private collections. Yet he does not see the ancient land of Peru yielding many more treasures for anybody, including collectors.

A few days after meeting the collector Aldo Valerga, I met at a café in San Isidro with our mutual friend, an experienced loot dealer known by his nickname Nancho. He asked me not to use his full name.

"There was always interest among a certain sector of collectors for Peruvian antiquities, but after Sipán that sector grew a great deal. I guess we came into fashion," he said. A nervous, chain-smoking man in his late forties, Nancho always had a few Polaroids of freshly looted ancient textiles made of llama wool or feathers that he or his friends were selling. A few of these textiles looked extremely valuable. Usually they had been restored at one of the semilegal private laboratories in Lima where conservators, often moonlighting museum specialists, repaired looted goods.

Nancho had taken top-quality textiles abroad once or twice as a courier but found he didn't have the stomach for that kind of work. Typically he would sell to European diplomats stationed in Lima or to big-scale buyers of antiquities such as Apesteguía. To do business in Europe or North America, it was essential to have your contacts established before traveling, he said. "It's like selling drugs. If you're going to take all the risk of transporting the merchandise to Europe, you're not going to go to a park in Amsterdam and sell it to the first person who comes along. You already have your buyers. You have it all set up."

He lit another cigarette and smoked it with a world-weary air. "Everything is being sold the first time. People don't want things that have already been in somebody's collection. That's like wearing used clothes," he said. "That sensation of new things coming out of the ground, that's what keeps the market going."

I visited one of the conservation laboratories he mentioned on an out-of-the-way street in the artsy neighhorhood of Barranco. A woman asked me a few questions through a remote intercom and then buzzed me in, and once inside I met two people standing around a fabulously valuable 1,200-year-old Wari man's shirt spread out on a table on parchment paper like a patient undergoing surgery. One similar to it had been offered at Sotheby's in 1999 at $250,000. When a collector brought the shirt around to the Barranco laboratory a few weeks before, it still had that acrid smell of a corpse. They had cleaned it and now they were delicately rethreading it where it was "burned," that is, frayed by years of decomposition, the woman told me. She had studied textile conservation with a Belgian specialist and had worked in museums but found a better way to make a living in the antiquities trade.

"The market for the best textiles is always strong," she said. "The prices go higher and higher."

Like looting, archaeology was never quite the same after Sipán, as a field of study or as a profession. More than any single site, Sipán helped moved the geographical focus of the field away from the Mediterranean world, where it had been since the birth of modern archaeology in the nineteenth century, and toward the indigenous societies of the Americas. Spectacular finds in the Mayan heartland of Guatemala and southern Mexico have strengthened that trend since, but in 1987 it was Sipán that brought attention as never before to the research potential of the ancient Americas. In Peru itself, the sudden intensification of looting brought on by Sipán began to transform the practice of archaeology in surprising ways. It had the effect of forcing researchers to concentrate more on tombs and grandiose mausoleums, particularly those likely to yield rich artifacts and metalwork. Sites based on everyday life were now passé. After Sipán, the research dollars went to the ancient lifestyles of the rich and famous.

"Sipán changed everything. It had a huge impact on how we do our jobs," said archaeologist Cecilia Jaime Tello at the Universidad Nacional Mayor de San Marcos, whose work has focused on the monumental ruins known as El Paraíso, built about 2000 B.C. in the Chillón Valley, a short drive north of Lima. As at Caral and other large, archaic sites, there is little in the way of objects to excavate at El Paraíso. It was built before the development of ceramics or metallurgy, a city where energy and creativity was channeled into agriculture and muscle power to make colossal stone platforms, ramps, and walls.

"After Sipán, people wanted to excavate only tombs and left aside projects dealing with daily life," she said. "They were serious projects, I'm not denying that. But after a while if you were an archaeologist who wanted to gain a reputation, or you just wanted research funds, it was like you had to excavate tombs. Villages, residences, daily life, all that was neglected. People who had spent their whole careers excavating other kinds of sites had to leave them and do their research only on tombs."[9]

Research institutions had become interested only in metalwork, the glitzier the better. It was harder for researchers to justify their work by filling museum vaults with pottery shards or household objects.

"Now archaeologists look for gold," archaeologist Peter Kaulicke of Lima's Universidad Católica told me. "That was part of the whole change in attitude brought by Sipán. It was a catalyst." The new rage in the looting business was seeping into its alter ego, the archaeological profession.[10] Not that those changes were entirely unwelcome. A specialist in early Chavín culture in the northern highlands, Kaulicke saw how Sipán energized a profession that was drained and demoralized by lack of funding, destruction of study sites by looters, agriculture, and urban sprawl, and the indifference and incompetence of officials in the INC, which has final authority over Peru's archaeological resources and a sad history of allowing key pieces to be damaged or "lost" in its vaults. Archaeology took an ever-higher profile in the public mind. Stories of "lost cities" found in the jungles, Inca mass graves, and newly discovered *huacas* appeared constantly in the Peruvian press. Some reports were exaggerated, to be sure, but they served to show how Peruvians were attuned to the depth and richness of their ancient heritage, probably to a greater degree than at any time in their history. Few would dispute that Alva's work at Sipán, together with the work of a few other prominent archaeologists, was responsible for that.

"Sipán showed how projects involving large numbers of people and resources could bring great results," said Kaulicke. "Before Sipán, people thought tombs were boring to excavate, lots of ceramics and nothing else. After Sipán, we all knew what tombs might contain. We were looking for tombs."[11]

In his house on Santa Fe's posh north side, surrounded by the treasures gathered over a lifetime of collecting, John Bourne took one last look at the golden monkey head that he said Ben Johnson had sold him. Bourne had brought his little beauties from Los Angeles to Santa Fe when he moved there around 1990, the time of Johnson's downfall and the long and ugly court cases that caused so much pain to some of Southern California's best collectors.

Bourne had managed to keep a low profile over the years, and now, with his collection in Santa Fe, museum directors had been courting him. Stanley Marcus, the department-store magnate and benefactor of the Dallas Museum of Art, had flown Bourne to Dallas and fêted him in hopes of winning his collection for that museum, according to one associate. But Bourne loved New Mexico and felt loyal to the state's premier cultural institution, the Museum of New Mexico, a statewide complex of history, art, and anthropology museums. He had been in contact with the director of one of those museums, Thomas Chávez, of the Palace of the Governors, about the possibility of donating his collection of pre-Columbian treasures, as well as part of the funding for a new annex to the museum, a building dating to the 1600s on the city's busy main plaza.[12] The museum had offered to name the new annex after Bourne,[13] a gracious offer although perhaps a bit incongruous for a man so shy of publicity, who was little known outside his circle of friends and collectors. Yet someday the bulk of Bourne's collection might be housed in that annex.

Strangely, one institution that did not pursue his collection was the Museum of New Mexico's own Museum of Indian Arts and Culture in Santa Fe, one of the most distinguished institutions of its kind in the country. It would seem like the natural place for Bourne's collection, instead of the Palace of the Governors, a Spanish-colonial edifice that is officially New Mexico's state history museum. Did the curators at the indigenous art museum think Bourne's collection was legally a bit too problematic? To be sure, some of his pieces had the telltale signs of looting: no precise findspot, no record of archaeologists having excavated them, no history of having been in any other collection. Did that scare off the museum? Could his pieces bring the wrong kind of publicity? These were the rumors, never confirmed, that, before too long, would be flying through Santa Fe's large and influential arts community.

On February 13, 1995, John Bourne signed a deed of gift for the monkey's head to the Museum of New Mexico, according to documents obtained under the U.S. Freedom of Information Act.[14] Those documents make it difficult to deny that Bourne should have known the monkey head was looted and exported in violation of Peruvian law, and the director of the Museum of New Mexico, Thomas Livesay, who also signed the deed, should have known, too. Under "Description of Gift," Bourne affirmed that it came from La Mina (or "La Mira, ca. 300 A.D.," as someone wrote), the site ransacked in 1988 in the looting free-for-all that followed Sipán. As Moche potentates, La Mina and Sipán were neighbors and almost exactly contemporaneous, and both met the same fate 1,600 years later. It was unusual enough for a donor to state a specific provenance for an ancient relic, stranger still for that provenance to be a notorious den of grave robbers.

On the same deed Bourne also donated a small pectoral disc from Panama in gold repoussé, dating from A.D. 800 to 1200. This one had no provenance at all. The total value of them both was listed as $122,500, with the deed noting that the value was "deductible from the donor's taxable income in accordance with the provisions of federal income tax laws."[15] The federal government had, in effect, retroactively financed the looting of La Mina.

It was the last time Bourne would look at the monkey's head in his own home, because on that day in 1995 it went to its new home at the Palace of the Governors in downtown Santa Fe. He couldn't quite bring himself to part yet with his golden rattle from Sipán.

Chapter 7

THE DEALER

JANUARY IS VACATION time for the Peruvian wealthy and middle classes, time for beach, *cebiche*, and double pisco sours. Raúl Apesteguía, art collector, supplier to European and American dealers in Peruvian antiquities, the man whose Sipán pieces had been seized in Miami a year before, was in good spirits as he planned to receive friends for dinner in his apartment on the thirteenth floor of a high-rise in the Lima district of San Miguel. Things were looking up again for Raúl. Friends had seen him out and about, and he had been entertaining a steady stream of buyers in recent weeks. He had regained his reputation as jeweler to the stars by lending another one of his authentic Inca necklaces to Keiko Sofia Fujimori, daughter of Alberto Fujimori, for the president's second inaugural ceremonies six months before.

It was January 26, 1996. Apesteguía was hosting his ex-wife's father, Argentine painter Liber Fridman, who was visiting from Buenos Aires. At about 6:30, Apesteguía told Fridman he was going up to his other apartment, a penthouse two floors above, where he had his pre-Columbian collection, to shower and change. By nine o'clock, dinner was ready but Apesteguía still hadn't come back down. The dinner guests had arrived. They called him on the phone: no answer. Finally they went up to the fifteenth floor and opened the door with an emergency key.

The apartment was in complete disarray. Lying on the living-room floor, with a bullet through his head, was Apesteguía. Some of his ancient

Peruvian pots lay broken on the floor. He had bruises on his neck and face. Apesteguía had put up a fight before he was murdered. Neighbors reported seeing a group of at least two men and one woman descending in the elevator, carrying boxes. They seemed to be in a hurry.

Coincidentally, Alva's brother-in-law, Luis Meneses, lived in the same building. Meneses, a lawyer, later told Alva that he saw the police activity and went up to Apartment 1502 that evening, found the door open, and wandered in. He was surprised to see that the police had disturbed the crime scene by moving objects around and that they had apparently not brushed for fingerprints. The police put the motive down to robbery and advised Apesteguía's family not to pursue investigations. Powerful people were behind the murder, the police warned the family ominously, treating the case like a drug-world rubout, refusing to investigate and suggesting that the collector had it coming.

"They told us they had an idea who did it, but that there were a lot of powerful interests involved. Best to leave it, they told us," said Apesteguía's son Gabriel, a tall, lanky man in his twenties with sad eyes who kept sitting down and getting up restlessly during our interview. Cowed by the brutality of the killing, that was exactly what the family did.

Apesteguía's murder shocked the Lima art world. The most obvious explanation was that he had taken the blame for the Miami bust. But some friends said the motive was yet another deal gone wrong, that he had unwittingly sold a load of fake stone carvings as Moche originals to a group of smugglers who took it to Europe. When the fakes were revealed and the smugglers demanded their money back, Apesteguía balked. The fakes were so good that even he was fooled. According to two people close to Apesteguía, the source of the fakes, perhaps unwittingly, was none other than Pereda, the Trujillo buyer who handled the first group of Sipán pieces and most likely the man who sold him the Miami rattle.

In the galleries and living rooms of the Lima bourgeoisie, the motives mattered little. Apesteguía's murder meant that collecting Indian antiquities was no longer merely a diversion for the European-blood aristocracy, a pastime for connoisseurs to dabble in, like decorating or horseback riding. Now it was seen as a mean, dirty business with all the violence and intrigue of Peru's other big illicit industry, cocaine. Police seizures, U.S. Customs sting operations, smuggling mafias, and now murder—the antiquities-dealing business was looking less and less like Lord Elgin's hobby and more like the Medellín cartel. Just as Sipán had transformed looting and archaeology, so it had changed collecting, making it a dangerous game that people entered at their peril. Eight years later, people still talked about the killing in hushed, frightened tones and immediately begged off any knowledge of who did it or why.

Gabriel and his sister, Irene, who lived in Argentina, sold what was left of their father's collection soon after his death, about fifty pieces, to a single buyer. Neither shared their father's interest in collecting and were happy to get rid of the objects. Gabriel, a computer programmer, kept just two works from his father's collection, a pair of colored etchings by contemporary Argentine artist Antonio Seguí, both of them dark, brooding, nocturnal landscapes. When I visited, he had them hanging on the wall in his ground-floor apartment in an old converted boardinghouse near the cliffs overlooking the Pacific, a foggy ocean breeze shaking the petals off the geraniums in the windowboxes. There were no pictures of his father anywhere. Only after the funeral did Gabriel learn that he had been hurriedly sent to Buenos Aires as a child so that he wouldn't learn of his father's humiliating jail spell in Lurigancho, that his father had spent a career associating with smugglers and had paid for it with incarceration and then with his life. A whole career in crime was revealed to him.

"My father never told us anything about what he was doing, what he was collecting, whom he knew. He almost never let us into the apartment where he kept his objects. All we knew was that people were coming to see him, buying and selling, buying and selling," said Gabriel, in the lilting Argentine accent of his mother. "I guess he wanted to protect us from that world."[1]

Although he had sounded angry at Denis Garcia when he called again about the backflap, Bazin was actually overjoyed to hear from him. Everything Bazin said, in fact, had been an act, including his name. (Bazin is his real name but not the one the gang knew him by, which he says he does not remember.) He was not about to undergo heart surgery; he invented that story on the spur of the moment because he had retired from the FBI on March 31, 1997, after twenty-eight years of service, seventeen in stolen art recovery, and needed a convincing story to turn the case over to his partner, Bob Wittman, who had learned the basics of undercover work from Bazin. The reason Bazin and his partner at the restaurant in Miami had read the letter about the backflap aloud was because they were wearing hidden wiretaps. And Bill Becker, the aging con man who connected Bazin with the warehouse gang and later tried to muscle his way into a share of the money for the backflap, had been an FBI informant all along to avoid serving time after being convicted in a Virginia gambling racket. No matter how many people Becker had swindled over the years, he had played an indispensable role in starting the process that might one day restore to the Peruvian people a national treasure.

One thing Bazin said was true. He had bought the Chavín headdress only to get the real prize, the backflap. In 1994, when he first made contact with the Miami men, he had sent Garcia's snapshots of the back-flap to Donnan at UCLA to ask him if it was authentic. Donnan called back immediately.

"This is it. This is the legendary piece that we had heard about. Go for it," Donnan told him, according to Bazin's recollection.[2] Bazin immediately set about laying a chum line for the backflap, and the first big piece of bait on that line was the U.S. government's money that he paid for the Chavín headdress.

"There was this interesting double-bait going on," said Bazin, now in retirement on the New Jersey shore. "We were using the crown to get to the backflap, and they were seeing if we could be trusted to buy the back-flap by selling us the crown."

A few months before his retirement, Bazin learned why the ware-house gang had stopped calling. Someone had blown his cover. Bazin be-lieved that Becker had betrayed him because he was convinced that Bazin was going to pay real money for the backflap, as he had for the headdress, and Becker was unhappy that he wasn't going to get a share. Bazin, how-ever, had no intention of paying for the backflap. When the time came to haul it in, he would have a meticulously planned police operation ready to confiscate it by force before any money would be paid. And if he *did* re-cover the backflap by paying for it, Becker wouldn't receive a single dol-lar. The only thing to which he was entitled in exchange for turning FBI snitch was the privilege of not spending his old age in jail. Like others in a long succession of people who touched, saw, or heard about the backflap, Becker saw it as a holy grail of wealth and opportunity that was going to make him instantly rich. When he became convinced that everyone but him was going to gain from the sale of the backflap according to Bazin's sources, he told the warehouse gang that Bazin was an undercover FBI agent.[3]

In testimony involving a later, unrelated criminal case that was re-ported in the news media, a more complex explanation emerged. In an-other of his endlessly creative enterprises, Becker had teamed up with another federal parolee named Sammy Kaplan to steal a yacht from a Mi-ami marina by posing as a repossession agent in 1992. It all went wrong when the two men whom Becker had hired to pilot the yacht double-crossed him and stole it themselves. (They were later arrested and con-victed.) When Becker offered his services as an FBI informant, his former cohort Kaplan was one of the people he betrayed, and Kaplan, still furious at Becker's handling of the yacht affair, then spread the word through or-ganized crime circles up and down the east coast that Becker was an FBI mole. Kaplan admitted as much under oath at his trial in April 1995, in which he was convicted.[4] If word reached the warehouse gang, it wouldn't have taken a great leap of logic for them to conclude that Becker's friend the art dealer was an undercover agent.

The backflap sting was about to collapse. It would have fallen through right then and there, if only someone had told Denis Garcia. The warehouse gang must have had a bitter falling-out with him, because they evidently never told him that Bazin was FBI. Bazin never knew what the dispute was about, and Garcia won't say, but it's tempting to conclude that they fought over the money from the Chavín headdress deal. Bazin had paid $175,000 for the piece, yet Garcia, who acquired it from Luis Peralta and arranged for its smuggling into the United States, received only $35,000 or $40,000, according to one of his associates.[5] Like Michael Kelly in the first shipment of Sipán treasures, Garcia had assumed virtually all the risk, received only a fraction of the money, and learned the hard way that there really is no honor among thieves. No wonder he wanted to do the backflap deal himself.

Just before his retirement, Bazin learned of yet another furrow in this endlessly fertile case. The "Monet" that Becker wanted to sell him actually *was* a Monet, an authentic and little-known work by the French impressionist master. It was believed to have been taken from Europe to Cuba shortly after the Second World War and thence to Miami. According to Becker's recollection and court transcripts and U.S. Parole Commission reports unearthed by a Baltimore *Sun* reporter, Becker sold the painting and collected a $1.2 million finder's fee.[6] New York gallery owner Guy Wildenstein called Bazin back to tell him that further inspection had shown the painting to be authentic and that he intended to purchase it.[7] (Wildenstein declined to confirm or deny that he was the buyer.) With the $1.2 million fee, Becker was able to hire an expensive legal team, including a former U.S. Attorney for the District of Columbia, Joseph di Genova, but it was not enough to keep him out of jail for violating the terms of his parole. He was convicted again and stayed there until May 2001. The Monet remains in a private collection.

Bazin's failure to get the backflap took a bit of the shine off his otherwise brilliant career at the FBI, at least in his own eyes. His superiors had reacted with great reluctance to the idea of paying $175,000 of U.S. taxpayers' money for the Chavín headdress, with no guarantee of getting the backflap or anything else later. The money "walked" and was not recoverable. Agents occasionally did the same thing in undercover narcotics work, paying millions of taxpayers' dollars for cocaine in order to infiltrate a drug ring "and then they throw it all in the goddamned furnace," as Bazin pointed out to his superiors. This time, at least they had a real artifact, sitting in the FBI warehouse in Woodlawn, Maryland. Still, it did not look good, and as Bazin gazed out over the Atlantic in his happy retirement, he wondered what ever happened to the backflap and if he had done something wrong, been too insistent with the warehouse gang, or not insistent enough.

The case that had outlived his career was coming to a head. He had laid the groundwork, and now the backflap might finally be within reach.

PART TWO

PART TWO

Chapter 8

THE ACTUAL OBJECT

I should wish to have examples in the actual object, of each thing, and architectural ornament—of each cornice, each frieze, each capital—of the decorated ceilings, of the fluted columns—specimens of the different architectural orders and of the variant forms of the orders,—of metopes and the like, as much as possible. Finally everything in the way of sculpture, medals and curious marbles that can be discovered by means of assiduous and indefatigable excavation.

LORD ELGIN, 1801

I opposed, and ever will oppose, the robbery of ruins from Athens, to instruct the English in sculpture (who are as capable of sculpture as the Egyptians are of skating).

LORD BYRON, 1821

THE FIRST THREE decades of the life of Thomas Bruce, seventh earl of Elgin, read like the genteel intrigues of a novel by his contemporary Jane Austen, a life of dashing gentlemen and demure ladies, class envy, and provincial mores. A Scottish nobleman born in 1766, Elgin (pronounced with a hard "g") first brought his ambition to the British army, where he rose quickly to the rank of lieutenant colonel and created his own regiment, the Elgin Highland Fencibles. He hankered to make his mark in society and, for a few years, he did everything right. He joined the House of Lords from Scotland at the age of twenty-four, served with distinction as a representative of the crown on diplomatic missions in Vienna, Brussels,

and Berlin, and built a splendid country home in Fife. He had torn down
the modest home where his father lived and, on the same plot, hired an architect to build a mansion named Broomhall. There Lord Elgin would live
with his new wife, Mary, and impress his taste and status upon her affluent
parents, the Nisbets. Elgin had good reason to woo the Nisbets, for he
hoped one day to marry their fortune to his. He was a man of some means,
but not rich, with perhaps more drive than talent, and the construction of
his grand estate had forced him into the first of a string of debts that would
dog him throughout his life.

Like everyone before and since who has gone beyond his means in
building a home, Lord Elgin found that once he had built his palace, he had
to furnish it like a palace. A Roman urn or two would not do, nor would
seascapes or mythological scenes by fashionable salon painters. This was a
man of discernment, a member of the rural nobility and relentless self-
promoter who, over the years, wrote repeatedly to the British royal court
to ask for a more elevated title than the one he had. (He was born an earl
but, as a Scotsman, had to be elected to the House of Lords as one of sixteen Scottish representative peers. A full-fledged, United Kingdom peerage would have meant a lifetime seat and a mark of royal favor.) In 1799
Elgin finished work at Broomhall and, though he never received the
grander peerage he sought, was appointed by King George III to be
Britain's new ambassador to the Ottoman Empire. The timing was good.
Britain's power in the eastern Mediterranean was in the ascendancy, and
Elgin could use his influence to bring home authentic Greek antiquities or
at least plaster casts that would make him the envy of his peers and crown
him as Britain's undisputed leader in collecting. In the process, he believed
he could raise the standards of British sculpture and design by exposing
the country's artists to the highest achievements of Hellenic art.

He and his wife set out on the British warship *Phaeton* in September
1799, accompanied by a dozen secretaries, servants, and maids, several of
Mary Elgin's dogs, thirteen large trunks, a traveling library, and a cargo
hold full of belongings and gifts for the sultan. The plunder began even before they arrived. As they waited at the entrance to the Dardanelles for fa-
vorable winds to take them (on a Turkish ship) to Constantinople, the lord
sent a group of soldiers ashore to the village of Sigaeum, on the Asian side,
to rip out two slabs of marble carved with ancient Greek inscriptions and
sculptures. The pieces had attracted the attention of European travelers for
nearly a century, but local inhabitants had resisted their removal out of fear
that it would bring plagues and misfortunes on the village, a Greek colony
dating from antiquity. Residents had even deliberately damaged some of
the sculptures and marred the inscriptions to try to make them less valuable
to Europeans. Elgin and his party dismissed the protests as superstitions,
bribed a military authority with gifts of diamonds and, despite the wailing

protestations of Greek priests at the site, had the pieces removed and loaded on the *Phaeton*. The modern era of antiquities looting had begun.[1]

Elgin enjoyed more influence and prestige in Constantinople than any foreign envoy ever had, and he used it aggressively to advance, among other interests, his personal agenda for the removal of antiquities. In 1800 he sent a group of his agents and contract artists, led by Italian landscape painter Giovanni Lusieri, to Athens, then part of the Turks' Ottoman Empire. After months of delays and balking from local authorities, Lusieri and his team were allowed in February 1801 on to the Acropolis, the rocky crag looming above the city, to begin making drawings of the ruins. They gravitated toward the largest structure on the hill, the Parthenon, a battered shrine to the goddess Athena built in the golden era of Greek art and statecraft in the fifth century B.C. and decorated with friezes and sculpted panels known as metopes, which were believed to have been carved in part by the legendary Phidias.

Over the intervening centuries the Parthenon had been used as a Christian church, a mosque, and an ammunition depot. It was in this last incarnation that it suffered its most grievous damage, in 1687, when a Venetian force lobbed cannonballs at the structure during a siege by the Holy League powers against the Muslim Ottomans. The ammunition inside ignited and set off a huge explosion, killing three hundred people, knocking out twenty-eight columns of the Parthenon, and destroying much of its stone artwork. Athens fell and Christian troops rifled through the blasted rubble of the ancient structure. The Swedish general who ordered the attack professed remorse. His wife wrote later that "it dismayed His Excellency to destroy the beautiful temple that has existed three thousand years and is called the Temple of Minerva! In vain however: the bombs did their work so effectively that never in this world can the temple be replaced."[2] She was right, because from then on the Parthenon was a ruin, its integrity so compromised that by the time Elgin's agents arrived, it did not even look like a single structure.

By August 1801, after several months of drawing the ruins, Elgin's agents in Athens were tired of being barred entrance to the Acropolis at the whim of local authorities, tired of the daily payment of bribes, and tired of having to wheedle and cajole for the right even to erect scaffolds and make plaster casts. His lead agent in Athens, an Anglican chaplain named Philip Hunt, wanted the real thing.[3] At the suggestion of Elgin, the ruling pasha in Constantinople issued an order known as a firman that granted Elgin's agents unfettered access to the Acropolis. It was unclear from the wording whether the firman granted permission to remove sculptures from the site. Unfortunately, the original document is lost, as was the original Italian translation until the preeminent Elgin scholar, William St. Clair, dug it up among Hunt's papers in the 1960s and published it in full in 1998. In

St. Clair's opinion, the document "confers no authority to remove sculptures from the buildings or to damage them in any way."[4] Yet the ever-resourceful Hunt convinced the local authorities that it gave the British team in Athens the authority to do precisely that, and so Elgin's agents began pulling down friezes and metopes from the Parthenon itself with ropes and tackle, as well as excavating fallen sculptures from the ground around the monument and removing them from nearby buildings where they had been reused in construction.

When Elgin himself arrived in Athens, he went to the Acropolis and, like Lord Byron later and other men of Britain's Romantic generation, was shocked by what he considered to be the Turks' shabby treatment of the artistic and architectural glories of ancient Athens. He ordered his men, with the help of paid Greek laborers, to step up the pace of removal. Many western European travelers over the years had taken as a souvenir the odd piece of ancient Greek marble—a carving or a sculpture—but Elgin took the plunder to a completely new level. Over the next eight years his team removed over seventy-five meters of the frieze, which ran around the outside of the Parthenon, some of it on the ground and some still in place, depicting scenes from Athenian life and ritual. They took fifteen of the ninety-two metopes depicting scenes from a battle between Greeks and centaurs, some still considered among the finest sculptures ever made. All these were carried by donkey cart down to the port of Piraeus, packed in wooden crates with sawdust, and held in a warehouse while they awaited British naval ships to carry them to England.

Except for the shipping, which was paid by the British state, the whole operation was financed out of Elgin's own pocket. Dozens of smaller sculptures, carvings, pieces of columns and pediments, and various other "curious marbles" got mixed in as well, some from the Parthenon and some from Elgin's travels over the rest of Greece, from which he sent back streams of plundered antiquities. In the end, Elgin got about half the Parthenon's surviving artistic elements.

Judging historical figures by today's ethical standards is always a cheap shot, but one is struck nonetheless by the vandalism involved in creating what are regarded today as some of the world's great museum collections. The sculptures known as the Aegina marbles, dating from about 500 B.C. in the transition period between Greek archaic and classical, were ripped from the ruins of a temple in 1811 by a group of four men led by British architect Charles Cockerell. People living near the site implored them to leave it alone, convinced that calamities would follow. Cockerell and his three mates bribed a local official with forty pounds sterling and sent the objects to port at night to prevent the Turkish overlords from finding out, packing them on a ship that took them to Malta. They are now in the Glyptothek in Munich. Elgin was convinced the French would dismantle the Parthenon themselves the moment they had the chance and ship its contents to the Louvre, which, with Napoleon's conquests, was filling with plundered art from all over Europe.

Outfoxing the French was not Elgin's only problem. One of the ships carrying his looted treasures from the Parthenon sank in a storm off the island of Cythera in 1802. Sponge hunters hired by Elgin's agents used ropes to haul the friezes from twelve fathoms down on the sea floor and onto a beach, where they were covered in sand and seaweed to protect them from the weather. The whole operation took two years, and we can only guess at the damage done to the marbles.

By then, Elgin's posting in Constantinople was nearly over, and he headed home to Britain in January 1803, choosing unwisely to travel overland across France during a brief peace between Britain and France. When war broke out again, Elgin and his wife were taken prisoner and banished to a village in the Pyrenees. When he finally reached London, in 1806, he found that his wife (who had been released a year earlier) had taken up with another man, a neighbor in Scotland, leading to a bitter and scandalous divorce trial. Elgin's own health was declining, too, from the effects of what was probably syphilis.

The one bright spot was that his marbles were, for a time, the toast of London. Few Britons had ever seen authentic classical Greek sculpture, and Elgin's collection caused a sensation and confirmed the notion that the Roman variety to which English taste was accustomed was in fact an inferior imitation. Artists, politicians, society gentlemen, and celebrities thronged a drafty shed near Piccadilly to see Elgin's work. The voyeurs included the actress Mrs. Siddons, subject of a famous Gainsborough portrait, and painter Benjamin Robert Haydon, who hailed the marbles as "truly the greatest blessing that ever happened to this country."[5] British artists ecstatically declared they would have to unlearn everything they had been taught about depicting the human form and reeducate themselves with the example set by Phidias. Haydon brought around his friend John Keats, inspiring the poet later to write the sonnet "On Seeing the Elgin Marbles," which captured something of the rapture the carvings induced in people:

> *So do these wonders a most dizzy pain*
> *That mingles Grecian grandeur with the rude*
> *Wasting of old time —*

Elgin's standing soon began to fade, however. Despite the admiration of the aesthetes, an opinion started to take root in British society and press that Elgin had abused his position as ambassador to remove and ship the sculptures. Yes, the Ottomans were guilty of neglecting the ruins of ancient Athens, but Elgin had gone too far. Much of the criticism was motivated by envy and spite; with a cold and distant manner, Elgin seems to have made enemies more easily than friends, and many of his harshest critics were former associates. Through the second decade of the nineteenth century he found himself increasingly shunned in fashionable society and denounced by the many British intellectuals who considered themselves supporters of Greek nationalism. In the nascent Greek struggle for autonomy from the Ottomans, they saw a renewed flicker of pride in the glories of ancient Athens, and Elgin's plunder had degraded, in their view, the most potent symbol of that struggle, the Parthenon. Lord Byron led the charge, expressing his distaste for Elgin's project and antiquarians in general in his satirical poem "English Bards and Scotch Reviewers":

> *Let Aberdeen and Elgin still pursue*
> *The shade of fame through regions of virtú;*
> *Waste thousands on their Phidian freaks,*
> *Misshapen monuments and maim'd antiques;*
> *And make their grand saloons a general mart*
> *For all the mutilated blocks of art.*

Byron avoided Elgin in London society settings and seems to have regarded him as something of a vulgarian, a crass showman. Dislike turned to rage, however, when the celebrated poet reached Athens in 1809 for the first of his long sojourns to the nation whose independence he championed so passionately. There Elgin's agent, Lusieri, gave Byron a tour of the Parthenon. Byron saw the blank spaces where friezes and metopes had been wrenched out. At the harbor in Piraeus, he saw fifty crates holding Elgin's marbles — the last of the ambassador's shipments.[6]

Like many people since who have descended to the bottom of the looting industry, Byron reacted with fury. In "The Curse of Minerva," which he started writing while still in Athens, the goddess Athena appeared before the poet and denounced Britain for sending a man to steal what past invaders, the Turks, and barbarians had spared:

> *I saw successive tyrannies expire.*
> *'Scaped from the ravages of the Turk and Goth,*
> *Thy country sends a spoiler worse than both.*
> *Survey this vacant, violated fane;*
> *Recount the relics torn that yet remain: ...*
> *The insulted wall sustains his hated name:*
> *For Elgin's fame thus grateful Pallas pleads,*
> *Below, his name — above, behold his deeds!*

Faced with this denunciation, Byron disowns the act of plunder. He pleads:

> 'Daughter of Jove! In Britain's injured name,
> A true-born Briton may the deed disclaim.
> Frown not on England; England owns him not:
> Athena! No—thy plunderer was a Scot.[7]

The terms of today's discourse on cultural heritage owe much to Byron's attacks on Elgin and, specifically, these lines. With lacerating clarity, Byron gave voice to the unprecedented idea that culture was an intrinsic thread in the fabric of a people's identity and that the object gave form and life to that identity. With his references to violation, robbery, and ownership, Byron expressed an early inkling of the idea that cultural property could be governed by international law. His denunciations of "Phidian freaks" and "mutilated blocks of art" prefigured the notion, now held by every archaeologist alive, that antiquities lose much of their meaning when they are wrenched out of context by looters. The fact that these ideas, some of the most important elements in the modern conception of culture, were expressed first in verse was a tribute both to the power of poetry and to the influence, charisma, and integrity of Lord Byron. Unlike some of Elgin's other critics, he did not cart home his own stash of antiquities. Although like many European travelers he scratched his name into the ruins now and then, he lived by his principles and denounced the pillage of cultural assets with uncanny prescience. He wrote:

> [W]hen they carry away three or four shiploads of the most valuable and massy relics that time and barbarism have left to the most injured and most celebrated of cities; when they destroy, in a vain attempt to tear down, those works which have been the admiration of ages, I know no motive which can excuse, no name which can designate, the perpetration of this dastardly devastation.[8]

The poet died in 1824 in the Greek port of Missolonghi at the age of thirty-six, giving his life and body to the Greek cause in one of the emblematic moments of Romanticism. One traveler after another who visited Greece echoed him in expressing shock and dismay at the damage done by Elgin. A member of the Princess of Wales's entourage on a visit in 1814 recounted all the damage and depredations done to the Parthenon over the centuries and then added with a sneer: "Another modern came, out of love to the arts, to accomplish the work of destruction the Venetians had begun."[9] It was obviously Elgin, and coming from someone of the royal court, a confidante to the future Queen Caroline, such words must have cut deep. Elgin's reputation never recovered.

By the time of his antagonist's death, Elgin was close to bankruptcy. He had gone deeply into debt to finance the removal and storage of the marbles, and the retrieval at sea had proved wildly expensive. He had long since abandoned any idea of sending them to Broomhall. Hoping perhaps that if he couldn't be an arts collector, he could at least be an arts patron, Elgin in 1816 offered the lot to the British government for £74,240, just enough to cover his costs. The government offered £35,000, take it or leave it. Elgin protested but the state refused to budge. He sold the pieces, the British state gave them to the British Museum, and Elgin spent the rest of his life fleeing creditors, eventually moving to France, where he died in 1841. Unrepentant to the end, he wrote:

> [T]he impulses which led me to the exertions I made in Greece were wholly for the purpose of securing to Great Britain, and through it to Europe in general, the most effectual possible knowledge, and means of improving, by the excellence of Grecian art in sculpture and architecture. My success, to the vast extent it was effected, will never cease to be a matter of the utmost gratification to me.[10]

Perhaps Elgin realized by then that the deepest effect of his sculptures would be felt not in art, as he had hoped, but in architecture. Many writers have attributed the rise of neoclassical design, with its pillars, pediments, and decorative friezes, in Britain and North America in part to the influence of the Elgin marbles and the drawings and plaster casts of them that abounded on both sides of the Atlantic.[11]

The enormity of this influence is hard to comprehend now precisely because it is so ubiquitous. In Washington, D.C., most major public buildings built between about 1820 and the outbreak of World War One bear some architectural imprint of ancient Athens as expressed in the casts and sculptures that Elgin brought to Western eyes. The Washington Monument, the obelisk around which the city revolves, bears a chunk of marble from the actual Parthenon, donated by the Greek government in 1845. Nearby is that Parthenon lookalike, the Lincoln Memorial, and a few blocks away is a large-scale replica of the Elgin Marbles in the Corcoran Gallery of Art. And so on. What a rich irony of history that America's favorite architectural idiom of civic virtue, stability, and progress for most of a century, the Greek Revival look, owes its existence partly to an act of "dastardly devastation" at the ancient shrine of democracy, the Parthenon.

Thus was born the first modern wrangle over the destruction of cultural property. Reading the opinions of Elgin, Byron, and their contemporaries, one is struck by how little the terms of debate have changed since. The Elgin Marbles have lost none of their power to symbolize, for some, the excess and rapacity of collectors, and for others, the virtue of rescuing cultural treasures from the neglect of those, like the Ottoman Turks, unworthy of them.

An authority on art law, John Merryman, wrote in 1985 that if a court of law were to rule on whether the British Museum or the government of Greece had proper legal title to the marbles, the court, on balance, would probably rule in favor of the museum, with the long passage of time since their removal being a key element in its favor. Yet the real significance of the case is not the legal arguments one way or the other, but its symbolic resonance for the many countries with claims, justified or not, on art in alien hands, as Merryman acknowledged. "The Elgin Marbles symbolize the entire body of unrepatriated cultural property in the world's museums and private collections," he wrote.[12]

Greece proclaimed its independence in 1822 and, with the help of British, French, and Russian forces, succeeded in expelling the Turks from Athens by 1830. As the fledgling Greek state fought through the nineteenth century to unite the Greek-speaking nation dispersed across the Aegean, the Parthenon became a riveting symbol of national redemption. Angkor in Cambodia, Machu Picchu in Peru, and other ruins would play similar roles in subsequent generations; places of past glory whose bouts of exploitation by foreigners or their agents made their power as symbols of wounded national pride all the more potent. The Greek government banned exports of antiquities in 1833, one of its early acts as an independent state.[13] Travelers who followed in Elgin's footsteps were disappointed to find they could not carry off antiquities so freely anymore, and an illicit trade sprang up in which dealers chopped up pieces into easily concealed chunks. A French tourist wrote in 1854, "[T]hey cut it up into pieces and retail a statue like mutton."[14]

In 1898 the Greek government, through its minister in London, requested the return of the marbles (denied).[15] Greece today demands the return of what it views as its stolen property at virtually every international cultural forum, often with the support of countries that feel they, too, have been stripped of their treasures by colonial powers. In 1983 the Greek actress and Culture Minister Melina Mercouri, who waltzed through a Greek postcard of sailors, broken dishes, and ouzo in *Never on Sunday*, ran her fingers over the marbles in the chilly splendor of the British Museum and, in front of television cameras, wept. Easily dismissed as melodrama, Mercouri's gesture nonetheless showed the power of the modern image to bring freshness and relevance to a debate more than a century and a half old. The Greeks, and the late Mercouri in particular, have been so successful in keeping the Parthenon Sculptures (as the Elgin Marbles are now officially called by the British Museum) in the public eye that it seemed perfectly appropriate for *The New York Times*, in an editorial in February 2002, to urge their return to Greece, and that thirty-two members of the U.S. Congress have sponsored a resolution calling for their repatriation.[16]

"These most precious treasures were literally snatched. And this barbarism was not committed by the Turks but by the then British ambassador to Turkey, who, using bribes and the corruption of the Turkish employees, obtained a permit to commit this vandalism," Mercouri said in 1982. She was responding to Lord Avon, who, speaking for the British government, said Elgin had in fact saved the marbles from destruction and that the British Museum was as important to world culture as the Acropolis and therefore as appropriate a locale to hold them. "I am very happy that Lord Avon is interested in the safety of the Acropolis Marbles," replied Mercouri, "since safety was not among Lord Elgin's priorities, for the first shipment was tragically lost at sea."[17]

As the Parthenon marbles enter their third century in Britain, their steward is Neil MacGregor, director of the British Museum and first line of defense against what, to British ears, must sound like tiresome demands for their return.

With the patient deliberateness of a courtroom attorney (he once practiced law, in fact) and without condescension, MacGregor explained that a museum forms a worthy context around objects that, for whatever reason, have been alienated from their original place. As an argument it has an obviously self-serving ring, but after a few hours among the Rosetta Stone, the Meroë head of Augustus, and the legions of other classical masterpieces in the echoing halls of the British Museum, you see his point.

"One has got to recognize that their life as part of the Parthenon is over," he said in his office one gloomy December day. "They can't get [the marbles] back onto the Parthenon because it is a ruin and because atmospheric conditions don't allow it, so the argument that one normally makes for gathering things together in the original ensemble, that you are restoring or recovering the work of art, cannot apply any longer. It seems to me rather a fortunate accident of history that about half of what survived is in Athens and the remaining half in London."[18]

When we spoke, Greece was proposing a new tack: a permanent loan arrangement in which the marbles would be housed in a new museum on the Acropolis, with British Museum conservators sharing in their upkeep. It could all be very European and amicable, in a continent of shared heritage and atrophying borders, and it had the support of a growing number of people in Britain itself, including several Labour members of parliament.

MacGregor would have none of it. "Look, it was the Greeks who decided to make this a foreign policy issue. We would normally expect to discuss this kind of question among museums. That's what happens normally in Europe and America," he said. "I think everybody in the museum community feels that once you start unpicking global museums, universal museums like this one, then you set a very, very dangerous precedent. Once you start taking out major elements because of political pressure, then you are certainly going to stimulate other political pressures for other unpickings."

Did he have any other demands for repatriation on his desk, then?

"No. None at all."

Museum directors all over the United States cite the example of the British Museum in refusing to return objects that are plainly and recently looted. Two directors have personally made that argument to me. Did that not bother him?

He shifted uncomfortably in his chair. "One cannot answer for how people cite one's behavior. This museum's argument has always been very clear, that [the marbles] have a purpose here which they can fulfill nowhere else, and that is to provide part of the universal story of humanity which this museum exists to tell." he said. "And if that's the basis on which other museums are refusing to return things or are reluctant to return things, if they're citing that as an example, that's an example I cannot support, obviously."[19]

In selling the marbles to the British nation, Elgin began a long tradition of collectors getting the state to finance, directly or indirectly, their plunder of antiquities. The state becomes buyer of last resort for pillaged art that the collector cannot maintain due to legal or financial hardships.

In the United States today, tax laws perform much the same function by allowing collectors to donate looted goods to museums in exchange for a deduction.[20] When a collector donates a work of art worth more than $20,000 to a charitable institution such as a museum and claims a deduction for its value, the Internal Revenue Service's Art Advisory Panel reviews the claimed deduction and rules on its validity. The panel is comprised of art historians, dealers, and museum curators, and its rulings become the official position of the IRS. Despite its name, the panel is not advisory; it has real power to adjust claimed deductions up or down, depending on the panel's assessment of the artwork's value. What happens if a collector claims a deduction after donating an artifact that has been looted from an ancient site? The IRS says the panel reviews the provenance information provided by the donor, along with the artwork's condition, size, and market track record, but the panel examines 250 to 300 claimed deductions and photographs of the works in question at each of its meetings, which happen two to four times a year, so it can hardly be expected to look very carefully. The panel's proceedings are secret, but non-

Western art listed by its culture of origin (and not by the name of an artist) has accounted for over half the art reviewed by the panel in some recent years. For example, in 1997 the panel looked at 185 objects claimed for charitable contributions that were classified as coming from "Africa, Oceania and the Americas," compared to 95 for "Painting & Sculpture" of any origin, and 29 for "Far Eastern and Asian Art." A similar story in 1998: the panel looked at 184 artworks claimed as charitable contributions and classified as "Africa, Oceania and the Americas," compared to 41 paintings and sculptures and 0 listed under Far Eastern and Asian Art.[21]

What this brief digression into tax law is meant to show is that the deduction-for-art system has been used by collectors to donate not just "art" as most people would understand it—objects created as art by identifiable artists—but also a large flow of non-Western artifacts. And the great majority of such artifacts on the market have no documented provenance. Tax breaks are, of course, not the only reason collectors donate art. But the tax advantage plainly has contributed to the influx into American museums of artifacts which one can only suspect have reached the market through illicit means.

U.S. art museums have repeatedly found themselves in trouble for holding looted antiquities. Some cases are famous, others known only to a few interested archaeologists, preservationists, and officials from the unlucky countries whose treasures have been robbed, and many more cases surely never come to light. The Metropolitan Museum of Art in New York has faced one charge after another of receiving loot over the years, but in terms of brazenness there is no case quite like a fifteen-piece set of Roman silver that Italian authorities believe was looted in Sicily in 1980. Archaeologists working at a site known as Morgantina began hearing reports that *tombaroli*, Italian for looters, had found a *"servizio d'argento,"* a silver service, including two unusual, tapered cylinders that looked like the horns of a miniature bull. In 1984 the Met put on display a new acquisition: a silver set including two horns dating from the third century B.C. that it bought for a reported $2.7 million. The Met was vague about where it came from ("Taranto or in eastern Sicily"), which doesn't prove it was recently looted but does mean it wasn't excavated by an archaeologist.

Crimes against cultural property in Italy are investigated by the Comando Carabinieri Tutela Patrimonio Culturale—the art police, which performs investigative and enforcement duties. The organization is well financed, well armed, and well versed in using satellite imagery to track looting. It's the envy of poorer countries like Peru, with rich cultural assets and few resources to mind them. The mere mention of the Italian art police is enough to make an American art museum director sharpen her tone of voice. As of 2003, Italy was demanding the return of allegedly looted goods from at least seven U.S. museums on the basis of evidence gathered by the art police, and threatening to bar those museums from receiving traveling shows of any Italian art if they didn't cooperate.[22] In the case of the Met silver service, the Italian art police gathered testimony from the *tombaroli* who allegedly found the silver and who testified that the pieces also included a medallion with the face of Scylla, similar to a piece at the Met. The art police asked University of Virginia archaeologist Malcolm Bell, who had directed excavations at the site since the 1970s, to investigate the recently uncovered damage to the Sicilian site and to pinpoint when it happened. Bell found what he believed to be the looter's two holes and a curious bit of evidence inside one of them: a 100-lire coin dated 1978. Apparently it had fallen out of a looter's pocket. Using dating techniques learned through a lifetime of archaeology, Bell was able to establish that the digging took place between 1978 and 1981.

"We found a great deal of evidence to substantiate the police case, including very solid evidence for the date of excavation," Bell says. The physical evidence would seem overwhelming, yet the Met says it has seen no proof that the pieces were looted. They resemble the looters' descriptions? Perhaps they saw pictures in the Met's bulletin of recent acquisitions, Met officials said.[23] The pieces remain in the Met's collection today.

In 1993 the Met ended a long dispute with Turkey over the Lydian Hoard, a collection of objects including bowls, pitchers, and incense burners in gold, silver, and bronze, plus carved marble sphinxes and fragments of paintings that had been torn from the walls of tombs, about 360 artifacts in total. They had been buried in the tombs of royalty and noblemen in west-central Anatolia in the era of the legendary King Croesus of Lydia, in the sixth century B.C., and stayed there until 1966, when grave robbers found them. Within three years, most of the stash had been acquired by the Met, and even Director Thomas Hoving said he believed "the stuff was illegally dug up."[24] Instead of putting these fabulous artifacts on public display, however, the Met packed them away to its basement for storage where, except for infrequent and unpublicized displays of select pieces, they stayed until 1984.[25] When most of the collection finally went on permanent display that year, the Met labeled it the "East Greek Treasure," even though the pieces were of distinctively Anatolian style, not Greek.[26] The misnomer was "for purposes of obfuscation," Hoving confessed.[27] Turkey was not fooled and brought a civil suit to demand the whole collection back. The museum sought to have the suit dismissed because, it contended, the statute of limitations had run out while the pieces were sitting in the basement all those years. The Turks persisted and, with their American lawyers, came up with a novel kind of evidence: statements by the looters themselves. Some of them had been convicted in Turkey, so, if they remembered digging up the artifacts, why not use their testimony to buttress Turkey's case?

Lawrence Kaye, a U.S. attorney for the Turkish side, explained how this worked: "Many of the thieves were found, interrogated, tried, and convicted, giving statements to the police both at that time and again years later during the investigation which led up to assertion of the [Turkish government's] claim. Thus, we had 'eyewitnesses' who were able to recall some of the more memorable items."[28] One thief recounted how he blew open the entrance to a tomb, was lowered down into it, and handed objects up to his comrades; he later recognized some of those objects in the Met's glossy acquisitions bulletin.[29] As a strategy, it brilliantly turned the antiquities trade against itself, and it worked. The museum, after six years of dilatory tactics, returned the collection to Turkey in 1993 through an out-of-court resolution. The pieces are now in the Museum of Anatolian Civilizations in Ankara. They might have joined the Elgin Marbles in the ranks of eternal stalemates over cultural property if not for this fortuitous piece of evidence and the lawyers' astute use of it.[30]

The Turks' legal fees reached a tidy $2 million, according to the former director-general of Turkey's museum service, Engin Ozgen. But he had no regrets. "We wanted to send a message," he said. "We think we have [the entire collection] now, but for all we know the Met may still have some of it in the basement."[31]

The Weary Herakles is a Roman marble statue of the second century A.D. from the ancient city of Perge, on the south coast of Turkey. Nearly life-size, it shows the hero Herakles standing in a strikingly unheroic, naturalistic pose with knees crooked and eyes cast down, resting on his club draped with an animal skin. The statue broke into two roughly equal parts, although exactly how and when this happened is not clear. The bottom half, excavated in 1980 by archaeologists at the remains of a Roman-era villa at Perge, along with several intact statues, shows the figure's lower torso and legs. It is currently in the Antalya Museum in Turkey. The twenty-seven-inch upper half, far more valuable because it shows his bearded face and shoulders, was bought in the early 1980s by the late American collector Leon Levy and his wife, Shelby White, and later donated by them to the Museum of Fine Arts, Boston.

Citing Turkish law of 1906 asserting state ownership, as well as basic principles of museum conservation, the Turks have asked for restitution of the upper half so that the two fragments can be rejoined to form an integrated whole.

The Boston MFA has refused to consider the Turkish petition, and in public statements the institution has practically challenged the Turks to sue. Museum officials no longer question whether the two pieces are part of the same whole; with curators and Turkish government officials watching, casts of the two fragments were placed together at the MFA in 1992. They joined perfectly. The MFA maintains, rather, that the statue may have broken in ancient times and the upper half taken from Turkey long ago, before Turkish law established state ownership of archaeological resources.

Yet if the museum or Shelby White, one of the top antiquities collectors in the United States, has any evidence to show such a provenance, they have not made it public. The break appears to be fresh, so the physical evidence would suggest a recent looting job.[32] The best evidence for pillage, however, is the fact that the upper half of the torso was unknown to the world before 1981. The conclusion is inescapable: either someone kept it extremely well hidden for the better part of a century—yes, those grandmothers do hoard a lot of priceless antiquities in their attics—or it was illegally removed from Perge and smuggled before 1980. That's the choice: grandmother's attic or looters.

I spent a long time gazing at the Weary Herakles in Boston, contemplating how well it symbolizes the mutilation of culture by the antiquities trade. The hero has been broken across the middle, the two fragments now continents apart. It has the look of a trophy, like the formaldehyde-stuffed head of a tiger mounted on a wall in a hunting lodge. A great work of art is always greater than the sum of its parts, and this piece shows how the reverse is also true, for when you know that the rest of it is elsewhere, the upper torso cannot help but look diminished. If indeed the upper section was stolen, we have no way of knowing if the thieves knew that they were getting only half the piece (although specialists say the fault line across the torso does not appear to be intentionally made). But we can say for sure that if it had been excavated properly by archaeologists, as the bottom half was in 1980, the Weary Herakles would be in one piece today.

In 1997 the government of Guatemala began a campaign for the return of its most flagrantly plundered antiquities in U.S. museums, in some cases with legal advice from the same New York law firm (Herrick, Feinstein) that the Turks had employed in their battle with the Met. The remains of the Mayan civilization, which flourished for nine centuries, had been looted pitilessly since the early 1960s. Although the pillage was unusually well-documented,[33] the Guatemalans had been too immersed in civil war ever to make a sustained pitch for restitution.

The campaign's first success was the grudging return in 1998 of a carved wooden lintel that looters had ripped from a temple doorway in a late-classical Mayan site known as El Zotz around 1970 and that found its way to the Denver Art Museum in 1973. The lintel was in poor and fragmentary condition, and the museum quickly signaled to Guatemala that it had no intention of returning anything else.

"I don't think the museum wanted to trumpet it. We did it on a voluntary basis and we're certainly not interested in returning objects on a wholesale basis," a curator at the museum said.[34]

Next came the center section of an elaborately carved, limestone stele that was about to be sold at Sotheby's in 1998. The piece's origin came to the auction house's attention after a Harvard archaeologist, Ian Graham, noticed that the sawed-off fragment matched perfectly a missing piece of a stele at a Mayan site known as El Perú, which Graham found in 1971. The site had been heavily looted by then, and twenty-seven years later, the missing fragment was on the auction block. Sotheby's reportedly advised the piece's owner to surrender it voluntarily to the Guatemalans or risk a lawsuit. The owner agreed, and the piece went back to a museum in Guatemala City.[35]

Not much more has followed. The Kimbell Museum in Fort Worth, the Art Institute of Chicago, and the Cleveland Museum of Art, among other institutions, all have in their permanent collections Mayan artifacts smuggled out of Guatemala since 1960. In some cases, we know the pieces were looted because they have identifying glyphs or marks that reveal them as being from a particular site. This is one of the special risks, well-known to buyers of Iraqi artifacts, of purchasing antiquities that come from literate societies: the buyer can be betrayed by the object. For example, Kimbell and Cleveland each have a stele that identifies the object as coming from El Perú; a fragment of a third stele from the same site was the one to be auctioned at Sotheby's.[36] Archaeologists who mapped the site found evidence that all three pieces had been looted about the same time in the 1960s. They may have been hauled out by the same looters in one continuous orgy of plunder.

Collectors became infatuated in the late 1960s with Guatemalan stone carvings, some so obviously chainsawed or hacked out of their original place that they still had chop marks on them. Like French Impressionist paintings and a Calder on the lawn, Mayan stonework became one of those things that good art museums in America just had to have, and looters in the jungles of southern Mexico and Guatemala worked overtime to meet the demand. One stele, in the Minneapolis Institute of Arts, was so brutalized by looters that its director at the time said he was embarrassed to have it. "The object was obviously mutilated in the process of being removed from its original site. It is in wretched condition now, hardly enjoyable to look at," he wrote.[37]

It was reports like these of the ransacking of Mayan sites that led Congress to enact one of the first laws restricting the flow of cultural property into the United States, the Pre-Columbian Monumental or Architectural Sculpture or Murals statute of 1972, which prohibited the import of pieces of aboveground structures from most of Latin America without a permit from the source country. Much hailed at the time as an example of sensible cooperation, this law probably helped curb the influx of stelae and wall carvings, as did a court case around the same time, *United States vs. Hollinshead*, in which an art dealer was convicted under the National Stolen Property Act after trying to sell to the Brooklyn Museum a well-known Mayan stele that had been stolen from an archaeological site. But neither that case nor the 1972 law did anything to stop museums from acquiring artifacts looted from *underground* sites, artifacts unseen by anyone alive until found by the looter. That trade continued unabated. Continually over the next decades, and still occasionally today, Guatemalan officials received tipoffs from U.S. archaeologists about previously unknown artifacts that appeared suddenly on display at museums, either newly acquired or brought up from storage. Some pieces could be traced to an individual site; most could not.[38]

In December 1997, the Boston MFA opened a new permanent gallery with a group of thirty-four Mayan artifacts, including a set of vases depicting magnificent scenes from Mayan royal courts. Antiquities traders and archaeologists knew the MFA had had the vases since 1989 but, like the Met's Turkish stash, they were rarely put on extended public view. When the collection was finally in 1997, it was clear that the pieces bore all the hallmarks of loot—no precise provenance, no record of having been in any other collection. The Guatemalan government instantly demanded to know how the pieces, among the greatest examples of Mayan art anywhere, had arrived in Boston. After aggressive reporting by *The Boston Globe*, the museum revealed that a collector named John B. Fulling had brought the pieces from Guatemala between 1974 and 1981 (in violation of Guatemalan law, if so, whether Fulling knew it or not). They were bought in 1988 by one of the museum's trustees, Landon Clay, who donated them to the MFA.[39] He would have been entitled to a large tax write-off.

Within days, Guatemalan officials were in Boston to examine the pieces. The nation's consul general in New York at the time, Fabiola Fuentes Orellana, and its deputy minister of culture, Carlos Flores, met with museum director Malcolm Rogers in January 1998 to request the pieces' return. The museum could keep the vases for a long, face-saving loan of perhaps three years, and Guatemala would be happy to lend the MFA top-quality pieces in the future from the nation's own museums, they told Rogers.

"And [the museum officials] said, 'How much will you pay us for them?' They were actually asking us to buy back something that was stolen from us," Fuentes told me. "Carlos and I looked at each other in disbelief. What are we supposed to do, take the museum to court? Guatemala is a poor country. We don't have that kind of money . . . nor should we have to go to court to recover what has been taken out of our country and into the United States in violation of your laws and ours."[40]

———

Such is the attitude of the institutions supposed to be custodians of the world's cultural heritage. They stand accused of acting as agents of its destruction. Rogers declined to be interviewed, but his spokesman denied that he demanded money for the pieces.

"We would take any claim seriously, but we would require evidence of clear proof of theft before we could consider any such request [for return]," said the museum's deputy director for curatorial administration, Katherine Getchell.[41] "Clear proof of theft" is, of course, what no government can ever produce with regard to clandestinely excavated and smuggled art. Getchell pointed out that the museum takes excellent care of the vases, and indeed they look gorgeous on the MFA's green velvet behind shatterproof glass. Everything, in fact, that the museum says to uphold its case is absolutely true. The vases *are* kept securely and presented with clear and complete didactic material. They *are* the only masterpieces of ancient Mesoamerican art that most people in Boston will ever see. Yet here the argument is one of values, not evidence. By accepting the donation of these pieces, the museum sends a message through the long chain of dealers, middlemen, and grave robbers that American museums want plundered art, and anyone who has spent time with looters knows that they receive that message.

Faced with these realities, museum directors swing between defiant bravado in public, and in private a gnawing concern that fast-and-loose acquisitions habits in the past may have done lasting damage to museums' standing. Philippe de Montebello, director of the Metropolitan Museum of Art, swerves a bit defensively from one attitude to the other in a single conversation. He asserted to me that his museum's acquisition policies were tighter than during his predecessor's time, yet dismissed people who questioned those policies as "people who hate museums."

"We are sick and tired of biased reportages that depict museums as if we were hoarders of objects, as if we were putting them away in caves," he fumed in an interview over the phone. "In fact, we present these objects to the public and we write about them a hell of a lot more than the archaeologists."[42]

Montebello acknowledged that "there is far greater focus and alertness to the issues of provenance"[43] than during the time of his predecessor, Thomas Hoving. A charismatic, impetuous man who imagined antiquities buying like big-game hunting, Hoving confessed to a "near-sexual pleasure" from one of the Met's most notorious purchases ever, the Greek libation vessel known as the Euphronios krater. When, in 1972, Hoving arranged for the purchase of the "hot pot," as it became known, he said publicly that it was owned by a European family that "had it since around the First World War and that goes back a nice long time."[44] Twenty years later, in his memoirs, he freely admitted what many people suspected all along: the piece was almost certainly looted in Italy the year before the Met bought it for $1 million.[45]

The krater marked the end of an era, Hoving wrote. It was "perhaps the last monumental piece ever to come out of Italy, slipping in just underneath the crack in the door of the pending UNESCO treaty which would drastically limit the trade in antiquities."[46] He believed it was one of two illegally excavated Euphronios pots that hit the market in the 1970s, the other finding its way into the Levy and White collection.[47]

"The museum has never done anything illegal. You had better believe that. We are no more illegal in anything we have done than Napoleon was when he brought all the treasures to the Louvre," Hoving said at the time.[48] It was this sort of cavalier, contemptuous attitude toward the problem of looting by people in positions of public trust that was often cited over the next two decades by supporters of tougher U.S. laws to stop the inflow of looted goods. A front-page controversy at the time, one whose impact has been largely forgotten, the "hot pot" purchase likely contributed more than any single event to the hardening of U.S. law on antiquities smuggling, a trend that began around the same time and reached a plateau with the 2001 Memorandum of Understanding banning unlicensed antiquities imports from Italy.

The rise in the 1990s of the issue of Holocaust art added to pressure on museums for more transparency in how they acquired art. Paintings, sculptures, and prints that had been stolen by the Nazis and their allies from Jewish Holocaust victims wound up on the U.S. art market, and sometimes in American museums. The Holocaust art controversy exposed an amorality in 1940s acquisition policies that was so complete as to seem almost unbelievable by current standards. Chastened museum directors now talk much more about accountability, and some of the more sensitive ones worry that their institutions' tone-deaf attitude in the past has eroded public trust.[49]

"Too often museums have been linked to scandal or questionable practices. And people are beginning to wonder about museums, about what and whom we stand for. We are on the verge of joining other distrusted professions—lawyers, politicians, the clergy, and corporate executives." So said James Cuno, director of London's Courtauld Institute of Art and later director of the Art Institute of Chicago, at a conference of museum directors in 2002.[50] The conviction that museums should be, in Montebello's words, "a great encyclopedia" of human artistic achievement has not changed.[51] Yet at a glacial pace, museums are finding that goods without a sound provenance can be more trouble than they are worth.

"We're careful now. We're much more aware of the problems of provenance, and the legal department is always reminding the curators involved in acquisition of antiquities about the need to avoid legal problems," said Martin Lerner, the Met's chief curator of South and Southeast Asian art. "This of course means that there are a lot of things out there on the market whose purchase is ruled out for us. We simply can't buy them." Sometimes they creep in anyway. Lerner had to remove a tenth-century Khmer stone head from the Met and return it to Cambodia after a picture of it appeared in a UNESCO book of photographs featuring pieces stolen from standing monuments at Angkor, the kind of irrefutable proof that exists in only the rarest cases. "We'll return things if it's very clear that it was stolen. In this case, there was no question it was the same piece. It had to go back."[52]

Restrictions on the flow of cultural property go back at least to 1464, when Pope Pius II prohibited art exports from the Papal States.[53] It was only in the nineteenth century, though, that the idea that ancient monuments were assets worth preserving integrally became common currency among cultural and intellectual elites in Western capitals. Even if such lofty ideas were not always enforced by governments, and they usually weren't, they were reflected in laws around the globe barring exports of ancient art or asserting state ownership of ancient sites, discovered and undiscovered. Laws in Peru (1893), Mexico (1897), El Salvador (1903), Turkey (1906), Lebanon (1933), Iraq (1936), Italy (1939), to name a few, varied widely in scope and many were toughened up later with more restrictive laws, but they had as a common goal the assertion of state protection of archaeological assets. In the United States, the rather tepid equivalent was the Antiquities Act of 1906, a classic piece of Theodore Roosevelt–era conservation law that made it a crime to collect objects or damage historic sites on public or Indian land and motivated largely by reports of damage to the Mesa Verde cave dwellings in Colorado.[54] Private property was not covered and still is not, making the United States one of the few countries in the world with no national legal protection for undiscovered archaeological resources on private land (although some states have such laws). This is why someone selling a $1.3 million estate in Texas can boast in a real-estate ad that the property includes "archaeological sites with 6,000-year-old Indian artifacts and an early 19th century family cemetery," a public invitation to pillage that would be inconceivable in most other countries.[55]

After World War Two, discourse about cultural property took a sharply more antagonistic turn. The debate that had simmered along since the Elgin affair intersected with the nationalist, anti-Western rhetoric of the decolonization movement. Looting had become not just bad taste in the eyes of some, but a potent symbol of cultural subjugation and imperialism. This new focus led to a groundbreaking treaty, the UNESCO Convention on the Means of Prohibiting and Preventing the Illicit Import, Export and Transfer of Ownership of Cultural Property, at UNESCO's general conference in Paris in 1970.

The UNESCO convention was the first major piece of international law to treat looting-for-profit as a global problem. The agreement committed those countries that signed and ratified it to use local laws and police forces to stop private collectors or museums from acquiring cultural objects that had been illegally exported from other countries, and to seize and repatriate those objects. The goal, as stated in the treaty, was to discourage looting by inhibiting the market for cultural goods—a market-based solution in the best sense. If a looter in Italy dismantled a Roman mausoleum and sold its contents to an art dealer who then shipped the goods overseas in violation of Italian law, the country that received the goods was supposed to confiscate the pieces and return them to Italy. It would no longer be solely up to Italy, as a source country, to stop the problem. The heart of the agreement was Article 9, in which the convention envisioned how this enforcement mechanism would work. A country whose archaeological patrimony was under attack from commercial looting could call upon other states to impose import restrictions on the kinds of goods being pillaged. This opened the way to the tough, bilateral treaties that later became the backbone of U.S. efforts in the diplomatic sphere to curb the loot trade. As to what constituted cultural property, the treaty gave some general rules but left the specifics up to each state.

For most buyer countries in North America and Europe, the treaty marked the first formal acknowledgment that they were implicated, as the text stated, in the "impoverishment of the cultural heritage of the countries of origin."[56] The responsibility for the problem could no longer be dropped, Elgin-style, at the doorstep of spineless and corrupt overlords. Pious as it sounded, all of humanity had a stake in this problem.

The United States, which succeeded in softening some of the convention's language in Paris, was one of the early signatories and, with the exception of Canada, the only major buyer country to sign and ratify for nearly fifteen years. Not many people seem to have realized it at the time, but it was one of the great moments in constructive American multilateralism. The fact that the United States signed the treaty so quickly while Europe balked was the result of a confluence of factors that, in the early twenty-first century, already seems deeply alien. American foreign-policy makers used to look rather more favorably on the concept of a rules-based international system than they do today, and museum and dealer communities had not yet found their voice. In April 2003, when the theft at the Baghdad museum hit headlines, the Met's Philippe de Montebello was able to ring up the White House's top political adviser, Karl Rove, to press for better U.S. military protection of the museum. In 1970 museum directors did not have that kind of clout, or, if they did, did not exercise it. Nor did dealers. Reading accounts of the proceedings in Paris by the American delegates, one is struck by how little heed the U.S. team seems to have paid to the business interests involved. The idea that cutting off the flow of illegally excavated goods might deprive dealers of a vital share of their business scarcely seems to have entered the negotiators' minds. They believed, naïvely, that "reputable" dealers did not touch looted goods and therefore would not be hurt by restrictions on their trade, continually drawing a distinction between the illegal trade and "the values of legitimate commerce in art objects."[57] Only later did it become clear that the legitimate trade and the illegal trade were, in fact, largely one and the same. In Paris, the U.S. delegates took the dealers at their word.

Europeans, by contrast, had no such illusions. They had long traditions of collecting, large and well-established dealer communities, and museums that feared the convention could somehow be used to pressure them to empty their galleries. The United Kingdom and Switzerland did not even bother to attend the Paris conference, and those European governments that did attend often fretted that the treaty would stigmatize "good-faith" buyers of antiquities, legal or not.[58] Not a single European country with a large antiquities market (that is, excluding source countries such as Italy and Greece) ratified and implemented the treaty until France became the first to do so in 1997. The convention thus began a trend toward antiquities dealers in Europe gaining a distinct competitive advantage over their counterparts in America. By 1990, the same Turkish vase or Peruvian pot that was perfectly legal to sell in Berlin could be considered stolen property in Boston. This difference, accentuated over the years by progressively stiffer American legislation and court precedents, turned more of the business over to Europeans, who could receive looted goods and then resell them at a profit to American dealers, often with a fresh "European" provenance to disguise the fact that they were looted. That was how Swetnam brought the first shipment of Sipán artifacts to Los Angeles in 1987.

But that was in the future. At the time of the UNESCO convention, most people in the business seem to have regarded it as, at best, a well-intentioned irrelevance and, at worst, an annoyance. Karl Meyer, in 1973, quoted an anonymous American dealer who wore his bad ethics on his lapel: "If they ratify the Unesco Convention, then what? I know several indigent counts who would be delighted, for a price, to swear that any piece of mine was part of the family collection for centuries. I bring my things from Europe, and who is going to deny it? The treaty won't end the trade, it just means more trouble."[59]

It was in this atmosphere of mild condescension, mixed with the fading goodwill of postwar internationalist feeling, that the Senate gave its unanimous advice and consent to the UNESCO convention in 1972. The vote sent it on a long and tortuous path to ratification.

The convention had some inherent shortcomings. At American insistence, it was not retroactive.[60] Anything removed from its original place or demonstrably on the market before 1970 was not affected, European fears that it might trigger pressure for wider repatriation notwithstanding. The convention had no built-in policing mechanism, and this led to the widespread assumption that it was unenforceable. Thousands of freshly looted pieces crossed borders stashed in shipping containers or suitcases every year, and there was no reason to think a piece of paper signed in Paris would change that.

Also, the convention was not self-executing. Each country had to pass legislation for the agreement to take effect within its borders. The Senate's vote in 1972 had been little more than a pat on the back to the U.S. negotiators. For the convention to have legal force in the United States, Congress had to pass implementing legislation, and that was where antiquities dealers mobilized to try to water it down. In 1975 they set aside their long-standing fractiousness and suspicion of each other and formed the American Association of Dealers in Ancient, Oriental and Primitive Art, later renamed the *National* Association, or NADAOPA, whose purpose was to lobby Congress to eviscerate the UNESCO convention.

In a key victory for the new lobby, supporters of the treaty agreed to create a Cultural Property Advisory Committee, whose job would be to advise the State Department's Assistant Secretary for Educational and Cultural Affairs on whether to grant requests from source countries for restrictions on the import of archaeological material and what their scope should be. The assistant secretary would have the final say. The committee would have eleven members: three from the dealing community, three from the academic community (mostly archaeologists), two from museums, and three members of the "general public" who were, in practice, usually people with ties to the collecting or museum communities.

The committee thus had a working majority in favor of unrestricted imports of antiquities. If you combined the three seats for the dealing community with the two from the museum community, plus only one of the three seats for the general public, you had the six necessary to keep the archaeologists on a short leash. It wouldn't be a sure thing, but the committee's composition alone looked a reliable bulwark against any onerous barriers to antiquities imports.

An even better concession came in the form of statutes of limitations. Any material or artifact that had been displayed publicly by a museum and announced in the institution's literature that was open and available to the public would be exempted from the law after three years. This put the burden on source country officials (people like Fabiola Fuentes Orellana) to keep close tabs on museum exhibits and literature or risk losing the possibility of gaining back valuable, looted antiquities. The expectation was that they would tire of flipping through auction catalogues and acquisition bulletins. Also, once artifacts had been in the United States for twenty years, even if they had not been publicly displayed for even a day, they would cease to be covered by the law if the owner could show that he purchased them "without knowledge of their illegal origin."[61]

By the early 1980s the association and its most prominent supporter, Senator Daniel Patrick Moynihan of New York, believed they had succeeded in defanging the convention so much that it would be essentially unworkable in the United States. Moynihan and his staff wrote the final bill. He had been U.S. ambassador to the United Nations during some of the nastiest criticism of the United States and Israel, including a 1975 resolution equating Zionism with racism, and he viewed the UNESCO convention in much the same context. "It's just the Third World flagellating America," he told a witness at a hearing.[62]

Blunted by the primitive-art dealers' lobby and by Moynihan, the Cultural Property Implementation Act finally passed the Senate in 1982, twelve years after the Paris conference. President Ronald Reagan signed it into law on January 12, 1983.

For a long time, enforcement of the treaty went nowhere, as predicted. The Reagan administration had little interest in the subject of cultural property, except as an element in its anticommunist campaigns, and it was in this context that it granted El Salvador's request of 1987, filed under the terms of the UNESCO convention's Article 9.

Meanwhile, some voices in academia reinforced collectors' views and gave them intellectual heft. Led by John Merryman of Stanford University, they held that antiquities were best in the hands of people who would take care of them—i.e., collectors—and that the market would solve the question of how to protect cultural property. According to this group, who called themselves "cultural internationalists," looted antiquities flowed to market like water to the sea, and restrictions on the outflow of artifacts in source countries were doomed to failure. Such laws only encouraged forgeries, which distressed collectors, and turned honest dealers into criminals by forcing them to work outside the law.[63] These advocates rarely accompanied their argument with calls for restraint by collectors, appeals to responsibility, or any call for sacrifice at all from collectors while at the same time upholding the market's right to extract a vital sacrifice from source countries, namely, their cultural heritage. Except for the occasional boilerplate lament over the damage done by grave robbers (usually a few Hail Marys to Guatemala), they rarely recognized looting as a problem at all and certainly not one of any urgency. Merryman wrote:

One way that cultural objects can move to the locus of highest probable protection is through the market. The plausible assumption is that those who are prepared to pay the most are the most likely to do whatever is needed to protect their investment. Yet the UNESCO Convention and national retentive laws prevent the market from working in this way. They impede or directly oppose the market and thus endanger cultural property.[64]

Thus the more that source countries tried to protect their cultural property, the more they actually harmed it. As for the damage caused by looters, Merryman looked on the bright side: "Illegal excavations may reveal important works that would otherwise remain hidden; smuggling may save works that would otherwise be destroyed through covetous neglect."[65] Others in this group tried to shift the blame away from looters and onto the archaeologists, who were caricatured as egghead elitists too full of themselves to comprehend the damage they were doing. As curator Gillett Griffin of the Art Museum at Princeton University wrote:

> Archaeology, as with many sciences, has put itself on a pedestal—it has become sacrosanct. Archaeologists, like art historians and critics, write using a technical jargon which makes their reportage impenetrable to the lay masses. . . . If archaeologists do not publish soon after excavation, their material loses meaning and is withheld from the scholarly community. If they are careless about interpreting and recording what they excavate, they can, in effect, be more destructive than looters, for they leave nothing for salvage.[66]

It was Sipán, a world-class case of the kind of illegal excavations that Merryman and others found so benign, that finally brought a real hardening of U.S. law on antiquities. Sipán was the spark that led the federal government to crack down. It took nearly a decade but the CPIA of 1983 led to a bipartisan body of federal regulations aimed at discouraging Americans from buying the products of pillage. Even more important, a spate of court cases in the 1980s contributed to the growing atmosphere of unease in the antiquities industry. One of those cases involved New York dealer David Bernstein, who in 1980 flew into Dulles International Airport outside Washington on a flight from Peru with suitcases full of 700 antiquities including textiles that reportedly were so freshly dug they still reeked of tombs.[67] The whole load was seized. After two years of legal wrangling, Bernstein pleaded guilty to a misdemeanor charge of making a false statement to government employees; he had declared the value of the artifacts as $1,785 whereas a Smithsonian archaeologist who inspected the shipment on behalf of U.S. Customs estimated its value at $1.5 million. Bernstein was sentenced to a year's probation, 200 hours of community service, and a $1,000 fine, a punishment which, an archaeological journal sniffed, "hardly seems to be a severe deterrent to traffickers in millions of dollars worth of antiquities" but which sent a signal that "the import of illicit objects to this country will henceforth be more difficult."[68]

At the time, Bernstein was "a naïve 34-year-old Jewish kid from Great Neck who never had any problem with the law," as he described himself, and a former Peace Corps volunteer in Peru. He never returned to Peru after the Dulles incident, but he continued to be a player in the pre-Columbian market, selling at his Manhattan gallery one of those marvelous monkey heads that Moche scholars believed to be from the looted mausoleum of La Mina.[69] Bernstein maintained the head came from "an old collection."

"The Sipán artifacts were of very high quality, but what followed was even better," he said. "The main collectors want what's new and exciting."[70]

In May 1990, the Bush administration reacted to fallout from the Sipán case—a large smuggling network had been disarticulated and only one person, David Swetnam, had been convicted—with the emergency ban on the unlicensed importation of artifacts from the Sipán region of Peru.[71] The area was being "pillaged, or in danger of being pillaged, in crisis proportions."[72] By then, the Sipán site itself had been fenced off and placed under twenty-four-hour guard, so it was unlikely to produce any fresh merchandise, but it was well known that the area for miles around had come under attack from looters. Eleven months later the government banned the unlicensed import of antiquities from the Petén region of Guatemala, effectively stopping the legal import of most Mayan artifacts, and in 1993 another emergency order prohibited the import of antiquities from the Niger River valley of Mali.

The Clinton administration was left in the mid-1990s with a crazy quilt of emergency import bans, some applying to arcane corners of the world but a few, like Sipán and the Niger basin, that crimped valuable segments of the trade. On the advice of the State Department, the Democratic administration moved toward creating bilateral agreements that would cover nearly all antiquities from a given country and make it simpler to repatriate confiscated goods. Again, El Salvador was on its toes and, in March 1995, obtained the first of the new, wide-ranging prohibitions. And again, the ban applied to antiquities whose effect on the market had largely run its course.

Meanwhile, the State Department's Cultural Property Advisory Committee, the board whose creation the antiquities trade had insisted on to ensure its voice would be heard, hit a crisis in late 1993, when the government of

Greece discovered that a New York antiquities dealer, Michael Ward, was taking bids starting at $1.5 million for a collection of Mycenaean gold that the Greeks charged had been looted from a site called Aidonia and smuggled out of the country. The Greeks demanded Ward give it back. The case bore some uncanny parallels with Sipán. Looters discovered tombs and emptied their treasures, but they missed one tomb, and its later excavation by archaeologists yielded objects strikingly similar to those in Ward's Manhattan gallery. The Greeks learned of the impending sale when Boston University archaeologist Ricardo Elia saw a newspaper article about Ward's "rare gold baubles" and alerted the Greek embassy in Washington.[73]

It would have been just another case of dubious antiquities on sale in America — except that Ward was a sitting member of the eleven-member Cultural Property Advisory Committee, whose job it was to advise the U.S. government on ways to stop the sort of trade in which Ward was alleged to have engaged. In an unusual out-of-court settlement, he was eventually allowed to donate the whole stash to a Washington-based organization called the Society for the Preservation of Greek Heritage, which would then be free to return it to Greece. Ward could recoup his costs by deducting the acquisition from his federal income tax, reportedly a savings of $125,000.[74] Once again, it seemed the American government was retroactively financing the looting of ancient sites. It looked like a good face-saving arrangement for Ward and the Greeks, who would not have to wade into litigation, but then someone pointed out that the purpose of such tax breaks was to improve U.S. museum collections for the public, and since the pieces were going straight back to Greece, U.S. taxpayers were being stiffed. It looked unseemly. So Ward's collection was put on public display in Washington, D.C., for exactly four days, with a similar token exhibit in Dallas, before being wrapped up and sent back to Greece. The Greeks were happy, Ward was a bit less happy, and U.S. taxpayers were left sweeping up the broken plates.[75]

Ward denied to the end that the hoard was from Aidonia, calling it "a totally made-up provenance," despite overwhelming scholarly opinion to the contrary.[76] Those who disagreed with him included the distinguished archaeologist James Wright of Bryn Mawr College, who had worked extensively in Aidonia and the nearby Nemea Valley and heard accounts from villagers in the area that bootleg excavators had struck a major tomb in late 1976. The gold they found was shipped to Germany or Switzerland in trucks carrying the region's succulent apricots, according to the accounts. "I have often wondered over the past fifteen years if, when, and how this material would show up in the market," Wright said.[77] Now he believed he knew.

Yet Ward was defiant. "There's no proof that those pieces really came from that place," he said. "This case has nothing to do with scholarship and everything to do with politics."[78]

It was not the first time a dealer would plead "scholarship" in his defense and accuse those who dared to interfere with the trade of playing politics. Ward's term on the committee ended shortly after the Mycenaean gold incident, which gave opponents of the antiquities trade the best ammunition yet to claim that it was still bent on pillage and smuggling with impunity. An embarrassed Clinton administration began to shy away from naming antiquities dealers to the advisory committee and looked instead for merchants in antique furniture, Old Masters, anything but ancient art, especially from problem countries like Greece.

If anyone was hoping the return of the Ward merchandise might discourage looters in the Aidonia area, he was disappointed. "We found a robbed Mycenaean chamber tomb in the Nemea Valley in 2001, which I excavated in collaboration with the [Greek government's] Archaeological Service in 2002," said James Wright. "While digging it, tomb robbers began to rob another cemetery directly to the north; a total of three tombs have been disturbed."[79]

Convinced that the 1990 Sipán agreement was still insufficient, Peruvian government officials began pushing for a stronger commitment from the Americans against smuggling, with a deal that would apply to a much wider range of artifacts. The Peruvians struck at just the right time, in the aftermath of the Ward case. In June 1997, after two years of off-and-on discussion by the advisory committee, the Peruvians got what they wanted: a bilateral agreement that applied to the country's entire ancient heritage. It was a milestone in cultural-property policy, probably the strongest statement of action against looting by any government since the UNESCO convention itself. It made only one passing reference to Sipán, for this agreement applied to virtually every kind of artifact, object, or trinket from the vast sweep of Peruvian pre-Conquest history, seven thousand years of progress from hunter-gatherers to Pizarro's landing in 1532. For the first time, Spanish colonial artifacts were also covered, although only those objects that showed indigenous cultural influences or were related to evangelization of the Indians.

"Peru asked for and received protection for its 'entire cultural heritage.'" said James Fitzpatrick, legal counsel to the primitive-art lobby NADAOPA. "Two forces seem to be at work here—domination of the committee by the archaeologists, who oppose collecting, and the heavy hand of State Department politics."[80]

As of June 11, 1997, virtually no antiquities could legally be imported from Peru into the United States without the impossible-to-obtain legal pedigree from the Peruvian state. The agreement was officially known as the "Memorandum of Understanding Concerning the Imposition of Import Restrictions on Archaeological Material from the Pre-Hispanic Cultures and Certain Ethnological Material from the Colonial Period"—or simply the MOU.

By now it was clear that curbing the loot trade was no politically correct plot by left-wing, third-world flagellators, as the antiquities trade tried to portray it. Like it or not, it was the policy of successive U.S. administrations, Democratic and Republican, and however timidly or belatedly applied, these policies were slowly changing the climate in which antiquities were bought and sold. They showed the power of government to combat a global problem whose existence had been known for decades but which most people had glibly assumed had no effective solution. More MOUs like the one with Peru were soon on the books, bans on the import of unlicensed archaeological goods from Canada, Mali, Guatemala, and Nicaragua, plus emergency orders banning the import of two more hot targets for looters, Khmer stone sculptures from Cambodia and early Byzantine ecclesiastical art from Cyprus.

"Frankly, if looted or stolen artifacts appear in U.S. museums and auction houses, they can harm our bilateral relations with other countries," said Thomas Pickering, the State Department's undersecretary for political affairs.

By late 2000 ten countries had asked the United States for import restrictions; eight had received them, and those for a ninth, Italy, were pending. Dealers were plainly being outflanked on the advisory committee. Those who filled the three designated slots on the committee drifted off, resigning with a mix of anger, apathy, and bewilderment.

"All the right questions are always discussed, but our government interprets information in such a way that the committee can always come out in favor of an embargo," said Gerald Stiebel, a dealer in French furniture who left the committee in October 2000. "Every time an important issue came up, it was like being in a trial where one side had a lawyer and the other did not. They say that dealers who make money in the field of antiquities shouldn't serve because they have a conflict of interest, but most of the other people on the committee had backgrounds in areas like historic preservation or conservation or Native American repatriation. So the committee is stacked against collecting in ways that may not be immediately evident."[81]

Frederick Schultz, new president of NADAOPA and a rising star in the business, expressed the dour mood in a 1996 speech to the American Association of Appraisers. "There is an adage in the art business that goes like this, 'Businessmen spend their time talking about art, and artists spend their time talking about money,'" he said. "To which I might add an amendment, 'Art dealers spend their time talking about the law.' This is a most distracting and annoying recent development, and those of us who deal in objects that are found in the ground are being distracted and annoyed to a greater degree than anyone else."[82]

Not much seemed to be going right for dealers and collectors. At Moynihan's prodding, President Clinton appointed Shelby White, former owner of the upper half of the Weary Herakles, to the advisory committee in 2000. Many assumed that the appointment was in exchange for Moynihan's early and strong support for Hillary Clinton's Senate run that year. Angry protests ensued from archaeologists and their supporters, who kept her nomination bottled up in State Department review until the administration ended and the nomination died.

In its last days, the Clinton administration acceded to a request from Italy and granted it an MOU.[83] The *terra santa* of antiquities collecting was now off-limits. Before being imported into the United States, art from a list of twenty-four broad categories covering everything from Roman busts to Etruscan vessels and Apulian vases now had to have a license issued by the Italian government showing that the pieces had not been recently looted, stolen, or rerouted through a third country. To casually buy looted antiquities in Italy and take them home to America was now to face almost certain seizure and forfeiture on arrival. Dealers who had made careers out of importing Italian antiquities that had no more provenance than a wink and a collector's scribbled note suddenly wondered whether they could stay in business and spread rumors that the MOU was in exchange for Italian cooperation in fighting drug trafficking.

Dealers and museums pleaded with the incoming Bush administration to reverse or back off enforcement of the Italian rule, in private and public realms. Some trotted out the free-trade rhetoric of the 1980s and again pretended not to see the connection with looting.

"Some argue that free trade in cultural property only encourages looting and pillaging of archaeological sites. But when an ancient object is offered to a museum for acquisition, the looting, if indeed there was any, has already occurred. Now the museum must decide whether to bring the object into its public collection where it can be preserved, studied, and enjoyed and where its whereabouts can be made widely known," wrote James Cuno, as director of Harvard University Art Museums, in a revealing essay. "With the signing of the accord with Italy, we have been backsliding on our principles for the protection of cultural property and the international movement of works of art. It is not too late to rethink our position. It would not be the first Clinton policy to be rethought by the new administration."[84]

When Cuno, an influential figure in American art, pleaded with the Bush administration to restore "international movement of works of art," he was not talking about what most people would consider art: objects made as art, by an artist, to be viewed, enjoyed, and studied as art. He was not talking about museum loans. He was talking about objects *stolen from graves*, archaeological sites, or ancient standing monuments, since these were the only kinds of objects covered by the Italian MOU that he was denouncing. In Cuno's view, agreements like the Italian MOU, whose stated purpose was to protect cultural property, actually harmed it ("backsliding on our principles for the protection of cultural property") because they impeded museums from acquiring it. Such was the ethical warp in which the directors of America's most prestigious art museums continued to think about antiquities.

To Ricardo Elia, archaeologist at Boston University who had worked in Italy since the 1970s, it would have been easy to dismiss the Italian MOU as too little too late, but at least it was something. He had testified in Washington in favor of the agreement.

"I saw thousands and thousands of Apulian vases coming onto the market in the 1970s, '80s, and '90s. They all came from a pretty small area, all undocumented and unprovenanced, and a lot of them found their way into museums despite the full knowledge among museums that they were looted and illegally exported. They kept buying them anyway," he said. "Museums have changed their policies, a lot of them. They've done it kicking and screaming, but they've done it, and they're much more circumspect about what they acquire. But the Met, the Boston MFA, Cleveland, they're resisting change with a vengeance."[85]

Collectors and curators dismiss him as an alarmist Cassandra or a scold, but Elia almost alone among researchers has actually taken a coldly quantitative approach to looting. In one study he focused on Apulian red-figure vases, which date mostly from the fifth and fourth centuries B.C. and originate almost entirely from south Italy. Although they have captivated collectors for over two centuries with their depictions of myth and classical theater, Apulian vases made a splash on the international market starting in the late 1960s. Elia believed their sudden popularity was due to the fact that Etruscan mausoleums, long a favored source of artifacts, were nearly exhausted after a century and a half of plunder.[86] Using information from published university and commercial catalogues, Elia was able to show that, in 1992, there were at least 4,284 Apulian vases circulating worldwide that were unknown before 1980. Of those, 31 percent appeared in private collections, 25 percent in museums, and the rest were still circulating on the market. There was only one possible source for so many undocumented, genuine vases appearing suddenly on the market: an upsurge in clandestine looting of ancient sites in southern Italy, which indeed had been documented by Italy's art police. Elia had, in effect, documented the supply and the demand, or, as he wrote, "a virtual flooding of the international market with previously undocumented Apulian vases, as well as extremely robust collecting, both by museums and especially by private collectors."[87] One museum alone, the Getty in Los Angeles, had acquired more than seventy Apulian vases between 1971 and 1987. He reviewed every Sotheby's catalogue published from 1966 to 1998, from both its London and New York offices, and found that 85 percent of the Apulian vases offered listed no previous ownership history whatsoever. His conclusion: Sotheby's had "direct links to large-scale, commercial sources of undocumented Apulian vases."[88]

Public pressure and a touch of outrage were needed to make museums act responsibly, in Elia's view. "We need to change the attitude much as the attitude has changed about wearing furs or smoking in public," he told a conference. "I haven't got to the point of advocating throwing red paint on looted pots in museums yet, but I really do think the focus needs to be on the public appreciation and esteem we give to collectors who are, after all, taking a common heritage and rendering it a private object."[89]

The Italian MOU was bad enough, but nothing could prepare the American antiquities trade for the shock that came in February 2002, when Frederick Schultz, president of NADAOPA from 1996 to 2001, was convicted by a New York jury for conspiracy to smuggle and sell Egyptian antiquities derived from a looting racket that stretched from the barren hills of the Sahara to New York. The goods included a sculpted head of the pharaoh Amenhotep III, which Schultz's British business partner, Jonathan Tokeley-Parry, dipped in clear plastic and painted in gaudy colors to resemble a cheap tourist trinket and deceive customs authorities. Schultz sold that piece for $1.2 million in London after two American museums turned it down at $2.5 million.

Schultz at first denied knowing of Tokeley-Parry's smuggling activities, but a paper trail uncovered by British authorities in their prosecution of him showed the American dealer's involvement. Tokeley-Parry often referred to Schultz as "004½" and signed himself "006½," and indeed their correspondence often sounds like the script from a bad James Bond movie. Tokeley-Parry wrote to Schultz:

> Tuesday I'm going south . . . ask for Mr. Johnson (that's me) or leave a message with Makhmoud Ibrahim (Ali's brother). Talk Italian, or veiled speech.

Any news of the big cheque? We now need it urgently; the boys have just returned from the hills above Minea, which is bandit country . . . and we are offered a large hoard. It should be possible to flip some items over, and take the ones you would prefer, but we shall need the money to put down.[90] . . . If you can put down deposits so as to keep me in funds, I'll be able to turn everything over to you—on consignment or sales, as preferable. I'm looking forward to 1992. As you say, when we aren't playing f****** bankers and insurance salesmen, it really is fun, this great game. (Have you read Kipling's 'Kim'?)[91]

There is, also from the same tomb, a pair of wooden Striding Figurines with bases, and another complete limestone, but smaller. I am trying for all of these and whether I get them depends on how soon you can get some money over to me.[92]

Schultz urged his partner on, often in the tone of a benevolent patron.

Am very pleased indeed that you are finally getting back the Two Lands [Egypt] for more clobber. . . . My borrowings against my stocks and my large interest payments made over the past two years were done on your behalf, so that you could have ready ammunition on the battlefield. . . . I encourage you to . . . come back to the idea of turning the objects over rapidly. It is in the velocity of sales that we shall all make our fortunes, not in squeezing every last penny from each transaction.

Of course, to get the greatest things of all take a lifetime of hunting. You may never get anything quite like AIII again, nor shall I. But we will get other things. We will get them because we make it our business to know how to do that and because we take the many risks required.[93]

The cash sums that Schultz wired to Tokeley-Parry and his associates were plenty to keep looters busy: $99,000 in 1992, $25,000 in 1994, $52,000 later the same year, $93,500 in 1995,[94] and so on. The two had concocted a story about how the artifacts came from a "Thomas Alcock" collection, creating labels attributing the pieces to the fictitious Mr. Alcock (actually the name of Tokeley-Parry's great-uncle) and baking them in an oven and staining them with tea bags to make them look older.

Not since the Sipán trial had so many dirty trade secrets come to light. One dealer who knew Schultz testified that it would be unfair to single out him for conviction because dealers ignored laws against smuggling all the time. "I hope it's not true," Judge Jed Rakoff replied. "But if it is true, the prosecutors are going to be very busy."

Tokeley-Parry had already been convicted, in 1997, in Britain and served three years of a six-year sentence for smuggling and passport fraud. Egypt sentenced him in abstentia to fifteen years' hard labor.

Schultz's attorneys based their defense on the assertion that Tokeley-Parry was a hardened liar and that Schultz was unaware of Egyptian laws on antiquities. That last argument brought derision from one of the prosecutors, who said in his final arguments, "Anybody who has been in this business for ten minutes, much less ten years, has to know that Egypt owns all of its antiquities."[95]

The Schultz case alarmed antiquities dealers like none other for several reasons. First, the government of Egypt had not actually sued for the return of the pieces. The case was initiated by federal prosecutors, who charged Schultz with violating an American law dating from 1934, the National Stolen Property Act (NSPA), by importing goods owned by the Egyptian state. That act made it a crime to receive or sell, in U.S. or foreign commerce, goods known to the holder to have been stolen, and the jury believed Schultz knew. As the judge said, "If an American conspired to steal the Liberty Bell and sell it to a foreign collector of artifacts, there is no question he could be prosecuted."[96]

Second, the case clearly reaffirmed the McClain precedent dating from 1979 which, while saying American courts do not enforce foreign laws, held that national laws asserting state ownership over cultural property can apply in U.S. courts, as long as those laws are clear, publicized, and enforced. At the initiative of Moynihan and the antiquities lobby, legislation had been introduced in Congress three times in the 1980s to amend the NSPA to overturn McClain, and each time it died in committee.[97] The McClain line of reasoning had been criticized, studied, and bandied about in court for over twenty years, and no one was sure whether it would hold up in court again. In the Schultz case, it did.[98]

Third, it showed that the lack of a bilateral treaty was no bar to prosecution, since the United States and Egypt had no MOU or emergency agreement. And fourth, the case was handled in New York, the capital of American antiquities dealing, setting a precedent that federal courts elsewhere would likely follow.[99]

For archaeologists, the case brought some rich satisfaction that their dire warnings to Congress, the media, and anyone else who would listen about how the antiquities trade operated not only proved correct, but fell short of reality.

"It's a bit ironic," said Ric Elia. "I was there in 1999, when Italy was in Washington seeking important restrictions for looted material. Schultz was testifying as the president of NADAOPA about how horrible the agreement was and that he didn't know of any looting going on at Italian archaeological sites."[100]

Eighty antiquities seized from Schultz, Tokeley-Parry, and their accomplices were returned to Egypt, according to Egyptian newspaper reports.[101] They included a pair of false door panels from the tomb of the royal hairdresser Hetepka; British police had found them hidden under a bed at the home of an associate of Tokeley-Parry. The head of Amenhotep III was not returned, however: it was being held as collateral for a bank loan to Egypt.[102] Schultz appealed all the way to the Supreme Court, but his conviction stuck, and he was sent to serve a thirty-three-month sentence in federal prison at Fort Dix, New Jersey. He was due to be released on December 24, 2005.

As the Schultz ruling and the Italian MOU demonstrated, the United States had somehow become the world's most dynamic enforcer of the spirit and letter of the UNESCO convention. On the international stage, this was a strange case of casting against type. Derided so often as unilateralist cowboys, the Americans were leading the way on cooperation, prosecutions, and police action to stop the loss of cultural property, while European governments were dithering or demanding the right to import antiquities unfettered. Deeper still was the irony that the United States, which had contemptuously withdrawn from UNESCO in 1984 after accusing it of anti-Western bias and corruption, was now taking the most prominent role in implementing that U.N. organization's proudest achievement, the 1970 agreement on cultural property.

By the end of 2003, exactly one hundred countries had signed and ratified the UNESCO convention, including that shoppers' mart of plundered goods, Switzerland. Germany, Belgium, and a few other major European buyer nations were still boycotting it, though. International negotiators forged another treaty with similar aims, the Unidroit Convention of 1995, with language aimed at assuaging European demands for specific provisions for compensation for good-faith buyers, though still relatively few have signed on. The United Kingdom ratified the UNESCO convention in November 2002, by which time the British Museum had long since stopped acquiring antiquities without an undisputed, pre-1970 provenance.[103]

In the United States, defenders of the antiquities trade were well aware by then that their problem wasn't in Congress or the White House. Their tormentors were scores of officials whom they had never heard of, all through the middle echelons of federal government—assistant prosecutors, FBI agents, State Department officials, customs inspectors, the list went on and on—who, to the surprise and dismay of the antiquities lobby, actually enforced the law. It was the revenge of the bureaucrats. It had become impossible to talk to anyone in the antiquities industry without hearing complaints of overzealous law enforcement and the government's supposedly antimarket bias.

"Much of the problem does not flow from deliberate policy but from overreaching law enforcement, from politics," said Ashton Hawkins, retired legal counsel to the Met.[104]

The Hoving-era bravado was gone. As for dealers, the public persona they took was now one of businessmen chafing under the weight of onerous regulation.

"This is now a highly regulated market. The high end of the dealing community is very sensitive to issues of provenance," said NADAOPA co-counsel William Pearlstein. "It's a hostile, I think needlessly hostile, environment in which to do business."[105]

Sting operations, airport seizures, criminal prosecutions—it was a long way from the alluring, glamorous business that dealers had entered in their youth, and no one could miss the parallels with the narcotics trade. The Clinton MOU with Peru had been in effect for less than three months in September 1997, when Bob Wittman received another phone call at the FBI office in Philadelphia from Denis Garcia. The last time they talked, Garcia had told Wittman he could finally bring the backflap from Peru to "el Hombre de Oro."

Now Garcia had some more news: he had a business partner, a young man from Miami named Orlando Mendez, whom Garcia claimed was his nephew. Orlando speaks better English than I do, Garcia told Wittman, half in jest because Garcia's English, although accented, was good enough. Garcia and Mendez were reluctant to discuss details on the phone and wanted to meet Wittman in person the next day.[106]

Yes, I would be delighted to meet you tomorrow, Wittman told them. But I can't go to Miami so you will have to come here. The men balked but they agreed. They were already growing anxious to make the sale, and that meant for sure that this time they could bring in the backflap.

Chapter 9

THE SMUGGLERS

ORLANDO MENDEZ KNEW nothing about smuggling. Born in Puerto Rico in 1966 of prosperous Cuban exile parents, he'd spent a dissipated, party-animal youth among swimming pools and bottles of rum, and now he wanted to get serious by raising some money to help solidify his Miami business, a company that rented construction equipment for southern Florida's booming real-estate industry. He had a young wife, a son, and an engineering degree from Florida International University.

When Garcia, father of a close friend of Mendez but no relation, offered him a piece of an interesting business deal that involved some travel, Mendez liked the idea. Family, friendship, and business ties all meshed in the Miami exile community, and Mendez believed he could trust the father of his good friend. It was a risky job, Garcia confessed, but it could bring them potentially a million dollars if it all went right. The deal involved taking a piece of gold from Peru to a buyer somewhere in the United States, exactly where to be decided later. Garcia told him how he had sold the Chavín headdress in a quick, clean sale to Bazin, and he was sure this deal to Bazin's colleague would go just as smoothly.

The linchpin of Garcia's plan was his boyhood friend, a Panamanian diplomat named Frank who, with his diplomatic passport and immunity from prosecution, could bring the piece through U.S. Customs without fear of inspection. Garcia believed that diplomats were the safest and most reliable couriers for bringing valuable artifacts into the country and that they could do so at will.

"If you can get yourself a diplomat, that always works quite well," Garcia told Mendez, according to the latter's recollection.[1]

They first had to buy the backflap from Garcia's contact in Lima, Jorge Ramos Ronceros, and that's where Mendez came in. Mendez would have to pay $100,000 of his own funds, some of it borrowed from his parents, to buy the piece and then he would regain it all plus a huge profit upon the sale of the piece. Garcia knew Mendez came from a wealthy family. Mendez accepted all this.

"I was the money guy," said Mendez some years later, with a dejected shrug. A compact man of few words, with a wrestler's body and a scar on his chin, he was thought by many people to be Garcia's bodyguard. He was actually the paymaster. He didn't worry too much about the legality of the deal in these early stages. Someone owned an object and someone wanted to buy it, so what could be wrong with that? He looked at it as an adventure and a business deal.[2]

Garcia and Mendez took a flight north and, on the sultry afternoon of September 5, 1997, drove in a rented car down the New Jersey Turnpike to the meeting place that Wittman had suggested: the rest stop at Exit 7A. Known as the Richard Stockton rest stop, it was about halfway between New York and Philadelphia and so would be easily accessible by them all. With cars whizzing past, Garcia and Wittman met each other for the first time and then Garcia introduced his "nephew," Mendez. At ease with Wittman as they discussed details of the deal, Garcia now and then would turn to Mendez for a translation into English of some word or phrase.

Wittman was accompanied by a man he said was his business partner—in fact Spanish-speaking FBI agent Aníbal Molina—and both were suited up with microphones to record the whole meeting. Not far away, an FBI surveillance team lurked in a vehicle, videotaping the meeting and listening to the conversation.

Garcia had an interesting twist on the backflap's past. He told the agents it had been owned for a time by the former president of Peru, Alan García, who had acquired the piece during one of his presidential visits to Sipán and, when he left office, turned it over to his "uncle" Ramos Ronceros. To Wittman, it was an intriguing story—and one that turned out to be completely false, fabricated by Garcia with the aim of whetting el Hombre de Oro's interest in the piece. Mendez stood listening to his cohort spin this tale, "a total crock of shit," he later called it. Garcia invented many canards, but this one found its way later into the press and court documents in both the United States and Peru and later sent investigators in both countries on a costly and embarrassing chase for evidence that did not exist.

The two men told Wittman their friends in Peru had the backflap in their possession and that the Miami men could get it into the United States on a few weeks' notice. They repeated that it would cost $1.6 million, all in cash. Wittman, the agent masking as art broker, agreed to all their terms.

"I would have paid much more than that. I would have paid anything," said Wittman later.

The two smugglers looked relaxed, and Wittman could tell that he had won their trust. He was curious as to how they planned to smuggle the piece out of Peru and into the United States. Their contacts in Peru would take the piece on a flight to Panama, they told him, and from there a Panamanian national named Frank would take it into the United States. Frank would act as "the mule" or human transporter in drug-traffic slang. They didn't tell him much about the mule, except that he was planning to spend his vacation at home in Panama in a few weeks' time.

Mendez had one more question: Was Wittman an undercover cop?

"No. Are you?" he asked.

Mendez looked relieved. Of course not, he said.

Denial of risk is part of the enabling psychology of the person committing a crime. "For some reason, people who engage in this kind of business think that if you ask the person if he is an undercover agent, and he lies and says that he is not, then they can't use the evidence against you," Wittman told me. The way he described the suspects he had met over his career, I could tell that he respected many of them, even feared them, but not when they asked him dense questions like that.

The four men shook hands and drove their opposite ways back down the turnpike. One detail that had yet to be settled was exactly where they would hand over the backflap to Wittman and Molina, once it was in U.S. territory. As they approached the spiky skyscrapers of Philadelphia, Wittman assumed they would be contacting him soon with information on how they wanted to proceed on that detail.[3]

After nine years in undercover work, Wittman had developed a good feeling for the psychology of art thieves. He knew they might seem self-assured, confident, even cocky during those first contacts, but as the day of the deal drew closer, they would grow more nervous and anxious to wrap it up. Part of his job would be to reassure them, give them reason to keep their trust in him, keep them from taking fright and backing out, give them enough rope to hang themselves.

The first time I met Wittman, at the FBI office in Philadelphia, I saw quickly why someone would trust him in a deal like this. I had come prepared with a long list of questions, but pretty soon it was Wittman who was asking the questions. With an FBI press agent sitting there and monitoring our conversation like a stern mother, I asked about a certain American expert on Peruvian archaeology who had been accused of taking money from an art collector to whitewash the provenance of Moche art in an American museum. Wittman immediately asked me who told me this (although I was sure he knew). If I asked him about something he wasn't prepared to talk about, he would pause, smile, and wait for me to go to the next question. He was quick in conversation, quick to spot little contradictions or ambiguities. He was someone you wanted on your side, someone for whom you had better be prepared.

In Wittman's youth, his parents ran an antique store, a background that gave him a lifelong interest in art and a confidence with the subject that helped him later in undercover work. "When I'm doing a case I can talk in detail about art, and they'll say, 'He can't be a cop because how the hell would a cop know about that?'" he told me. After joining the FBI in 1988, Wittman took university courses in modern art history, learning to distinguish, for example, not just between a Miró, a Picasso, and a Braque, but also the distinct phases of those painters' oeuvre and gaining the knowledge that would allow him to convince corrupt dealers he was one of them.

Wittman is one of the FBI's certified undercover agents and the only one currently working full-time in art theft, an area that has gained visibility lately with the crackdown on antiquities smuggling. These agents undergo a rigorous training program at the FBI complex in Quantico, Virginia, that includes psychological profiling and role-playing in scenarios like penetrating a money-laundering network or gaining the confidence of drug dealers, plus more prosaic tasks such as writing reports and testifying in court. Once on the job, the agents are tested again every six months to measure their psychological stability. The work carries unique and often unbearable pressures that burn out even the toughest agents and give it a reputation as one of the most stressful jobs in law enforcement. Those who do it talk about it less as work than as a torment.

"I drove myself crazy doing undercover work," said Bob Bazin, who nonetheless did it for seventeen years until his retirement. "I could stand it for only two or three days at a time. Before going into a room to do a deal, I'd ask myself, 'What if they ask this? What do I say if that happens?' You have to become this person that you're not, and you have to make it believable, and after a while you're not even sure who you are anymore. It is unbelievably stressful work."

Bazin had cracked a series of well-known art heists, though his name rarely appeared in the news media. One was the theft of a Rodin sculpture from the Philadelphia Museum of Art in one of the first armed robberies of an American museum, and later another sculpture coincidentally also by Rodin, a study for the Burghers of Calais, which was lifted from the Wharton School at the University of Pennsylvania. He found the latter work where stolen art and those who traffic in it often wash up, Miami, where it was being sold in a room at the Fontainbleau Hotel. Wittman had worked with Bazin, learning undercover technique with him, getting a feel for the psychology of the thief, and now he was hoping to bring Bazin's last case, the backflap, to a conclusion.

"You're alone with people who are breaking the law, and you've got to create a rapport with them," said Wittman. "You can't entrap them. You can't suggest they do anything illegal; they've got to do it by themselves. You've got to get to know them personally, build a relationship, and if you don't do that you're not going to be successful. If you're standoffish, if you make them feel like it's all fake, they're going to know it. You've got to befriend them. And then you betray them."[4]

Garcia called Ramos Ronceros in Peru that night with the news that the backflap had a buyer at last. In late September, first Garcia and then Mendez flew to Lima to coordinate the backflap's final journey to what they thought would be a collector's home in Philadelphia.[5]

Garcia's contacts in Lima were curious: he had been obsessed with the backflap since 1994, and now, three years later, he was finally buying it. What took him so long? He had been in a terrible airplane accident, he told them, and had been struggling to recover from his life-threatening injuries. Maybe he thought this would engender some sympathy, but no one in his family or circle of Miami friends knew anything about a plane crash. It was another one of his tall tales.[6]

Ramos Ronceros required his full $100,000 up front before he would release the backflap from his living-room display cabinet.[7] A wire transfer of any amount over $10,000 required the American bank involved to notify federal authorities, and a transfer of $100,000 from the United States to a narcotics center like Peru would certainly have raised suspicion, but Ramos Ronceros had a solution for this. He had a bank account in New York. He gave the account number to Mendez, and Mendez, with a phone call from Ramos Ronceros's office, ordered a transfer of $100,000 from his account in Miami to the Peruvian's account in New York.[8]

That accomplished, Ramos Ronceros then demanded a commitment to receive *another* $175,000 before he would hand over the backflap, but that tranche could wait until after the deal was done. The smugglers would deposit it after they had sold the backflap in Philadelphia. The ever hardnosed Ramos Ronceros would send his assistant and general fix-it man, Juan Carlos Salas, to accompany them to New York and ensure that they paid Ramos Ronceros the rest of the money. For his efforts Salas would also get a cut: $100,000.[9]

"They kept asking for more money. It went on and on. It was four or five days of grueling negotiations," Mendez recalled. "For a long time we didn't even know if we were going to get the piece." The Peruvians continued to place new conditions, insisting that more handlers would need to be paid off, squeezing out more money for more people.[10] When Mendez saw the backflap in Ramos Ronceros's office, he was intrigued to find that the piece still had bits of the original textile still stuck to it. In ten years of being shuffled around from owner to owner, no one had given it a thorough cleaning. Except for the broken-off rattle attachment, it still looked much like it did the day Ernil hauled it up from the pit.

"It was gorgeous. It was the most amazing thing I had ever seen," said Mendez.

During a break in the negotiations, Garcia and Mendez went to see the treasures of Sipán at the Museum of the Nation in Lima. The hundreds of objects that Alva had excavated, plus some of those seized from the Bernal brothers, had returned from their tour in the United States and Germany and happened to be on display at an even larger exhibit called "Sipán: All the Mystery" just when the smugglers were in Lima. For most Peruvians, it was the first time they had ever seen the famous artifacts. Garcia and Mendez jostled among the crowds looking at the golden rattles, the ear spools, the golden backflap excavated from Tomb One, its label describing it as the largest piece of metalwork from the tombs. Soon, they knew, they would have an even bigger one.

Mendez got no satisfaction from this. He sat glumly in taxis in Lima's chaotic traffic jams, watching the shoeless children beg for coins, the dilapidated storefronts, the buses belching smoke, and felt a mix of terror and despair wash over him. He had no criminal record, no brush with the law ever, and he wondered what he had gotten himself into. He felt a few dim pangs of remorse that he was taking something so valuable from these impoverished people. He tried to keep his mind on the money.[11]

A few more days of haggling and the Miami men finally had the backflap. A complicated operation involving nearly a dozen people to smuggle the piece into the United States then swung into operation. The first task was to get the piece past Peruvian Customs controls. Although at the time such border controls were not stringent (they are much stricter now), the risk of such a valuable piece falling into police hands was simply too great. Garcia enlisted the help of an old friend from Chiclayo, Guillermo Elías Huamán, a retired colonel in the Peruvian police. They had known each other's families since Denis's days in Chiclayo in the 1970s and had swapped visits between Peru and Miami over the years. Now in Lima, Elías Huamán took his old friend Denis out to dinner along with his sullen, introverted friend,

Orlando Mendez, who never said more than two or three words but was rumored to be the son of Cuban millionaires.[12]

A man of indigenous features in his late fifties with the physique of a sack of potatoes, Elías Huamán had worked a police detail at the airport in the 1970s and, although he did not work there any longer, had the right contacts to clear a package through customs with no questions asked. His fee for this service was $5,000, tiny compared to the promised $1.6 million, but Garcia kept him in the dark about that.[13] And the ex-policeman would have to wait until after the deal to collect his tip. With Garcia paying his roundtrip airfare, Elías Huamán would fly to Garcia's house in Miami and wait there with Garcia's wife and children until the deal was done. Elías Huamán didn't mind waiting, though; he could do some shopping for himself and his family.[14]

On the morning of October 1, Garcia, Mendez, and Elías Huamán met at Lima's Jorge Chávez International Airport, Garcia holding the backflap in his carry-on bag, his "James Bond bag," as Elías Huamán jokingly called it. Everyone seemed relaxed and confident, and Mendez carried a few plastic bags with souvenirs.[15] Elías Huamán accompanied Garcia and Mendez through airport controls, having seen to it that there would be no problems. They all boarded the Copa Airlines plane for the four-hour flight. On arrival at Tocumen airport in Panama, Elías Huamán walked alone to the gate for his connecting flight to Miami while Garcia and Mendez headed for the exit for their rendezvous with Frank. Panamanian Customs officers waved them through; their local contact had apparently seen to that, using his influence to make sure there were no hitches. And influence he had, for their contact in Panama was Francisco Iglesias, the Panamanian consul general in New York, whose son was married to the daughter of the country's president, Ernesto Pérez Balladares.

Iglesias met them in the airport terminal and accompanied Garcia and Mendez to an apartment in a modern building in Panama City for the handover. Iglesias asked to see the backflap and they opened the suitcase. Scrubbed and washed by Ramos Ronceros's men, the piece gleamed like the sweat of the sun, and the bits of textile were gone. Here it was before the diplomat's eyes, a masterpiece of pre-Columbian metallurgy wrapped up in underwear, T-shirts, and bath towels. The eyes of the decapitator glared up at them, its mouth in a snarl, one hand holding a knife and the other a severed head.[16]

Iglesias closed the suitcase again, the backflap inside, and carried it home with him, telling Mendez and Garcia to meet him at the airport the next day.

Known to his friends as Frank, Iglesias had the easy charm and gracious manners of the perfect Latin American diplomat. Born in Cuba, where he and Denis Garcia were friends, he had emigrated to Panama and married a woman of that country's upper class. He thrived at the cocktail parties, dinners, and social events that constituted a big part of his job as consul in New York. He was liked and respected by his colleagues, and, although consular officials had ample opportunity to skim off money for services rendered, he was not known to be corrupt. But among Panamanian officials he had a reputation for a certain frivolity. He kept comfortable hours at the consulate, was usually seen in expensive suits and made sure everybody knew that he was a close friend and in-law of the president. His son and the president's daughter had married a few months before in a lavish ceremony that filled the social pages in the Panamanian press. It was the president himself who appointed Frank Iglesias to the coveted post, bypassing many experienced diplomats who resented the consul ever since.[17]

The next day Iglesias, Garcia, and Mendez boarded a Continental Airlines flight to Newark, the backflap in the consul's checked luggage because it was too big to fit in his carry-on. He flew in business class, Mendez and Garcia in economy. Iglesias had placed his diplomatic business card on the exterior of the suitcase carrying the backflap to indicate to customs officers that, because of his diplomatic status, it was exempt from inspection. Once in Newark, they had no problems whatever bringing in the piece.

Elías Huamán, meanwhile, had flown from Panama to Miami to stay at the home of Garcia's wife and children, where he would wait until he got his money.[18] The men had known each other for over twenty years, but they were not good enough friends for Elías Huamán to trust Garcia to wire or send him the money in Peru. Everyone, it seemed, mistrusted everyone else.

That day or the next, Mendez and Garcia in New York called Wittman to tell him the backflap had landed. Salas had also arrived separately and was staying at the same hotel as the smugglers, the Doral Court Hotel, near Times Square, to keep close tabs on the smugglers and ensure that Ramos Ronceros's share of the money made it safely into his bank account.[19]

Now they had to decide where to do the sale. Iglesias had wanted Wittman to come to the Panamanian consulate on New York's Avenue of the Americas with the $1.6 million in cash, and they would hand over the piece to him inside the security of the consulate. Garcia relayed Iglesias's proposal to Wittman, but Wittman balked. He knew this would make it impossible to make any arrests. As a diplomatic legation, the consulate was Panamanian sovereign territory and therefore U.S. agents could not enter without written permission from Panamanian authorities, and merely asking for that permission could blow the whole operation. But of course he could not tell this to Garcia because he was supposed to be an art dealer.

So with the phone in his hand, Wittman thought fast and came up with a solution.

"We'll want to authenticate the piece, and the authenticator is old and not in good health. He doesn't like to travel. You'll have to bring it down here," said Wittman.

Garcia was silent. They knew Wittman wanted to have the piece authenticated, but they did not anticipate this being an impediment to doing the deal on their turf. Also, Wittman told him, he would not want to walk down the street in New York carrying a bag with $1.6 million in it.[20]

Mendez and Garcia eventually agreed to do the deal on neutral ground: once again, the rest stop at exit 7A on the New Jersey Turnpike.

Wittman said he and his "business partner" Molina would inspect the backflap at the rest stop and then they would all drive to the Adam's Mark Hotel in Philadelphia, where the elderly "authenticator" would be waiting. Once the authenticator had given his seal of approval, Wittman would hand over $800,000 in cash. Then he would drive to a nearby bank with all or some of the smugglers, as they liked, to withdraw the remaining $800,000 to complete the deal.[21]

Mendez and Garcia agreed to this. They wanted to get the piece off their hands. Wittman could hear the anxiety in their voices, the nervous yearning to finish the deal. They did not have a lot of cash after Ramos Ronceros and his men cleaned them out in Lima, and they were living on Chinese takeout food.

As a final confidence-building measure, Wittman sent them a statement from the bank confirming that $800,000 was on deposit and available for withdrawal. It was $800,000 of American taxpayers' money, borrowed from FBI coffers and deposited at the bank to lure three art smugglers to their next meeting, on Tuesday, October 7, 1997.

Chapter 10

THE CONSUL

WITTMAN AND MOLINA were racing down the New Jersey Turnpike for their meeting with the smugglers. They arrived a bit early. A surveillance team suited them up again with listening devices and parked nearby to videotape everything. Then the two agents stood outside their rental car in the parking area, waiting for the two smugglers with whom Wittman had done business before, and their new associate, the anonymous Panamanian. Wittman knew the man worked at his country's consulate but assumed he was a secretary or a driver, at most some low-ranking official. A high-ranking diplomat would never get involved in such risky activities.

Suddenly a large gold sedan, more like a limousine, came toward them. Wittman was baffled. This was nothing like the car Garcia and Mendez had shown up in before. Then he noticed the diplomatic plates.

Garcia and Mendez alighted from the car, and then a man in a suit with well-coiffed hair and glasses stepped out of the driver's side and came smiling toward Wittman.

"How nice to meet you," said the man, as smoothly and charmingly as he had done with new acquaintances at a thousand cocktail parties.

They shook hands and the man handed Wittman his business card and gave another to Molina. Beneath the Panamanian national seal, it read: "Francisco Humberto Iglesias, Consul General."

Bob Goldman, the assistant U.S. attorney, was sitting in his office in
Philadelphia waiting anxiously to hear from Wittman, with whom he had
been working on the case since the summer. Goldman was a lean, plain-
spoken man with a bushy mustache like that of the young Rough Rider
Theodore Roosevelt, whom he admired and of whom he kept a photo
tacked to his office door. When he learned back in August that the mule
bringing in the backflap was a Panamanian diplomat, he had called Justice
Department headquarters to ask if he could arrest a foreign consular
diplomat, possibly the consul himself, for smuggling. What Goldman received was a quick education in the complexities of the Vienna Convention
on Consular Relations, a rather obscure piece of international law dating
from 1963 that granted a wide range of privileges to diplomats appointed
to work in any country's consulates abroad, including immunity from arrest "except in the case of a grave crime," exemption from inspection of
diplomatic bags, immunity from being forced to give evidence or testify in
trials in the host country, and the inviolability—that is, police may not enter without permission—of the consulate's premises.[1] (It was that last rule
that Garcia and Iglesias surely had in mind when they asked to sell the
backflap inside the Panamanian consulate, and Wittman's refusal of this
request should have set off their alarm bells.) Under the terms of the convention, Goldman would have to file written charges before the arrest—
and that was impossible because Garcia had not given them the diplomat's
name or title.

Goldman's higher-ups in Washington advised him to go ahead anyway
with the investigation, leaving up to him the decision of whether to arrest
the diplomat, if the chance arose.

"They found it fascinating. Their attitude was, go for it," Goldman recalled. The diplomat's immunity was "limited to acts committed in his role
as a consul, and I don't think the government of Panama would be able to
say that part of his official acts as consul was smuggling."[2] As the day of the
deal approached, and as Wittman and Goldman gathered more and more
evidence against Garcia and Mendez in the form of tape-recorded phone
conversations, the paucity of their evidence against Iglesias became clearer.
They could not, at this point, show that he had brought the backflap into
the United States and, if he had that he knew it was illegal to do so. Also,
was smuggling a "grave" enough crime to annul his immunity to arrest? All
this would complicate any prosecution, would surely be raised by the diplomat's defense lawyers in court, and might even bring dismissal of the elaborately built case against Garcia and Mendez if a judge thought Goldman
was acting too rashly in indicting the diplomat with them.

Standing in the parking lot, Wittman could barely conceal his surprise at the seniority of the diplomat. Denis Garcia had some powerful friends.

Iglesias popped open the trunk of the car to reveal a large black suitcase. One of the smugglers opened it up and there, wrapped up in T-shirts, underwear, and filched hotel towels, lay the backflap.

The two agents looked at it with satisfaction but did not touch it, and they congratulated the smugglers on successfully bringing the piece into the country. Now it was for the authenticator to confirm the piece's pedigree. With the "buyers" leading the way in their car, they all headed down the highway for the thirty-minute drive to the Adam's Mark Hotel on City Avenue, on the western edge of Philadelphia. As he drove along, Wittman spoke on his cell phone with Goldman to keep him abreast of what as happening, telling him there was no sign the smugglers were armed and that the deal had so far gone pleasantly. Goldman in turn was on the phone with an official at the Justice Department in Washington with the startling news that the Panamanian diplomat he had spoken of was none other than the consul general in New York, who was about to be caught *in flagrante delicto*. In the car behind them, Mendez, Garcia, and Iglesias were sweating through their shirts, swearing and bickering about which of them had let the agents draw out the sale like this while unwittingly committing yet another federal crime, the interstate transportation of stolen property, as they drove over the bridge into Pennsylvania.

First Wittman's car and then the gold limousine swung into the hotel's giant parking lot. All five men got out.

Within seconds, police were upon them. About fifty FBI and U.S. Customs agents clutching submachine guns jumped out from vans and behind cars and wrestled all three suspects to the pavement. Before Garcia and Mendez had any idea what was happening, their bellies were on the ground, an agent's knee was planted in their backs, and handcuffs were being shackled over their wrists. All they could see was the black tar of the pavement, all they could hear was shouting.

Iglesias cursed and trembled as FBI agents pulled him up from the pavement. He stammered that he was a diplomat, that he had immunity to arrest, that he had no idea he was doing anything illegal. He looked "thunderstruck," said Wittman. He was not arrested because, for all the FBI or Goldman knew, it was the consul's secretary who had actually brought the piece into the country and the consul had merely given the smugglers a lift. Goldman had obtained a judge's all-purpose arrest warrant, known as a John Doe warrant, for Garcia and Mendez, but not for Iglesias, who was allowed to drive home alone in his limousine. "He sure looked happy when we told him how to get back on the highway," Wittman said later.

Wittman retrieved the suitcase carrying the backflap from the back of the car and brought it to the FBI's evidence vault downtown. The piece's journey was far from over. He called the University of Pennsylvania Museum of Archaeology and Anthropology and asked them to send a few professors down to FBI headquarters right away to certify whether the piece was authentic. They didn't have to be the world's greatest specialists on Moche art, just knowledgeable enough to satisfy a judge that the suspects should be kept in custody. Within an hour archaeologists Clark Erickson and Steve Epstein and museum keeper Lucy Fowler-Williams were on their way.

"So we walk into a conference room with the FBI seal on the wall and a table, and the only other object in the room is a suitcase. If you went to K-Mart to buy the biggest, cheapest, ugliest plastic suitcase you could find, this would be it," Erickson recounted. "And all these FBI agents were standing there looking at the suitcase. They opened it up and it was full of underwear and T-shirts, and then they took out this big piece of gold."[3]

The three scholars passed this strange piece amongst each other, looking it over carefully. It had obviously been scoured with Ajax or some other abrasive material, or maybe steel wool. It was real gold, all right, but it was in such awful condition that they couldn't be sure about its age.

"So is it real?" asked one of the agents.

Erickson, Fowler-Williams, and Epstein, who was an expert on pre-Columbian copper smelting, said they believed it was an ancient artifact, and not a modern copy, but that they would have to subject it to chemical analysis to be sure. That would take a couple of weeks.

No way, the agents said. We've put a lot of resources into this case, we've got the judge waiting and we want to go big with this, they said. "You got to tell us right now. Is it real or not?" asked Wittman.

Erickson examined it some more, the agents almost literally breathing down his neck. Then he thought he recognized, low on the blade, an imprint left by scrubbed-off textiles, an imprint that could only have been made over centuries of pressure. "You can't fake that. That's when I knew it was real."

Yes, the archaeologists finally said, it was real. But Erickson was an authority on early pre-Columbian agriculture, not art, and Epstein, despite his expertise on copper, wasn't so confident in judging the authenticity of gold, nor was Fowler-Williams. To be absolutely sure of the piece's origin, Erickson suggested to Wittman's aggravation that he show it to a few more experts.

So Wittman called pre-Columbian art consultant Robert Sonin, formerly of the Brooklyn Museum, and a renowned detector of fakes who would tell collectors for a fee whether their artifacts were authentic or not. Usually they weren't, and Sonin had seen a lot of phony Peruvian gold circulating on the market lately. Wittman was so worried that the smugglers might have consulted Sonin about the backflap that, when he called the art expert, he did not say he was from the FBI or even give his real name until he was sure Sonin had no previous knowledge of the case. Sonin was no bleeding-heart preservationist, and that fact would give his opinion credibility. "I'm pro-looter. I'll bet there isn't more than one in 5,000 Peruvians who wouldn't sell whatever national treasures he could get his hands on, if he could get a few bucks for it," he once said.[4] When Sonin walked into the FBI's conference room in Philadelphia and looked at the backflap, it took him no more than a few seconds to give his verdict. It was definitely real.[5]

It would have been tough to contradict Sonin's opinion in court, but still Wittman was taking no chances. Fakes were sophisticated and common, and if there were any question about the authenticity of the backflap, the indictments would be trashed and so would Wittman's reputation. He needed a few more endorsements. So the backflap went back into a car trunk—this time Wittman's—and down the highway again with another agent riding along with an assault rifle to the home of archaeologist Elizabeth Benson. An art history professor at American University, author of one of the definitive books on the Moche, and an old acquaintance of Alva, Benson disliked getting involved in smuggling cases like this, even as a consultant, but she invited Wittman into her dining room outside Washington one evening and contemplated this slab of gold on her table.

People who saw the backflap in those years usually fell into one of two categories: either they thought it was going to make them rich, a glittering piece of El Dorado that sparkled the eyes of its beholders, or they thought it was a ghastly example of Moche excess. Benson, an elderly woman with cotton-candy hair and a gentle voice, fell into the latter category. To her, it was "that thing they found on the New Jersey Turnpike."

"Compared to other objects [from Sipán], it did not have the precision of detail. It was bigger but not as fine," she told me a few years later in Chiclayo.[6]

Wittman showed it to a few more experts in the Washington area. The piece was so enormous, heavy, and ostentatious compared to anything else ever seen in its class, like a grotesque caricature of Moche goldwork, that plenty of people, like Erickson, had initial doubts about its authenticity. But everyone confirmed it was real. The danger from Wittman's point of view was that the defense might find and pay a self-styled expert who could introduce just enough doubt about the authenticity of the piece in court to persuade a judge to throw out the case. (If the backflap really *had* been fake, then attempted fraud charges might apply.) By showing the piece to so many people, he was trying to snow any such attempt under the weight of scholarly opinion and avert any cracks from appearing in the

Iraq, 2003. Susanne Osthoff, archaeologist, with a guard, holding a cylinder seal freshly excavated by looters, rear, at Isin. *(Roger Atwood)*

Looters at Isin, southern Iraq. *(Roger Atwood)*

Faces carved from ancient stone structures at Angkor, Cambodia. Note the roughness of the chiseled surface, suggesting a recent looting job. *(Werner Romero)*

Beheaded stone men on the east causeway into the Cambodian ruins of Angkor Thom. Few original heads remain; they are easy to saw off, transport, and sell. *(Werner Romero)*

At the bottom of the looters' pit in Sipán, Peru, archaeologist Walter Alva found an 1,800-year-old scepter that the grave robbers missed. *(Museo Tumbas Reales de Sipán)*

Sipán, Peru. The burial mound known as Huaca Rajada. The mudbrick platform where a Moche dynasty was buried is visible at left. *(Museo Tumbas Reales de Sipán)*

Brushes and tools in hand, archaeologists excavating the Sipán tombs. *(Museo Tumbas Reales de Sipán)*

The Lord of Sipán in his tomb. Note the gold-and-silver peanut necklace, the molded gold plate that covered his mouth and chin, and his skull at far right. *(Museo Tumbas Reales de Sipán)*

Excavation at Sipán. *(Museo Tumbas Reales de Sipán)*

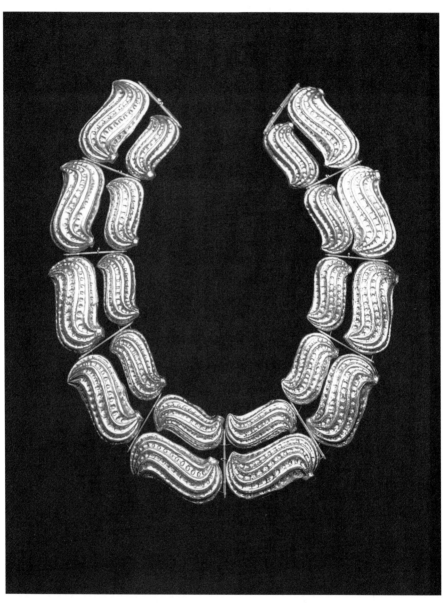

Cleaned and restored, the Sipán peanut necklace glistened at museum shows. *(Museo Tumbas Reales de Sipán)*

One of the golden monkey heads from La Mina. They dazzled collectors when they hit the U.S. market after 1988. *(Werner Forman /Art Resource, NYC)*

The master grave robber Ernil Bernal posing with his son in 1986. A year later he struck it rich in Sipán

Batán Grande, Peru. From their now-dilapidated mansion, the Aurich family directed the wholesale looting of a fabulously rich complex of pre-Inca burial mounds and cemeteries on their estate. *(Roger Atwood)*

The Aurich looting crews sunk more than 100,000 holes across the north Peruvian landscape, finding artifacts now in many U.S. museums. *(Izumi Shimada)*

By the end of its feudal reign over Batán Grande, the Aurich family was using bulldozers to extract pre-Hispanic treasures by the ton. The damage could still be seen in 1975. *(Izumi Shimada)*

"It was a gold rush," said one witness, after 1987. Looters' holes pockmark the land near Sipán. *(Museo Tumbas Reales de Sipán)*

Moche men in battle, depicted here in a roll-out drawing from a pot dating from circa A.D. 400. Note backflaps and rattle attachments on the victorious soldiers. *(Donna McClelland)*

The Sacrifice Ceremony: The Moche lord, upper left, drinks the blood of captives from a goblet, while priests draw blood from other prisoners, below right. *(Donna McClelland)*

The Chavín headdress, a 2,200-year-old gold artifact, in its machine-gun case. The piece was the smugglers' bait for a larger prize—and a near-disaster for the FBI. *(Robert Bazin)*

Philadelphia, 1998. Alva receiving the backflap in a ceremony with Peruvian ambassador Ricardo Luna, center, and FBI official Wayne Comer. *(Beverly Schaefer, Reuters)*

One of ten gold rattles from Sipán, manufactured circa A.D. 200, looted 1987, seized by U.S. Customs in Miami, 1995. It was almost identical to a piece confiscated . . . *(Museo Brüning)*

. . . by the FBI from a museum in New Mexico in 1998. *(Museum of New Mexico)*

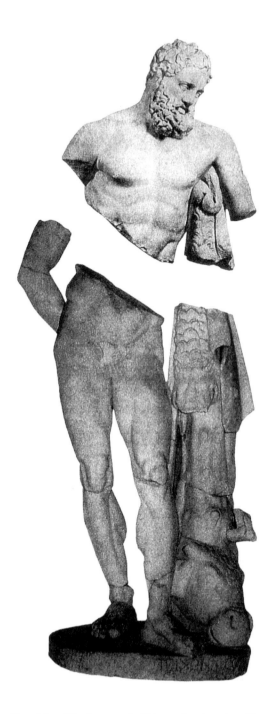

The Weary Herakles: The bottom half is at the Antalya Museum in Turkey, the top half at the Museum of Fine Arts, Boston. *(Ozgen Acar)*

Looters at work near Huacho, Peru, with a thin, metal pole to find tombs.
(Roger Atwood)

Robin, a professional grave robber, holding a freshly looted ceramic pot. He dug through five other tombs before finding this urn, which, because of the crack at right, was unmarketable. *(Roger Atwood)*

A pillaged pre-Conquest graveyard near Chilca, Peru, and uprooted human bones. *(Roger Atwood)*

Walter Alva in front of the new Sipán museum in Lambayeque, 2004. *(Museo Tumbas Reales de Sipán)*

consensus, a bit like a defense attorney polling a jury after it has issued a guilty verdict.

"We've got what we think is $1.6 million worth of stolen art in the car, and if you make the arrests and it turns out to be fake, you've got egg on your face. You want to have the right charges," said Wittman.[7]

Agents took the still-stunned Garcia and Mendez to an FBI booking room in downtown Philadelphia immediately after their arrests. They glowered at Wittman and Goldman as they entered the sterile little room that afternoon. Goldman introduced himself as el Hombre de Oro and offered his card to Garcia. Garcia looked at the name and laughed. "Very good, very good," he muttered.[8]

"That sort of broke the ice," Goldman recalled. They began to talk, Garcia accompanied by a Spanish-speaking public defender until his own lawyer arrived. Only slowly, over hours of questioning and recollections, did Garcia begin to comprehend how elaborate the FBI's case had been: the Chavín headdress, Becker, Bazin and his heart surgery, the meeting in New Jersey, the whole thing had been a gigantic scam. Every word he had said to Bazin and Wittman had been taped. Most of their meetings had been filmed. He had spent nearly four years with his every movement and phone call under FBI scrutiny and had had no idea.

Now he had no option but to cooperate, and soon he began recounting in detail the whole operation. They had bought the backflap in Peru from a man who everyone said was Alan García's uncle, handed it over in Panama to the consul Iglesias, who then brought it in through Newark in his diplomatic bag and was supposed to receive $100,000. It became clear that Iglesias's role in the conspiracy was deeper than Goldman or Wittman first realized. They soon began writing indictments for all three.

Denis Garcia still couldn't quite part with his mendacious story about Alan García, the former Peruvian president, having owned the backflap. He told it to his lawyer and it found its way into an FBI press release issued two days later, parts of which were translated into Spanish by international news agencies and quoted by news media all over Latin America. The story would be repeated for years to come by ordinary Peruvians, to the understandable annoyance of the former president. His rule had ended in 1990 in a chaotic atmosphere of strikes, hyperinflation, and "dirty war" tactics by security forces against guerrillas, but in the late 1990s, from exile in France, he was planning a political comeback. Whatever his sins, owning a stolen treasure from Sipán was not one of them, although the charge was still raised by his political foes when he ran unsuccessfully for president in 2001. He wrote a letter to Goldman denying he ever owned the backflap.[9]

Mendez meanwhile sat fuming in his cell, refusing to talk to anyone, awaiting the arrival of his pregnant wife, his parents, and an attorney from Miami. One of the most damning pieces of evidence had been plucked from his wallet when he was prone on the pavement—a handwritten card with the amounts of money to be paid to each person in the whole racket, including Ramos Ronceros and Iglesias. He was still shaken by the suddenness and violence of the arrests.

"We're down on the ground, we've got these guys on top of us, guys all around us, they're shouting and waving these big guns around," he said. "And it's like—have you ever felt like a total ass? I mean, like, instead of a face, you have two buttocks where your face used to be? That's how I felt. I am a total ass."[10]

Two days after their arrest, a judge ignored FBI warnings that the suspects were flight risks and released them both on bail, $300,000 for Mendez and $100,000 for Garcia. The two men returned sullenly to Miami to await trial.

Frank Iglesias drove back to New York and, two or three days later, fled the United States for Panama, never to return. On the basis of statements from Garcia and Mendez, a warrant was issued for his arrest on October 25 on charges of conspiracy, smuggling, and interstate transportation of stolen property. By then he was back at his family home in Panama City, disgraced and stripped of his post as consul general and his diplomatic status. Among his ex-colleagues in the Panamanian diplomatic service, the rumor was that his daughter-in-law's father, President Pérez Balladares, had personally called President Bill Clinton to beg him to allow Iglesias to resign quietly and go home.

The news could not be kept quiet for long, though. On Panama's Independence Day, November 3, the news broke on the front pages of the small nation's newspapers about the forced resignation and arrest warrant.[11] The scandal dragged on for days, and Pérez Balladares's government was forced to issue a statement practically disowning Iglesias. "For the sake of the country's good name and the accountability that characterizes the government's actions, it was decided to request his resignation," it said, noting the government's "firm intent to maintain the good name of Panama."[12] Friends and colleagues shunned him,[13] and newspapers across Latin America referred to him as the man who "took advantage of his prestige as a foreign diplomat" to engage in smuggling, as the Lima newspaper El Comercio wrote.

If Denis Garcia was telling all in Philadelphia about Iglesias's involvement, the disgraced consul got a measure of revenge in his own country. "I knew that Garcia had dedicated himself for many years to the business and trading of antiquities," he was quoted as saying in one report.[14]

The United States and Panama have no extradition treaty, so Iglesias cannot be arrested on these charges in his home country. To this day the United States has an international arrest warrant for Iglesias, meaning that as soon as he enters a country with which the United States has an extradition treaty he will be subject to arrest and deportation. In under two weeks he had gone from diplomat to international fugitive.

I obtained Iglesias's phone number from a friend at the Panamanian embassy in Washington, and when I spoke to him I received the usual spray of fury, denial, and self-pity that I had grown accustomed to hearing from people caught smuggling. He would not allow a full interview.

"I walked into this innocently because I had no idea it was illegal. Someone got me mixed up in this whole affair and made me the useful idiot. It caused me a lot of harm, and now I'd like to forget about it," said Iglesias. "Naturally I had no idea this was outside the law."

His ignorance of the law may be no defense in court, but it did sound sincere. International standards on antiquities trading had changed under his feet without his realizing it. Iglesias seemed to have the mentality of diplomats from another era, when they were elite emissaries free to gather objects and trinkets during their missions abroad and take them as gifts for the powerful or as personal vanities. It was as if someone had issued an international arrest warrant for another diplomat who used his position to ship antiquities, Lord Elgin.

Hoping to establish the whereabouts of Mendez and Garcia through the whole operation, Wittman asked the Doral Court Hotel in New York for its full guest list. Indeed, Mendez and Garcia were on it, listed as sharing a room. They were about to receive over a million dollars for the backflap but they wanted to economize on the room. And then Wittman noticed another name: Juan Carlos Salas, the messenger of Ramos Ronceros. Someone, presumably someone in Garcia's family, tipped him off as to what had happened and he left New York in a hurry. Wittman was bitterly disappointed. Salas's arrest would have been the coup de grace in a case that had come together nicely. Goldman tried later to bring Salas from Peru for trial but, at this writing, has been unsuccessful.

Elías Huamán quietly slipped out of Miami the day after Garcia was arrested, with Denis's own son taking him to the airport. The FBI apparently never learned of his presence in the United States, which Elías Huamán did not reveal until nearly two years later in his testimony in a related Peruvian trial.

A federal grand jury indictment was issued for Mendez and Garcia, written by el Hombre de Oro himself, Bob Goldman, charging them with one count each of conspiracy, interstate transportation of stolen property, and smuggling. Another indictment followed in absentia for Iglesias for the same three charges. There was no trial. Mendez and Garcia pleaded guilty to all three charges and were each sentenced to nine months in jail, a light sentence for the value of the goods they smuggled, but neither had any previous arrest and cooperated enough with the FBI, so the judge was lenient and allowed them to serve their sentences at halfway houses in Miami.

"They let me go to work during the day, but every night it was back to the halfway house," Mendez said. As we sat among potted palms in the breezy, pink-and-turquoise lobby of a hotel on Miami Beach, he recounted how the experience had sharpened his Catholic faith and taught him the kind of lessons one learns only through the commission of great mistakes.[15] He had been back home in Miami on bail for a few days, he recalled, when his wife suddenly went into labor and gave birth prematurely to their second son, Michael. The baby weighed less than a pound, small enough "to fit in the palm of my hand." For a time Michael seemed to be improving, but after forty-four days of life in a bubble in the neonatal intensive care unit, he died. Mendez was there. A nurse advised him to go hold the tiny dead body. Mendez balked but the nurse insisted, saying, "Just do it. Someday you'll thank me." He walked down the hall to the intensive care ward and saw the baby's still-warm corpse, lying in a crib. "And I picked him up and I looked down at him, and I saw the figure that was inside the backflap, the man holding the knife and the head. I looked at my own baby, and all I could see was that face in the backflap," Mendez said. A look of exhaustion and sorrow and terror crept over his face like a shadow. "That was when I knew the backflap had gotten into my blood."

Walter Alva was stunned by the recovery of the backflap—stunned that smugglers could walk into such a trap, that such a large metal object could make it past Lima airport controls, stunned by the meticulousness of the FBI's planning and execution.[16] Unlike Wittman, however, he was not surprised that the mule had been a high-ranking envoy. Alva, like everyone else in Lima, knew that diplomats were among the top buyers and shippers of looted antiquities.

Alva flew to Philadelphia in November to see the legendary piece at last and add his pebble to the mountain of validations of its genuineness. He met Wittman and Molina for the first time and came away impressed with their earnestness, but he recalled a strange feeling of disappointment when he saw the piece itself in the basement of an FBI building in Philadelphia. It was in even worse condition than he had imagined. It was so scratched and scrubbed it looked like the bottom of a kitchen sink, and like his nemesis Poli, he noticed immediately that the piece had been mutilated. Somewhere on its long journey from the Moche burial pyramid to the New Jersey Turnpike, the back of the decapitator rattle had been bent so much that it snapped off. The small, severed scrap lay there with the backflap. Conservators could repair a lot of damage, but he didn't think they would be able to fix a wound as deep as that, and nor should they. Plans were already under way for a new museum in Peru dedicated to the Sipán site, and Alva knew the backflap would be a star exhibit that would highlight the damage done by the loot trade. One tip of the blade had also been slightly bent back, as if it had bumped up against something.[17]

Before returning to Peru, Alva went to Sotheby's annual pre-Columbian auction in Manhattan. As each piece of metalwork, ceramic pot, and woven textile swung into view on the dais, almost none with any specific information on their provenance, Alva could feel himself getting angrier and angrier. A spectacular Peruvian south-coast textile was brought out before the crowd of collectors, dealers, and curators, and bidding climbed higher and higher until it finally sold for $240,000. Alva stormed out.

"I thought it was disgusting. I felt like holding up a banner saying, 'People who care about culture don't buy looted antiquities,'" he said.

Garcia and Mendez were serving their sentence by the time Alva returned to Philadelphia on July 15, 1998, to receive the backflap in a ceremony with Peruvian Ambassador Ricardo Luna, Erickson, and the head of the FBI office in Philadelphia, Wayne Comer. As local television reporters crowded around him, Alva fumbled in English to try to find a way to explain the significance of the backflap and its return to Peruvians.

"It's as if—it's as if someone stole the Liberty Bell!" he said.

Wittman attended the ceremony but kept to the back of the room to ensure he wasn't filmed; it could ruin his cover for future undercover cases. He had been interviewed and quoted at length in Peruvian media but never photographed. Oddly enough, the ceremony took place in the Egyptian hall at the University of Pennsylvania's Museum of Archaeology and Anthropology, where an exhibit on the backflap and the Moche was to open the next day and last for three weeks, with the piece itself as the star of the show. The backflap was now officially owned by the Peruvian government and loaned by it to the museum, but this did not prevent Peruvian reporters from protesting bitterly that the treasure's return to Peru should not be delayed by even one day. Such was the emotional power raised by the backflap.

It was nonetheless a good place for the exhibit because the UPenn museum was the first U.S. institution to renounce publicly the purchase of antiquities that did not have a full pedigree, complete with documentation on previous owners, legality of export, and place of origin. The museum's stand in April 1970 became known as the Philadelphia Declaration and drew much attention and praise—and almost no imitators among art museums until the mid-1980s. Even now many major institutions have balked at signing on to its principles.[18] Erickson, Alva, and Fowler-Williams co-curated the show and made it as much about the depredations of looters in northern Peru as about the Moche, and the result was an eye-opening counterpoint to the traveling Sipán extravaganza a few years before, with the highest attendance levels of a summer exhibit in the museum's history.[19]

Alva carried the piece back to Lima in a protective crate, and on August 14, 1998, it was put on display to the Peruvian people for the first time, in the Museum of the Nation in Lima. Behind glass on black velvet, the backflap lay in the same room where, a year before, Garcia and Mendez had admired the other treasures of Sipán. Alva was now able to study the legendary artifact for the first time. Even without complete chemical analysis, he realized from the gold's weight, color, and texture that it was between sixteen and twenty karats—a staggering amount of precious metal bearing in mind that pure, unalloyed gold is twenty-four karats and that anything, including wedding bands and chains, over fourteen karats is popularly called gold.[20]

In a dusty neighborhood of cement row houses on the outskirts of Chiclayo, Samuel Bernal was sitting on a beat-up couch and watching his old television when he saw a report on the handover of the backflap in Philadelphia. Seven years had passed since he last saw the piece. When he heard the price, $1.6 million, he started sputtering with rage again about all the money that he, his martyred brother Ernil, and the benighted village of Sipán had lost. Alva was holding the piece in his arms like a baby.[21]

"Who got the money for all that gold? Where did it all go? That's what I want to know. All into the pockets of that jackal Alva, that's where," Bernal shouted at me, recalling the day he learned the fate of the backflap. He stormed out of the room and then came back in and shouted some more.

The backflap case showed everybody who bought, sold, or traded antiquities that the gentlemen's activity of dealing in loot was now no minor transgression. It was not a question of a person's or an institution's "ethics" anymore; it was a felony. People who engaged in such dealings would go the way of Frank Iglesias or later Frederick Schultz, professionally wrecked and disgraced for life. Nor was it any place for dabblers, people looking to turn some dollars on the side. Looters would still rip through tombs, but much of the cross-border dealing went deeper underground, and some of the weaker-willed dealers simply left the antiquities business.

With the convictions to prove it, Wittman was able to say, "It showed that if you deal in smuggled pieces, you're going to get convicted."

Barely a month had passed since Alva left Philadelphia, carrying the crate with the backflap inside and trailed by a bevy of Peruvian TV cameras, when Wittman received a phone call at his office from an archaeology professor at an east coast university. A colleague of the professor had seen a collection of ancient Latin American art at a museum in Santa Fe, New Mexico; one artifact and possibly three others looked strikingly like pieces from Sipán. He had mentioned his concerns to a colleague, and now that professor was tipping off the FBI to what looked like another case of looted Sipán artifacts finding their way into the United States.[22]

The professor who called the FBI begged Wittman to keep his name quiet, and he is still anonymous out of fear of being sued for defamation by the collector who donated the pieces to the museum. The professor could be tagged an FBI snitch and troublemaker and be barred access to museum collections for research, a courtesy commonly extended to scholars. His fear was not groundless: the Metropolitan Museum of Art for many years barred Malcolm Bell from examining the Morgantina silver set after he told *the museum*, not law enforcement, of his concerns that the set might be looted.[23] When I called by telephone to the person whom I believed was the FBI informant, he spoke in the third person: "That person fears legal action. That person could have serious legal problems."

One of the four pieces was a golden rattle. It was similar to the one attached to the backflap, and it was virtually identical to the one seized by U.S. Customs at Miami airport in 1995. Atop the *huaca* at Sipán, it would have been worn with the backflap by the Moche lord during the blood rituals of prisoner sacrifice.

These pieces, among those bought by Johnson and then sold to the collector John Bourne, were not in the hands of two-bit smugglers. They were held by a publicly financed museum, the Palace of the Governors unit of the Museum of New Mexico in Santa Fe. They were on public exhibit.

Chapter 11

THE GOLDEN RATTLE

IT'S AMONG THE finest small collections of pre-Columbian art anywhere. In a gallery at the Palace of the Governors, dimly lit and hushed but for a viewer's occasional gasp, fourteen shelves hold grinning Mayan deities, a 1,500-year-old ceramic incense burner from Guatemala, a brawny stone man from Costa Rica dating from about A.D. 900, grasping an ax in one hand and a trophy head in the other. There's a 1,300-year-old ceramic man from the Remojadas culture of Mexico, standing proudly with the flayed skin of a woman draped over his shoulders and enigmatically holding out his hand. Nearby stands an Aztec wooden skull mask.

Museums often prattle on about a collector's "singular vision" or "exquisite taste" when they receive a private gift like this. In this case, it's true. Culled from three thousand years of indigenous Latin American civilizations, the seventy-four artifacts on display show an uncommon taste for the violent, the eccentric, and the carnal. To spend an hour looking at this collection is to be drawn into a forbidding world of warriors, growling dogs, and decapitating monsters. Every piece brims with character and vitality; not a single one looks damaged, cracked, or abraded. This collection dazzles.

Four pieces drew the archaeologist's attention. One was a golden monkey's head, the size of a plum, with its eyes delicately formed in minute pieces of shell and turquoise, its mouth stretched open in a scream. Tiny holes in the back of the piece indicated that it would have been worn as a bead in a necklace or pendant. Two other pieces in question were twin ear spools made of gold, turquoise, and shell inlay, both depicting marching Moche warriors holding shields and clubs.

The fourth piece, a semicircular golden rattle, was by far the most incriminating. The rattle (or "bell ornament" as it was called in the museum catalogue) had been hammered and pressed while still fresh out of the furnace by Moche craftsmen to form the backflap's decapitator god, grimacing and brandishing a *tumi* knife in one hand and a man's head in the other. It was a fearsome image, and, in this particular form, one that was uniquely Sipán.

There were at least six other ancient Peruvian pieces on display in the gallery, but only these four bore hallmarks of Period III Moche, of which Sipán was the best-known site. Not a single piece on display gave a specific provenance, archaeological history, or other sign it emerged from any place but a looter's pit, but that was hardly unusual among museums.

The Palace of the Governors clearly had some explaining to do. It was one thing to have private collectors holding looted Sipán items. Here, if the anonymous archaeologist-cum-informant was correct, was a taxpayer-supported museum exhibiting items whose import had been specifically barred by federal law, the 1990 emergency order on Sipán.

In September 1998, Wittman called the FBI office in Santa Fe and spoke with Special Agent Brian Midkiff, who had worked on cases involving violence on Indian reservations and white-collar crime but had little undercover experience. Wittman recounted to him the basic outlines of the case. It seemed that while he was snaring the backflap and while Miami customs investigated who shipped the Sipán waist rattle, an identical treasure from the same site had been on public view in Santa Fe since May.

Wittman sniffed a criminal case, the prime suspects of which would be those who brought the pieces into the United States and sold them to the collector, although it would be the collector who stood to lose his investment, without compensation. The backflap case had consolidated Wittman's reputation as the FBI's specialist in art theft, and the Mendez and Garcia prosecutions had demonstrated how simple it would be under the Clinton MOU to seize and repatriate looted Peruvian artifacts and convict those who trafficked in them. As he drove from the airport in Albuquerque through sagebrush country up to Santa Fe, Wittman thought he might have a few more items to return to Peru soon. He wondered if looters and smugglers were starting to get the message.

"If they were dealing in smuggled goods then, we thought they were probably still doing so," said Midkiff, a man with the soft drawl of an Alabama upbringing who, in his early thirties, had ambitions to make his mark in the agency. "We thought we had a criminal case here."[1]

The Palace of the Governors was built by Indian laborers under Spanish rule around 1610 and, although not much of the original structure survives, it is considered the oldest public building in the United States. A sprawling, low-slung mansion built of timbers, adobe, and stucco, the palace had a tortuous history like few buildings in the country. When the Pueblo Indians revolted against Spanish rule in 1680, settlers took refuge inside its cavernous rooms and courtyards until the Indians starved them out and attacked them as they fled hundreds of miles to the south. Indians warriors and families occupied the palace and turned it into a traditional, indigenous settlement, a living throwback to a century before, until the Spaniards marched back into New Mexico and reconquered it thirteen years later. All traces of the Indian occupancy were painted over and the palace was turned back into the colony's executive residence and office, first under the flag of Spain, then Mexico, the Confederacy (for five days in 1861), and the United States until 1909, when the territorial legislature voted to convert the building into a history museum. That year, workers digging a basement beneath the palace to install a boiler found large collections of human bones, where the Indians had buried their dead. For days, workers turned up one skeleton after another. New Mexicans built their state history museum literally astride the bones of their ancestors.

In this hallowed building Wittman and Midkiff met on September 29 with the director of the museum, Thomas Chávez, a tweedy, earnest man with the nasal twang of a New Mexico native. He greeted the agents in his modestly furnished corner office overlooking the city's adobe rooftops, then bathed in early autumn light. Chávez was a historian, educated at the University of New Mexico, who had written several well-regarded books on Southwestern history. The agents told him that his collection contained artifacts that the FBI believed were looted from a Peruvian tomb, and they wanted to know where they came from. Chávez told them they were from the home of John Bourne, an elderly, reclusive antiquarian who lived in Santa Fe. Neither Chávez nor the museum had any particular background in pre-Columbian art before receiving the Bourne bequest, but Chávez had wanted the museum to emphasize the state's ancient cultural connections with indigenous societies to the south and so accepted it.[2] He pledged his cooperation with the FBI agents on whatever they wanted.[3]

Chávez could not have been entirely surprised by the FBI's interest. Experts in the field of pre-Columbian art had warned him that there might be some "repatriation concerns," as he put it, about several pieces in the collection. Chávez had broached these concerns to Bourne, yet the collector did not seem worried. He had donated one of the four pieces in question, the monkey head, to the museum in 1995 and loaned the rattle and the twin ear spools in May 1998 with the intention of later donating them, Chávez told the agents. The same was true for the rest of the collection: some donated already, others slated to be donated later, a common practice in art museums to maximize the donor's tax benefits. Until Bourne donated or otherwise transferred ownership of the loaned pieces to the museum, they were still formally his property, although in the custody of the museum.[4]

As for the four pieces that interested the FBI, Chávez said Bourne had implied to him, but had not exactly said, that he had inherited them from his father.[5] Chávez did not indicate that he had asked Bourne for any substantiation of this claim, such as a photograph or document. Nonetheless, a perhaps skeptical Chávez told him that if the pieces had entered the country improperly, the museum could be obligated to send them back to Peru.

"I told him, if these pieces are stolen, if they're not legit, they're going back. That was our agreement. A lot of things come in here illegally [to New Mexico]. I mean, we're right on the border," Chavez recalled in an interview in 2002.[6]

Bourne had donated only a small portion of his collection. He had enough, in fact, to fill an entire new wing of the museum, which Chávez hoped to build if the state legislature would approve the financing. "He wants to donate it. He's old, he's alone, he lives by himself, and he doesn't want to get robbed," Chávez said.[7] As often happened, a public museum was to be the ultimate repository of an aging collector's antiquities.

To the FBI agents, Chávez seemed forthcoming. He pointed out that his museum had returned hundreds of items sacred to U.S. Native American groups. Midkiff described Chávez's attitude: "It was like, we'll do whatever we can to repatriate these, we have repatriated many things before to Native American groups, and we'll be willing to do so again this time. He was very cooperative."[8] When the agents asked if they could see the pieces in question, Chávez responded, "Of course. What are you asking me for? It's open to the public."

The agents walked down the stairs to the exhibit hall and saw the pieces. The gallery guide noted blandly that they were from "Northern Peru, A.D. 200–500." Only a trained art historian could say for sure, but Wittman thought they resembled previously seized Sipán pieces. Then he and Midkiff drove to the home of John Gilbert Bourne, collector.

Bourne lived alone in an area of tasteful homes which by local ordinance all had their exteriors done in the warm, chocolate brown color of Southwestern adobe style. Yet instead of the communal jumble of traditional adobe communities in the Southwest, with houses built almost on top of each other, these houses were separated by fences and well-tended lawns and gardens, American suburban style.

When Midkiff and Wittman arrived and rang the bell, Bourne acted surprised to see them and courteously invited them in. He was a tall, white-haired man in his early seventies with the nervous, preoccupied air of one who does not receive many visitors. As the agents stepped into his elegant living room, art and ancient treasures on shelves and tables all around them, Bourne chattered about his youthful exploits in Latin America, how he developed a taste for pre-Hispanic artifacts and how he discovered lost cities in the jungles of Central America.

Wittman asked if they could look around. The agents had no warrant, so everything they did had to be with Bourne's consent. Bourne agreed, and the agents inspected a few more rooms in the house. Wittman didn't see anything that seemed obviously Sipán. The agents then asked Bourne where and when he bought the four Peruvian pieces on exhibit at the Palace of the Governors. He bought all four, he said, in 1987 from a man named Ben Johnson.

So much for inheriting them from his father.

Bourne said Johnson had called him in 1987 and told him he had some interesting pieces from a recently discovered Moche site. Bourne was intrigued. A few days later, two men unknown to Bourne showed up at his house in Los Angeles with the items to sell. Bourne did not remember the names of the two men, if he ever knew them, or was not prepared to tell the FBI. Bourne bought all four pieces in cash, no receipts.[9] In museum documents later he assessed the value of the monkey's head at $120,000, the golden rattle $80,000, and the ear spools $40,000 the pair, figures presumably similar or identical to what he paid.[10]

The next day, Wittman and Midkiff returned to tell Chávez that they were going to remove the four pieces suspected of being from Sipán. Again, Chávez reacted with disarming folksiness. "I asked them, what are you taking them away for? They're not going anywhere, they're in good hands here. But they said, sorry, that's the way it has to be," recalled Chávez.[11]

With the FBI agents present, museum staff took the pieces from public view, trussed them up in tissue paper, and handed them over to Midkiff, who took them to the FBI vault in Albuquerque, where evidence seized in criminal proceedings in New Mexico and worth more than $5,000 is kept.

Tellingly, the FBI cited not the Customs code of 1990 for seizing the pieces but the National Stolen Property Act, a criminal statute, and this, to the consternation of the museum, was what appeared in the press the next day. Bourne's statement that he had bought the pieces in 1987 meant that the 1990 code could not apply because it was not retroactive. They had, however, entered the United States after the precedent set by the McClain ruling of 1979, in which a dealer was convicted under NSPA for dealing in pieces that had been smuggled out of Mexico in violation of that country's laws declaring state ownership over archaeological assets. The dismissal of the civil case against Ben Johnson in 1989–90 had undermined the applicability of that precedent to Peru because the judge in the case deemed that Peru, unlike Mexico, had not adequately established the state's ownership over its ancient riches. Although an appeals judge later ruled that the McClain precedent might indeed be valid in Peru's case, the judge let the dismissal stand because of supposed doubts about the origin of the pieces.

What this all added up to was a difficult, complex case that, if prosecuted at all, would have to rely on some creaky and unreliable legal precedents set well before the 1990s crop of bilateral U.S.-Peruvian accords. It might have been unethical for the museum to receive looted property, but it would be difficult to prove it was illegal. Still, with Sipán's notoriety, Bourne would have had a tough time selling the pieces. What he owned, and what he gave the museum, was not so much pre-Hispanic artifacts as a legal hot potato. Wittman had seen cases like this before, of collectors unloading legally dodgy pieces on obtuse museums.

"What else are you going to do with it? Sell it? If you donate, you get a tax deduction, and then it's the museum's problem," he said.[12] With this in mind, Wittman thought, there was a decent chance the museum would voluntarily repatriate the pieces to Peru and save itself some bad publicity and possibly a trial. Chávez's statements to the press suggested he was tilting in that direction. He was cooperating with the FBI, and the Museum of New Mexico system had been returning culturally sensitive pre-Columbian objects to U.S. Native American groups for over a decade, as Chávez continually pointed out. What Chávez did not always add, however, was that the museum was *required* under the federal Native American Graves Protection and Repatriation Act of 1990 to return most skeletal remains, funerary items, and culturally significant goods to tribes that formally request them. The law did not apply to sacred or sensitive items claimed by indigenous groups outside the United States. Yet of all museums that could be accused of holding plundered pre-Columbian art, this one, with its experience in repatriation, seemed like the best candidate to act ethically and return the loot.

There was another compelling reason why this museum, more than any other, would understand why Peru would want the pieces back. Around 1720, Native American artists working in Santa Fe, possibly in the Palace of the Governors itself, painted two large bison skins with scenes from the recent history and daily life of their community. The paintings have an epic power that is hard to convey in words. One depicts a battle in 1720 between Spanish troops and combined French and Pawnee and Oto Indian forces along the banks of the Platte River in what is now Nebraska, a battle in which the Spaniards were routed and their commander, Pedro de Villasur, killed. The painting shows the Indians mounted on horseback and confidently holding rifles, one of the earliest depictions of them with Western firearms. It shows Villasur in his death throes, lying on his back with blood spilling out of his mouth and onto his red Spanish uniform in startlingly graphic and lifelike tones. Survivors of the battle straggled back to Santa Fe to tell residents what had happened, and this painting is based on their accounts. The second painting, which is in worse condition, shows scenes from Native American family and social gatherings, hunting, and wildlife like jackrabbits, bison, deer, mountain lions. Taken together, the paintings give a vivid sense of the resilience of indigenous traditions while New Mexico was a Spanish colony.

Some time around 1750, the hides fell into the hands of a Swiss Jesuit missionary, Father Philipp von Segesser von Brunegg, who must have recognized their great artistic value because within a few years he had sent them home to Europe. (He shipped a third bison-hide painting as well, but its whereabouts are unknown.) They reached his family in Lucerne and were handed down from generation to generation in the Segesser clan for over two centuries, until the early 1980s, when New Mexico museum officials got wind of the paintings and approached the family to negotiate their return. The Segessers at first demanded $2.5 million but later settled for $400,000, a price well below market value for pieces that were both captivating works of art and invaluable historical documents.

In 1988, after three years of negotiations, the Segesser family of Switzerland returned the two bison skins, which, although they required some restitching and restoration, were in good condition. The Segesser Hide Paintings, as they are known, now occupy their own gallery in the rear of the main courtyard at the Palace of the Governors, the museum's other prize exhibit along with the Bourne collection.

The bison-hides case was a textbook example of the benefits of repatriation. It restored to the people of New Mexico a piece of their cultural heritage, and no one questioned the hides' importance to that heritage merely because New Mexico didn't know of their existence before 1980. No one scorned the New Mexican claim as "cultural nationalism." It took an important work of art out of a private setting, where it could be appreciated by a few, and put it into a public setting, where it can be appreciated by everybody, especially those who might derive from it pride in the achievements of their ancestors. Could people in Switzerland fully appreciate the value of bison hides cut by Native Americans and then painted, with extraordinary attention to accuracy and detail, to bear witness to a decisive moment in their history? Of course they could, but it was also reasonable to expect that New Mexicans would find an emotional resonance in the pieces that might escape people elsewhere.

Chávez himself used such arguments before the New Mexico legislature to persuade it to allocate money to buy the skins from the Segessers. He viewed regaining the hides as one of the triumphs of his twenty-one years as chief of the museum.[13] Like Melina Mercouri weeping for the return of the Elgin Marbles, or the Hungarians seeking the return of the Crown of St. Stephen as an assertion of their independence while under Soviet occupation, Chávez sought to have an essential document in the history and culture of his people returned to its place of origin. And he had won. With that kind of background in repatriation, both as practitioners and beneficiaries, surely the Palace of the Governors could understand the emotional freight of Peru's pleas and return artifacts pillaged from a site that had become a point of pride to Peruvians like none other.

"We knew where they came from and what they were," Chávez was quoted as saying in the *Santa Fe New Mexican*.[14] The FBI could hardly have found a more complaisant subject. Chávez wrote that he welcomed the confiscation, or "retention," as the FBI called it publicly. "I, as the director of the Palace of the Governors, consider this action the proper thing to do and I am pleased to be a part of this process."[15]

It looked like all four pieces might soon go the way of the Philadelphia backflap: on a plane back to Peru, without a penny of compensation for the unwary American buyer. But then Bourne, his lawyer, and the antiquities lobby struck back.

To build a case to present to the local prosecutors, the FBI needed to establish that the pieces were indeed from Sipán and at least go through the motions of gathering criminal evidence. The FBI never ascertained the identity of the two dealers whom Bourne claimed appeared at his house in 1987. The obvious suspects would have been Swetnam and Kelly, the original Sipán smugglers, but they were believed to be no longer in the business and were apparently never contacted.

Proving the pieces were from Sipán would not be so simple. It is usually impossible to "prove" that an artifact has been looted from a particular grave. A looter breaks into a tomb, he grabs the first valuable thing he sees, he sells it. No one else alive has ever seen the tomb, so how could anyone except the looter know where the loot came from? This reality has been the defense of professional pillagers and collectors for generations. The ransacking of standing monuments, such as temples and churches, is easier to prove because there will be witnesses or photographs showing what stood there before. But pieces from underground sites comprise the vast majority of ancient artifacts in American museums and private collections today precisely because it is so difficult to prove that they were excavated improperly or illegally.

Sipán, however, was no ordinary case of pillage. Its contents were so distinctive and so unlike anything ever found that provenance could be proven by a kind of comparative art history. Did the pieces in Santa Fe match pieces seized by Peruvian police or excavated later by archaeologists at the same site? To answer that question, the FBI needed the expert opinion of the man who excavated Sipán. They needed Walter Alva.

In less than a year, Alva had left his family in the tranquil town of Lambayeque four times to fly to the United States to identify or receive confiscated Sipán art from the Americans. The FBI and U.S. Customs were clearly on some kind of roll, and something was also afoot in the antiquities market. The Sipán racket had crept out from behind the dark veil that had covered it since the well-publicized trials in Los Angeles and the executive order of 1990, now with a different cast of dealers and much higher prices. The seizures of the Chavín headdress, the backflap, the Sotheby's necklaces, and the Miami crate, and now the public display of a looted Sipán rattle in New Mexico, all suggested that people had concluded the controversy had blown over and that they could resume business as before.

Although he was delighted to bring these seized pieces home, all the recovery runs to the United States were an unwelcome distraction for Alva, who, with his wife, Susana Meneses, was drawing up plans and rounding up financing for the upcoming Sipán museum. These trips certainly kept Sipán, and him, in the news. As his passport filled up with U.S. immigration stamps and he grew accustomed to having Peruvian TV camera crews and reporters trailing after him, he had become much more than an archaeologist. He was a cultural ambassador, a reluctant advocate for the ancient heritage of his poor and marginalized country against what he perceived as the rapacity of the antiquities trade in the northern colossus. It was a role that inspired contempt and fear among antiquities dealers, and envy among more than a few cultural figures back home.

The FBI invited Alva in his role as Sipán's chief archaeologist to come to New Mexico and offer his opinion on whether the pieces came from the site. The Peruvian government officially designated him as its envoy in the matter.[16] Apart from the legal issues, Alva and Chávez had a lot in common. Both were provincial museum directors from academic backgrounds, running small but prestigious public institutions. There could be a gentlemen's agreement to hand over the pieces, perhaps after a lengthy, face-saving loan to the New Mexico museum. Alva might even give a public talk on the Sipán excavation and turn his visit into a cultural event. The whole thing could be done, like much business in the museum world, with a handshake and a wink, clearing the decks to allow the FBI to pursue the leads given to them by Bourne.

Before leaving, Alva talked on the telephone with Chávez about their impending meeting.

"I was confident we could reach an agreement for the return of the pieces quietly, like gentlemen, without harming the image of the museum," Alva said three years later. "No one likes to be accused publicly of showing stolen property."[17]

When Alva arrived in Santa Fe in mid-October, he found that Chávez had suddenly soured. According to Alva, who was staying at a hotel a few blocks from the museum, Chávez at first refused to take Alva's phone calls and when he finally did, he told Alva he was too busy to meet him and bluntly told him he had no intention of returning the pieces.[18] No matter what he had said on the phone earlier, Chávez now resented the archaeologist's presence in Santa Fe, which he felt was aimed at pressuring him into doing the FBI's bidding. He was incensed by the FBI's snooping around and the way the whole controversy had played out in the press, where he thought the coverage suggested his museum had been duped into receiving stolen goods.[19]

Bourne and Chávez had heard about the Sotheby's case in 1994 and how the auction house was cudgeled by the Peruvian and U.S. governments into returning two necklaces that Alva asserted were from Sipán.[20] Determined to prevent another slide like that, Bourne hired the same New York lawyer, Carl Soller, who had represented the phantom Swiss company Transrover that was supposed to receive the Miami crate. Bourne was footing the legal bill to hold on to all four pieces,[21] and if Alva thought he was going to come to Santa Fe and take whatever artifacts struck his fancy with the FBI's blessing, Bourne was going to teach him a lesson.

Midkiff meanwhile had checked the pieces out of the FBI vault so that Alva could inspect them. Alva had already decided that the golden rattle was unquestionably from the looted tomb on the basis of photographs. In his view, to deny the rattle was from Sipán would be like denying that the jewels of Tutankhamen were from Egypt. In an affidavit to the FBI, he wrote that such rattles were "exclusively originating from the tombs of Sipán. There is absolute assurance that this ornament originated from the tombs, and was removed between January and February [1987] by looters."[22]

Like the backflap, the rattle was made of gold alloyed with small amounts of copper to lower its melting point during the forging process and give it durability once finished. The endlessly inventive Moche devised lost-wax, electroplating, and welding techniques, pushing the working of metal to its limits,[23] but the gold Sipán rattles would have been manufactured through a somewhat simpler method. Artisans placed a hot, freshly forged ingot onto a mold and then hammered it to conform to the mold. If the ingot went hard during the hammering, the craftsmen would heat it some more to soften it and then slide it back on the mold for more hammering, a process known as annealing. The ingots would have been forged in a small furnace stoked by men sitting around it and blowing through long, copper tubes, for the Moche did not use bellows.[24]

All ten rattles would have been made on the same mold, probably in quick succession because the mold, like any stencil, would deteriorate over time. Once hammered into shape, the rattles were folded in half to give them the semicircular form that allowed them to hang over the user's waist string. They were made as indivisible, identical parts of a whole, at the same time and by the same goldsmiths, and all buried together with the Sipán monarch in his tomb about A.D. 250, where they remained until it was ransacked in 1987.[25]

As he and Midkiff looked over the pieces, Alva could barely believe the coincidence of finding two of the looted rattles in the same year. He had now accounted for six—three with Poli, one seized in Miami and now in Peru, one with the Chilean millionaire Carlos Cardoen, and now another. This suggested strongly that the tomb struck by the Bernal brothers had originally contained a set of ten golden rattles, the same number as that with the Old Lord of Sipán, the elderly Moche ruler buried at the bottom of the pyramid whose tomb Alva and Chero had excavated in 1989. Some of the finest indigenous American art ever found came out of that tomb, and it saddened and amazed Alva to think what might have been lost in the looted tomb a few meters above it. The pieces seized in Philadelphia, Miami, and now Santa Fe were adding evidence that the looted tomb had more in common stylistically with the tomb of the Old Lord of Sipán than with the later Lord of Sipán's. Alva already knew that whoever had been buried in the looted tomb had been a man of unrivaled power and wealth. What he believed he was seeing now was a clear, artistic continuum from one generation in a Moche dynasty to the next.[26]

This also meant that there were probably four more golden rattles from the looted tomb out there somewhere, Alva thought. Maybe they were stashed away in a some collector's china closet, maybe they had been destroyed or lost in shipment. They might even be still buried under Ernil Bernal's chicken coop.

Next Alva looked at the ear spools. They might have been from Sipán but, careful not to overreach, he told the FBI that, as a field archaeologist, he was not completely sure and would need to consult with other experts in Moche iconography. Although he did not tell the FBI at the time, he felt the ear spools had been partly "reconstructed" by art forgers, with the decorative panels made of a mix of authentic and modern materials.[27] Plenty of workshops in Peru performed this kind of embellishment. The style of the ear spools hinted that they were made at the time of the Sipán burials, with the spade-shaped war clubs carried by the tiny warriors especially reminiscent of Sipán. Similar pieces had been excavated at the site, but not identical ones. The evidence of Sipán provenance here was essentially circumstantial; the pieces had been sold by Sipán dealer Johnson at about the time when Sipán pieces were entering the market, according to Bourne's recollection. Alva abandoned any hope of regaining the ear spools, telling an interviewer there was "no exact proof that they are from the tomb because the archaeologists didn't see these items."[28]

Alva had no doubt that the screaming monkey head had been looted from a Moche site and smuggled out of Peru. It was an unforgettable image, a masterwork of Moche metallurgy, and no archaeologist had ever excavated anything remotely like it.

Yet it was not unique, and Alva knew it. Similar monkey heads, no doubt part of the same necklace, had been circulating in affluent circles in Peru since about 1990 and were assumed by dealers to be looted from La Mina. One was said to have passed through Apesteguia's hands. The now-defunct American magazine *Connoisseur* ran a photograph of a gold monkey head in 1990, along with several Sipán pieces from the Bernal brothers' stash including peanut beads, disc-shaped beads similar to the ones seized at Sotheby's, and a feline mask. All the pieces looked to be in horrendous condition—scratched, scrubbed, corroded sometimes almost beyond recognition. The magazine, whose editor at the time was former Met director Thomas Hoving, ran the pictures with a fanciful-sounding account written by a Peruvian photographer who claimed that he had bumped into Ernil Bernal in Chiclayo a few days after the looting of the tomb and that the master looter had gamely invited him to photograph everything they found.[29] The photographer, Heinz Plenge, did indeed know Bernal, but Alva believed the pictures were taken at the home of Apesteguía or other collectors after Bernal's death; Plenge's story would have allowed the collectors to stay discreetly in the background, and Bernal wasn't around to contradict it.[30]

Photographs of two monkey heads from the same series appeared soon after in a glossy, coffee-table book published in Lima and edited by a renowned collector and scion of one of Lima's most prominent families, José Antonio de Lavalle, a close friend of Apesteguía.[31] The book contained appreciative essays on the Moche by Alva himself, as well as by Donnan and New York art dealer André Emmerich, among others.[32]

Thus by the time he arrived in Santa Fe, Alva had had long exposure to the monkey heads of La Mina and knew they had circulated among the elite of Moche art collectors for nearly a decade. He must have known they did not come from the Sipán tomb. Why, then, did he say in his FBI affidavit that they were "with almost absolute certainty" from Sipán?[33]

The answer to that question was that the 1990 U.S. Customs order did not bar the importation of objects merely from Sipán and was never intended to apply to objects only from that site. Rather, it covered an amorphous "Sipán Archaeological Region," the precise boundaries of which were never made public, if they existed at all. The reason for extending protection to a wider region in the vicinity of Sipán was to cool the explosion of looting that had enveloped the north coast following the Bernals' discovery, much as the El Salvador agreement applied to a Cara Sucia Archaeological Region that actually covered eight separate archaeological sites, all under attack from looters, over an area covering sixty-six square miles.[34] It would seem obvious that La Mina should be included in the Sipán Archaeological Region. Less than forty miles away from Sipán as the crow flies, La Mina dated from precisely the same period as Sipán, closely resembled it in style, and was looted only a year later. As repositories of Moche art, they were born and died at almost the exact same moments in history. If the designation of an archaeological region, as opposed to a single site, had any meaning at all, then it would have to apply to La Mina.

In light of this, Alva thought the case for the return of the rattle and the monkey's head would be self-evident. His case was undermined from an unexpected quarter: Christopher Donnan.

The UCLA professor had a long and complicated association with Sipán. In 1986 he had fought off armed bandits with a .38 pistol as they tried to overrun his dig site near Jequetepeque, an episode that increased his aura of fearless dedication and provoked inevitable comparisons to Indiana Jones, which he professed to dislike.[35] He earned Alva's undying friendship and appreciation by coming up with money for the Sipán excavation during its first chaotic months and shepherding through the National Geographic Society two grants worth a combined $92,000, which kept the project alive. At the time, Donnan had been excavating his own site at Pacatnamú, south of Sipán, and drove up now and then in his pickup truck to see Alva's progress. He happened to be present at key moments, including the discovery of the Lord of Sipán's coffin. Donnan was the author of several brilliant books on the Moche world and the acknowledged expert on its iconography, and both Alva and the Sipán project gained great stature in his reflected glow.

Yet Donnan's close ties to collectors had brought him much criticism. Not many of his colleagues would say so on the record, but many felt his single-minded dedication to cataloguing Moche art in private collections, whatever the circumstances of its removal from the ground, gave him a certain tone-deafness to the ethical problem of collaborating with loot buyers. He made no secret of his visits to the homes of collectors to photograph their holdings for the UCLA archive of Moche art. He made no financial gain from these visits, but the collectors did. Donnan's attention raised the value of the artifacts, confirmed their authenticity, and, according to some critics, encouraged the acquisition of more. It also undermined the argument that archaeologists gave for opposing looting, that individual items lose their cultural and historical value if assessed outside the matrix from which they emerged.

A stately, distinguished-looking man with white hair, Donnan defended his ties with collectors as a necessary evil and said it was no different from working with museums. "If you don't record the stuff before it gets dispersed all over the planet, then for scholars today and for those in the future, you just compound the loss caused by the looting in the first place," he said. "At the Met, the Munich museum, Art Institute of Chicago, ninety-nine percent of the [pre-Columbian] objects there have no provenance. It's all looted. I don't know why people have this idea that just because it's in a museum, that the object has somehow become sanctified."[36]

Donnan had no illusions about the damage done by looting. "I would say ninety-five percent of the ultimate usefulness of an object is lost when it is looted," he said. "Look at the Vicús culture. I don't think there are more than five pieces from that whole culture that have been excavated archaeologically. The looters got it all. So we either study what looters found or we throw that whole culture down the memory hole. That's the choice."[37]

No collector or dealer was beneath Donnan. At the invitation of Swetnam, Drew, and Poli, he had photographed pieces looted by the Bernal brothers even before the police saw them and later worked so closely with the American smugglers that he became the target of a U.S. Customs probe on suspicion of complicity.[38] No charges were ever brought against the archaeologist but the episode brought him some extremely hostile press. An article in *Art & Antiques* in 1990 called Donnan an "advance man" for the smugglers and recounted how he showed slides of the Sipán loot to a shocked audience at the Institute for Andean Studies in Berkeley.

"It was like being in a porno theater," one archaeologist was quoted as saying. "You heard panting from all sides."[39]

It was Donnan's enthusiastic confirmation of the authenticity of the backflap that first set the FBI on the hunt for the piece. His standing among U.S. law enforcement as an identifier of Moche loot was unrivaled. His support for Alva's position on the New Mexico artifacts would have greatly helped his efforts at their recovery.

Nonetheless, according to museum director Chávez, Donnan expressed in writing his view that the monkey head was not from Sipán and that Sipán was notable for its *lack* of monkey imagery.[40] Strictly speaking, this was true. Donnan had seen about five similar monkey heads in private collections in the past, and he believed them to be from La Mina.[41] Neither Samuel Bernal nor Poli remembered seeing any monkey imagery from the Sipán tomb, either. But Donnan's opinion rested on a strictly literal and narrow definition of what was meant by Sipán, much narrower than the definition taken by the U.S. government in its 1990 Customs code. It was the kind of technicality that one would expect from a collector, not an archaeologist.

The question remained as to why Bourne told the FBI he had bought an artifact in 1987 that, if from La Mina, could not have reached him before 1988. Either his memory was faulty or he wanted the FBI to think he had bought it earlier than he actually had.

Nothing else in the Bourne collection interested Alva. When he saw it at the Palace of the Governors, he was struck by what the gallery guide described as a gold Chimú mask. It may well have been gold, but he was sure it was a modern fake.[42]

The stakes were growing higher for the museum. A story in the *Santa Fe New Mexican* quoted a source inside the Museum of New Mexico as saying the seizure could affect the museum's professional accreditation and ability to win grants. This brought a sharp response from Ed Able, president of the Washington-based American Association of Museums (AAM), who called the comments "irresponsible and inaccurate."[43] Chávez also wrote the newspaper to denounce the "ill-spirited" museum official whose "anonymous words . . . smack of character and institutional assassination."[44]

Alva left message after message for Chávez, but the director still refused to return his calls. The two FBI men assumed he was under pressure from the wealthy donor-collector Bourne not to yield. Alva walked the streets of Santa Fe, his boredom relieved only by an outing with Midkiff to see Indian cave dwellings at Bandelier National Monument in the piney hills outside town. Alva waited in vain for Chávez to discuss the confiscated pieces with him, stewing at what he felt was a crude affront.

It was clear by now that there would be no gentlemen's agreement. But there was a gentleman: Midkiff, who suggested a dinner for the two museum directors at a Santa Fe restaurant at which he hoped Chávez would at least agree to shake Alva's hand. Alva had had enough and was leaving the next day, so this was the last chance. Chávez agreed and chose the restaurant, Jack's, on the third floor of a modern building a few blocks from the central square.

The evening was an almost comical fiasco. Chávez says he and his wife arrived at the restaurant to find Alva, Wittman, Midkiff, and their translator, who was Midkiff's secretary, already eating. Feeling slighted, they went to another table and stayed there. Midkiff says Chávez, his wife, and two of their friends whom he did not recognize were already seated at the restaurant when the Alva group arrived. He says he went over and invited Chávez and his group to dine with Alva, but Chávez refused. The two parties dined at separate tables, glaring at each other across the dining room like feuding clans.

After dinner, the agents managed to get Chávez and Alva to agree to meet at a bar across the street. Chávez went there with his group, but by the time Alva and his group finished their meal, the archaeologist was so incensed by Chávez's snub that he refused to go in. So Wittman and Midkiff went into the bar and told Chávez that Alva was outside, that he was leaving the next day, and that he would like to speak with Chávez. The museum director emerged from the bar, and there on the sidewalk, they at last shook hands and talked alone in Spanish.

Chávez told Alva he would not return the pieces because he had seen no proof they were looted.

"And why should I give them to you anyway? How do I know you are who you say you are?"

Alva said he represented the government of Peru and had the documents issued in Lima to prove it, had been invited to Santa Fe by the FBI, and that the pieces had no business being in his museum. "And if that's not good enough for you, fine, don't give them to me," Alva said. "I'm asking you to agree to send them back later because they were stolen from the Peruvian people."

At the mention of the word *stolen*, Chávez spread out his arms and legs as if preparing to be frisked, as if Alva were accusing him of receiving hot property. At first mystified by the gesture, Alva then laughed at the ridiculousness of it. Chávez said he felt intimidated by the presence of the FBI agents, and by then his wife had emerged from the bar and tried to calm them down, as if these two middle-aged men might be about to brawl.

With their conversation getting more and more heated, they finally turned and walked away from each other, fuming.[45] It was now a bitterly personal standoff between two men, two museums, and two cultures. That evening, accompanied by Midkiff and Wittman, who were startled by the fury of the usually mild-mannered archaeologist, Alva walked down the street to the offices of the *Santa Fe New Mexican* to tell the reporter who had been following the controversy, Hollis Walker, that the Palace of the Governors had become a repository of stolen property. The rattle and the monkey head were both looted from Moche tombs in Sipán and "they belong in their place of origin," he said.[46]

Midkiff knew this would destroy any possibility, if there was any left, that the museum would ever cooperate in returning the pieces. The battle between the bearded Peruvian and the local museum had become the talk of Santa Fe. But now it was war, and Midkiff thought Alva might regret this particular move.

"It was his decision to go to the press," said Midkiff. He understood

Alva's feelings, though. "It was like Chávez didn't even want to sit with him, like he wanted to make some kind of statement. It was a strange evening and very, very awkward."[47]

The story came out under the headline: "Archaeologist: Museum Items Were Stolen." Chávez was furious. Three and a half years later, he still fumed at what he perceived as Alva's indiscretion.

"Alva wanted to do a reverse looting," said Chávez. "It was pretty clear he just wanted these things for his own museum. He had a vested interest in bringing those things home with him and I had a vested interest in keeping them here, and what I wanted was a neutral person who could say whether these things were from Sipán. Alva was not that neutral person."

In his view, Alva and the FBI had formed an alliance to browbeat him publicly into acting against the best interests of his museum. "If they wanted to handle this properly, what are they doing giving newspaper interviews? I don't know why they ran to the papers but I didn't like it."[48]

Alva flew back to Peru the next day. The four pieces were still in the FBI vault and he despaired of ever seeing them in Peru. Friends and associates said he considered Santa Fe to be the most unpleasant and humiliating experience of his long career.

"What that museum did was launder stolen property," said Alva. "It was clear Chávez was not going to help. He was on the side of the collector, not on the side of a country that has been stripped of its patrimony. I was outraged and surprised that this could happen in the United States."[49]

He had one small consolation, again courtesy of the FBI. In the first week of December 1998, the agency restituted the golden Chavín headdress to the Peruvian embassy in Washington, four years after Bazin bought it from the Miami gang, and the embassy sent it to Alva at the Brüning Museum in Lambayeque.[50] Ironically, the headdress had entered the United States at about the same time as Bourne's set of treasures, in the late 1980s or 1990. The only difference, from Alva's point of view, was that one had been culled from its smugglers while the other had been laundered through the museum system. If the ex-convict Becker had not happened to bring Bazin into the deal, that headdress, too, might also have wound up in a museum behind an insurmountable barrier of glass, lobbyists, and lawyers.

Back in Peru, Alva wrote a letter addressed coldly to "Doctor Chávez" and stating with dignity and eloquence his case for the restitution of the pieces:

We understand that the prestigious museum you direct has fulfilled its mission by receiving and displaying these objects that were donated or lent by a local collector, who probably bought them in good faith in the

United States. Bearing in mind the importance of these archaeological pieces for our cultural heritage, and current international agreements, I would ask you to accept our request for the formal return of these works to our country.

He had modified his original stance that the monkey head probably originated from the Sipán tomb:

The ritual rattle with the image of a Mochica deity known as Ai-Apaec possesses a style that is unmistakably and exclusively that of Sipán. An identical piece was seized by Customs in Miami. The monkey head also bears the style of other objects from the tomb, and we have data on its provenance, among them a photograph published some years ago. This evidence and a review of archaeological literature indicate that prior to the looting of Sipán, no similar materials had been found.[51]

As if to underscore that he had tangled with powerful interests, Alva received a reply to his letter not from Chávez but from the office of the Attorney General of New Mexico, which represented the museum in its efforts to sway the federal prosecutor's office from filing suit against the museum. Assistant Attorney General Sally Malavé wrote to the archaeologist that the rattle still belonged to Bourne, so the state had nothing to say on that matter (despite Chávez's repeated public statements that the collector planned to donate the rattle to the museum). As for the monkey's head:

Neither Dr. Alva nor the FBI has provided to the Museum any plausible evidence that the seized monkey head is from Sipán . . .

Based on the current information available, there is no way to know with any degree of certainty that the monkey head is or is not from Sipán.

As trustee over objects of historical, archaeological, and ethnological interest to the people of New Mexico, the Museum would be remiss to release the monkey head to Dr. Alva on behalf of the government of Peru without there having been presented sufficient evidence that the monkey head is without question from the Moche culture ruins at Sipán.[52]

The Peruvian government meanwhile added its voice. Its embassy in Washington wrote to Assistant U.S. Attorney Paula Burnett in Albuquerque, calling the return of Sipán artifacts "a national priority for the government of Peru" and the pending repatriation of the Santa Fe pieces "an important test of the resolve and efficiency of law enforcement agencies and their international efforts to fight the illegal traffic in stolen cultural property."[53] The letter was an obviously heartfelt reaffirmation of Peruvian feeling but, coming as it did two months after Alva's retreat from Santa Fe, rather tardy.

Under pressure from all sides, Burnett seemed to be looking for a compromise. Again, the stumbling block was the monkey's head. She sent Bourne's lawyer, Soller, a copy of Alva's affidavit on the origin of the pieces and asked "whether you agree that there is sufficient basis to return the rattle to Peru."[54]

Soller did not. He instead denounced the seizure of the pieces in the same tone of aggrieved impatience as he had in the Miami case. Writing to Burnett, he charged that the FBI had "improperly and illegally removed these items" and said the case had "reached the point where we now demand that you return the pieces to the location from which they were taken"[55]—by which he meant the museum, not Peru. The fact that the pieces were exported without the knowledge of Peruvian authorities reinforced the collector's claim to the pieces, not weakened it, Soller implied. "Since there is no one who has knowledge of the time the pieces left Peru nor knowledge of the time the goods were imported into the United States, the Government cannot claim that there was any violative activity relating to any of the three items," he wrote.[56] No one could prove the pieces entered the United States after 1990, so whether they were from Sipán or not was irrelevant, Soller said.[57]

By this argument, Soller would seem to be acknowledging that the pieces might have been illegally removed from Peru, but that this was Peru's problem, not the United States'. Frederick Schultz's lawyers would try a similar defense two years later, only to see their client convicted in criminal court under the National Stolen Property Act. Also a court in New York was wrestling with a similar case at almost the exact same time as the New Mexico prosecutors. In November 1995, U.S. Customs agents seized a fourth-century B.C. gold libation bowl known as a phiale from the Fifth Avenue apartment of retired financier Michael Steinhardt, who had paid $1.2 million for the piece in 1991. The agents were acting on a request from the Italian government, which alleged that the phiale appeared on the market in the late 1970s, was Italian state property, and had been illegally exported. In a civil forfeiture trial prosecuted by the U.S. Justice Department, a federal judge ruled in November 1997 that Steinhardt's phiale had to go back to Italy. Complicating the case was the fact that Steinhardt's dealer, Robert Haber, was judged to have made false statements on a customs declaration by claiming the piece was from Switzerland (whose laws on export of antiquities are more lenient than Italy's) and was worth $250,000. The AAM, with Ed Able at the helm, led a coalition of museum organizations filing friend-of-the-court briefs in support of Steinhardt. Yet the ruling stuck. Steinhardt appealed all the way to the Supreme Court but never recovered the phiale. It is now in a museum in Sicily.

The Steinhardt ruling sent a chill through the collecting community, and it could have offered the New Mexico prosecutors pointers for winning forfeiture for the Peruvian pieces (although, on Steinhardt's appeal, it was the fact of the false declaration on the customs form, and not Italy's ownership claim, that cost him the phiale). Yet they still viewed the Gray decision in Los Angeles as an insurmountable barrier to the applicability of the National Stolen Property Act in Peru's case. It was as if Peru was beneath the law.

In late 1999, the U.S. Attorney's office in Albuquerque made its decision: it would not prosecute. The pieces would be returned to the museum. For the first time in a major antiquities case since the Gray decision, Peru had lost. In a state where cases of stolen Native American bones and artifacts make front pages and rile public opinion as nowhere else, denying the restitution of pieces such as these must have been an unwelcome task, and the prosecutors' correspondence reflects much ambivalence. Assistant U.S. Attorney Sasha Siemel, who took over the case from Burnett in April 1999, wrote to Chávez that he was letting the museum have the pieces back, but Siemel added:

This decision does not necessarily end the matter: Peruvian expert Dr. Walter Alva has identified origin of the monkey's head as the Sipan site, thereby arguably making them subject to return to Peru, while the museum has experts who assert that the monkey's head is not probably from Sipán, but may be from the La Mina site instead, and therefore arguably not returnable to Peru.[58]

In practice, it did end the matter. An FBI agent retrieved the pieces from the vault and returned them quietly to the Palace of the Governors in January 2000, where they remain on exhibit at this writing.[59]

The rattle is the only known Sipán artifact in the permanent collection of any museum in the world outside Peru. The monkey's head is, to the best of my knowledge, the most recently looted pre-Columbian object with a precise find-spot (La Mina, looted in 1988) in any museum in the United States. As Siemel's letter above suggested, the museum experts' affirmation that the monkey head did not come from Sipán weighed heavily on the decision not to pursue the case. The museum took Donnan's stand as vindication of its refusal to deal with Alva.

"Alva and the FBI came up here making all these accusations, saying this stuff had been stolen from his site. But the curator from UCLA, the guy who did the big exhibit of Sipán, said it wasn't from that site. So if Alva is still insisting they're from Sipán, he's wrong, period," Chávez, candid as ever, said a month after the return of the pieces.[60] "I've got the world's greatest expert on the Moche on my side and I've got the New Mexico Attorney General's office. What else do you want?"[61]

Whether Donnan meant it that way or not, his stand on the monkey's head was construed to mean that he doubted the rattle was from Sipán, as well, although its true origin was well known to both archaeologists. "Oh yeah, I think it's from Sipán," he told me.[62] Donnan had been present at the excavation of similar rattles at Sipán. A photograph of an identical rattle — or perhaps even the same one, it's like trying to tell identical twins apart by photographs — illustrated an article by Donnan himself in 1992 in Lavalle's book, where it was duly attributed to Sipán.[63]

Midkiff remained bitter about how the collector and the museum teamed up, in his view, to prevent stolen property from being returned. It was his first brush with the ways of the antiquities trade. Sitting in jeans and a sweater in the FBI office in Santa Fe, he recollected the case with an air of shattered idealism.

"It almost makes you sick to return something when you know it's wrong. But you present everything to the U.S. attorney's office and then it's their decision," he said. "It's unfortunate that our investigation didn't prove what it needed to, but I think we made a statement that we will investigate these matters."[64]

"We did everything we could. We did a lot to get them [the museum] to do the right thing here," said Wittman.[65]

Peruvian officials at the embassy in Washington and in Lima explored bringing their own civil case against the museum, along the lines of Turkey's suit against the Met over the Lydian Hoard that ended in a settlement. They decided against it because of the great expense to hire counsel, while the MOU had yielded such spectacular results at little cost to Peru. Money spent to battle the antiquities lobby in court might be better spent building roads and schools to combat the poverty that leads young men to loot. As one official in Lima told me, "Everything we have gained in terms of cultural property in the United States has been through the diplomatic channels and the police. The courts lead us nowhere."[66]

John Bourne, the elusive collector, left Santa Fe during the height of the scandal and moved temporarily to California, according to someone familiar with the case. He declined to talk with me but sent me a letter stating his views, with a swipe at the FBI. Its confiscation of the pieces, he wrote, was

based on an allegation by *one* individual. However impressive that individual's credentials might be, the FBI did not deem it necessary to engage or even request advice from any other known expert in the pre-Columbian art and artifacts field to determine whether the allegations had any basis in fact before confiscating and holding them for nearly two years. It was certainly a classic case of FBI presumption of guilt with no factual background to support its premise. It was necessary to expend a very significant sum of money to obtain the release of the items[.] . . . The items would still be in FBI custody had legal advice not been sought in order to refute the specious allegations. After the issues in this matter had been resolved and it was established that the items had not come from the alleged Peruvian site, the local FBI personnel continued to exert pressure on Museum of New Mexico officials to return the item that the Museum owned to Peru. The Museum did not bow to that pressure.[67]

Bourne could take some pride in the fact that he had scored one of the few recent, categorical victories against the cultural retentionists, as people like Alva and Elia were now disparagingly called. A naked attempt to shame a museum into giving up valuable artifacts had been stopped cold. The FBI's "presumption of guilt" had been exposed.

I asked Ed Able of the AAM, which lobbies in Washington for the interests of museums, about the Santa Fe case and got an answer that made me wonder if some museum people hated archaeologists so much that they couldn't even think straight.

"The difference between us and the archaeological researchers is that they would like the piece to be reburied where it was found. They want to rebury those objects in situ. And that's not what museums do," he said. Archaeologists want to rebury objects in the ground? I wasn't sure if he was joking. "By putting these things on exhibit, museums are in a way performing a service," he went on. "If these things remain in private collections, they remain out of sight and the donor countries [Peru, for example] won't know about them. The donor country will never find out if it's never exhibited."[68]

So museums were actually helping to curb the trade in looted objects by acquiring them and putting them on exhibit, so that the source countries could then demand them back. Except that the museums won't give them back.

Chapter 12

THE JAGUAR'S HEAD

UNDER THE TERMS of the 1997 MOU between Peru and the United States, one of the conditions for U.S. help in recovering Peru's looted cultural property was that Peru show good-faith policing efforts within its own borders to control the outflow. Exactly what steps it was supposed to take, and how they would show their progress to the satisfaction of the Americans, was not spelled out. But the agreement would come up for renewal every five years, and if either party thought the other wasn't holding up its end in the fight, it would have the option of canceling the MOU.

The fact that collectors inside Peru were able to buy and collect antiquities at will had always been used by U.S. dealers and collectors to attack the MOU. Their attitude, expressed by their representatives on the advisory committee, was that the Peruvian state was not exercising control over its cultural assets, so why should the Americans? Ironically, with the FBI's success in scoring the backflap, opponents of the MOU had more ammunition to assert that Peru had failed to apply even the most basic controls on the outflow. Smugglers had managed to push the biggest piece of Peruvian gold ever known past airport controls in Lima and onto a plane.

Public statements by U.S. and Canadian officials reflected a growing exasperation with the Peruvians. "We're not able to help source countries control this if they don't have adequate export controls. We need them to help," said one.[1] All front-page news in Peru, the backflap and Miami cases contradicted the image of cool authority and order that Fujimori's quasi-military government was trying to project and exposed the degree to which the venality of airport inspectors contributed to the pillage.

"The MOU has been quite useful, but Peru needs to show that it is taking action on protecting our cultural property. We need to do more than we have been accustomed to doing," said Luis Repetto, who was Fujimori's last director of the Instituto Nacional de Cultura, in 2000.[2] Late in 1999, Repetto got the government to train inspectors at airport X-ray machines to recognize ceramic and metal artifacts in passengers' carry-on luggage. If the image of a *huaco* flickered on their screen, the inspectors were supposed to send the traveler to a desk at the airport that would be staffed twenty-four hours a day by an archaeologist and an art historian. If both agreed the piece was real, they would have the power to confiscate it.

Before my late-night flights to Miami, I often stopped by the INC desk at Lima's international airport to see what they had turned up. They usually had a trinket or two. Once, before a 2 A.M. flight, I found two bright-eyed students from Universidad Mayor de San Marcos who, a few hours earlier, had confiscated an eight hundred-year-old Chimú pot from a departing tourist who said he had no idea it was real.

"He kept saying, 'I paid only thirty soles ($10) for it. How could it be real?' He'd been up in the north in Trujillo, where the real ones are so abundant they're cheaper than the fakes," said one of the students, Juan Carlos Rodríguez. "The first time you get caught, you get a warning. But we take your name, and if you get caught again, you may be fined."

They seem so touchingly out of proportion to the problem, but the airport inspections have actually turned up several hundreds pots and the occasional metal artifact over the years (as well as many fakes that the buyer thought were real). The authentic pieces go to the Museum of the Nation, where most end up gathering dust in the basement, along with thousands of other humble artifacts excavated by archaeologists, seized by police, or left by collectors who tired of them. The defenders of Peru's cultural heritage hope that, with enough seizures, visitors will stop buying authentic trinkets and that Peruvians will stop selling them. It was this sort of death-by-a-thousand-cuts strategy that Repetto and other Peruvians hoped to apply to the antiquities trade.

"We may be catching only a small fraction of what's leaving the country, but before we didn't stop anything," said Repetto, a brisk, imposing man with a background in museum design whose office was on the top floor of a Lima skyscraper housing the Museum of the Nation and the INC. It's an ugly, concrete-and-glass box built as the Ministry of Fisheries in the 1970s, when the Peruvian economy was hauling in revenue from a boom in production of fishmeal, an animal feed. As an export product, fishmeal had declined in the years since, while culture and antiquities, both legal and illicit, had increased in visibility, and in 1990 President García turned the building into the nation's cultural headquarters. Construction of the building had partly obliterated a pre-Hispanic *huaca* that was one of forty-one such ancient burial mounds within the city limits of Lima, Repetto told me matter-of-factly, as if untroubled by the irony. A vestige of the demolished *huaca*, a small mud-brick hump, still stood wedged between a parking lot and a housing development.

Repetto had no illusions about the reach of the MOU. "The big-time shippers send more overland to Bolivia and from there to the United States so the goods will not be seen to be arriving directly from Peru," he said. "It's like drugs; you pressure them on one avenue, they look for another."[3]

Airport X rays cannot detect the current motor of the market—textiles—and smugglers know it. One experienced textile shipper I met in Lima was a Peruvian woman I will call Jacqueline, who came to pick me up one evening in her silver Toyota with tinted windows all around. She wore dark glasses, and as we drove around in her car whose pitch-black interior smelt cloyingly of strawberry fragrance, I couldn't tell how she could see where she was going. When she traveled to the United States, she often carried two or three pre-Columbian textiles at a time wrapped up in jeans and blouses, she told me. She never had problems, from either Peruvian or U.S. inspectors. Once, on a flight to Atlanta with her young son, she began shaking with fear when a Lima airport inspector saw something funny in her carry-on bag and ordered her to open it. She was carrying some Inca weavings inside.

"I was so scared, but when I opened the bag, it turned out they had seen my son's toy gun. That was all! I was so relieved," she said. The weavings arrived safely in Atlanta. They had survived for centuries buried in dry coastal Peru, and unless kept under careful climate controls, they will deteriorate and eventually disintegrate in the moist air of a place like Atlanta.

In January 1999, the Peruvian state initiated its own probe into the backflap crime and issued indictments for the four men implicated by Garcia and Mendez in their statements to the FBI in Philadelphia.[4] Though the investigation, such as it was, has yet to bring a conviction, the testimony by the four offered a sad picture of the casual betrayals, secret deals, and bottomless greed behind the trafficking of Peruvian antiquities.

The testimony was led by investigating judge Hilda Piedra. (In Peru, as in other countries with Napoleonic legal traditions, judges cross-examine witnesses and perform functions that under English common law would be carried out by prosecutors.) She asked Guillermo Elías Huamán under oath if it was true, as Garcia charged, that the ex-policeman was to receive

$5,000 for taking the backflap through airport controls. Elías Huamán replied:

> I have no explanation for why he would say that, and in the papers I have learned that they will get a prison sentence of twenty-five years, and maybe through some trickery, his lawyers have won him some benefit.
>
> PIEDRA: But the information given to us by Denis Garcia has been verified on all counts, so what's your explanation?
>
> ELÍAS HUAMÁN: I don't have an explanation, it's all a lie, and don't think anyone can prove that he gave me some money because I never got a single dollar from Denis Garcia . . .
>
> PIEDRA: What exactly did Garcia's invitation to you consist of?
>
> ELÍAS HUAMÁN: Denis Garcia arrived on the 23rd [of September 1997] and told me a friend of his named Orlando Mendez was coming from Miami and he explained to me who he was . . . that he was the only child of a millionaire, and he [Denis] offered to let me stay in his house in Miami and of course that would include room and board, and he offered me the air ticket, only to me.
>
> PIEDRA: Do you know how much a ticket to Miami costs?
>
> ELÍAS HUAMÁN: About $500.
>
> PIEDRA: As a policeman, didn't you think it strange that someone would offer you a $500 gift?
>
> ELÍAS HUAMÁN: No, because when Denis Garcia came to my house, he always stayed with us and we fed him, sometimes with his wife, and after having him so many times at our house it seemed normal that he would invite me to his. . . . He was my friend, but only so to speak because in light of these events, Denis Garcia is no longer my friend because he harmed me over something that I had nothing to do with, and he did it so they would reduce his sentence from twenty-five years to nine months. He knows everything about my family because I've known him for many years, but he never gave me any money. . . .
>
> PIEDRA: You say you didn't know that Denis Garcia was carrying the backflap on that trip. Why do think he invited you to come along when he happened to be carrying the backflap?
>
> ELÍAS HUAMÁN: I don't know, I don't know why he invited me along, it seemed normal to me after all the times that he and his family came to stay with us. And I can't say more because I can't enter his mind.[5]

Later in his testimony Elías Huamán blurted out that on the same trip he was carrying six ceramic *huacos* in his carry-on bag. During the stopover in Panama, he handed off the pots to a waiting associate.[6] He claimed the pots were modern copies of pre-Columbian vessels, but if so, why make this unprompted confession? Presumably he thought Garcia or Mendez had told the FBI about it, or maybe he thought the FBI had found incriminating artifacts in Garcia's house that might be tied to him.

Juan Carlos Salas, alleged bagman for the backflap's former owner, Ramos Ronceros, tried out various alibis when asked what he was doing in the Doral Court Hotel in New York at the same time that Garcia and Mendez were in the hotel preparing to sell the backflap.

> It's true that I was in the city of New York in that hotel on the day in question, for reasons of tourism. Also I was going to make the most of my time there to get those gentlemen to take me to an interstate company that sold used buses. With regard to what they've said about me, that I was there while they were negotiating the sale of the backflap, I deny it categorically. I was never aware that they were negotiating the sale of that object and the only explanation I can find is that they want to implicate other people to reduce their sentence.

At that, Salas's lawyer interrupted him to remind him of yet another reason, prompting Salas to say:

> Let me add that the reason for my trip to New York was because it was a prize for my youngest daughter for having finished her high school degree and it was her vacation time.[7]

When Peruvian police inspected Salas's home, they found nine authentic pre-Columbian artifacts, a fact that would seem to bolster the idea that Salas and Garcia were cohorts in smuggling. This finding, taken with Elías Huamán's delivery of the *huacos* to Panama and Garcia's history, suggest that the backflap was not the once-off, get-rich-quick scheme that the FBI believed it was but rather the last and grandest operation of an experienced racket. The FBI, which was not aware of the testimony by the Peruvians in the case, knocked down more ducks than it realized.

Salas was asked in his testimony why he introduced Garcia and Ramos Ronceros:

> I introduced him to Garcia because he [Garcia] told me he knew collectors.
>
> PROSECUTOR: In that conversation, what exactly did they talk about?
>
> SALAS: He [Ramos] said he had a very old and priceless piece of gold, they talked about prices, and Garcia said he would come back in fifteen days with the information about his company and also to see about the sale of the piece. . . . That was in 1994.

PROSECUTOR: Why did the backflap transaction take more than two years?

SALAS: Because Garcia couldn't come to an agreement with Ramos Ronceros until 1997.[8]

"The company" he was referring to was, of course, the FBI front company, which in 1994 was represented by Bazin. Salas still did not fully comprehend the extent of the ruse.

An indignant Ramos Ronceros testified on October 19, 1999, barely concealing his contempt for the whole process. He constantly interrupted the judge, contradicted himself, and brazenly recounted how he made sure he had his $100,000 before releasing the backflap.

PROSECUTOR: Wasn't it true that the price you charged Denis Garcia for the piece was $275,000, but that he was able to pay you only $100,000?

RAMOS RONCEROS: The agreed price was $100,000, all paid up front through a bank transfer. . . . I made sure it had been deposited all right. Garcia, Salas and Mendez, who was the one with the money, and yours truly were all there.[9]

He denied having any knowledge that Garcia and Mendez were going to smuggle the backflap out of Peru, an assertion contradicted by Mendez's deposit of $100,000 in Ramos Ronceros's New York bank account. One must wonder whether Ramos Ronceros was relying on his political connections, rather than the coherence of his testimony, to clear his name.

Wittman and Goldman traveled to Lima in October 1999 at the invitation of the Peruvian court for what proved to be a good-natured encounter of clashing legal cultures. In a room with a scribe sitting at an ancient typewriter, Goldman showed the card taken from Mendez's wallet with the amounts of money to be paid to each person and recounted, through a translator, everything Garcia had said about the deals in Lima. Neither got the impression that the Peruvian end of the case was leading anywhere, and for Goldman, with twenty years' experience as a prosecutor, Peruvian standards of evidence seemed so exasperatingly high that he wondered how anybody ever got convicted. "For there to be a case they have to see you do it," he said. "They have to have a physical witness to the crime as it takes place. Even a confession isn't enough."[10]

Their skepticism was partly justified. After the investigative phase of the trial, a state prosecutor formally asked the judge to convict Elías Huamán and Salas to five and four years in prison, respectively, and order them to pay 30,000 soles (about $10,000) each. The prosecutor, Ricardo Saavedra Luján, declined to ask for prison terms for Ramos Ronceros or

Bacigalupo because he deemed they had no knowledge the piece would be exported.[11] Apart from the Bernal brothers, Ramos Ronceros was the only person to earn any cash from the backflap.

The case marked one of the few times when antiquities smuggling in Peru brought judicial penalty—or would have, if the prosecutor's request for prison terms were ever enforced. Four years later, and after the collapse of the Fujimori government, it remained unacted upon in the byzantine halls of Peruvian justice, the case officially still open.

"It was that Cuban dog who accused me, but it's all false. And now they want to try me and throw me in jail with the *terrucos?* No, this isn't justice, this isn't justice," Elías Huamán told me. The *terrucos* are left-wing guerrillas. For a former policeman, that prospect, however remote, must be humiliating.

Goldman and Wittman could not leave Peru without seeing the place that had occupied them for so long. They flew to Chiclayo with Alva, saw the Sipán treasures at the Brüning Museum, and then ventured with Alva to see the *huaca*. Alva, who had not visited the town in more than a year, showed them the cavity where the Lord of Sipán's tomb had been and the spot where the filled-in looters' hole had been, before leading them to the top of the *huaca*. There, rising above the swaying sugarcane plants, they could see the roof of the Bernal homestead.

The backflap case added a furious edge to Alva's protests over the destruction of Peru's heritage. At a symposium in the Peruvian national congress in 2000, attended by many of the country's top cultural figures, its foreign minister, and the president of the congress, Alva lectured them that Peru's archaeological record was disappearing out from under them and that all the police seizures in the United States were making Peru look foolish. He lambasted the prosecutor's office for failing to seek a prison term for Ramos Ronceros, the police for not bothering to investigate the murder of his friend Apesteguía, and the whole Peruvian state for not doing more to protect historical sites from pillage.

"The mafias continue to work at will," he said. "With what moral authority can we ask foreigners to return archaeological pieces when we don't know how to take care of them ourselves, and can't even punish those involved in these cultural crimes?" His voice rising in anger yet tinged with sorrow, he said: "Invasions of archaeological sites go on with impunity. At this rate, we can be sure that within five years we will have lost eighty percent of our surviving patrimony, and all that will be left are the most important monuments that are . . . incorporated into the tourist trade."[12]

In the past twenty years, he estimated, Peru had lost more of its archaeological wealth than in the previous four and a half centuries, the entire period since the Spanish conquest.[13] It had failed to take the most basic step, he said, of asserting beyond all ambiguity and enforcing state ownership of the country's undiscovered archaeological assets. As a result, Peru faced disasters in foreign courts, such as the Los Angeles decision, "where Judge Gray ruled practically in favor of the smugglers and collectors using precisely this weakness in our laws, because we don't define with absolute clarity the ownership of the Peruvian state over its patrimonial assets."[14]

It was a daring and devastating indictment of the indifference of the Lima political elite, who shared the responsibility for allowing the despoiling of Peru's cultural heritage by the Peruvians themselves. He had punctured the hypocrisy and stale nationalism that ran through their arguments.

Yet here and there in the hinterland, something was changing.

One day in November 1996, two men working at a livestock ranch near the village of Leymebamba, on the rainy eastern slopes of the Andes, rested from their chores and sat on a hill by a lake known as Laguna de los Cóndores. Farmers had hacked this part of the ranch out of the cool, montane forest only a few years before, and the men still didn't know all the terrain. They sat chewing coca leaves and gazing across the water at the cliffs on the other side.

They saw something they hadn't noticed before. Tucked into the side of a cliff was a tiny patch of red, like a painted stone. One of the men recognized it as a *chullpa*, an ancient funerary house similar to those built into ledges all over the region by the Chachapoya people who inhabited its canyons and cloud-soaked ridges for five centuries before being subdued by the Incas in the 1470s. *Chullpas* were difficult to reach, and they seldom contained more than mummies, pottery, and simple wooden implements. But that didn't stop these men who earned a few dollars a day. There might be gold and silver inside, they said.

A few days later, they hacked a path through the woods and clambered up the cliff until they found themselves standing at the entrance to a tomb built into the ledge. They went inside and saw about twenty bundles, most of them stacked against the rock face, and a huge array of pots, masks, and wooden objects. They took a few ceramic pots, wrapped them in plastic, and hid them on their way back to the ranch. A week or so later they returned to their lucky find, and again a few days later. They found other ledges nearby, with more mummies, and with each visit they used machetes to chop open the mummies to look for gold or silver. All they found inside were layers upon layers of textiles wrapping the bones of men, women, and children, so they grabbed more objects lying amongst the mummies: pots, idols, wooden figures with big faces like masks and tiny bodies, things they could sell for the equivalent of a few dollars at most.

One day the other ranch hands saw them coming home with long, wooden staffs and rice sacks full of gourds, pots, and wood carvings. Take us to where you found those things or we'll tell Don Julio, the ranch owner, the other workers told them. So the next day, they brought two other ranch hands along, and then a third.

"Every time we cut open a mummy, we would look through it but there was never anything. There were pots and gourds all over the place. We took those," said Miguel Huamán, one of the second group. A nervous, twitching man of nineteen at the time, he watched his mates curse the tattered mummies and throw them over the cliff and into the lake three hundred feet below, shouting "Miserly mummies!"

Don Julio Ullilén, the ranch owner, soon got wind of the pillage and joined in, according to the original looters. But when he realized that the first two looters had made off with the choicest items, he confiscated all their booty that he could find. One of the original looters went to the police to report this theft and was promptly arrested, as were the other four. Ullilén was not arrested or charged, though; he was a powerful and influential landowner.

From that moment on, Laguna de los Cóndores became the site of Peru's hottest rivalry between grave robbers and archaeologists since Sipán. The local office of the Instituto Nacional de Cultura sent historian Peter Lerche with local authorities and police to assess the damage and inventory what was left at the site. But they had no way of giving the remote site permanent protection, as it was a ten-hour ride by horse from the nearest settlement. And by then, word was out. News of the mummies and funerary offerings appeared on front pages of newspapers all over Peru, and hundreds of people from nearby provinces were soon taking buses to Leymebamba and trekking to Laguna de los Cóndores to see the chullpas, and some to loot them. They clambered up the cliff and crowded into the mausoleum, some of them rummaging through the bundles.

When archaeologists Sonia Guillén and Adriana von Hagen reached the chullpas in July and arranged permanent protection, they found a complete mess. Looters had tried unsuccessfully to burn the tombs and everything in them to destroy the evidence, and pieces of textiles, bones, and broken pottery were strewn about. Many of the items inventoried by Lerche were gone. Still, like Alva in Sipán, they realized that, bad as it was, it could have been worse. The bundles had been kicked and thrown about but most were intact, and there were funerary offerings all around the ledges that had escaped looters and the curious.

Slowly the sheer size and importance of Laguna de los Cóndores became clear. This was no Sipán, with its glittering artwork made for the elite, but a place where people of a simple, outlying culture left their dead with the everyday objects they used in life. There were kitchen pots, sandals, tweezers, combs, rope, clothing, cotton slings for hunting, bone flutes for entertainment, and the remains of food offerings, including corncobs and the bones of llamas and guinea pigs, an Andean delicacy served on special occasions today. There were also about thirty *khipus,* knotted-string devices used for recordkeeping, probably the closest thing to writing that Andean cultures devised. *Khipus* were rare. Untold thousands of them were lost or destroyed in the Spanish Conquest and tossed aside as garbage by generations of looters, including the ones who looted these *chullpas.* The wife of the ranch owner had washed one of the largest *khipus* in laundry detergent, bleaching out the colors that are a crucial part of the information conveyed. Yet even with what remained, the site yielded one of the largest collections of *khipus* ever discovered.

Von Hagen and Guillén found a total of 223 funerary bundles, all containing bodies trussed up with rope and textiles, plus the skeletal remains of a further one thousand people laid to rest at seven different ledges on the same cliff. In the whole site, they found only one mummy in its original place, which they could tell was in situ from the impression in the earth below.

The Chachapoyans practiced a kind of open-air embalming. The ledges where they left their ancestors had just the right mix of dryness, sunlight, and airflow to prevent decay of bodies and belongings. After six centuries, they were in remarkably good condition.

"They deliberately chose a site to enhance preservation," said von Hagen. In its day, the cave must have been a busy place, more like a shrine than a cemetery, where people regularly left food, drink, supplies, and household objects for the dead. It might have functioned as a kind of oracle, with relatives talking to the mummies and divining messages back from them. Across the lake, archaeologists found the ruins of a large Chachapoyan town, nicknamed Llaqtacocha ("lake town" in Quechua) by von Hagen, that would have faced straight into the necropolis. The living thus nourished and paid obeisance to their neighbors, the dead.

Thankfully, these looters weren't very savvy about what the antiquities market wanted. Among pieces they spurned were colorful weavings and carved wooden figures with strikingly abstract features, pieces now on display in the museum that Guillén and von Hagen created in Leymebamba. When I visited the museum, they and a team of researchers had brought the mummies to a climate-controlled laboratory and were painstakingly unwrapping about a dozen of them, with the rest due to be X-rayed. Hundreds of bundles, most about the size and shape of a Spanish ham, rested all trussed up in their original rope and textiles on shelves. One revealing detail about their contents was the number and size of bird nets, which the Chachapoyans used to gather feathers for use in ornaments and textiles. One net found with the body of an adolescent boy measured ten by twenty-three feet. The Chachapoyans took huge volumes of birds and may have been the source of many of the gloriously gaudy feathers adorning the Inca regalia that so impressed the Spaniards.[15]

What was really different about Laguna de los Cóndores, however, was what happened to the original looters. They were tried and convicted for the crime of grave robbing in what were believed to be the first convictions of their kind in Peru's history. The five were fined the equivalent of $750 each, about a year's wages, and served short spells in jail.

"If I heard of anybody finding a *chullpa* now, I would tell them to stay away. Don't go near it. Tell the police or tell an archaeologist, but don't listen to your friends who say you'll get rich from the dead. The dead bring only curses," said Miguel Huamán, taking a break from sweeping floors in the museum where Guillén gave him a job. He then launched into the story of his life, how his mother abandoned him and his siblings, how he never went to school and starved as a child, how he bounced from job to job until Ullilén hired him to fix fences and cut wood, all leading to his fateful encounter on the ledge with the dead. A tear slipped down his olive, bony cheek. With the prematurely old look of a man who has been working since a very young age, he's been paying off his fine since February 2001 and expects to be doing so for many years more.

The convictions and the looters' repentance won widespread publicity, but archaeologists had some surprisingly mixed feelings. They would have much rather the onus of the law fell on collectors.

"In this business only the poor get punished. We don't call the rich looters, we call them *collectors*," said Guillén. The department of Amazonas, of which Chachapoyas is the capital, is one of the wildest and most sparsely populated areas of the Peruvian Andes, yet even there archaeologists struggle to keep a step ahead of, or at least not too many steps behind, the looters. One researcher found apparently undisturbed *chullpas* near Chachapoyas but, since he lacked permission from the INC to excavate, could only photograph them. When he returned to the site a few days later, INC permission in hand, looters had found and damaged the site.

"Every time I come to Leymebamba I hear another report about tombs discovered by *huaqueros* somewhere," said von Hagen, who divides her time between an apartment in Lima and the museum in Leymebamba. "There's so much out there, and the INC never does anything about it. What can we do?"[16]

At every level of the illicit antiquities trade, from the remotest valleys of Peru to the galleries of New York, one is constantly struck by the breadth of its impact and the volume of merchandise it moves. No other export industry reaches so deeply and so destructively into so many corners of the world.

There has been no serious attempt that I know of to assess the value of this trade. Estimates in print have ranged from $300 million to $6 billion a year, a spread that reflects more the dispersed nature of the trade and the degree to which it has escaped official scrutiny than any real understanding of its magnitude. To gauge its size, we are left with anecdotes and impressions from the people who work in its shadow—dealers, looters, archaeologists, and increasingly local police departments as they tackle a vast underground trade most of them never knew existed.

In November 1999, a man phoned the New York Police Department's anonymous tip line to say there was something funny in a garage on Pitkin Avenue in Brooklyn. Police thought he was talking about drugs, but when they swept in with bulletproof vests and a search warrant, what they found was not cocaine but a quarter-ton sculpture of a jaguar's head wrapped up in newspaper and packed in a wooden crate. They found some smaller pieces as well, but the stone jaguar head, previously unknown to archaeologists, drew the most attention. It had been freshly hacked from a Mayan tomb, probably near the Pacific coast of Guatemala, according to art historians later consulted by the police. They were intrigued by the sculpture. In contrast to most such pieces showing a jaguar eating a person, it instead depicted a man apparently emerging *from* the maw of the feline.

On the day of the bust, police were unsure of exactly what they had and finally loaded the piece onto the flatbed of a truck and brought it to headquarters in lower Manhattan, where it stood like a hunting trophy in the courtyard while police figured out what to do with it. The family renting the house on Pitkin Avenue convinced police they had never even noticed the crate, and the previous renters had disappeared. No arrests were ever made, and the N.Y.P.D. detective in charge of the case, Rubén Santiago, admitted to me two years later that investigators had drawn a blank. One New York dealer I talked to said the case bore the hallmarks of a deal gone wrong; the garage was probably a drop-off point for the piece on its way to or from nearby Kennedy airport.

Police finally delivered the sculpture, still in its original crate, to the Guatemalan consulate on Park Avenue South. When I went around to see the jaguar head one morning, I was greeted by the consul, María Luz de Zyriek, a pretty, smartly dressed woman with a subdued seriousness who was busily helping immigrant workers fill out their applications for new passports and identity cards. While embassies have the more glamorous job of representing their home country in foreign capitals, Latin American consulates in the United States act more like a city hall for their country's local immigrant community. And in this city hall, De Zyriek had the job of mayor.

"My husband is an American with a Polish name. That's how I got that surname," she told me with an understanding smile, as if Americans always asked her that and she assumed I would, too. We jostled past the crowds of passport seekers and entered what had once been a reception room, with a plush wine-red carpet and a perfectly draped blue-and-white flag of Guatemala, but which had been converted into a loot room. On shelves and tables all around, there were close to one hundred pre-Columbian vases, bowls, and figurines, and a large and expensive-looking stone stele carved with what looked like Mayan hieroglyphs. Beneath a window in the back of the room, sitting in its crate of wooden slats like a caged zoo animal, was the stone jaguar head. It was badly eroded and looked like it had been chopped off about halfway down the jaguar's torso. Caught in its toothy jaws, a person emerged headfirst with outstretched arms while screaming in agony or liberation or perhaps transformation, as if something were struggling to be born.

I looked around at the other artifacts in amazement, ran my eyes up and down the stele, and asked the consul where all these things had come from.

"They're pieces the police dropped off, most of them," she said. "We get them quite often. Some others I had to go pick up myself after they had been confiscated. We've been working with the police to get them to recognize Guatemalan artifacts and now whenever they find something they bring it to the consulate. Every so often we ship them back to the archaeology museum in Guatemala." How long since the last shipment? "Oh, a few months." There were pieces seized by police in New Jersey, Ohio, and all over New York, among other places, she told me. Once, she had to take a nine-hour train ride to the Canadian border to retrieve some Mayan artifacts that had been seized in Quebec. The Canadians insisted on personally handing over the pieces to a representative of the Guatemalan government, and, as the unofficial custodian-general of Guatemalan loot, she was the one sent to receive them.

"I had to spend the night there, and then it was nine hours back the next day," she said. "I had them all carefully wrapped up, like babies. These things break so easily."[17]

De Zyriek still had not sent the jaguar home with the other waves of artifacts because its size and weight made it too expensive to ship and insure. The consulate had tried to interest some American museums in exhibiting the head, possibly as a way of highlighting the damage caused by the illicit antiquities trade. None were interested. In December 2001, after two years in red-plush exile in New York, the jaguar head finally went home to Guatemala's central morgue of captured loot, the National Museum of Archaeology, where it is known as *la cabeza de jaguar de Brooklyn*. The antiquities trade had erased its true provenance and given it a new one: Brooklyn.

"We don't know exactly where it's from and we may never know, although we have specialists who will try to find out," Fernando Paniagua, director of Guatemala's Registry of Cultural Assets, told me. "We had never heard of this piece until it appeared in Brooklyn."[18]

I should not have been so surprised to see all those artifacts in the consulate. The basements and back rooms of diplomatic legations of other source countries fill up periodically with confiscated loot. The Peruvian embassy in Washington has held up to three hundred looted artifacts at one time before their repatriation to Lima, according to a diplomat who worked there. The embassy of Honduras received a single load of 279 seized and surrendered artifacts in September 2003,[19] and even Cara Sucia, the Salvadoran site that was the subject of the first U.S. loot import restriction, had a comeback of sorts when a routine customs check in San Francisco turned up forty artifacts from that site and nearby ruins in 2000. Twenty-six Mayan stone and ceramic pieces worth some $165,000, seized in Miami in 1998 but not returned because their shippers began litigation to keep them, were sitting in a U.S. Customs warehouse beneath the World Trade Center in New York on September 11, 2001. They survived the attacks intact and were finally returned to the Guatemalans in 2003. The list goes on and on. Pre-Columbian pieces have been disproportionately represented in seizures because of the plethora of bilateral deals and because they usually arrive in the United States straight from the source country. Treasures from Italy, Greece, and Turkey, for example, are more likely to sojourn in a European laundering point for a few months or years before continuing on to the United States, making their illegal origin that much more difficult to prove.

All ripped out of archaeological sites, these pieces were found by authorities not looking for them, looking for something else, or acting on a lucky, anonymous tip. We can only imagine the volume of what *is* getting through, but it must be staggering.

Why are these pieces repatriated, but not the Mayan vases at the Museum of Fine Arts, Boston? The simple answer would be that the vases entered this country before the two governments signed a bilateral agreement banning their import. The MFA got them in before the bell.[20] Even if that is true—and the MFA has yet to make public any documents showing it is—one need not be a cultural property fanatic to see the disingenuousness of the argument.

To the advocates of Guatemala's cultural heritage, American art museums have acted like high-class fencing operations. Both the vases and the jaguar head are Mayan artifacts, all looted and shipped illegally out of Guatemala. If the vases had been seized in Brooklyn instead of the jaguar head, they would surely have gone to María Luz de Zyriek's reception room and back to a museum in Guatemala, and then somewhere a middleman who is paying young men to destroy Mayan sites would get the message, however belatedly and indirectly, that it does not pay to deal in plunder anymore. Instead, the message that daily finds its way down the long chain of smugglers and pillagers to Robin and his looting colleagues all over Latin America is that the better the loot, the more U.S. collectors will pay for it.

Wittman walked with a hundred disguises through the layers of the art theft underground like Dante's narrator in *The Inferno*. Back in the glutted art market of Santa Fe, he posed as a connoisseur of Navajo artifacts to win the trust of two dealers whose shop on the main square, across from the Palace of the Governors, offered religious items including medicine pots and bullroarers plundered from graves or otherwise taken illegally from reservations all over the Southwest. Teaming up with a Norwegian police agent who posed as a rich European collector, Wittman heard the dealers weave colorful stories about the pieces' supposed ceremonial powers and then charge astronomical prices for them. The two dealers, Joshua Baer and Thomas Cavaliere, pleaded guilty and later took out a two-page ad in *American Indian Art* magazine to apologize. The items confiscated from them were reported to be worth about $400,000, but in cases like this the monetary value is, of course, barely relevant. Some of the items were so sacred that, after being repatriated to tribes in New Mexico and Arizona in 2003, they had to be purified by Indian shamans of the defilement caused by being held by alien hands.[21]

Occasionally the flow went the other way. Wittman joined forces with Goldman again in 2001 to go to Rio de Janeiro where, with the cooperation of Brazilian authorities, they threatened an art dealer with criminal charges in the United States unless he gave up three original paintings by Norman Rockwell that had been stolen from a gallery outside Minneapolis in 1978. The works included the original of a famous calendar reproduction of three wet boys pulling on their shirts and running past a NO SWIMMING sign. The dealer was keeping them in a farmhouse in Teresópolis, in the hill country north of Rio, and had been discreetly offering them for sale to U.S. galleries and the Norman Rockwell Museum in Massachusetts. He gave up the paintings and, in exchange, was not charged.

It was seize-and-send-home operations like the backflap that still drew the most attention. Wittman wasn't sure if they were doing anything to stop looting on the ground, but he detected a steady change among the most established antiquities dealers. Little by little, they were getting cold feet. There was more risk, more liability, more lawyers.

"There have been a few high-profile prosecutions, and I think the top-end dealers are getting afraid to deal in this material," said Wittman. "Or they'll find new ways to get around it. They'll get smarter."[22]

PART THREE

PART THREE

Chapter 13

THE BRIGADES

A SHORT, STURDY man in his fifties with skin burnished from a lifetime working in northern Peru's sugarcane fields, Gregorio Becerra re-members the days when his father used to bring home ancient ceramic pots to their home in the village of Úcupe. Birds, faces, fruits, animals—the whole pantheon of Moche pottery themes stood on their living-room shelf, where his father would place the perfectly preserved vessels he and his buddies dug up. Usually they found them tilling fields, digging wells, or dredging irrigation ditches in the fields around Úcupe, a village in the lower Zaña River valley, about forty minutes' drive south of Chiclayo.

"Everyone had a few pots in his house in those days. They were nice decorations," said Becerra.

But in the late 1980s, something changed.

"It became a business. Outsiders came. They came from the city, and you'd see them out in the hills digging up everything they could find. They'd take it all away and sell it," he said.

And so the modern looting industry came to little Úcupe and a hun-dred villages like it up and down the coast of Peru. People who used to ex-cavate pots as backlot hobby or family activity at Holy Week, as much a part of local social life as fishing or football, watched first with bafflement and then anger as professional grave robbers descended on their lands to search for pieces to supply the exploding international market for Peruvian antiquities. Poor, neglected, marooned by the collapse of sugar prices like boats left by a falling tide, these villages suddenly found themselves living literally on top of a commodity hotter than sugar ever was. They were living on top of ceramics—Moche ceramics from the first millennium A.D. that, for a time, had collectors in their thrall.

Now Becerra is the leader of his village's *grupo de protección arqueológica*, or *la grupa*, a citizens' patrol formed in 1994 and armed with binoculars, a dirt bike (which has not worked for a few years), one revolver, and one shotgun but whose most important weapon is the eyes and ears of people living in the adobe homes around Úcupe's fields and sand dunes. The mission of the "archaeological protection group" is to stop people from occupying the land and plundering what lies beneath it. They scout the land, chase away bands of looters, or they surround them and tie their wrists with rope until the police arrive, and they seize their tools—shovels, poles, buckets.[1]

Alva, his wife, Susana Meneses; and his deputy director at the Brüning Museum, Carlos Wester, organized the patrols in the early 1990s in response to the phenomenal growth of commercial looting in the Moche heartland. In doing so, they took a cue from rural Peru's long tradition of ragtag peasant militias known as *rondas campesinas* that have fought scourges like cattle rustlers, bandits, and land squatters, as well as Maoist Shining Path guerrillas after their strong-arm tactics alienated the rural working class in parts of the Andean highlands. *Rondas campesinas* have been much studied by anthropologists and sociologists as living examples of local autonomy and self-reliance in the Peruvian countryside. This time the militias had a new enemy: looters hunting for ancient art, and the spark that lit the art market's desire for Peruvian antiquities as never before was Alva's own sensational excavation in 1987 of the tombs at Sipán, fifteen miles north of Úcupe. Pronounced OO-coo-peh, Úcupe is believed to be a word in Muchic, the lost language of the Moche, although its meaning has been forgotten. The village lies about midway between the two mother lodes of Moche art of the last twenty years, Sipán and La Mina.

"After Sipán many more people came," Becerra said, walking down the village's dusty main street. "They would set up their little shacks out in the hills, take out their cane liquor, and dig and dig until they found something. And then we said, enough."

Alva created the patrols in eight villages throughout the Department of Lambayeque, with about 350 people actively involved. From the start, the patrols had widely varying degrees of organization and success. Some villages took to the patrols quickly, others more slowly, and others, like Sipán itself, were so given over to the antiquities trade and hostile to Alva that he thought he could never enter the village without police escort, much less try to organize people to protect a community resource. Interestingly, the older villages with deeper roots in the land and traditionally Moche names had the more successful *grupas*, while communities populated mostly by the descendants of workers who migrated from other parts of Peru to work in the sugar fields tended to have weaker ones or none at all. Local police and politicians, after some reluctance, came around to supporting the *grupas* and the project advanced quickly. On June 30, 1995, about three hundred men and women from eight towns — Batán Grande, Coyúd, La Compuerta, Pampa Grande, Poma, Pomalca, Úcupe, and Zaña — gathered in the main square of Úcupe, next to its tiny, whitewashed chapel, and marched in quasi-military formation, although unarmed, to a dais where Alva, Wester, Meneses, and several local politicians sat. The male villagers looked lean, dark, and muscular in their denim, straw hats, and work clothes, while the women wore skirts and sandals with their hair pulled back in ponytails.

Alva stood before the crowd and held up a megaphone.

"By our ancestors, do you promise to protect our archaeological monuments?" his voice boomed.

First a confused murmur wafted from the crowd, then some random shouts until finally the crowd erupted in a definitive, "Yes, we promise!"[2]

To reach Úcupe, one leaves the bustle of Chiclayo and crosses the barren contours of the coastal desert with its blank hills, clumps of hateful little weeds, and distant charcoal mountains that rise up like a vision of hell. It rarely rains here, so nothing is eroded. The rocks are sharp, the dunes are parched, sand blows up and over the road in powdery billows. Truck stops, abandoned tires, and gravel pits sprawl along the highway. In the time of the Moche it was these empty, forbidding plains that divided the different potentates into their power spheres, each in its own valley, and even today driving across this landscape of death feels vaguely disconcerting. A small dog lay by the highway, panting, apparently abandoned, waiting for starvation to come over it.

Finally the highway descends to the Zaña River, where the women of Úcupe wash clothes and children splash among the water lilies. Goats nibble on weeds by the banks, and swallows dart over the placidly flowing water. The road crosses a bridge and climbs past some rocky bluffs overlooking the river and then the village appears, a collection of single-story brick-and-adobe homes spread out along the highway, with unpaved streets that stretch back for miles into the farms and sand dunes that separate the village from the Pacific coast a few miles to the west. The streets are clean, and papaya trees and vegetable plots, some demarcated by neat lines of white stones, occupy the spaces between the houses. The impression is of a village that is poor but organized.

Carlos Wester and I drove in the Brüning Museum's Land Rover through the village and a short distance into the fields where the unmistakable shape of a burial mound protruded. Unusually tall and steep, it had a prominent notch on its summit that gave it the shape of a cleft chin. We parked and climbed the thirty feet or so to the top, where we looked out over algarobo trees, grazing goats, and the village off in the distance. It was possibly the first more-or-less undisturbed burial mound I had ever seen in Peru, all the others having been damaged or destroyed by urban sprawl, roads, agriculture, or pillage. The *grupa* deserved the credit for this, Wester said.

"If you come to this village to loot, they'll chase you out before the police even get here. People have become aware of the value of preserving the *huacas*. Inside this one, there are probably some good things, mostly ceramics I would think. It's probably about contemporaneous with Huaca Dos Cabezas," said Wester, referring to a Moche site about thirty miles south, where Donnan had worked. "Someday we'll excavate this *huaca*, and until we do it's well protected."

Known as Huaca de Úcupe, this 1,800-year-old Moche burial mound stood unmolested, while similar sites less than twenty miles away have been demolished by looters. Wester and I drove next to the slopes of a conical mountain known as Cerro Corbacho, about ten miles north of Úcupe. The land, unpatrolled by the *grupa*, was pockmarked with holes and trenches dug by generations of looters until its Moche and Chimú cemeteries were exhausted. Uprooted bones, tufts of hair, useless pieces of tattered textile, cigarette butts, plastic bottles, all the detritus of pillage lay around, unquestionably the fate of the Huaca de Úcupe if not for the patrols.

Despite their success in the Moche heartland, the idea of citizens' patrols to curb pillage is still in its infancy. Turning poachers into wardens takes time, a thorough knowledge of local customs and sensitivities, cooperation from the police, and roots in the community that not a lot of archaeological researchers have. In Peru, I knew of nobody else doing anything like it. Other countries are experimenting with the idea, including the West African nation of Mali, where the elected former president Alpha Oumar Konaré, himself a trained archaeologist, has supported creative, grassroots solutions to fight pillage, including citizens' patrols. "It's a strategy focused on looking proactively to preserve sites and rescue them from depredation, instead of focusing on repatriation," said Susan McIntosh of Rice University in Houston, who has helped organize the *brigades de surveillance* near Djenné, in Mali.

In Lambayeque, Alva calculates that the brigades have seized about four thousand objects from looters. So far they have worked only on a small scale, and he knows the brigades have to some extent pushed the looting problem elsewhere. But they have prompted villagers to see their archaeological riches as a resource worth protecting, like clean well water or good grazing land, rather than as a windfall to exploit.

A few days later I returned to Úcupe on a bus to see the patrols in action. Gilberto Romero, another leader of the patrol, met me at the bus stop. A man with a gravelly voice and a sleepy smile, he had a manner so mild that I was surprised to learn he doubled as a security guard for the local sugar cooperative and, as such, was licensed to carry a gun. He was the only member of the antilooting patrol who regularly carried a weapon although, he told me, he had never fired in anger at looters. "I've fired in the air before to scatter them, but never at a looter. This isn't a war," he said. I was glad of that.

Becerra, Romero, and I hired a motorcycle that had been fitted with a passenger seat just wide enough for the three of us. With a young driver named Julio, we drove along a rutted dirt road past fields of spicy red-pepper plants and sugarcane. Now and then Romero would point out a bare, sandy hill and explain that it was not a hill. It was another *huaca,* an entirely man-made structure weathered by so many centuries of wind and sun that it was indistinguishable from a natural feature.

"We have virgin *huacas,* never been touched and known only to us," said Romero, shouting above the sound of the engine.

Since the creation of the patrol in 1994, the village had divided into those who actively patrolled the fields in shifts and a much larger group who acted as spies. "There are about twenty of us active in the *grupa,* but directly or indirectly I would say 90 percent of the people in the town collaborate with us." Everyone keeps an eye on the *huacas* as they work in the fields or tend the goats, reporting any outsiders, he said. "There are always a few people in town who still want to dig up pots to sell, but we keep an eye on them. We know who they are."

What would happen if they saw illicit diggers?

"If we see somebody digging, we call the museum"—the Brüning, where Wester answers the phone—"and then they call the police. If the police can't get here fast enough, we detain them ourselves. A month ago I detained three looters and all their tools. We let down our guard for an hour and before we knew it they were digging," said Romero. "It's like that here. You go to lunch and you come back, and there they are, digging."

We bounced along past fallow fields and groves of scraggly algarobo, a species related both biologically and etymologically to the Mediterranean carob and source of a prized hardwood used by the Moche to build the coffins of their rulers. We stopped and walked through the trees to a shallow, sandy depression where, jutting up from the sand, stood a line of four sticks, each about a foot high. There was nothing to explain what the sticks meant—no signs, no labels, no markers of any kind.

Underneath those sticks lies a Chavín-era wall, part of a rectangular building dating from about 200 B.C., festooned with ceremonial warrior characters in red, ocher, and black paint. Alva and Meneses excavated the site in 1983. They ascertained the dimensions of the building, photographed the murals, and then refilled the whole site with sand to protect it from the elements, later publishing their findings about the site in a German scholarly journal.[3] Now Alva relied on the patrols to protect it from a much worse threat: professional pillagers, who in a few nights could dig up the wall, cut it up into bite-sized chunks, and sell it all to art dealers in Lima.

The Murals of Úcupe are well known. Their image appears on postcards and Peruvian tourist pamphlets, and now and then tourists come around the village asking to see them. But no visitors are allowed because the murals' exact location is a secret, known only to the *grupa* and a few researchers who excavated it, and marked only by the line of sticks. Alva himself probably could not find it now without help from the patrol.

"As long as we don't have the resources to excavate and protect them, better to leave the murals underground and thus guarantee their long-term preservation," Alva told me a few days later in Lambayeque. "If we show it, we lose it."

I asked Gilberto and Gregorio where the looters usually came from. "They come from neighboring towns, Chiclayo, some from Trujillo," Gilberto told me. "Always people from outside. And mostly they are people from Cayaltí."

Much larger than Úcupe, Cayaltí is a market town about twelve miles due north of Úcupe. One reaches it by driving up the Zaña valley, passing the ruins of the Spanish colonial settlement called Zaña, which was wrecked by waves of pestilence, slave rebellion, pirates, and finally floods in 1720 and abandoned. The tidy modern village of Zaña stands on a hillside a prudent distance away. A bit beyond, one crosses the pillaged wasteland of Cerro Corbacho, and later crumbling lines of mud-brick walls built by the Chimú nearly one thousand years ago and irrigation ditches that, Wester told me, follow the path of those dug by Moche excavators one thousand years before that. Peru's layers of history are all here, grafted uneasily one upon the other.

After more sugarcane fields, the town of Cayaltí, built around a rambling, wooden mansion once owned by the Aspíllaga family, appears. Like their neighbors the Auriches and other families in Peru's feudal *ancien régime*, the Aspíllagas lost everything in Velasco's land reform of the early 1970s, their mansion and all their sugar plantations expropriated and turned over to a workers' cooperative. Thirty years later, the cooperative went bankrupt, the Aspíllagas have long since left, and residents say the town has no jobs to offer its young people.

Now Cayaltí is known as a looting center, a clearinghouse for antiquities plundered from all over the region and bought and sold here with impunity. It's a busy town of woodworking shops and pirated video stands, where fruit sellers and prostitutes in clingy black pants stand in the street and little cafés sell sandwiches and warm Cokes. One day as Carlos Wester and I drove into town, he pointed out two men walking along beside a horse-drawn cart carrying hay.

"The older one, he's been arrested several times for looting. We know who he is," said Wester, a burly, handsome man with a mustache whom you might confuse with an off-duty policeman if it weren't for his gentle temper. As for his information, it's better than that of the police. With a network of informants in villages all around the Department of Lambayeque, he follows the local grave-robbing groups and has kept tabs over the years on brothers, families, and whole clans that are in the business. His spies inform him of where looters operate and who's digging, even if they are prominent local officials. In 1998, thanks to a tip from one of Wester's spies, the sitting Minister of Education in Fujimori's government was arrested while digging with his family in a Chimú cemetery near Batán Grande, leading to a national scandal and the minister's eventual resignation. Alva and Wester received endless phone calls from the Presidential Palace in Lima, pressuring them to stop talking to the press about the arrest and to fire the unarmed guard at the site who called the police, but the damage was done. Now and then Wester has posed as a buyer to snare loot salesmen in the act and report them to police, once entering a dealer's house in which the treasures were piled up on a bed, but he can't do that much anymore because people recognize him. Developing spy networks, tracking suspects, organizing stings—it's not what you would expect the director of a prestigious museum to be doing, and I told Wester so.

"There's no choice. We can sit on our hands and do nothing, or we can get dirty trying to stop this problem, because if we don't, someday there won't be any archaeology left in this country because there will be nothing left to excavate," he said. Wester wrote his doctoral thesis at the Universidad de Trujillo on the Gallinazo culture, which flourished in the valleys south of Trujillo for a few centuries before it was subsumed by the Moche around A.D. 100 in a process that archaeologists have discerned mostly through subtle variations in pottery design and patterns. If left to looters, the physical remnants of the Gallinazo culture would have been obliterated.

As we drove through Cayaltí's crowded streets in the Land Rover, Wester told me he couldn't get out because he might be harassed by people. The windows were not tinted and he drove rather quickly so passersby wouldn't get a look at my face, either. The town's social hierarchy was no longer based on sugar but on loot, he told me, with grimy tomb diggers at the bottom, small-time dealers and mules above them, and at the top, antiquities traders who sold to Peruvian and occasionally foreign collectors who came to town to buy. Certain shops doubled as sales centers. A carpentry shop and a bakery were known as fronts for loot salesmen. A taxi stand at the edge of town was a distribution center, he told me.

I returned to Cayaltí a few days later and wandered through town, letting people think I was a loot buyer and asking around for *antigüedades* in the places where Wester told me I could find them. It didn't take long. A dealer named David took me to an alley behind his house, where he and another man offered me point-bottomed Inca pots, a broken Moche portrait vessel, and an exquisite little ceramic jar no bigger than a perfume bottle in the shape of a spondylus seashell. All freshly dug up, he told me. (The pieces were authentic. I bought an Inca pot and the broken portrait vessel for the equivalent of $3 each and took them to Alva at the Museum of the Nation in Lima, and he confirmed they were real. I donated them to the museum.) David asked me politely, was I a museum director? Like loot sellers everywhere, he boasted, whether truthfully or not, that he sells his best pieces to museums. He claimed that the son of the late owner of Lima's Gold Museum, Miguel Mujica Gallo, occasionally came to town in a big black car to look at what he had to offer.

"*Aquí todo el pueblo huaquea,*" he said. Everybody loots here. Now and then he rode on his motorcycle about nine hours down to Lima with some of his choicest pieces wrapped up in a knapsack and sold them to a woman who would then put them in the window in her shop in Miraflores or, for the best pieces, sell them to exporters. He believed that, along with the authentic pots he sent, the woman also sold a lot of fakes in her shop to distract the police if they should come around asking questions—all the more reason, he said, to buy in Cayaltí. "In Lima, the pieces are fake and expensive. Here they're authentic and cheap." By the time I took the bus back to Chiclayo that evening, two more dealers had offered me some lovely artifacts, all authentic and cheap, just like David said.

The hills outside Cayaltí are pockmarked with the cavities of emptied graves. The former president of Cayaltí's sugar cooperative, Manuel Ramírez Rojas, was arrested for looting in 1996 along with four other men, and two more looters were detained in 1999 carrying ten gold and silver artifacts, according to local press accounts.[4] In January 1996, an antilooting patrol in nearby Zaña detained three grave robbers from Cayaltí and turned them over to police.[5] The seizures went on and on, until the storage rooms at the Brüning Museum were overflowing with pots seized by antilooting patrols or police, or handed in by repentant collectors who took Alva's message to heart.

The people of Úcupe spoke with disgust about how residents of Cayaltí, Sipán, and other villages had let their ancient sites be destroyed. "No respect for their ancestors," a woman from Úcupe told me, shaking her head as we waited for the bus, after I remarked to her that I had spent a day in Cayaltí.

Cultural preservation is not Úcupe's only motive for creating its patrimony police. The two towns, Úcupe and Cayaltí, are divided by a bitter land feud in which farmers in the former fear that people from the latter will descend on their lands, start erecting houses, and then petition a judge for legal title. Whole towns are born this way in Peru. Squatters take over idle private land by the light of the moon, and months or years later they present authorities with a fait accompli and ask for their community to be incorporated as a town. This is how, in 1989, the Tupac Amaru shantytown outside Lima, subject of a *National Geographic* cover story in 2002, established itself smack on top of an enormous Inca graveyard with thousands of funerary bundles.[6] In the dunes and fields around Úcupe, looters are considered the advance guard of the squatters. It's a lamentable battle of poor-against-poorer but one whose outcome may well determine if the heritages of Úcupe and other towns like it are preserved or destroyed forever.

"People come from Cayaltí with the excuse that they want to work on the farms. Some of them have family members here," said Romero. "But to us, everyone who comes from Cayaltí is a looter. And after the looters come the invaders."

"We have extinguished looting in this area, because after the looters come the cattle rustlers, the thieves, and the land invaders. All the bad elements," said Becerra.

Alva and Wester had managed to hitch the cause of cultural preservation to the villagers' wish to prevent their lands from being occupied by squatters. The pressure for arable land and rivalries between neighboring communities for control of it had existed for years on the north Peruvian coast. These archaeologists had astutely exploited, if that's the word, the conflict to benefit the cause of historic preservation with results that archaeologists elsewhere could only dream about.

The night before Wester and I went to Úcupe, the *grupa* had found a band of about 120 squatters in the hills outside the village. A *traficante de tierras*, a land trafficker, had charged the squatters a fee to take them all in pickup trucks to a spot where, the trafficker believed, they would not be detected. But they were detected, and early that morning the members of the *grupa* surrounded the squatters and called the police, who chased the squatters away before they could start erecting houses with mats and sheets of plastic. Most of the invaders were allowed to leave voluntarily. A few who had put up resistance were still in detention the next day at the police station in Mocupe, the first major town heading south from Úcupe, when Wester, the leaders of the *grupa*, and I went to the station. The would-be squatters were sitting on their haunches in a courtyard, men in sneakers and dusty jeans with bony limbs and sad, stoic eyes. They were unemployed and hungry and most of them came from Chiclayo, looking for a piece of farmland that they could not afford to buy.

"The farmers [in Úcupe] want all the land for themselves. Look how much land they've got, kilometers and kilometers of it," one told me. "There is no more land anywhere, but they won't let us live here. That's the way it is in Peru, *hermano*."[7] He wasn't aware that the area was an archaeological zone and didn't seem to care.

The other squatters straggled back to Chiclayo. I saw a few of them wandering down the highway, carrying rolls of plastic that flapped in the wind, the plastic they had hoped would be the walls of their new homes. The *grupa* had done its job, carrying out citizens' arrests of these people whose crime was to be desperately poor. As we stood in front of the police station, Wester patted the *grupa* leaders on the shoulders and congratulated them. Another victory for culture property. I was amazed, and frankly a bit frightened, by how single-minded he was in his dedication to preserving the ancient tombs beneath the sand. For him and the *grupa*, there was no other way.

The leaders of the patrols have constantly feared that the fight against looters and land squatters will become more violent.

"Usually they go peacefully, but once we detained a group of eight *huaqueros* who threatened to come back and kill us all. For several days we were under police protection," said Romero, owner of the revolver. The patrols shouldn't have to rely on archaeologists, he said. He wanted the police to train and arm them, essentially turn them into a vigilante group, a citizens' militia similar to those that fought in the highlands against Shining Path. Tension between land squatters and farmers has been simmering for years in the Zaña valley, a rich archaeological zone outside Cayaltí where Alva excavated ancient funerary complexes in the 1970s and where, in January 2003, a battle broke out on the former Aspíllaga sugar plantation. Farmers and squatters attacked one another with machetes, stones, and blunt weapons, and when it was over there were eight people dead and seventeen wounded.[8] The people of Úcupe may have mixed motives for protecting their land, and forming popular militias will have its own perils, but it is clear that the idea that ancient sites have an intrinsic value to a community has taken root.

"When I was a boy, people knew nothing about the importance of these objects we found," said Becerra. "We didn't know what the pre-Columbian cultures were. Moche, Chimú, Chavín, we'd never heard those names. Now everyone knows them. They teach them to the children in school."

An organizer to the bone, Becerra had been recently laid off from the sugar cooperative because he was accused of trying to organize a union. It wasn't true, he said, but he smiled and held my elbow for a second when I told him I was a member of a union (for journalists, the Communications Workers of America). He lived now on money sent to him by his son, who was in the military, but he had also reopened a barbershop that once functioned in the front room of his house, and he was cutting people's hair again. After a few hours in the fields one hot December morning, he led me into his home, past an ancient, leather-seated barber's chair with its hanging strap and an old black-and-white photograph of his parents on the wall, and motioned to a chair for me to sit down. The room had an air of humble formality, and his voice a melancholic sweetness so characteristic of the north coast. He noticed me studying a Moche-looking pot on his shelf.

"A replica," he added quickly.

Looters are feeling the pinch. Every professional grave robber I met said that activity was declining in the north because of stepped-up police protection and the antilooting patrols. "You might be digging and then Walter Alva comes around to get you," said Rigoberto, Robin's friend, who, sitting in a Lima park, pulled out swatches of Inca textiles that some of his mates had found. The trade had moved to the south, where grave robbers were extracting the gorgeous textiles of which collectors never tired, he said.

Rigoberto introduced me later to Gloria, a woman he sometimes worked with, who said she was an *empresaria*, a businesswoman, who had loose gangs of looters who extracted *mercadería*—merchandise, the word she used—from burial mounds near Nazca and her hometown of Ica, a five-hour drive south of Lima. As a businesswoman, she has succeeded not because of investment in her product or marketing but mostly because she happened to be in the right place at the right time when the tastes of the antiquities market tilted away from ceramics and toward south-coast textiles.

"I have my *huaqueros* who go out and find the merchandise. It's not hard to find good looters. What is hard is finding looters who are good and that you can trust," she told me in a toney Lima café, running her fingers now and then through her dyed red hair. What she meant was that it was difficult to find looters who would not, upon finding a good piece, try to cut a deal on the side with another buyer.

Young men rip into *huacas* and graveyards all night and, in the morning, after washing (she insists they wash first) they come to her house with textiles they have found. Usually they are of the Inca, Ichma, or Chiribaya cultures. She usually then sells the textiles to traders who take them out of the country or, for the inferior ones, sell them locally. She works her looters hard, but they come to ask her for jobs because she is known to pay them well. Occasionally specific requests reach her. For example, she learned through one of her local middlemen that someone in Europe was in the market for a good-quality pre-Inca mantle. She didn't know how much the buyer was willing to pay; that was between him and his dealer. After a few months digging, her boys found a piece that seemed suitable, and she sold it for $10,000, the most she ever earned from a single piece. It helped to have advance orders to move the merchandise quickly, she said, although it was impossible to predict whether they would be able to fill specific orders or if a competitor would beat them to it. You could call it customized looting, but it was a bit more fortuitous than that.

What happened if her looters did not find artifacts good enough to sell? "They've got to look for a job somewhere else. It's like any job," she said. Her team typically had six men, sometimes more, working nightly. There were perhaps fifty people like her in Ica with full-time teams of grave robbers working for them, she said. If all fifty of them had the same sized looting crews, then there would be approximately three hundred people in this one city working nightly to empty tombs. And if the same thing were happening in only fifty other towns across Peru, then the number of nightly tomb raiders would reach fifteen thousand.

Alva has never heard of Gloria yet he knows that she, her looters, dealers, and foreign clients are snuffing out some of the last undiscovered physical remains of one of the world's great ancient civilizations, the Incas. "The last decades," he said at a conference in England in 1999, "have seen the black market flooded with textiles from the south coast Chiribaya and Inca cultures, of which we archaeologists know hardly anything."[9]

Alva offered a balance on the success of the patrols at the conference, held at the University of Cambridge, where archaeologists and their sympathizers from about two dozen countries came to read the usual jeremiads against looting, the same people talking in the same old tone of querulous indignation. The title of one paper was "One Damn Illicit Excavation After Another: The Destruction of the Archaeological Heritage of Jordan." People looking for grassroots solutions to the problem had been watching Peru's experience, and Alva was able to tell them the patrols had confiscated 3,200 artifacts up to that time, while "the number of vandals at some sites has declined from more than one hundred to a furtive few [and] networks of local dealers have been broken up."[10] The scale of the problem was great, but so was the boldness of a few Peruvian archaeologists to combat it.

Chapter 14

RECOVERING THE PAST

The irony, Sally thinks, is that the apartment is hideous in a way she associates with macho flamboyance, with its Lucite coffee table and brown laquered walls, its niches in which spotlit Asian and African objects (Oliver surely thinks of them as "dramatically lit") suggest, despite their immaculate and reverential display, not so much connoisseurship as plunder. This is the third time Sally has been here, and each time she's felt the urge to confiscate the treasures and return them to their rightful owners. She feigns attention to Oliver while imagining herself entering a remote mountain village amid cheers and ululations, carrying the age-blackened antelope mask or the pale green, faintly phosphorescent porcelain bowl in which two painted carp have swum for ten centuries.

MICHAEL CUNNINGHAM, *THE HOURS*

THE WORLD IS not condemned to lose its cultural heritage. We face the destruction of ancient sites around the world not because of some inexorable rule of human nature, but because private and public institutions have let them be destroyed. The U.S. government has moved only belatedly and reluctantly to curb the antiquities-dealing industry and still erases with its elbow what it has written with its hand by allowing collectors to donate pillaged artifacts to museums in exchange for tax write-offs. Museums have ignored their own ethics statements and bought looted pieces on the open antiquities market, and even if they have cleaned up their acquisitions practices, as claimed, they have yet to make amends for practices that contributed to the incalculable damage to the world's heritage over the past three decades. The public has failed to demand accountability from museums in disclosing where their antiquities came from. Governments in source countries, with few exceptions, have neglected to talk to their own people and tell them about what can be gained by preserving the ancient sites in their midst rather than letting looters destroy them. Nearly every institution with a stake in this problem has shirked its responsibility to leave future generations with the tools and resources with which to expand our knowledge of the ancient world.

The biggest obstacle to stopping the looting of the ancient world is overcoming the feeling that it is inevitable. At every stage of the illegal antiquities trade, from the lowliest looter to the millionaire collector, one finds weary resignation and glib assumptions that nothing can be done to stop the trade. As long as there are rich buyers, there will always be poor looters willing to supply them, goes the familiar refrain. Everybody knows the antiquities trade is demolishing the world's archaeological record, and everybody feels that nothing can done about it.

Yet something can be done about it. A lot can be done.

We saw an example of how decisive international action can curb the illicit trade in the aftermath of Saddam Hussein's downfall. Governments, police, cultural institutions, and dealers cooperated quickly to circulate descriptions and pictures of Iraqi artifacts that had been stolen from the National Museum of Antiquities. Customs agents at ports of entry in the major buyer countries were alerted. The result was that the fifty or so artifacts stolen from the museum's main galleries became impossible to sell. They were too famous, and within a year most of them had been returned or recovered by U.S. forces in Iraq. At this writing, at least four thousand of the perhaps thirteen thousand items stolen from the museum's storage rooms have also been recovered—a good record of recovery. True, all those pieces were tagged and catalogued by the museum, unlike freshly excavated artifacts from archaeological sites all over Iraq. But an encouraging number of those have been confiscated and returned as well, caught in the same net that had been set for the museum artifacts. The ad hoc Iraqi recovery effort shows that with the right mix of agile detective work, resolute government policy, and a commitment by responsible dealers and art museums to put the interests of preserving a shared resource before their own, much progress in stopping the antiquities trade can be made quickly.

What sort of world awaits us without stronger action to curb the antiquities trade? Fast-forward to the year 2050. Around the world, there are no more ancient sites left to excavate. Nearly every tomb, temple, village, or dwelling left by humanity's great ancient civilizations has been ransacked, stripped down, or destroyed. Their buildings have been left in ruins, their memory obliterated, their artwork dispersed among thousands of private collections and museums. Of course, the marquee archaeological sites are all still there. The Valley of the Kings in Egypt, the Angkor complex in Cambodia, Pompeii, Petra, Machu Picchu, Tikal—they are alive and well, packed with tourists and lavished with hundreds of millions of dollars in preservation grants, depicted on billions of postcards and snapshots. But only a few miles from those sites, the ravages of the international antiquities trade are everywhere: piles of pottery shards, bones, and debris where ancient villages have been dug up, heaps of brick where dynamite brought down stone temples, giant holes that show where looters gouged out tombs. Around the world, from China to Peru to Italy, ancient sites have been destroyed before trained specialists could even look at them, much less excavate them. Archaeology as a profession is dying because there is nothing left to study. In the coastal deserts of Peru, archaeologists find there are no more pre-Conquest tombs or towns worth excavating because they have all been ransacked by commercial pillagers. In Cambodia, bar a few famous sites, all that is left of the majestic stone cities of the Khmer Empire are headless Buddhas and a few walls still standing with the rough surfaces where looters chiseled off tenth-century carvings and friezes. At universities and in governments, in the media, and in ordinary conversations, people ask why. Why did people living in the early twenty-first century let this happen? They'll ask this in the same aggrieved tone with which we ask today how we allowed so much tropical rain forest to be destroyed, so many big mammals to become extinct, so many of our architectural treasures to be lost, so much degradation of the things that connect us to the past, enrich our lives in the present, and constitute our greatest legacy to the future.

There are plenty of archaeologists who, although deeply concerned about the loss of information caused by looting, do not think this dire scenario will ever happen. To them, the world's archaeological resources are practically infinite. I disagree. Whole countries are being stripped of their archaeological endowments by the antiquities trade, as Guatemala has seen and as Alva has warned the Peruvians is happening to them, and there is no reason to think it will not swallow up more cultures until intact ancient sites become, if not unheard of, extremely rare. The day is not far off when an archaeologist can go through an entire career without seeing a single unpillaged site. That's a realistic possibility and whether we realize it or not, we are moving toward it with alarming speed.

Governments responded to the looting problem with the UNESCO treaty of 1970, and although that proved more effective and durable than anyone had any right to expect, the antiquities trade has changed a great deal since then and the international legal framework to combat it has not. Goods move faster, suppliers are in closer contact with buyers, airports now stand where before there were barely even roads. Commerce has been globalized, made massive, and streamlined. The rise of container shipping, in which goods are moved in self-contained metal cells stacked on freighters, has allowed traders to move antiquities in volumes scarcely imaginable thirty years ago.[1]

Here are some concrete and achievable steps that can be taken by governments in cooperation, by the U.S. government alone, by the private sector, and by governments in source countries to hold on to some of the world's shared ancient heritage. Some of these recommendations have been aired before by other people, and some are entirely or substantially original.

First, the multilateral measures:

- A five-year worldwide moratorium on the sale or purchase of antiquities without a clearly verifiable provenance dating from before 1970 or an export certificate from the country of origin. The international outcry over looting in Afghanistan and especially Iraq makes this old proposal, long spurned by antiquities traders, politically feasible at last. A simple assertion of provenance —"it belonged to my grandmother"—is not good enough. To be verifiable, a provenance must include documentation that can be corroborated independently or by photographic evidence. Sure, such documentation can be forged, but then a dealer would risk a criminal charge for fraud. How would the moratorium be enforced? The practical reality is that it can't be, unless legislation to enforce it is passed in each country. National governments could sign their names to a moratorium at a multilateral conference à la Paris 1970 and then it would be up to them to decide whether to enact implementing legislation. Some will, most probably won't. But like the ivory trade ban, the moratorium on the trade in undocumented antiquities should be widely publicized by nongovernmental organizations to bring moral pressure to bear on dealers, museums, and auction houses. Sotheby's and Christie's have taken great pains to stress that they do not want to encourage looting; here is their chance to prove it.

- An indefinite worldwide moratorium on trade in undocumented antiquities made of gold, silver, and other precious metals. Ancient gold objects should be treated like ivory or fur from animals in danger of extinction, with no legal trade in it except in exceptional circumstances. Closing down the market for gold and silver objects would do more than possibly any other single measure to stop pillage because looters toss away every other kind of object to get to small but phenomenally valuable amounts of gold, as Sipán and La Mina showed. Every dealer, auction house, and museum should know that when they buy, sell, or receive an undocumented gold artifact, incalculable damage has been done to all the other archaeological resources around it. Also, when precious-metal objects are large and so well known that they cannot be sold, the temptation to melt them down can be too great to resist; this has happened at least twice with Peruvian gold artifacts.

- Repatriation on demand of all human remains and international prohibition of trade in ancient body parts. Many museums now accept the repatriation principle for remains from sites within their own countries; it should be applied now to remains from outside their borders as well. Museums in the United States must by law send most Native American human remains back to the tribe involved, if asked, and all museums should do the same for remains whose origin can be clearly linked to a particular country. It is hard to see any compelling scientific reason for keeping ancient human remains, and yet they linger in some of our institutions. When Peruvian archaeologist Sonia Guillén visited Yale University's Peabody Museum in the 1990s, she discovered that human remains taken from Machu Picchu in 1914 by explorer (and Yale graduate) Hiram Bingham were being used in osteology demonstration classes.[2]

For all their failings, the U.S. government and Congress have a thirty-five-year-old tradition of bipartisan support for responsible, global action to combat the pillage of ancient sites. Here are some steps they can take to build on that tradition and close the loopholes in existing legislation:

- Creation of a committee within the Internal Revenue Service to assess the provenance status of antiquities in cases when collectors want to donate artifacts to museums to gain a tax advantage. The goal is to stop the laundering of looted antiquities through the tax process. This committee would work like the IRS's existing Art Advisory Panel, discussed in Chapter 8, which appraises works of fine and decorative art that collectors want to donate or leave as inheritance and which has the power to adjust the claimed value up or down. For example, if you donate a cheap painting to your local museum and claim a deduction worth $500,000, the panel will rule against you and assess your painting, and hence your deduction, at its real value. Same for inheritances; if you inherit a $500,000 painting and claim on your tax form that it was worth the price of the cheap painting, the Art Advisory Panel can increase the painting's appraised value and hence your tax liability.[3] I propose that all works or art, donated or inherited, that are claimed for a tax advantage and are more than 250 years old (the period stated in the Cultural Property Implementation Act of 1983) be evaluated by a second committee, the Antiquities Advisory Panel, which would evaluate whether the owner of the piece has proper title to it and a documented chain of ownership dating to before 1970. If he does not, the panel would have the power to reject the claim and, in the most flagrant cases, recommend a criminal inquiry. The committee should include representatives from law enforcement and the archaeological community, with representatives from source countries (or their embassies) in a consulting role.

- Legislation requiring antiquities dealers to keep detailed records, subject to inspection, on the origin of all goods they import, buy, or sell, with descriptions, prices, and names and addresses of suppliers. This provision was included in the original UNESCO treaty of 1970 but unwisely dropped in the Cultural Property Implementation Act. By requiring antiquities dealers to leave a paper trail, the government can deter illegal dealing of the kind for which Schultz was convicted. As Marina Papa Sokal of the City University of New York wrote, "Here's an analogy: businesses are required by federal law to maintain certain financial records, which are subject to audit by the tax authorities; and though this record-keeping doesn't make it impossible to cheat on one's taxes, it does make it more difficult."[4] Presumably most antiquities dealers are already keeping such records anyway; this law would require them to make the records available to tax or customs authorities on demand.

- Amend the CPIA to end the requirement that other countries first request a bilateral deal on antiquities before the United States will impose "emergency import restrictions." This change is needed because when a country's cultural heritage faces a true looting emergency, the country often doesn't have a functioning government. The United States should be able to ban imports of antiquities from such countries without waiting for a government to reconstitute itself and make a request, a process that could take years. The best example is Iraq. After the demise of Saddam Hussein, the United States banned imports on an ad hoc basis, but we are bound to see more cases of collapsing governments and antiquities hunters running wild. Looting has become as much a part of war's aftermath as CNN and blue-helmeted peacekeepers—as demonstrated in Cambodia, Guatemala, Afghanistan, and Iraq—and U.S. policy needs to be able to respond more quickly to that reality.

- Amend the CPIA to end the five-year limit on the Memoranda of Understanding with source countries and allow them to stay in effect for ten years or, better yet, indefinitely. Although the five-year terms are renewable, the period is short enough for dealers to hold onto to illicit material and wait it out. Also, the renewal process itself gives dealers an opportunity to try to pressure the government to weaken or abolish agreements. We're sure to see such an effort in early 2006 when the Italian MOU comes up for renewal. The interests of dealers are already represented on the advisory committee through the three seats guaranteed to them; there is no reason they should have this extra edge.

- Legislation to require taxpayer-supported museums to disclose publicly the provenance of all future acquisitions or risk losing federal funds. To protect confidentiality, the name of the last owner of the piece and the price paid (if the museum purchased it) need not to be disclosed. This law would force museums to be more accountable and responsible in their acquisitions and end the wide berth of secrecy that some museums have taken as a license to acquire works that, as we have seen in this book, have no business being in the United States and much less in a publicly supported institution. Most museums say they conduct due diligence on the origin of every acquisition and require full documentation; this law would require them to make that documentation public and available. There may once have been reasons to grant museums a degree of secrecy enjoyed by no other public institutions and not even publicly traded companies, which must declare the source and value of all their major assets. But there is no longer. The public interest in stopping the pillage far outweighs the privacy interests of museums, and if they are not willing to disclose the source of their antiquities, then we can only assume that the museums are complicit in the destruction.

The countries where antiquities originate could also do more to stem the illicit outflow. Although some, as we have seen, are working hard to control the hemorrhage of their treasures, there are a few steps that could be taken.

- The controlled, licensed sale by source countries' governments of some artifacts excavated by archaeologists, with the funds used to finance future excavations and community projects nearby. In most source countries, all objects excavated by archaeologists go to a government-owned museum or cultural institute. Those institutes could decide which items could be sold into the open market, photograph them, and keep records on who buys them. The controlled, legal sale of any antiquities is anathema to most source countries, including Peru. But it would do more than any other measure to separate legitimate collectors from those who buy the products of pillage,

and it would show that source countries are also willing to try new solutions. The proposal could apply to artifacts that are not so significant from a historic or artistic point of view that they must stay in
their country of origin. Of course, these will not be the investment-
grade artifacts that some collectors want, but that's the whole point. It
would allow a legal, legitimate antiquities market to develop, com-
prised of people who love art more than status and want to help stop
the pillage. The biggest obstacle to a plan like this is political: in most
source countries, the idea of selling even a few antiquities into the
open market is akin to treason. "Impossible, legally impossible," an official at Peru's Instituto Nacional de Cultura told me.[5] The basement
of the institute's headquarters was stacked to the ceiling with objects
excavated by archaeologists but deemed too ordinary to put on public
view. Peruvian museums have thousands more. Many of them are
nevertheless beautiful and valuable objects. Why not sell a small portion of them to raise money for controlled excavations and museums?

- Creation of a seal-of-approval system for antiquities excavated by archaeologists and available for sale. In most source countries, this plan
  could not be enacted unless the above recommendation were enacted
  first. Objects taken by looters wouldn't have the seal. Even if only a
  small number of artifacts on the market carry the seal of approval, it
  would begin the crucial task of separating looted antiquities from
  those that have been legitimately excavated.

And finally,

- A commitment by archaeologists and other scholars not to collaborate
  with collectors who continue to buy or otherwise acquire undocumented antiquities. This should extend to writing catalogues, gallery
  guides, or scholarly articles about objects that the writer knows or
  strongly suspects are looted. Many archaeologists already refuse to
  help institutions that hold hot artifacts, and some researchers report
  their suspicions to authorities, as we have seen. But too many archaeologists still disregard the fact that, by writing about undocumented
  artifacts, they raise the value of the object, confirm its authenticity,
  and encourage further looting. They shouldn't do it.

None of these recommendations has any claim to being the magic bullet to end the illicit antiquities trade. All of them have some inherent draw-
back, flaw, or loophole, but taken together they can start to address a
complex, global problem that is perhaps not as intractable as it seems. To
stop the pillage of ancient sites is to demand proud museums change their

time-honored ways of acquiring art, force dealers to give up a lucrative share of their business, ask governments in buyer countries to resist pressure from the antiquities lobby and enact tougher legislation, and persuade officials in source countries to abandon some of their most cherished and chauvinistic assumptions about their own cultural property. It will require confiscating a lot of objects to which dealers and collectors feel they are entitled, sending some people to jail, and putting a lot more out of business. And in countries where people have come to depend on looting as a livelihood, it might cause some economic dislocation.

The most frustrating reality about any effort to stop the antiquities trade is that, even if it succeeded, we wouldn't actually see tangible gains. Stop the ivory trade, and you've got more elephants running around. Stop the international use of land mines, and you'll save lives and limbs. By closing down the illicit antiquities trade, we would actually be *losing* those artifacts that might otherwise have entered the market and given pleasure to their buyers. Much of the inertia that has characterized campaigns against the loot trade owes to that fact. What we gain by stopping the pillage is the knowledge that these sites can someday be excavated scientifically and that, when they are, we will all broaden our understanding of ancient life and be able to look at the excavated objects in the context for which they were made. You could call it delayed gratification. Yet what it means is that everyone will be able to see and gain from those objects, not just those rich enough to buy them.

That's a hard sell to grave robbers living in poverty, but not impossible, as the people of Úcupe and other villages have demonstrated. Poverty alone does not lead people to want to devour heritage rather than preserve it; first you must have that peculiarly exploitative attitude toward the past. No matter how hard it is to get people in poor countries not to raid tombs, to sacrifice that resource for the sake of a greater good, it has proved even harder to convince wealthy collectors of freshly looted antiquities to make the same sacrifice. They are mindless consumers of heritage, depriving everyone alive and everyone who ever will live of part of the collective memory that makes us human.

Chapter 15

COMING HOME

AFTER FIFTEEN YEARS of being shuffled through airports, car trunks, boxes, rice sacks, and suitcases, the looted treasures of Sipán finally have a permanent home, of sorts. The new Royal Tombs of Sipán Museum opened to the public in Lambayeque on November 9, 2002. Starkly modern, with low, angular lines and painted a bright terra-cotta like the color of certain varieties of Moche pottery, the museum contained everything Alva found in the thirteen tombs at Huaca Rajada, all the objects meticulously catalogued and conserved. About 1,400 pieces were on display, including the sixty or so pieces known or strongly suspected to be from Sipán and seized by police from the Bernal brothers and the assorted smugglers and collectors they supplied. The very existence of the museum was a triumph of scholarship over the looting and predatory collecting against which Alva, at the age of 51, had fought for a lifetime. It should have been a richly satisfying moment for him.

Yet it was tinged with sadness. His wife, Susana Meneses, died of cancer seven months before the museum was completed. She was only fifty-four. Alva was devastated that she did not live to see completion of the project on which they had worked together for fifteen years. A woman of prodigious energy and creativity, she had, early in the Sipán excavation, settled the mystery of how the *huaca* was built, establishing that it was constructed in stages over several centuries with Chimú bricks on top of Moche bricks, later putting her keen talents as a draftsman to use in the new museum, for which she designed many of the galleries. She was known as much for her talents as for her fiery temper. Museum guards once had to restrain her from physically attacking Enrico Poli when he came to the Brüning in 1987 to warn darkly of assassination plots against her husband, hoping to scare him off the Sipán site.[1] Another time, Peru's tourist board, PromPerú, arrived at the museum to make a promotional film and brought along a pretty fair-skinned model to play the role of a museum employee. Meneses was furious and threatened to throw out the whole crew unless they allowed the museum employees to play themselves, which they did.

Just after they were married, Alva and Meneses had worked together in the hills above Chiclayo to explore the hulking stone ruins of a city dating from the second millennium B.C. In jeans and straw hats, they excavated the remote site of huge curtain walls, terraced platforms, and sunken plazas. They could not afford a car, so they cheerfully camped at the site for days at a time and sat on the ruins at night, looking at the stars. With careers in archaeology before them, Alva told her, they would probably never have a vacation or own a home, and indeed they never did. That was in the late 1970s, Alva remembered, well before big-scale commercial looting came to Peru. There was no need for an archaeologist to carry a pistol, no need to post lookouts or obtain police protection. Looting was mostly a family affair in those days, a few families digging up pots at Holy Week and selling them for a few soles. Those days were long gone.

They had discovered the painted walls at Úcupe in 1983 and then dejectedly filled them back again with sand and earth, hoping to return someday to excavate them further, a day that never came. Next came their work at the enormous mud pyramids at Túcume, north of Lambayeque, where they had to ask the local villagers to stop dumping garbage on the site. They had organized the antilooting patrols, traveled all over Peru together to talk about preserving cultural patrimony, raised money for the new museum. They were something unusual in Peru: a married couple who were also professional colleagues. They raised two sons, Ignacio and Bruno, now in their twenties and both studying archaeology. Friends knew that it was Susana who gave the usually apolitical Alva much of his passion and combativeness on the issue of looting. When Peru erupted in protests in 2000 against Fujimori's fraudulent reelection, she caught her sons and some friends marching off to a protest rally. They were carrying protest signs, plus bottles of water and hankerchiefs to counteract the effects of tear gas, and instead of trying to stop them, as they expected, she joined them and marched off to protest.

As work on the museum entered its final year, in mid-2001, fatigue and malaise began to creep up on Meneses. She was diagnosed with cancer but told few people about it. She and Alva worked closely on a project to build a life-sized re-creation of a Moche royal ceremony in the museum. The

plan was to have a low stage with a group of standing figures—in the end
there were thirty-five—made of fiberglass, dressed in re-creations of
Moche royal garb. The exhibit was to be powered by electricity so that
some of the figures could raise their arms, tilt their heads, and drink from a
golden goblet. It sounded a bit Disneyland to some people but it turned out
to be one of the museum's highlights, an original touch, and the design of it
caused a small sensation. To create this piece of mechanical theater, they
needed models. So Susana went from town to town around the Department of Lambayeque to find people who bore classically indigenous facial
features and would agree to allow a sculptor to take a plaster impression of
their whole body and then re-create it in fiberglass. She and Alva didn't
have much trouble finding subjects; for example, the model for a Moche
guard was a robust young soldier from a local army base. Soon word
spread around the region that the new museum was seeking volunteers
who looked Indian, and local people started showing up at the museum eagerly offering themselves as models, with Meneses, Alva, and Carlos
Wester looking them over like theater casting directors and asking what
they knew about their ancestry. They had to turn away most of them, but
they were delighted that the museum was causing so much excitement. It
was on one of these scouting missions to find a few last models in the village of Chongoyape, in early 2002, that Meneses collapsed and was rushed
to a hospital. After that her decline was terrifyingly fast. She died at home
on April 15, 2002, with Walter at her side.

He returned to work at the still-incomplete museum the next day. The
workers were sanding bricks, erecting windowpanes, asking him about
specifications on this or that. All just like before, and yet all completely
different.[2]

At Alva's request, the Instituto Nacional de Cultura, which officially
owns the museum, allowed her to be buried in the new museum's yard,
with a simple stone marker in the grass. On the day of the museum's opening ceremony, someone placed fresh flowers at her grave.

The museum is located about half an hour's drive from the village of Sipán.
Alva had come under some pressure to build the museum in Sipán itself,
but he parried the idea because the roads to the village were inadequate,
the village itself too isolated, and its people still too hostile to outsiders, and
to top it off the local sugar workers were known to erect barriers of logs
and burning tires across the only road to Sipán during strikes and protests.
Alva had also turned aside proposals from officials at the INC to load the
Sipán treasures into a yet-to-be-built annex at the Brüning Museum, as
well as proposals to build the new museum in Lima.

In the end, the Royal Tombs of Sipán Museum was true to Alva's vision in almost every important respect. Its design of slopes, platforms, and ramps suggested a *huaca,* and its vividly colored exterior hinted at the dazzling artwork inside. It was set on an eighteen-acre lot with rows of native crops like potatoes, corn, and squash on one side, harvested by local gardeners, and a shady grove of native algarobo trees with picnic areas and an outdoor stage in the rear, all meant to create a relaxed, community atmosphere that would celebrate indigenous heritage without sanitizing or trivializing it. The idea was to create not just a museum, not even a whole cultural destination, but a sense of self-worth among the descendants of the Moche and the Chimú who had lost everything—their language, their names, their oral traditions that had lasted for 1,300 years—under five centuries of Spanish and Republican Peruvian rule. It wasn't about rejecting the modern world. The descendants could still buy skin whitener in the drugstores in Chiclayo, still name their children Jacqueline and Ronald, they could, and did, still own microwaves, boom boxes, and televisions. Alva was aiming for a deeper and longer-lasting change in the way Peruvians thought about themselves and their collective identity, a task that intellectuals like Julio C. Tello and Luis Valcárcel had undertaken at moments in the twentieth century by writing books for the academic elite that extolled the achievements of the Incas and their forebears, but which few had achieved with the concrete success of Alva and his new museum.

"This museum exists not just to show objects, but to promote a sense of identity and self-esteem among the people, make them feel that they are really the heirs to a great culture. That's the goal, but it's so hard to get people to look at their past that way. Like in every place else in the Americas, these people were just crushed," Alva said.[3]

The museum was built with a budget of about $5 million, some paid by the Peruvian state but the largest share coming from the proceeds of the touring show of Sipán treasures in Germany, the United States, and Japan. "You're looking at the place where all the money from the touring show went. This is it," Carlos Wester told me one day as we stood in front of the under-construction museum. The government of Switzerland pitched in with a grant of $1 million.

Architecturally, it made no contrived attempt to "fit in" with the Spanish late colonial and nineteenth-century buildings around it. It looked unmistakably modern, and yet its main architectural elements—sunken plazas, ramps, multilevel platforms—all harked back to the *huacas* and monumental cities of Peru's ancient past.

Visitors enter by walking up a long ramp rising gradually to the top of the building, in the same way that priests of the Moche and other pre-Hispanic cultures ascended their structures. Once inside the building, you start at the top and work your way down, a path meant to evoke the archaeological process and to make you feel that you are "discovering" the

Lord of Sipán for yourself. The first exhibit offers a general overview of the Moche, with maps, diagrams, pottery, and artifacts from other sites illustrating daily life in that era, followed by the first glittering piece of gold from Sipán: the gold rattle confiscated by U.S. Customs in Miami, hanging in its own vitrine in the middle of a room. It gives a taste of the treasures to follow.

Next comes a section on the archaeological process, complete with the original trowels, brushes, picks, and other tools used at Sipán, beneath a huge photograph from the rough days of 1987 with Meneses, Chero, and Alva inspecting the tomb, workers brushing bricks, and a policeman standing nearby with a submachine gun. Some of the 1,130 ceramic jars found at the site stand nearby, some with the original llama bones and seeds found inside them, now restored and preserved.

The day before the museum opened, Alva gave a tour of the museum to a group of reporters in which I was the only foreigner. Dressed in a blue blazer and rumpled trousers, he looked tired, with his beard long, unkempt, and flecked with gray, and he'd lost some weight. He looked frankly like a man in need of a wife, but as he led us around I sensed that he knew how lucky he was. Few people got a chance to bring a career's work to fruition like this, to create an institution that embodied everything one had struggled for and then to have creative control over every inch of it.

"We wanted to give a sense of space, to highlight the objects, but not make it all about objects and nothing else," he said. "Usually belongings are exhibited in Peruvian museums as if they were decorations and curiosities. That's what we wanted to get away from. We wanted context."

A tall, balding man with the clothes and bearing that suggested a wealthy *limeño* accompanied Alva, adding commentaries now and then on aspects about the building. This man, I soon found out, was the architect of the museum, Celso Prado Pastor, who had designed the Brüning Museum in 1966 when he was a cub architect and who had had a long association with Alva. "There are so many museums in this country that try to cram in everything they've got. That's what we wanted to avoid. We wanted it low density and to bring the visitor gradually down to the tomb, make him feel part of the process."

As we descended stairs and ramps, moving downward layer by layer, there was an inescapable feeling of being inside a tomb. There were no windows, so the only light was artificial, cast by tiny, powerful lamps hanging from the ceiling with fiber-optic cables and casting the objects and their explanatory panels in a warm glow. Everything else was dark, heightening the sense of mystery and drama that Alva had been looking for. Yet keeping the building hermetically sealed to the outdoors was also for the security and well-being of the objects themselves. The temperature (71°F) and humidity (65 percent) were precisely calibrated to replicate conditions inside the tomb where the pieces had rested for nearly two millennia. Sunlight and changes in humidity levels could damage them irretrievably, an especially acute problem in northern Peru, where periodic El Niño disasters can drench the area in rain for weeks at a stretch.

Unlike the inside of a *huaca*, the museum galleries were spacious. With thirty-two thousand feet of exhibition space, there was none of the sense of cramping or dumping of objects that marred other museums in Peru, and in some places Alva seemed to have gone too far in the other direction. Certain spaces felt vacant, a bit underutilized. This was deliberate. Alva's hope was that the new museum would house more artifacts from Sipán—those yet to be excavated and those that might be recovered later from private collectors, most notably Poli, who was believed to hold between one-third and two-thirds of the surviving contents of the tombs looted by the Bernal brothers. With this much space, the museum would never need an annex or addition, even if it managed to get the ailing Poli's entire collection of pre-Columbian treasures; and it could still comfortably handle traveling exhibits. In Peru and abroad, Alva had seen enough bad museums to know what he wanted to avoid.

"I visited the Egyptian Museum in Cairo and there you see the problem," he told us. "The funerary offerings that accompanied Tutankhamen to his grave look awful. They're badly lighted, thrown together. They're presented as if they were on sale in a jewelry store."

Despite their polished, sophisticated look, nearly all the exhibition spaces at Alva's museum were designed and constructed by his own staff. Alva had hired an Italian firm with experience in museology to cut outlines on the lighting fixtures to conform to the shape of each object, so that only the object itself would be lit. But, unhappy with the firm's work and its prices, he canceled the contract and had his own staff do the work in-house. The result was superior and it saved several hundred thousand dollars, he said.

He led us over to the necklace of gold-and-silver peanut beads that hung in its own vitrine in the center of a room so that it was—for the first time in any museum—visible from all angles. The effect was stunning. The piece gained a sense of volume and voluptuousness that it lacked in 1994 at the American Museum of Natural History in New York and at the Museum of the Nation in Lima, where it had been displayed flat. "Every single object is full of meaning and symbolism, each one requiring detailed study, and by displaying them in the round, we're inviting the viewer to study them from all angles, just as researchers do," he said.

I had seen all these objects in three museums before—in New York, Lima, and at the Brüning—and yet every one of them looked fresh and exciting. I was amazed at how much difference it made to see the objects in three dimensions, in a glass case in the middle of space. All the showstoppers from the traveling Sipán exhibition were there—the gold-and-turquoise ear spools with their tiny warriors, the delicate pectoral necklaces of shell beads, the gold-and-silver scepter with its scene of a warrior clubbing a subdued prisoner, the thin sheets of gold that covered the Lord of Sipán's eyes, nose, mouth, and teeth. Everything was thoroughly explained but not *too* explained—"some museums get too technical," Alva said—thus creating an experience that was profoundly visual but, at the same time, meaty and informative. We descended past a decorative adobe wall into the galleries holding the objects from the tomb of the Old Lord of Sipán, with its rich array of backflaps, necklaces, and rattles, all ten of which floated in the air, suspended, in a glass case from barely visible fibers.

On the museum's third and lowest level lay the splintered, fragmentary remains of the man himself, the Lord of Sipán. His bones were the color of chocolate, shiny with the conservator's shellaclike liquid, with only his femurs in any state of completeness and his skull a delicate-looking shell the size of a large gourd. Set on the same, careful east-west alignment in which he was found, the man lay in a sarcophagus of brown marble and algarobo planks similar to those of the original coffin, covered by a pane of glass. Beneath him lay some of the mud-brick dust from his original tomb inside the *huaca*.

A guard stood nearby, admonishing the reporters against taking flash pictures.

"There are many ethical issues involved with showing dead bodies," Alva had told me a year before, when the sarcophagus was still under construction. "In designing it this way, our idea was to make it look as much like a veneration as possible and not exhibition. We show it with very low light, we give it a funerary connotation, and we try to make it feel as much as possible like a grave, because although this is a museum, it is also a mausoleum. The remains of an entire dynasty will be buried here."[4]

A month before the opening, Alva arranged the Lord of Sipán's final journey: the half-mile trip from the Brüning to the new museum. The restored bones were placed in a wooden coffin that was draped with the red-and-white Peruvian flag, as befits a deceased head of state, before four pallbearers lifted the coffin and carried it through the hushed streets of Lambayeque with a uniformed army band playing a funeral march. Alva, Wester, and various distinguished citizens walked slowly along behind the coffin and into the museum.[5] Later, without pomp, Alva and his staff carried the remains of the lord's various attendants, priests, and relatives, including the man who was probably his grandfather, the Old Lord of Sipán, to their final resting places in the new museum. Only the lord in the middle generation was missing, of course; his remains had been destroyed by the looters.

Alva escorted us into the museum's last room. Instantly something felt very different. It resembled everything that Alva said he disliked about other museums, with objects bunched up in glass cases, two-dimensional, bereft of explanation. This was the loot room, the place where the pieces seized by authorities in Peru and the United States over the years had washed up. Alva had presented them as well as he could but, being wrenched out of their original setting by looters, there wasn't much he could say about them without resorting to a fair amount of conjecture. Alva had turned the room into an exhibit on the destructive action of the antiquities trade, with panoramic color photographs of the pockmarked cemetery at Sipán and the devastation at Cerro Corbacho and an account of how the *huaca* was wrested from looters. The whole stash from the Bernal homestead hung in one case—the masks, broken peanut beads, and the golden goblet—and in another case rested the two necklaces from Sotheby's. Except for the rattle, which was on the top floor, all the Sipán pieces from Miami bust were there, including the fox head and gold feline mask, along with a photograph of Alva standing with Maria Capo and a few other customs officials beside the confiscated objects.

Alva believed that about half the objects in this room had at one time or another passed through Apesteguía's hands. In contrast to the impeccable state of most pieces in the rest of the museum, the ones here showed scratches, nicks, and abrasions or, like an ear spool that had lost its backing and all its precious stones, they had a mutilated look. The room had a strange feeling of anonymity, of odds and ends that had been thrown together and meant to impress but that left only a taste of alienation, fragmentation, and loss.

In the middle of the room, in its own vitrine suspended from the ceiling, hung the backflap. For the first time, I could see it from all sides and gain a real impression of its massive girth. It gleamed with a light of its own and seemed bigger somehow than the case in which it hung. It still showed the indelible scratches caused by scrubbing with Brillo pads, but I still could detect a faint impression of the textile weaving on the back that had convinced so many people it was authentic. A black brace discreetly held together the two broken parts of the rattle.

That evening, about five hundred of Peru's most prominent archaeologists, businesspeople, politicians, diplomats, and academics crowded into the museum's sunken front yard for the opening ceremony. Waiters served bottle after bottle of Argentine wine, and people lined up to congratulate Alva. President Alejandro Toledo and his wife, Eliane Karp, a Berkeley-educated anthropologist, arrived in a black limousine nearly as big as some of the houses it passed on the streets of Lambayeque. In the stately, colonial-era town of about fifteen thousand people, Alva was respected and admired more than any politician. But the villagers of Sipán had never forgiven him. A big crowd of them gathered that evening outside the museum's twelve-foot-high steel gates to try to spoil the party, carrying the same old banners ("Alva, give us back our jewels!"), hooting at the luminaries gathered inside the gates, and shouting to Toledo's car as he drove in, "Toledo, friend, Alva is your enemy!" The villagers still resented being shooed off the *huaca* in 1987 and now they had a new reason to get steamed: the museum had been built twenty miles away, in Lambayeque, and not in their village. Once again, they had been frozen out of the benefits that emerged from what they thought was their *huaca*.

On my visits to Sipán I had met Carlos Zapata, head of the community development committee and its highest elected official. A compact man in his thirties, he startled me sometimes with how articulate he could be in the language of victimhood. "They said they were going to build an on-site museum and where did they put it? In Lambayeque. They've given us no role and no participation," he had told me in Sipán, while we sat under a flimsy roof of woven reeds to take refuge from the sun. "First they took away our treasures and now they deny us the only opportunity we had for jobs here. They built a museum. Great. How about a decent school for Sipán?"

The last panes of donated Japanese glass had been fitted into the displays that very morning. Alva looked tired after days of final preparations. With a cool maritime breeze drifting through the crowd, he stepped up to the microphone to speak.

"For more than four centuries, the tombs of our ancestors have been despoiled and pillaged, and the objects that accompanied them to their graves have circulated around the world to become mere trophies for collectors," he said. He recounted how the looters broke into the burial pyramid in 1987 and destroyed the tomb of the Moche lord, "another black page in this history of destruction. Yet we assumed the responsibility of saving Sipán from still more looting." Thanks to the patient work of archaeology, Peruvians could now see the Lord of Sipán as their country's first identifiable ruler, he said, adding that there were certainly earlier rulers but that we will never know anything about them because their tombs were lost. He recounted how he, Susana, and their colleagues braved the threats and attacks from looters and their patrons and how they conceived this museum and mausoleum as Peru's most palpable victory over the antiquities trade, "the trade that every day mutilates more of our history."

Standing next to Toledo, Alva told the president there was one way he could now complete his work on the museum: order the confiscation of Sipán pieces belonging to private Peruvian collectors (with compensation, he clarified later).

"What we need, Mr. President, is a law that makes the Peruvian state a participant at last in the recovery of its heritage," he said. It was an obvious shot at Poli.

Amid thunderous applause, Alva stepped aside and Toledo came forward to speak. Born in the Andean highlands near Huaraz in 1946, Toledo was Peru's first elected president of indigenous ethnicity. Elected in 2001 after leading a popular surge of opposition to Fujimori's rigged and constitutionally dubious third election, Toledo had been raised in poverty in the fishing port of Chimbote, where he worked as a shoe-shine boy, but he was bright and charming and he was also a talented soccer player. He got a job as a reporter at Chimbote's daily newspaper and later won a spot at the University of California at San Francisco on a soccer scholarship with the help of some Peace Corps volunteers. In the Bay Area he completed his doctorate in education at Stanford and met his future wife, Eliane Karp, who spoke the Andean indigenous language Quechua better than he did and, as first lady, was given to verbal digs at the white Lima bourgeoisie. As president, Toledo liked to emphasize Peru's and his own indigenous roots. He flew to the Inca ruins of Machu Picchu the day after taking office as president in 2001 and symbolically repeated the whole ceremony: musicians wearing red ponchos played Andean panpipes while Toledo held a traditional Inca scepter known as a *varayoc* and gave thanks to "the force and the courage that the Apus and the earth gave me." Apus are mountain gods, and they sent good weather to make a gorgeous photo op that appeared in television and newspapers all over the world.[6] Toledo's staffers made no bones about the fact that the whole show was geared to bolster tourism and command a more positive image abroad for the country after the years of guerrilla violence and dictatorship under Fujimori. It worked splendidly.

Anybody who thought that Toledo's up-from-poverty life story might make him identify with Alva's themes of pre-Hispanic pride and identity was disappointed. Toledo was businesslike to a fault, focused as perhaps presidents should be on the potential for economic growth in everything. In his speech at the museum, he started out with the usual paeans to national culture ("a people without culture is a people without a soul") and then talked about the new museum as little more than a tourist attraction, reminding the crowd that he had promised to raise the country's foreign tourist influx to three million per year by the end of his term in 2006 and that this place would help him reach that goal. The museum, he announced, would be incorporated right away into all of the government's tourism campaigns and brochures. It had become, in Toledo's description, another tool to get foreigners to come and spend dollars.

"The world is getting smaller, and we can get many more tourists to come to this museum," he said. "Culture is not just something to see but something to sell—in the best sense of the word."

The crowd groaned. Toledo seemed tone-deaf to Alva's message, and he gave no reply at all to Alva's call for a crackdown on private antiquities collecting. (When I called Toledo's office a few weeks later to ask how the president viewed Alva's suggestion, I was told the president respected Alva but had nothing to say on the subject of private collecting.) When Toledo finished his speech, the crowd of Sipán villagers outside the gates heckled, chanted, and shouted, and although they were too far away to tell if it was against Toledo or Alva or both, it sounded like we might all have some difficulty getting past them on the way out. People looked at each other a bit nervously. Alva and the Toledos, bleached by the television lights, then walked over to the place where a bottle of *chicha*, a traditional fermented corn liquor used in Andean celebrations and rituals, hung from a post next to a copper reproduction of a Moche war club. The club was heavy and Karp, a delicate, red-haired woman, held it up a bit unsteadily until, with Alva's help, she whacked open the bottle to christen the museum. The liquor frothed and spattered all over the first lady, Toledo, Alva, and the rest of us standing nearby; suddenly we all smelled like *chicha*, as people have at Peruvian ceremonies for many, many centuries.

The museum was finished, and, if it was ever true that Peru did not have adequate institutions to house its own treasures, it was certainly not true any longer. Peru could claim to have a world-class museum infrastructure, with no fewer than three institutions in the Lambayeque area alone.

Alva, for the first time in a decade, felt he had time to return to his and Susana's first love, field archaeology. He and Chero had begun plans to excavate a site called Chotuna, a complex of ruins and *huacas* near the seaside a few miles outside Lambayeque that had mostly avoided destruction thanks to active vigilance by local residents. Chotuna was believed by many archaeologists to be the site referred to in legends first recorded in writing by a Spanish chronicler named Miguel Cabello Valboa in 1586. Cabello Valboa transcribed stories told to him by north-coast Indians about how, several centuries before the Spaniards, a man called Ñaymlap (the word is practically unpronounceable for most English speakers but it sounds something like nime-LAHP) sailed ashore in a flotilla of rafts with his wife, an entourage of forty attendants including a royal cook and conch shell trumpeter, and an idol made of green stone called the Yampallec, from which the name Lambayeque is believed to derive. He announced to the local people that he had been sent from afar to govern them, and he began a dynasty that lasted through eleven more rulers. The dynasty ended when the last lord of Ñaymlap's line was tempted by a sorceress to move the green idol, a sin that provoked thirty days of disastrous rains and flooding, after which his people rose up, killed him, and tossed him into the sea. After that, "a certain powerful tyrant called Chimo Capac came with an invincible army," Cabello Valboa wrote, and conquered the area.[7]

It sounded like a beautiful legend, but what made it unlike others recorded by the Spaniards was that there was some archaeological evidence to support it. Although there was no sign of a large seaborne disembarkation, researchers had found evidence of a new political order that spread from the coast over Lambayeque between A.D. 700 and 900, following the collapse of the last Moche state, at Pampa Grande.[8] The calamitous floods mentioned in the oral tradition as following the twelfth ruler might correspond nicely to an El Niño disaster known from sediment deposits to have occurred in the year 1100, and indeed there is clear evidence of conquest by the Chimú empire—"Chimo Capac"—shortly thereafter.

Cabello Valboa, the Spanish chronicler, wrote that Ñaymlap, upon reaching old age, instructed his descendants to spread a story that he had sprouted wings and flown up into the sky; that way, his followers would think he was immortal. They duly followed his wishes and, to keep up the deception, never even took his body outside his room, according to the story related to Cabello Valboa. He wrote:

> The time came for his death, and so that his vassals would not know that death had jurisdiction over him, his attendants buried him secretly in the same room where he had lived. They then proclaimed it throughout the land, as he himself had instructed, that he had taken wings and flown away.[9]

Incredibly, both the legend and the true story had been told for centuries, side by side, or rather somehow woven together into the same story, until it reached the ears of the diligent Spanish scribe. We know he must have transcribed it with some degree of accuracy because in 1782, another writer independently heard the same legend and wrote it down as well, and it was in most key respects identical to the version given to Cabello Valboa. The rest of the story, as told to him, maintained that Ñaymlap's descendants spread throughout Lambayeque, and again there is archaeological evidence to support the spread of a new culture known as Sicán, whose principal center was Batán Grande. The standing male figure on scores of ceremonial knives dug up by looters at Batán Grande and sitting in museums all over the United States is now believed by some archaeologists (though by no means all) to be, in fact, a representation of Ñaymlap.

Chotuna, or "Chot" as Cabello Valboa's informants called it, was thus the ancestral home, the point of creation of a new political order that swept over the north coast on the ruins of the Moche. Looters have damaged the burial mounds at Chotuna but not destroyed them, and somewhere inside them may lie the secret tomb of Ñaymlap, founder of the dynasty, the tomb whose existence Ñaymlap wanted to conceal. Alva hoped to find it. He might even find the green idol that, when disturbed, had brought so much ruin and destruction.

Epilogue

THE GOVERNMENT OF Peru awarded Bob Wittman and Bob Goldman the Order of Merit for Distinguished Service, a distinction for those who have served Peru in the area of arts, industry, or business, at a ceremony at the Peruvian embassy in Washington in July 2000.

Wittman played a key role in one of the largest FBI art-theft recovery operations ever in June 2002 when, at a Madrid hotel, Spanish police arrested two men who had stolen seventeen masterwork paintings from the Madrid home of Esther Koplowitz Romero de Joseu, the billionaire heiress to a construction fortune. The investigation had been handled entirely by Spanish police until the FBI's Eastern European Organized Crime Task Force learned that thieves were offering Pieter Brueghel the Elder's *Temptation of Saint Anthony*, one of the stolen works, as bait for the others, which included Francisco de Goya's *The Swing* and Camille Pissarro's *Landscape at Eragny*.

The FBI established contact with the sellers and set up a sting with Spanish police, offering to lend Wittman as an undercover specialist with enough knowledge to make him believable as an art appraiser. He flew to Madrid and introduced himself to the sellers as an American art history professor who would authenticate the stolen works on behalf of a group of anonymous Russian buyers. The buyers had the money, and Wittman, as their agent, was able to gain the confidence of the sellers, whom Spanish police believed to be the leaders of a criminal enterprise that had been dealing in narcotics, stolen cars, and guns across Europe for at least ten years. Professing a great interest in art, the Spanish gangsters and the charming American professor got along so famously in their meetings in a hotel lobby over glasses of Spanish wine that they asked him to join their enterprise as their full-time art consultant. They had planned to kidnap a British art historian for that purpose, they said, but Wittman would serve even better and save them the bother of kidnapping. They confided to him what they hoped would be their next hit: the Van Gogh Museum in Amsterdam.

The sellers told Wittman he would have to produce one million euros (about $1.2 million) in cash before he could see the Brueghel. He could have it on the spot or, if he wasn't satisfied with its authenticity, he could walk with the money. He could have nine more of the stolen paintings for an additional nine million euros—quite a steal, so to speak, considering that the Brueghel alone was worth at least $4 million. Wittman strung them out in negotiations over nearly two weeks, keeping up the illusion of a deal, keeping up his persona of a corrupt professor.

On the day of the deal, the entire hotel had been turned into a kind of elaborate theater. About one hundred Spanish policemen posed as maids, bellhops, garbage collectors, and bystanders all over the hotel as Wittman and two Spanish officers posing as his security detail sent by the Russian buyers waited in a suite for the two sellers to arrive. The sellers drove all around Madrid making sure they weren't being followed and used disposable cell phones to thwart surveillance, once calling to say they were ten minutes away when in fact they were in the hotel lobby. One of them took the Brueghel up to the suite where Wittman and the two others waited. Still posing as the art professor and dressed the part in a blazer and slacks, Wittman carefully examined the painting under a black light and pointed out the centuries of restoration, inpainting, and craquelure. Yes, it was an authentic Brueghel, he said. And you're under arrest.

The other gangster, allegedly the capo of the organization, was arrested in the lobby. A third man who turned himself in the next day confirmed what police suspected all along: he had been Koplowitz's security guard on the night of the robbery. It had been an inside job. She had been betrayed by her own security staff.[1]

Thomas Chávez left the Palace of the Governors in 2002, after twenty-one years as its director. He became director of the National Hispanic Cultural Center in Albuquerque after having been passed over to succeed Livesay as head of the Museum of New Mexico system. "Twenty-one years is too long to be doing anything, no matter how much you love it," said Chávez.[2]

His successor at the Palace, Frances Levine, wrote to me later regarding the Peruvian pieces confiscated and subsequently returned by the FBI. "This issue is delicate, and a matter that our museum is scrutinizing internally," she wrote.[3]

Brian Midkiff never returned to investigating antiquities and was transferred from Santa Fe to FBI headquarters in Washington in June 2002. He and his wife liked Santa Fe but they wanted better schools for their young son and thought they would find them in the Washington area.

Orlando Mendez has been slowly rebuilding his life and his marriage after the backflap nearly destroyed him. The $100,000 to buy the piece from Ramos Ronceros was his money. "I got involved in what I thought was a simple business deal, and it blew up in my face," he said.[4] He and Denis Garcia, who lives quietly with his wife in Miami, bumped into each other on the street once but otherwise have not seen each other or spoken since finishing their sentences.

Samuel Bernal lives with his new wife in Chiclayo and says he has finally given up alcohol but can't quite pull himself away from looting. A visiting Frenchman, perhaps a small-time smuggler, was arrested at the Chiclayo airport in March 2002 with some twenty-five Moche ceramic pots from the Sipán area. The Frenchman implicated Samuel, who has since been told by police to stay away from Sipán or he will be arrested. This means he cannot visit his father.

Samuel says he believes a few more gold objects left by his late brother, Emil, are still buried in the ground around the old house. Someday he plans to look for them.

Christopher Donnan, the UCLA authority on the Moche, became the subject of an investigation by the INC in late 2001 after he used a heavy frontloader, similar to a bulldozer, to clear sterile backfill at the Huaca Dos Cabezas in the Jequetepeque Valley. Peruvian news reports said the machinery damaged the monument, but Donnan vigorously denied this, telling the Lima daily *El Comercio*, "The only thing removed [with the frontloader] was dirt, without affecting the architecture of the monument. This is easy to prove." The inquiry ended without penalty or charges. Although the accusations against Donnan were probably unfair, the incident, recalling as it did the Aurich family's bulldozers, served to underscore the prickly sensitivity with which Peruvians now regarded the integrity of their ancient assets.

In 2003 the University of Texas Press published Donnan's study of Moche portrait vessels, *Moche Portraits from Ancient Peru*, which was based on minute analysis of more than nine hundred ceramic pots, only 5 percent of which were excavated by trained archaeologists. "The rest were wrenched from graves by looters in their haste to satisfy collectors' desire to own Moche treasures," a reviewer for *Archaeology* wrote. "Apparently, Donnan's approach is: If you can't fight the collectors, you might as well get what you can from them."[5]

Donnan increasingly saw that analysis of Moche ceramic vessels without any knowledge of even which valley they came from, much less the exact find-spot, was impeding progress in the task that had occupied him and a generation of other archaeologists since the late 1950s: understanding what was now widely considered one of the most sophisticated cultures of the ancient world. "We have the basic architecture, the basic outlines of what Moche society was like, no more than that," he said in a lecture at the Pre-Columbian Society of Washington, D.C. in 2004. "If we had only fifty portrait vessels, only fifty, excavated by archaeologists and with a precise provenance, then it would open up a whole new world in our understanding of the Moche." His archive at UCLA now had photographs of 165,000 Moche artifacts—more than 95 percent of them excavated by looters.

Robin, the happy grave robber named for Batman's sidekick, was arrested on the morning of September 17, 2002, near a burial mound known as the Huaca Malena, only a few miles from the place where he, Remi, and Harry dug the Inca textile that night with me. Robin and four other looters were hauled into a police station in the town of Cañete, where police made them stand for television and newspaper cameras in front of their shovels, knapsacks, and an assortment of ancient Wari ceramics and textiles that the police told the reporters had been seized with these five bedraggled looters. I saw their picture in *El Comercio*.[6] Robin held his head down, which gave him a sad and repentant look though, knowing him, I was sure he would have no regrets at all. I didn't recognize the men arrested with him. The newspaper account printed Robin's real name, Roberto Santos, making it the first time that many of Robin's friends and most likely the people arrested with him that night learned his true identity. Robin had been unmasked.

All five were released by a judge two days later (upon payment of bribes by one of the looters' buyers, Robin believed) and the case died. Robin returned home to Pampa Libre and drove a taxi in the nearby town of Chancay, resolved to stay out of looting for six months or so, at least until the police attention died down.

When I spoke to him on the phone some months later, he told me what happened. Police officers in a cruiser caught them entirely by chance as the five of them, holding their shovels and poles, emerged at dawn onto the Pan-American Highway and stood by the roadside trying to flag down a bus toward Lima after a disappointing night of digging up tombs. They had worked hard but discovered nothing of value, only masses and masses of skulls. He said they should have recognized them as a bad omen and stopped work immediately. It was the first time he had been arrested. He had no idea where police got all the Wari artifacts that appeared in the news pictures.

The *huaca* where they were arrested was barely a stone's throw from the one where they had taken me, the one he thought was so promising. I asked Robin, why weren't they still digging there?

"We found a few more things there, and then it stopped giving us merchandise," he said. "I guess we had taken everything out of it."

On October 9, 2002, a group of forty-five collectors, museum officials, and lawyers gathered in the Fifth Avenue apartment of collector Guido Goldman for the first meeting of the board of advisers of a new organization called the American Council for Cultural Policy, or ACCP. They included the collector Shelby White, legal scholar John Merryman, former director of the Kimbell Museum Edmund Pillsbury, and the retired counsel to the Trustees of the Metropolitan Museum of Art, Ashton Hawkins, who was reported to be the impetus for the group's creation. The group was clear about its goal: to stop the proliferation of legal obstacles to the flow of antiquities into the United States. Its leaders made a point of excluding dealers from the board of advisers to ensure that the new group would not be confused with the antiquities dealers' lobby NADAOPA, which had been so disgraced by Frederick Schultz's conviction and by the failure to stop the Italian MOU and a long list of other restrictions. The new council's aims, according to Hawkins, included pressuring the Bush administration to overhaul the 1983 Cultural Property Implementation Act and to persuade museums to get more involved in stopping "this Italian initiative, which is a direct threat."[7]

"We believe that legitimate dispersal of cultural material through the market is one of the best ways to protect it. We're interested in the protection of culture as much as the protection of legitimate collecting," Hawkins said.[8]

The new group endeavored to show that it had a larger agenda for cultural preservation, as well. In an unusual act of cooperation, a group of

ACCP advisers teamed up with McGuire Gibson and other archaeologists to meet with U.S. Defense Department officials at the Pentagon before the bombing of Iraq in 2003 to ask the U.S. military to take care not to hit Iraqi archaeological sites and museums in the coming war and then guard them after the bombing stopped. They got the first wish but not the second: sites and museums suffered almost no damage in the aerial bombing but were overrun with looters once Saddam fell.

Yet the ACCP's involvement with Iraq was remembered more for a serious faux pas. The council's treasurer, a lawyer and collector named William Pearlstein, was quoted in news reports as saying he believed Iraq's "retentionist" policies on antiquities should be relaxed under a new, post-Saddam government and exports of antiquities liberalized. Coming as it did after the Pentagon meeting, Pearlstein's comment suggested an unholy alliance between the U.S. government and dealers to allow a free-for-all of Iraqi antiquities exports, and it sent plenty of archaeologists and commentators, particularly in the British press, into a netherworld of conspiracy theories. Pearlstein was forced to apologize and say his remarks had been misinterpreted.[9]

The incident caused a moment of embarrassment for the new council—but only a moment. Under its influence, the Bush administration moved quickly to give collectors a bigger say in antiquities laws. When the State Department's powerful Cultural Property Advisory Committee resigned en masse after the looting of Iraq's National Museum of Antiquities in April 2003, President George W. Bush appointed a famed collector of pre-Columbian art named Jay Kislak, who had attended some ACCP meetings, to be the committee's new head. A millionaire banker and Republican Party contributor from south Florida, Kislak had turned his collection of Mayan, Olmec, and Aztec treasures and rare books into the heart of a charitable foundation at which scholars, by invitation only, could study and analyze the works. Kislak and his foundation represented everything to which the new ACCP aspired—political influence, social respectability, and a veneer of scholarship.

If collectors and art museums were trying to offer a more circumspect image, some dealers were still speaking the old language. The Taliban's destruction of the Bamiyan Buddha statues in Afghanistan in early 2001 and later the theft at the Baghdad museum were all the proof that antiquities dealers needed to argue once again that third-world countries were incapable of protecting their own treasures, which would be better off in the hands of adoring collectors. The source countries' claims were no better than anyone else's, they argued. Thirty years of legislation to combat the trade in pillaged goods had done nothing to change this transparently self-serving philosophy.

"One curious point in this debate is that the present-day population of so many archaeologically well-endowed regions consists of the descendants of the invaders who destroyed the very cultures whose remnants their modern governments now so jealously claim as exclusively theirs," wrote New York dealer André Emmerich in the days after the Iraqi museum looting. "Turkey's Adriatic coast [*sic*] is rich in ancient Greek art — but in the 1920s, the remnant of its Greek population was expelled in an early instance of ethnic cleansing. Most modern Latin Americans are descendants of the Spanish conquistadors who destroyed the Aztec and Inca empires and all their works within reach. Do these descendants have a better moral claim to the buried artifacts of earlier civilizations than the rest of humanity?"

Emmerich added a new facet to the argument: American exceptionalism. "We are a country of immigrants, coming from countries all over the world, and surely have a moral claim to reasonable access to the buried treasures of our common ancestors."[10]

The day after I visited Isin in May 2003, I walked back under Assassin's Gate and into Saddam's palace, with its monstrous rooftop busts of the dictator, and waited for two hours on his kitschy gold furniture to see the U.S. Army officer in charge of protecting cultural sites, Colonel Kessel, to tell him what I had seen. Isin was being destroyed by looters, I told him. The whole place had been overrun and was being dug up. Kessel stood on the polished marble floor in his boots and said nothing, turning away with a weary look that said he had heard this all before and was growing tired of it.

Two days later, a reporter for *The New York Times* went to Isin and found that the number of looters had swelled to about 150. The morning the reporter dropped in, the looters had excavated two large and intact urns, a vase, and "the leg to a statue of what might have been a bull or a calf, and countless small engraved artifacts," he wrote.[11] With reports of the looting of Iraqi ancient sites finally appearing in American newspapers, the U.S. Army began flying helicopters low over Isin and firing warning shots to try to shoo away looters in late May 2003. Flyovers at other archaeological sites in southern Iraq followed, and at one site the looters foolishly fired back, leading to a gun battle in which several looters were killed.

"That's all they can do right now," a U.S. Army captain told me in Baghdad. "After one or two incidents like that, maybe looters will start to get the message."

All over Iraq, the message seemed to be that the Americans were leaving the Iraqis to fend for themselves against relentless pressure from antiquities hunters, an inevitable process, perhaps, but one that still eliminated the only real barrier to the destruction. At Nimrud, the Assyrian ruins where looters had repeatedly broken in after Saddam's fall, the U.S. command withdrew Cory Roberts's platoon from the site in September—one day after it was declared a World Heritage Site by UNESCO.[12] The timing was terrible, but the withdrawal followed the installation of a new corps of thirty local guards, trained and armed by the Americans, plus the seven original guards contracted by the regional Antiquities Department, an Iraqi government agency left over from Saddam's day. U.S. army patrols were to check the site periodically.

"I believe that this constitutes ample security, and should problems arise, help is close at hand," said art historian John Malcolm Russell of the Massachusetts College of Art, one of the world's top authorities on Assyrian culture, who, as deputy senior adviser in Baghdad to the new Iraqi Ministry of Culture, helped organized the new corps. "The U.S. troops were only moved from the site after ample alternative security had been arranged."[13]

After seeing the thirty bullet holes in the guards' trailer at Nimrud, the chiseled-out carvings, and the terrified guards, I had my doubts whether the new Iraqi policemen would be able to face down the antiquities trade. Maybe they would. But there was no doubt that, nearly a year after the fall of Saddam, looted artifacts were still flowing out of Iraq in a drearily familiar assault on a nation just when it was most vulnerable and drained by war and poverty. It wasn't just the Americans and the British who had invaded Iraq; so had the antiquities trade, with potentially even greater consequences in the long term for the Iraqis' sense of identity and the integrity of their cultural heritage. Matthew Bogdanos, the hyperactive U.S. Marine colonel and Manhattan assistant prosecutor with a classics degree from Columbia who directed the investigation into the theft at the Baghdad museum, said in a long interview that more than 750 looted Iraqi antiquities had been seized outside Iraq in only six months since Saddam's fall.

"New York and London are the two hot spots," he said.[14] Artifacts looted from archaeological sites were being mixed up with those stolen from the museum, which numbered about thirteen thousand. "We are seeing that it is the same pipeline," said Bogdanos, "the same pre-existing art-smuggling architecture, if you will, that is being used both for items taken from the museum, particularly the basement, and these sites."[15]

ACKNOWLEDGMENTS

THIS BOOK BEGAN as an article entitled "Standing Up to the Smugglers" in the June 2000 issue of *ARTnews*, whose executive editor, Robin Cembalest, gave me the room and encouragement to keep exploring the subject in the pages of that magazine over the subsequent four years. My editors, Colleen Popson at *Archaeology* and Monika Bauerlein at *Mother Jones*, also helped me sharpen some of the ideas and narratives contained herein. To all of them, I offer my thanks and my conviction, reinforced through their example, that a reporter's editors are his best teachers.

I was blessed with the support of people and institutions whose enthusiasm for this book never flagged, even in those moments when mine did. The Alicia Patterson Foundation gave me a fellowship that allowed me to travel and do research, and I am particularly indebted to the foundation's executive director, Margaret Engel, for her encouragement and advice. My agent, Gary Morris, of the David Black Agency, believed in this book from its beginnings as an unsolicited query on his desk in New York and, with the patience of the best editors, helped me bang it into shape and found it a home. I thank my editors at St. Martin's Press, Joe Cleemann, Julia Pastore, and Tim Bent, for their persistence and good judgment.

Hundreds of people shared recollections and insights with me in interviews or informal conversations; to all of them, named and unnamed herein, I offer my thanks. I owe a special debt of gratitude to the archaeologists and historians quoted in this book, some of whom regarded the subject of looting as distracting, distasteful, or legally compromising and spoke to me only with great reluctance. Among them are Walter Alva and Carlos Wester, both extraordinarily generous with their time and scholarship, Izumi Shimada, Guillermo Cock, Ruth Shady Solís, Paloma Carcedo, Andrés Álvarez Calderón, Ellen Herscher, Thomas Chávez, Sonia Guillén, Adriana von Hagen, who made excellent comments on sections of the manuscript, and Cecilia Jaime Tello, who also allowed me to give a guest lecture to her archaeology class at the Universidad Mayor de San Marcos. In Britain, I was grateful to Neil MacGregor of the British Museum and Colin Renfrew of the University of Cambridge for interviews.

For their time and recollections, I am grateful also to Orlando Mendez, Gabriel Apesteguía, Vania Távara Palacios, Torkom Demirjian, Aldo Valerga, Enrico Poli, Hernán Navarro, Carlos Bernal Vargas, Samuel Bernal, R. Ascencio, Roberto Santos, Gregorio Becerra, and Gilberto Romero, among many others.

This book would have been diminished without the confidence and sincerity of many people in law enforcement who work, or formerly worked, to combat the illicit antiquities trade in the United States. First among them is Robert Wittman of the Federal Bureau of Investigation, for whose trust and recollections I am deeply grateful, all the more so because he works mostly under cover and incurred special risk in sharing his knowledge with a reporter. I have acceded to his request not to publish his picture in this book or even describe his appearance, and for that I ask the reader's indulgence. Robert Bazin, Brian Midkiff, Robert Goldman, Maria Capo-Sanders, and Ana Barnett, among others, were generous with their time and recollections. My thanks to Lawrence Kaye and Howard Spiegler of Herrick, Feinstein in New York and Patty Gerstenblith of DePaul University, Chicago, for their comments on portions of this manuscript and for helping me get comfortable with some of the complexities of cultural property law.

In Iraq I was grateful for interviews and help under often very trying circumstances from Susanne Osthoff, Donny George, McGuire Gibson, Muzahim Mahmud, the late Manhal Jabr, Abdulsadiq al-Abed, Lt. Cory Roberts, and Col. Matthew Bogdanos, among many others. Thanks also to Peter Maass and my unflappable interpreter, driver, and occasional bodyguard, Azher Taher Ahmad.

I tip my hat to the staffs of the Library of Congress, Washington, and the archives of *El Comercio,* Lima, and to everyone who had anything to do with the U.S. Freedom of Information Act. My thanks also go to those members of the foreign services of the United States, Guatemala, Peru, Panama, and El Salvador who granted me interviews, most of them in confidence.

In Peru, many friends offered ideas, contacts, and sympathetic ears, in particular Mary Powers, whose hospitality and friendship mean more to me than I can express, Manuel Mendieta, Amelia Morimoto, Hugo Coya, Rómulo de la Vega and David Strul, Jimmy Torres, the late Renzo Uccelli, and my "lazarus" in Chiclayo, José Olidén. Alfonso Valdés Vargas introduced me to the culture of Peru when I first arrived there as a correspondent for Reuters in 1989, and for that, plus his warmth and friendship in the years since, I offer my thanks.

I am grateful for special help from Audrey Baker, Gary Cohen, Hollis Walker, and Jane Evelyn Atwood. Phillip Wearne's energy, perspicacity, and humanity would have been inspiration enough for any author, but I was blessed also with his insights and probing comments at every stage of this book, including on the final manuscript. My mother, Nancy Atwood, offered loving support and an uncanny knack for finding articles and reports that I had missed. Finally, this book never would have been possible without my partner, Werner Romero, who gave me love, more patience than I deserved, and his insights on the law.

Those listed above share the credit for any virtues this book may have; all errors of fact, judgment, or taste are entirely my own.

NOTES

Most interviews noted below were conducted by the author in person; some were conducted by telephone. Dates of interviews are in month-day-year format. All other dates are spelled out.

Documents obtained through the U.S. Freedom of Information Act are noted with the letters (FOIA).

Introduction: Looters in the Temple

1. On the museum looting, see for example Andrew Lawler, "A Museum Looted," *Science*, August 1, 2003; Roger Atwood, "Inside Iraq's National Museum," *ARTnews*, vol. 102, no. 7 (summer 2003).

2. Portions of this introduction appeared originally in Roger Atwood, "Day of the Vulture," *Mother Jones*, vol. 28, no. 5 (September/October 2003). Osthoff and I estimated the number of looters at Isin that day, May 18, 2003, at sixty to eighty, not including those we saw leaving the site by truck, motorcycle, and bicycle. My information on the history of Isin is drawn from conversations with Osthoff and Joan Oates's book, *Babylon* (London: Thames & Hudson, 1986). The chief of the German excavation team was Barthel Hrouda.

3. These busts were unfortunately removed with cranes and tackle in late 2003 to be melted down for scrap. My thanks to Zainab Bahrani of Columbia University for this explanation.

4. Donny George interview, 05.12.03.

5. McGuire Gibson interview, 05.14.03.

6. Ibid.; Martin Gottlieb, "Looters Swarm over Remote Sites," *New York Times*, June 12, 2003.

7. Gibson interview, 05.14.03.

8. Genesis, 10:6–9, in which Nimrud is called by its old Assyrian name, Calah, or Kalhu.

9. Fernand Braudel, *The Structures of Everyday Life*, trans. Siân Reynolds (New York: Harper & Row, 1981), pp. 158–59; see also Jared Diamond, *Guns, Germs, and Steel* (New York: W.W. Norton, 1997).

10. In 1989 Russell began a comprehensive photographic record of the giant stone reliefs at the ruins of the seventh century B.C. city of Nineveh. His work was interrupted by the Gulf War and then by sanctions. The next Russell knew of the reliefs, they were showing up on the antiquities market, hacked apart and smuggled out of Iraq. In 1995 London businessman and collector Shlomo Moussaieff paid about $15,000 to buy one of the pieces, a relief showing prisoners of war towing a boat. He told reporters later that he bought the piece in a warehouse at the airport in Geneva and that he was unaware of its origin. When he offered the piece to the Bible Lands Museum in Israel for display, the museum sent a picture of the relief to Russell, who immediately replied that he had photographic evidence that the piece had been looted since 1990. Alerted to the piece's illegal origin, Moussaieff returned the piece to Iraq upon receipt of compensation from the Iraqi government. After that, dealers who knowingly dealt in looted Iraqi artifacts took much greater care. Pictures of two more pieces looted from Nineveh came Russell's way. He could not determine who had them or where, so he published a note in the May 1996 issue of *International Fine Art Reports* alerting dealers and museums to the presence of the pieces on the market. He never heard of them again. In 1996 a New York lawyer contacted Russell on behalf of a client to ask if ten more Assyrian sculptures up for sale were being sold legitimately. Russell replied they were not. They were all looted from Nineveh and he had the photographs to prove it. Again, he then lost all trace of the pieces. Since then, Russell has learned that in removing those ten pieces, "the looters destroyed whole slabs at Nineveh to extract the best-preserved bits." The loss is incalculable. See Russell's *The Final Sack of Nineveh* (New Haven, Conn.: Yale

University Press, 1998). On the Moussaieff case, see Dalya Alberge, "Collector to Fight Iraq over 'Stolen' Sculpture," *The Times* (London), October 29, 1998; Martin Gottlieb, "Of 2,000 Treasures Stolen in Gulf War of 1991, Only 12 Have Been Recovered," *New York Times,* May 1, 2003. Also on looting in Iraq, see McGuire Gibson, "The Loss of Archaeological Context and the Illegal Trade in Mesopotamian Antiquities," in *Culture Without Context,* no. 1, (fall 1997); Samuel Paley, "Nimrud, the War, and the Antiquities Market," in *IFAR Journal,* vol. 6, nos. 1 and 2 (2003).

11. On looting in the north, see John Simpson, "Why I Fear for the Safety of Iraq," *Daily Telegraph* (London), September 28, 2003, and Roger Atwood, "In the North of Iraq: Mosul's Museum, Hatra, and Nimrud," *Archaeology,* online edition, June 4, 2003.

12. The figures on recoveries of Iraqi artifacts outside Iraq are from Donny George of the Baghdad museum. Interview, 6.25.04. U.S. Customs declined to give figures on their seizure rates.

1: Looking for a Tomb

1. Throughout this book I use the term "looting" to mean the intentional and unscientific invasion of all or part of an ancient site for the purpose of commercial extraction of objects contained therein, legal or illegal. The term applies to either underground assets such as tombs or to standing monuments. Although it has not always been so, looting of ancient or archaeological sites is illegal under present-day law in most countries, including on private land; in the United States it is unlawful to disturb historical sites on government-owned or tribal land but not necessarily on privately owned land by the owner of the land. Depending on the applicable law and the timing of the acquisition, it is not always the case that those who have come into possession of what I refer to as "looted" items have committed an illegal act.

2. John Hemming, *The Conquest of the Incas* (New York: Harcourt Brace Jovanovich, 1970), pp. 62–63; Michael E. Moseley, *The Incas and Their Ancestors* (London: Thames & Hudson, 1992), p. 197.

3. Fray Martín de Murúa, *Historia general del Perú (1590–1611),* ed. Manuel Ballesteros Gaibrois (c. 1614; reprint, Madrid: Dastin S.L., 2001), pp. 202, 517.

4. J. Alden Mason, *The Ancient Civilizations of Peru* (London: Pelican Books, 1957), p. 49.

5. This was recounted to me by archaeologist Susan McIntosh of Rice University. Interview, 02.09.00.

6. Michel Brent, "Faking African Art," *Archaeology*, vol. 54 (January–February 2000), pp. 26–32.

7. David M. Pendergast and Elizabeth Graham, "The Battle for the Maya Past: The Effects of International Looting and Collecting in Belize," in *The Ethics of Collecting Cultural Property*, 2d ed., ed. Phyllis Mauch Messenger (Albuquerque: University of New Mexico Press, 1999), pp. 51–53.

8. Thomas Killion interview, February 2000; Roger Atwood, "Standing Up to the Smugglers," *ARTnews*, vol. 99 (June 2000), pp. 118–23.

9. See United Nations Educational, Scientific and Cultural Organisation (UNESCO), *Cent objets disparus: pillage à Angkor* (Paris: ICOM, 1997); Sarah Rooney, "Tomb Raiders," *The Times* (London), January 6, 2001.

10. Michael Freeman and Claude Jacques, *Ancient Angkor* (Bangkok: Asia Books, 1999), pp. 42–43. They write: "Damage caused to the sites during the period of civil war were comparatively few, as each Khmer faction respected the Angkor monuments. However, a major problem of theft arose at the beginning of the 1990s. Free-standing figures, lintels and pediments have been hacked away and removed, frequently via Thailand for sale to Western collectors."

11. Colin Renfrew, *Loot, Legitimacy and Ownership* (London: Duckworth, 2000), p. 36.

12. On looting in China and on Hong Kong's role as the valve through which antiquities flow, see He Shuzhong, "Illicit Excavation in Contemporary China," *Trade in Illicit Antiquities*, ed. Neil Brodie, Jennifer Doole, and Colin Renfrew (Cambridge, England: McDonald Institute for Archaeological Research, 2001).

13. Torkom Demirjian interviews, January 2000 and 02.13.02.

2: Twenty-three Feet Down

1. Portions of this chapter originally appeared in Roger Atwood, "Stealing History," *Mother Jones*, vol. 27., no. 3 (May/June 2002).

2. William H. Denevan, *Cultivated Landscapes of Native Amazonia and the Andes* (Oxford: Oxford University Press, 2001), pp. 139, 152.

3. Michael E. Moseley, *The Incas and Their Ancestors* (London: Thames & Hudson, 1992), p. 184.

4. Robert Sonin interview, 02.02.04; Heather Lechtman, "Traditions and Styles in Central Andean Metalworking," in *The Beginning of the Use of*

Metals and Alloys: Papers from the Second International Conference of the Beginning of the Use of Metals and Alloys, Zhengzhou, China, 21–26 October 1986, ed. Robert Maddin (Cambridge, Mass.: MIT Press, 1988), pp. 371–72; Sidney Kirkpatrick, *Lords of Sipan* (New York: William Morrow, 1992), p. 151.

5. Dorothy Hosler, "The Metallurgy of Ancient West Mexico," Maddin, ed., op. cit., pp. 328–30.

6. Moseley, op. cit., p. 223.

7. Walter Alva, "Discovering the New World's Richest Unlooted Tomb," *National Geographic*, October 1988.

8. José Bonilla interview, 12.11.01.

9. Alva, "Discovering the New World's Richest Unlooted Tomb."

10. Réna Gündüz, *El mundo ceremonial de los huaqueros* (Lima: Editorial Universitaria, 2001), pp. 126–27.

11. Ibid., p. 145.

12. Segundo Carlos Bernal (brother of Ernil Bernal) interview, 8.5.02; Kirkpatrick, op. cit., pp. 27–28.

13. Samuel Bernal interview, 07.21.02.

14. The area above the village cemetery had in fact been subjected to periodic waves of looting since at least the 1960s, according to villagers and archaeologists who have worked in the area.

15. Walter Alva interview, 12.12.01.

16. Ibid.; Kirkpatrick, op. cit., pp. 61–62.

17. Christopher Donnan, *Moche Art of Peru* (Los Angeles: Museum of Cultural History, University of California, 1978), pp. 86–93.

18. Juan de Matienzo, *Gobierno del Perú, obra escrita en el siglo XVI por el licenciado don Juan Matienzo, oidor de la Real audiencia de Charcas*, quoted in Susan E. Ramírez, *The World Upside Down: Cross-Cultural Contact and Conflict in Sixteenth-Century Peru* (Stanford: Stanford University Press, 1996), p. 141.

19. Izumi Shimada, *Pampa Grande and the Mochica Culture* (Austin: University of Texas Press, 1994), p. 14, which gives the figure of six thousand pounds (2,800 kilograms); Moseley, op. cit., pp. 178–79.

20. Ramírez, op. cit., pp. 127–29. The total of 642 is what I counted from the complete list, which Ramírez found at the Archivo General de las Indias (Seville) and presents in full in her fascinating book.

21. Kirkpatrick, op. cit.

22. Samuel and Segundo Carlos Bernal interviews, 07.21.02 and 08.05.02, respectively.

23. Narda Montalvo interview, 12.11.01.

24. Gündüz, op. cit.

25. Samuel Bernal interview, 07.21.02.

26. Heinz Plenge interview, 04.12.02.

27. Samuel Bernal interview, 07.21.02.

28. Ibid.; see also Heinz Plenge, "The Robbers Tale," *Connoisseur,* February 1990.

29. For the description of the discovery of the tomb, I am relying mainly on Samuel Bernal's recollection and on Kirkpatrick, op. cit., pp. 19–21. The timing of the pillage has been ascribed to various dates in the month of February 1987. Kirkpatrick's sources have it happening on February 6, perhaps the most reliable date since their memories of the events in question were still fresh. Samuel Bernal recalls it as "the first days of February."

30. Kirkpatrick, op. cit., p. 21.

31. My account of the raiding of the tomb is based on interviews with the surviving Bernal brothers and their father, and published accounts including Kirkpatrick, Plenge, et al.

32. Samuel Bernal interview, 07.21.02.

33. Kirkpatrick, op. cit., p. 73.

34. Ibid.

35. See, in particular, Carl Nagin, "The Peruvian Gold Rush," *Art and Antiques,* May 1990, and Kirkpatrick, op. cit.

36. Enrico Poli interview, 02.15.00.

37. The figure of five thousand sites is from a preliminary national census conducted by the INC in 2001. "Urge catastro de sitios arqueológicos," *El Comercio,* April 22, 2002.

38. Ruth Shady Solís interview, 02.16.01; on Caral, see John F. Ross, "First City in the New World?" *Smithsonian,* August 2002.

39. Poli interview, 02.15.00; Kirkpatrick, op. cit.

40. I am grateful to María Elena Córdova of the Instituto Nacional de Cultura, Lima, for providing me with a useful summary on the history of Peruvian cultural property law, April 2002.

41. Samuel Bernal interviews, 07.21.02 and 11.09.02.

42. Walter Alva interview, 12.12.01.

43. Samuel Bernal interview, 07.21.02.

44. Walter Alva interview, 02.15.00.

45. Bernal family interviews, 07.21.02 and 08.05.02.

46. Interview with Brüning Museum director Carlos Wester, 12.10.01; Samuel Bernal interview, 07.21.02; Brüning National Archaeological Museum, "Caso Gallardo," unpublished paper, undated.

47. "Panorama mortal," *Sí* (Lima), April 27, 1987; Carlos Bernal Vargas interview, 12.12.01.

48. Carlos Wester interview, 12.10.01.

49. King Juan Carlos and Queen Sofia were visiting Lima for an Ibero-American summit. The story of the expectation of their arrival was told to me by the head of the village's community development committee, Carlos Zapata.

50. Alva, "Discovering the New World's Richest Tomb"; Roger Atwood, "Stealing History," op. cit.

51. Carlos Bernal Vargas interview, 12.12.01.

3: The Excavators

1. Walter Alva interview, 05.06.02.

2. Kirkpatrick, op. cit., p. 65.

3. Julio C. Tello, quoted in *Memorias*, by Luis E. Valcárcel (Lima: IEP ediciones, 1981), p. 282.

4. Izumi Shimada interview, 07.19.02.

5. Walter Alva and Christopher B. Donnan, *Royal Tombs of Sipán* (Los Angeles: Fowler Museum of Cultural History, 1993), pp. 45–49.

6. Walter Alva, *Sipán* (Lima: Colección Cultura y Artes del Perú, 1994), p. 202.

7. Ibid., p. 44.

8. Susana Meneses de Alva, quoted in "El otro rostro de Sipán," by Rosella di Paolo, *La Tortuga* (Lima), November 28, 1989.

9. Kirkpatrick, op. cit., p. 98.

10. Di Paolo, op. cit.

11. Alva and Donnan, op. cit., pp. 51–52.

12. John W. Verano, "War and Death in the Moche World: Osteological Evidence and Visual Discourse," *Moche Art and Archaeology in Ancient Peru,* ed. Joanne Pillsbury (Washington, D.C.: National Gallery of Art, 2001), p. 121.

13. Samuel Bernal interview, 11.08.02.

14. Ibid. Bernal called the pots *"adornos no más,"* mere decorations.

15. John W. Verano, "Human Skeletal Remains from Tomb 1, Sipán (Lambayeque River Valley, Peru); and Their Social Implications," *Antiquity,* vol. 71 (1997), pp. 670–82; Alva and Donnan, op. cit., p. 55.

16. Alva and Donnan, op. cit., p. 65.

17. Ibid., p. 87.

18. Walter Alva, "The Royal Tombs of Sipán: Art and Power in Moche Society," in *Moche Art and Archaeology in Ancient Peru,* ed. Pillsbury, pp. 227–28.

19. Ibid.

20. Verano, op. cit.

21. Ibid., p. 104–06; Kirkpatrick, op. cit., 158–59.

22. Alva and Donnan, op. cit., p. 111.

23. Julie Jones, "Innovation and Resplendence: Metalwork for Moche Lords," in *Moche Art and Archaelogy in Ancient Peru,* ed. Pillsbury p. 210.

24. Alva, "The Royal Tombs of Sipán," op. cit., p. 226; Alva and Donnan, op. cit., pp. 120–25. This count does not include the footless adult male mentioned previously.

25. Alva and Donnan, op. cit., p. 158.

26. See for example Boyce Rensberger, "Tomb Yields New World's Richest Trove," *Washington Post,* September 14, 1988; Warren Leary, "Tomb in Peru Yields Stunning Pre-Inca Trove," *New York Times,* September 14, 1988.

27. Walter Alva, "Discovering the New World's Richest Unlooted Tomb," *National Geographic,* vol. 174 (October 1988); Alva and Donnan, op. cit., p. 215.

28. Steve Bourget, "Rituals of Sacrifice: Its Practice at Huaca de la Luna and Its Representation in Moche Iconography," pp. 103–04.

29. Alva and Donnan, op. cit., p. 213.

30. Walter Alva interview, 11.13.02.

31. Kirkpatrick, op. cit., p. 183.

32. Ibid.; Alfredo Narváez V., "La Mina; una tumba Moche I en el valle de Jequetepeque," *Moche: Propuestas y perspectivas,* ed. Santiago Uceda and Elías Mujica (Trujillo: Universidad Nacional de La Libertad, 1994); Alva interview, 11.13.02.

33. Alva and Donnan, op. cit., p. 220.

34. Alva interview, 11.13.02; Alva, *Sipán*, p. 193.

35. Alva, *Sipán*, pp. 200–04.

36. Alva interview, 11.13.02.

37. Enrico Poli interview, 02.15.01; Alva interview, 11.13.02. García declined to be interviewed for this book.

4: Backflap

1. Interview with Carlos Wester Torre, acting director of the Brüning National Archaeological Museum, Lambayeque, 05.16.02. Some reports have given the backflap's weight as 2.5 pounds, but that figure excludes the severed half of the rattle attachment, an integral part of the piece, as discussed later in this chapter.

2. Alva and Donnan, op. cit., p. 111.

3. Enrico Poli interview, 05.10.02.

4. Interview, in confidence, 08.05.02.

5. Alva interview, 11.13.02.

6. Paloma Carcedo Muro and Izumi Shimada, "Behind the Golden Mask: Sicán Gold Artifacts from Batán Grande, Peru," *The Art of Precolumbian Gold: The Jan Mitchell Collection,* ed. Julie Jones (Boston: Little, Brown); Izumi Shimada interview, 07.19.02; Juan Carlos Santoyo interview, 07.21.02.

7. República del Perú, Poder Judicial, declaración instructiva de Luis Eduardo Bacigalupo Remy, denuncia no. 754–98, March 18, 1999, pp. 188–96.

8. Alva and Donnan, op. cit., p. 39.

9. Donnan, *Moche Art of Peru*, p. 124.

10. Ibid.

11. Alva interview, 11.13.02. There was another, slightly larger set of rattles, possibly from another tomb on the *huaca* emptied by the Bernals. The gilded copper rattle confiscated from Gallardo in 1987 and currently on public view at the Royal Tombs of Sipán Museum in Lambayeque was from that series. None of the others has turned up so far, suggesting that those rattles numbered fewer than the solid-gold series.

12. Norton Simon, quoted in *The Plundered Past,* by Karl E. Meyer (New York: Atheneum, 1973), p. 145.

13. Nagin, op. cit.; Kirkpatrick, op. cit., p. 123.

14. *Peru vs. Peruvian Artifacts, et al.,* United States District Court, Central District of California, Case no. 88-6990-WPG, March 7, 1989.

15. Ibid.

16. Ibid.; Kirkpatrick, op. cit., p. 144; *The Gazette* (Montreal), April 12, 2000; Roger Atwood, "Standing Up to the Smugglers," *ARTnews,* vol. 99, no. 6 (June 2000); telephone interview with Kathryn Zedde, Department of Canadian Heritage, March 2000. The Vancouver inspection led to a long and complicated court case that highlighted the city's brief but intense role as a transshipment point for looted artifacts headed for the United States. Some of the ceramics released at the airport were sold to a Vancouver man, who kept them in a storage vault. When news of the operation and its relation to the Sipán case emerged in 1989 in testimony by Kelly and others, Canadian authorities ordered new inspections which revealed the pieces to be authentic, but only after a consulting archaeologist soaked the pots in water to remove the phony mud-and-ceramic casts still on them. The Vancouver buyer later took legal action to recover the pieces but lost. The case ended in April 2000 with the return of fifty-nine ceramic artifacts to Peru's acting ambassador in Canada, Amador Velásquez, in Vancouver. Five of those pieces had actually been determined to be high-quality replicas—fake artifacts first thought to be real, disguised as fake, pronounced to be real, and finally revealed as fake. One of Drew's suppliers had apparently conned him.

17. *Peru vs. Peruvian Artifacts.*

18. Ibid.; Kirkpatrick, op. cit., pp. 101–02.

19. *Peru vs. Peruvian Artifacts.*

20. Ibid.

21. Documents relating to this case were obtained from the U.S. Attorney, District of New Mexico, through the Freedom of Information Act. I am grateful also to FBI special agents Brian Midkiff and Robert Wittman for interviews in February and March 2002.

5: Gold Man

1. Nagin, op. cit.; Kirkpatrick, op. cit., tells the story in detail.

2. Santa Barbara Museum of Art, *Diverse Directions: A Collector's Choice* (Santa Barbara, 1987).

3. Kirkpatrick, op. cit., p. 191.

4. Douglas Ewing, "What Is 'Stolen'? The McClain Case Revisited," in Messenger, *The Ethics of Collecting Cultural Property*, pp. 178–80.

5. Kirkpatrick, op. cit.

6. *Peru vs. Peruvian Artifacts, et al.*

7. The use of looters' accounts as part of a strategy to prove the illicit origin of antiquities was later established in the case of the Lydian Hoard, a set of silver Anatolian artifacts looted in 1966, acquired by the Metropolitan Museum of Art in New York and demanded by the Turkish government, as discussed in Chapter 8.

8. *Government of Peru vs. Benjamin Johnson, et al.*, United States District Court, Central District of California, Case no. CV 88-6990-WPG, Memorandum of Decision, June 29, 1989; also, see Kirkpatrick, op. cit., pp. 192–93.

9. *Government of Peru vs. Benjamin Johnson, et al.*

10. *Peru vs. Peruvian Artifacts.*

11. The Peruvian government did, however, appeal the verdict in the Johnson case in September 1990 with a new lawyer, Edward M. Fox, although with the same result. By the time of the appeal, the Johnson case had been severed from that of the other defendants, and Johnson himself had died.

12. Ann Guthrie Hingston, "U.S. Implementation of the UNESCO Cultural Property Convention," in Messenger, op. cit., pp. 138–40. Technically the requesting country (in this case, El Salvador) does not ask for emergency restrictions, but rather for a bilateral agreement covering certain types of cultural property. The State Department may, at its discretion, impose emergency import restrictions if it sees evidence of ongoing looting in crisis proportions, but only after the country has requested a full-scale bilateral deal. The sluggishness of this system came under criticism from archaeologists and some members of Congress after the Iraqi looting emergency, as discussed in Chapter 14.

13. Ibid.

14. In 1999 Peru was number nine in the world, with total U.S. aid of $162 million. *National Journal*, June 10, 2000.

15. Kenneth Roberts and Mark Peceny, "Human Rights and United States Policy Toward Peru," in *The Peruvian Labyrinth: Polity, Society, Economy*, ed. Maxwell A. Cameron and Philip Mauceri (University Park: Pennsylvania State University Press, 1997), pp. 213–14; Reuters, October 7, 1989, in which Garcia told the author in an interview that the United States should put more money into economic assistance and less into military aid. "The most direct and real way of attacking the problem . . . of Latin American [coca] production is not through weapons and helicopters. . . . The United States should commit itself by investing billions of dollars in the next few years to substitute coca crops." García and his successor, Alberto Fujimori, were uncomfortable with the U.S. emphasis on a military approach to curbing drug trafficking, in part because of the effects on local public opinion and because they thought it might exacerbate leftist guerrilla insurgencies. Nevertheless, they welcomed cooperation in other areas, including loot smuggling.

16. *Federal Register*, May 7, 1990; 55(88): 19029–19030. It should be noted that, in March 1989, the U.S. government issued restrictions on the importation of textiles dating up to 1850 from the community of Coroma, Bolivia, at the request of the Bolivian government. This step followed news reports of Western tourists traveling to Coroma, waving wads of cash before village elders, and walking off with Inca-era textiles that were still being used in community festivals. The practice showed an intact continuity between ancient and modern-day ritual with few parallels in the Andes. Compared to the Peruvian and Salvadoran import restrictions, the Bolivian code was far more modest—only textiles, and only those that might originate from this particular village. *Federal Register*, March 14, 1989; 54(48): 10618–10620.

17. *Federal Register*, May 7, 1990, Department of the Treasury, Customs Service, 19 CFR Part 12.

18. *Washington Post*, May 9, 1992; January 27, 1995.

19. Museo Chileno de Arte Precolombino, *Moche: Señores de la muerte* (Santiago, 1990), pp. 15–26. Similar fox heads have been found at other Moche sites. See Christopher Donnan, "Moche," *Andean Art at Dumbarton Oaks*, vol. 1, ed. Elizabeth Hill Boone, (Washington, D.C.: Dumbarton Oaks, 1996), pp. 159–62.

20. Alva and Donnan, *Royal Tombs of Sipán*, p. 184; Samuel Bernal interviews.

21. Walter Alva interview, 11.13.02. Around the time of the Chilean show, an associate of Cardoen wrote to Alva, asking if he would be interested in coming to Chile to help construct a life-size replica of the Sipán tombs. Alva thought the request a bit odd but wrote back asking what sort of

organization would be funding the project. When he heard back that it was a private-sector initiative, Alva replied that he worked only with public institutions.

22. Josephson made the assertion in a letter published in *The New York Times,* September 4, 1993.

23. David Wilson interview, 09.24.02; *Dallas Morning News,* September 3, 1993; In 2003 U.S. Customs became the Immigration and Customs Enforcement, or ICE, within the Department of Homeland Security. ICE would not comment on the case. The author's request for documents on the case through the Freedom of Information Act was still being acted upon at the time of publication.

24. Alva interview, 12.12.01; Mark Rose, "Jewelry Repatriated," *Archaeology,* vol. 49, no. 5 (September/October 1996); interview with U.S. Customs special agent Dominick Lopez, 10.17.03.

25. Carol Damian interview, 09.10.03. The trade in human remains is literally a fellow traveler with the loot trade. In June 1999, an American was detained at Lima's international airport with artifacts including two mummies and three skulls of the Nazca culture, along with some five hundred shark teeth before boarding a Delta flight to Atlanta. El Comercio, November 6, 2000.

26. United States District Court, Southern District of Florida, Case no. 98-1432, Complaint for Forfeiture in Rem, June 17, 1998. Contrary to some reports, no sniffer dogs were involved in the seizure. For useful press reports, see Kevin Hall, "US Customs Returns Rare Artifacts to Peru by Jet," *Journal of Commerce,* October 9, 1998; Mike Toner, "Peruvian Artifacts Returned After 3 Years," Cox Newspapers, October 8, 1998; David Adams, "Ancient Artifacts, Modern Crime," *St. Petersburg Times,* October 9, 1998; Warren Richey, "New Efforts to Stop Plundering of the World's Past," *Christian Science Monitor,* June 16, 1998.

27. On Swiss free ports, see Barry Meier and Martin Gottlieb, "An Illicit Journey Out of Egypt, Only a Few Questions Asked," *New York Times,* February 23, 2004; the parallel with drug cases was noted with interest by experts on cultural property law. Lawrence Kaye of the New York law firm Herrick, Feinstein said: "More recently the U.S. has begun to apply another weapon, which they've adapted from the drug trafficking cases, where they seize property. In other words, artworks become the kind of property—such as the house owned by a drug dealer—that the state seizes." Kaye, quoted in "On the Trail of Stolen Art," by Melik Kaylan, Forbes.com, undated [2001].

28. Ana Barnett interview, 11.04.02.

29. Press reports said the government made only halfhearted efforts to bring Cardoen to trial because it feared he would reveal embarrassing details about the government's own arms sales to Iraq during the Reagan and Bush administrations. *New York Times*, August 8, 1995; Barnett interview, 11.04.02.

30. Internal documents relating to this case were made available to the author in confidence. John Atwood is no relation to the author.

31. I am taking some liberties with the timeline here to give a sense of continuity. Some of this action took place after events narrated in later chapters, as will become clear later. Maria Capo-Sanders interviews 11.05.02, 01.08.03; Ana Barnett interview 11.04.02; Walter Alva interviews.

32. Arturo Jiménez Borja, "Introducción a la cultura Moche," *Moche*, ed. Lavalle, pp. 15–16; Jones, "Innovation and Resplendence: Metalwork for Moche Lords," *Moche Art and Archaeology in Ancient Peru*, ed. Pillsbury p. 206. Art of the Vicús culture was also labeled by the local name for an ancient cemetery, Loma Negra, that was "discovered by local inhabitants," according to a Met gallery guide of 1992. It is by this name that the artifacts are displayed in the Met.

33. Maria Capo-Sanders interview, 11.05.02.

34. James Brooke, "Peru: On the Very Fast Track," *New York Times*, January 31, 1995.

35. República del Perú, Poder Judicial, declaración instructiva de Luis Eduardo Bacigalupo Remy. On Bacigalupo and horse racing, see República del Perú, Poder Judicial, declaración instructiva de Guillermo Antonio Elías Huamán, denuncia no. 754-98, March 26, 1999, pp. 201, 210–11.

36. Hugo Otero, a close personal associate of the former president, said García and Ramos Ronceros were of no blood relation.

37. *El Comercio*, May 31, 1991; May 5, 1991; December 3, 1995.

38. Denis Garcia's surname does not carry an accent over the "i" in U.S. legal documents.

39. República del Perú, Poder Judicial, declaración instructiva de Jorge Modesto Ramos Ronceros, denuncia no. 754-98, October 19, 1999, page numbers illegible.

40. Ibid.

41. "Que viva Chiclayo," by a composer known as D.A.R., was sung by the late Lucha Reyes.

42. Haydee Garcia telephone interview, 03.03.03; on the Auriches and their holdings, see Paloma Carcedo Muro and Izumi Shimada, "Behind the Golden Mask," in *The Art of Precolumbian Gold*, which includes two photographs taken in the "treasure room" about 1960. Shimada has counted 189 different objects in these photographs alone, mostly large gold beakers with embossed faces, plus a large *tumi* knife and a golden mask similar to one in the Metropolitan Museum of Art. These rare and intriguing photographs are also on display at the Museo Nacional de Sicán in the town of Ferreñafe, on the road from Chiclayo to Batán Grande. The story of the dinner guests being offered artifacts as party favors is told by archaeologist and Batán Grande native Juan Carlos Santoyo, among many others. Shimada interviews, 07.19 and 07.22.02; Santoyo interview, 07.21.02. The Aurich mansion still stands, in some disrepair, in the village of Batán Grande. It is owned by a private sugar company and unfortunately not open to the general public. I am grateful to Mr. David Silva for giving me a tour of it.

43. Garcia interview 03.03.3.

44. For the full text of Velasco's message and many other absorbing passages from the length and breadth of Peruvian history, see *The Peru Reader: History, Culture, Politics*, ed. Orin Starn, Carlos Iván Degregori, and Robin Kirk (Durham and London: Duke University Press, 1995).

45. Garcia interview, 03.03.03.

46. Ibid.; República del Perú, Poder Judicial, declaración instructiva de Guillermo Elías Huamán, op. cit., p. 209; Jorge Ramos Ronceros, op. cit., page numbers illegible.

47. Ibid.; Fernando Peralta (son of Luis Peralta) interview, 07.20.02; República del Perú, Poder Judicial, declaración instructiva de Luis Eduardo Bacigalupo Remy, p. 190.

48. Peralta interview, 07.20.02; República del Perú, Poder Judicial, declaración instructiva de Juan Carlos Ignacio Salas Arnaiz, denuncia no. 754-98, March 11, 1999, p. 532.

49. Peralta interview, 07.20.02.

50. Bill Becker, quoted in Jim Haner, "Career Criminal Faces Last Stand," *The Sun* (Baltimore), August 6, 1995.

51. Robert Bazin interviews, 07.31.03 and 09.08.03.

52. Bill Becker interview, 11.06.03.

53. Ibid.

54. Bazin interview, 07.31.03.

55. Ibid.

56. Robert Wittman interview, 03.04.02.

6: Lord of Sipán

1. Alva, "The Royal Tombs of Sipán," in *Moche Art and Archaeology in Ancient Peru,* ed. Pillsbury, pp. 233–34.

2. Ibid.; Alva interviews; The individual in this tomb was buried at roughly the same time as the lord buried in the looted tomb.

3. Alva, "The Royal Tombs of Sipán," in *Moche Art and Archaeology in Ancient Peru,* ed. Pillsbury, p. 235.

4. Alva interviews. 20.12.01 and 02.15.00.

5. Alva interview, 20.12.01.

6. Rita Reif, "Dazzling Jewelry from Peru's Mystery People," *New York Times,* August 28, 1994.

7. Mason, op. cit., p. 75.

8. Andrés Álvarez-Calderón interview, 03.21.02.

9. Cecilia Jaime Tello interview, 05.10.02.

10. There were, of course, some notable exceptions to this trend, such as the excavations at Laguna de los Cóndores, discussed in Chapter 12, and the excavation of thousands of Inca funerary bundles at the Tupac Amaru shantytown outside Lima in 2001–02 by UCLA's Guillermo Cock.

11. Peter Kaulicke interview, 02.15.00.

12. Thomas Chávez interview, 02.19.02.

13. Ibid.

14. Museum of New Mexico, Deed of Gift, Registration no. 1995.033.02, February 13, 1995 (FOIA).

15. Ibid.

7: The Dealer

1. My account of the Apesteguía affair is based on interviews with his son, 05.14.02, 05.15.02 and 10.06.03; with Walter Alva, 05.07.02; and with

other associates of Apesteguía who spoke in confidence; and on "Las joyas de Raúl," *Caretas* (Lima), February 8, 1996.

2. Robert Bazin interviews, 07.31.03 and 09.08.03.; Donnan, communication with author, March 2004.

3. Bazin interview, 07.31.03.

4. Haner, op. cit.

5. Orlando Mendez interview, 11.05.02; Haydee Garcia interview, 03.03.03; Fernando Peralta interview, 7.20.02.

6. Haner, op. cit. Becker remembered the finder's fee as $1 million. Interview, op. cit. Bazin interviews, op. cit.; the authenticity of the Monet was later challenged yet again, leading to legal proceedings. As with many paintings, its attribution may never be completely established, but what is certain is that a lot of money changed hands in the belief that it was authentic.

7. Bazin interview, 07.31.03.

8: The Actual Object

1. William St. Clair, *Lord Elgin & the Marbles*, 3d ed. (Oxford: Oxford University Press, 1998), pp. 30–31.

2. Mary Beard, *The Parthenon* (London: Profile Books, 2002), pp. 77–80.

3. St. Clair, op. cit., p. 87. Hunt wrote in a memorandum to Elgin that the firman should give the workers in Athens "liberty to take away any sculptures or inscriptions which do not interfere with the works or walls of the Citadel," wording intended to give wide deference to the Ottomans' use of the Acropolis as a military base but which would allow removal of any of the Parthenon sculptures that Elgin's agents subsequently took.

4. Ibid., pp. 88–89.

5. Ibid., p. 167.

6. MacCarthy, op. cit., pp. 112–13.

7. Citations are from Lord Byron, *Complete Poetical Works* (Oxford: Oxford University Press, 1970).

8. Byron, quoted in Fiona MacCarthy, *Byron: Life and Legend* (London: John Murray, 2002).

9. Her Majesty Caroline, Queen of Great Britain, *Voyages and Travels* (London: Jones & Co., 1821), p. 440.

10. St. Clair, op. cit., p. 260.

11. Ibid.

12. John Henry Merryman, "Thinking About the Elgin Marbles," *Michigan Law Review*, vol. 83, no. 8 (August 1985). A Stanford University law professor, Merryman finds the moral weight of Greece's arguments legally insufficient to justify the return of the marbles. Subsequent events have nonetheless undermined a few of the arguments Merryman offers in this influential article. He asserts that the marbles "are well-mounted, maintained and guarded" in London, an arguable proposition at the time, which was gravely undermined by later revelation of serious and irreversible damage done to the sculptures in a 1937–38 "cleaning" in which workmen, trying to make the sculptures look more classically white, scraped away much of the natural, protective patina on the stone and, in some places, a layer of the marble itself. The tools and chemicals they used were intended for polishing granite and grinding steel implements. Although the revelation of this "cleaning" caused some public controversy at the time, the most damning museum documents on it were suppressed until 1996, when St. Clair brought them to light, leading to an internal museum probe and a 1999 international conference on the episode at which opponents and supporters of the museum's position almost literally came to blows. On the Acropolis, Greece has begun construction of a modern and secure museum, designed by Swiss-American architect Bernard Tschumi, to reunite the Parthenon sculptures indoors and away from pollution. An empty space will show where the London pieces would be. Merryman states, "If the time should come when they would be safer in Greece, then the preservation interest would argue for their return." There can be arguments for and against the return of the marbles, none of them having anything to do with the modern problem of looting, but it would seem that the time has come. On the 1930s cleaning, see St. Clair, op. cit., and for the other side, Ian Jenkins, *Cleaning and Controversy: The Parthenon Sculptures 1811–1939*, The British Museum Occasional Paper No. 146 (London: The British Museum, 2001), and Jenkins "The Elgin Marbles: Questions of Accuracy and Reliability," *International Journal of Cultural Property*, vol. 10, no. 1 (2001); on the 1999 conference, see Beard, op. cit., pp. 168–73; on the Acropolis Museum, Michael Glover, "Olympic Effort," *ARTnews* vol. 102, no. 3 (March 2002).

13. St. Clair, op. cit., p. 319.

14. Edmond About, quoted in St. Clair, op cit., p. 320.

15. Merryman, op. cit.

16. "Return the Parthenon Marbles," *New York Times*, February 2, 2002.

17. *New York Times*, April 18, 1982.

18. Neil MacGregor interview, 12.06.02.

19. Ibid.

20. Various writers have noted the role of tax deductions in encouraging the donation of antiquities. Meyer, op. cit., p. 43, wrote: "[U]nquestionably, American tax laws have been a powerful factor in the postwar art boom. . . . One can question, however, whether those who give looted art to museums should also benefit, as they now do, from this exceptional provision—whether in effect, the American taxpayer should subsidize the devastation of archaeological sites."

21. Internal Revenue Service, *The Art Advisory Panel of the Commissioner of Internal Revenue: Annual Summary Report for 1997 and—1998* (FOIA). In 1997 the donors of these artifacts from Africa, Oceania, and the Americas claimed their total value as $984,575. The panel cut the assessment to $841,625. In 1998 the claimed figure was $593,090, trimmed by the panel to $450,290. It should be noted that the overall claimed value of the artwork classified as "Africa, Oceania and the Americas" is much smaller than that for paintings and sculpture in the years cited. The reason that the average value of the non-Western art is lower than the $20,000 minimum for review by the board is that the artifacts were donated as complete collections, with a single deduction claimed for the whole collection but each piece reviewed separately. Established in 1969, the IRS Art Advisory Panel also reviews art received as inheritance and declared in tax returns. In 2000 it accepted without adjustment 52.4 percent of the appraisals submitted by taxpayers. The panel works almost exclusively from photographs, not the actual works of art, presumably making it even more difficult for the panel to make any serious review of the provenance of a questionable artifact. Daniel Grant, "Appraising Appraisals," *ARTnews*, vol. 101, no. 5 (May 2002).

22. Hugh Eakin, "Looted Antiquities?" *ARTnews*, vol. 101, no. 9 (October 2002); Roger Atwood, "A Public Disservice?" *ARTnews*, vol. 102, no. 2 (February 2003).

23. Eakin, op. cit.; see also Alexander Stille, *The Future of the Past* (New York: Farrar, Straus, and Giroux, 2002), pp. 71–95.

24. Thomas Hoving, *Making the Mummies Dance* (New York: Simon & Schuster, 1993), p. 217.

25. The presence of the fabled Lydian collection in the bowels of the Met was publicly known, or at least rumored, from 1970 when *The New York Times* first reported on it. See Meyer, op. cit., p. 66.

26. Lawrence M. Kaye, "The Future of the Past: Recovering Cultural Property," *Cardozo Journal of International and Comparative Law*, vol. 4, no. 1 (winter 1996).

27. Hoving, op. cit.

28. Kaye, op. cit.

29. Lawrence M. Kaye and Carla T. Main, "The Saga of the Lydian Hoard," in *Antiquities Trade or Betrayed*, ed. Kathryn W. Tubb (London: Archetype Publications, 1995).

30. Ibid. Turkey's case relied also on documents yielded by the Met, which Turkey's lawyers said showed that the Met staff knew the true origin of the pieces, and on statements by archaeologists attesting to the stylistic similarities between the looted pieces and those excavated by archaeologists nearby. All these elements bore parallels in the case of the looting of Sipán. Kaye and Main wrote, "Resolution of the Metropolitan case was not easy, and, the significance of the Metropolitan's willingness to resolve the matter should not be underestimated. One of the world's great museums has deaccessioned a major collection and returned it to the sovereign nation to which it belongs."

31. Ozgen quoted in Mike Toner, "The Objects of Their Desire," *Orange County Register*, November 28, 1999.

32. On the Weary Herakles, see Mark Rose and Ozgen Acar, "Turkey's War on Illicit Antiquities Trade, *Archaeology*, vol. 48, no. 2 (March/April 1995); Nancy Wilkie, "Moynihan's Mischief," *Archaeology*, vol. 53, no. 6 (November/December 2000); and Colin Renfrew, *Loot, Legitimacy, and Ownership* (London: Duckworth, 2000).

33. See Clemency Coggins's articles, including "The Maya Scandal: How Thieves Strip Sites of Past Cultures," *Smithsonian*, October 1970, and Meyer, op. cit.

34. Atwood, "Standing Up to the Smugglers." The Denver museum acquired the lintel in 1973 and repatriated it because it was an architectural object. Although the museum believed the piece entered the United States before 1972, curators felt that keeping it violated the spirit of that year's pre-Columbian art act, said the museum's curator of pre-Columbian art, Margaret Young-Sánchez. Interview, February 2000. Herrick, Feinstein was not involved in the Denver case.

35. "Maya Stela Fragment Returned," *Archaeology*, Online edition, September 3, 1999.

36. Angela Schuster, "The Search for Site Q," *Archaeology*, vol. 50, no. 5 (September/October 1997).

37. Alan Shestack, "The Museum and Cultural Property: The Transformation of Institutional Ethics," in Messenger, op. cit., p. 95.

38. Fabiola Fuentes Orellana, Guatemalan consul general in New York, interview, 02.11.00.

39. John Yemma and Walter V. Robinson, "Questionable collection; MFA Pre-Columbian Exhibit Faces Acquisition Queries," *Boston Globe*, December 4, 1997.

40. Fuentes Orellana interview, 02.11.00.

41. "The government [of Guatemala] was here. There was a meeting, but they did not come up with any new information to substantiate their claim," Getchell added. Interview, 02.28.00.

42. Philippe de Montebello interview, 12.19.02.

43. Ibid.

44. Hoving, quoted in Meyer, op. cit., p. 305.

45. Hoving, op. cit., pp. 318–21.

46. Ibid., p. 318.

47. Ibid., p. 338.

48. Hoving, quoted in Meyer, op. cit., p. 193.

49. See, for example, Shestack, op. cit., in which the associate director of the National Gallery of Art, Washington, writes, "Museums, heretofore naïve about the looting and mutilating of archaeological sites or unconcerned about the problem, are finally becoming more sensitive to the issues." He adds, "Museum professionals are acquirers; we are inherently greedy collectors. Most of us go into the profession because the desire to accumulate and bring together objects of quality is in our blood."

50. Cuno quoted by Robin Cembalest, "A Matter of Trust," *ARTnews*, vol. 11, no. 102 (December 2003).

51. Michael Kimmelman, "An Enduring Elitist and His Popular Museum," *New York Times*, November 3, 2002.

52. Martin Lerner interview, 12.09.03; UNESCO, *Cent objets disparus*.

53. James A. R. Nafziger, "International Penal Aspects of Protecting Cultural Property," *The International Lawyer*, vol. 19, no. 3 (summer 1985).

54. The 1906 law was strengthened by the 1979 Archaeological Resources Protection Act, but again this also applies only to public and tribal lands. Messenger, op. cit., p. 277; Barbara Purdy, *How to Do Archaeology the Right Way* (Gainesville: University Press of Florida, 1996), p. 156. It should be noted that many countries with laws barring extraction of archaeological

resources from private land have little ability, or sometimes inclination, to enforce those laws. U.S. law is more limited in scope but generally better enforced.

55. From a real estate ad in *The New York Times*, January 10, 2003, p. D5.

56. UNESCO Convention, reprinted in full in Renfrew, op. cit.

57. Mark B. Feldman and Ronald J. Bettauer, *Report of the United States Delegation to the Special Committee of Governmental Experts to Examine the Draft Convention on the Means of Prohibiting and Preventing the Illicit Import, Export, and Transfer of Ownership of Cultural Property* (Washington, D.C.: U.S. Department of State, 1970), p. 3; see also Paul M. Bator, "An Essay on the International Trade in Art," *Stanford Law Review*, vol. 34 (1982), in which Bator, a Harvard University law professor and member of the delegation in Paris, recounts how the Americans rejected an early draft by the UNESCO Secretariat that would have called for signatory states to impose a total prohibition on the import of *all* cultural property older than fifty years. The Americans at the conference objected to such an overarching "blank check" approach, saying it would constrain private business and make the UNESCO convention unworkably broad, a document "designed for a Heavenly City in which everything is utterly orderly, tidy, and subject to perfect and all-encompassing controls," wrote Bator. With the benefit of thirty-five years hindsight, it seems clear such an approach would have served only to make the convention fatten the pile of useless and irrelevant documents churned out by UNESCO in those years. Instead, the U.S. delegation supported, and got, a more targeted, bilateral enforcement mechanism that ended up giving the treaty its teeth. "Thus, it was provided that, if the cultural patrimony of a state is in jeopardy, the state would issue a call for help. The parties were to undertake an obligation, upon such a call, 'to discuss and to take appropriate measures to help remedy the situation, including the application of appropriate import controls to items . . . of great importance.'"

58. As a member of Sweden's delegation stated: "It is obvious that the draft convention is based on a conception that purchasers of illicitly imported cultural property would seldom be in good faith (Cf. art. 7(g)). The Ministry of Justice [of Sweden] cannot share this view but finds it more realistic to believe that the cases of bona fide possession will be rather numerous." *Report of the United States Delegation*, op. cit., p. 75.

59. Meyer, op. cit., p. 15.

60. Bator, op. cit., Feldman and Bettauer, op. cit., p. 42.

61. Ninety-seventh U.S. Congress, Senate, Report No. 97–564, "Miscellaneous Tariff, Trade, and Customs Matters," September 21, 1982.

62. Kareem Fahim, "The Whistle-Blower at the Art Party," *Village Voice*, August 6–12, 2003. Moynihan died in March 2003.

63. See Nafziger, op. cit., and Bator, op. cit.

64. John Henry Merryman, "Two Ways of Thinking About Cultural Property," *American Journal of International Law*, vol. 80, no. 4 (1986), p. 849.

65. Ibid., p. 848n.

66. Gillett G. Griffin, "Collecting Pre-Columbian Art," Messenger, op. cit., p. 109.

67. The stench was remarked by, among others, American lawyer Fred Truslow, who represented the Peruvian government in the case, interview 5.21.02; David Bernstein interview, 06.09.04, in which he said he was not sure if it was the smell that tipped off customs agents, telling me: "It's possible. There is a certain, unique embalming odor. It could have been that."

68. Ellen Herscher, "Peruvian Antiquities: The Bernstein Case and Others," *Journal of Field Archaeology*, vol. 9 (1982), pp. 531–32, 276–77; Harris, in Messenger, op. cit.; Nafziger, op. cit.

69. A picture of the Bernstein monkey head, duly credited to the dealer, appears in *Archaeology*, vol. 56, no. 1 (January/February 2003).

70. Bernstein interview, op. cit. Bernstein further suggested that the monkey head might have originated from Loma Negra, a site looted in the 1950s.

71. Department of the Treasury, U.S. Customs Service, *Federal Register* Notice, May 7, 1990; 55(88), pp. 19029–30.

72. Ibid.

73. Elia, in panel discussion transcript, in R. H. Howland, *Mycenaean Treasures of the Aegean Bronze Age Repatriated: Proceedings from a Seminar Sponsored by the Society for the Preservation of Greek Heritage and Held at the Ripley Center, Smithsonian Institution, Washington, D.C., January 27, 1996* (Washington, D.C.: Smithsonian Institution, 1997), pp. 59–60.

74. Mary Williams Walsh, "Grecian Treasure: Back from the Grave?" *Los Angeles Times*, August 12, 1996.

75. Shareen Brysac, "Mycenaean Jewelry Goes Home," *Archaeology*, vol. 49, no. 3 (May/June 1996).

76. Michael Ward, in comments to author, 05.06.04; Renfrew, op. cit., pp. 44–45; on the parallels between Aidonia artifacts and the Ward collection, see James Wright, "Thugs or Heroes? The Early Mycenaeans and Their Graves of Gold," in Howland, op. cit.; and Mark Rose, "Greece Sues for Mycenaean Gold," *Archaeology*, vol. 46, no. 5 (September/October 1993).

77. Wright, quoted in Rose, Ibid.

78. Ward, quoted in Walsh, op. cit. Greek officials indicated in news reports at the time that they would have preferred to have the case go to trial because it might have revealed the inner workings of the antiquities trade and possibly the whereabouts of more treasure believed to be from Aidonia. "If we had gone ahead with the trial, we would now know the names, and we could have broken the chain from Greece to Munich and to the New World," Yannis Tzedakis, director of antiquities at the Greek Ministry of Culture, was quoted as saying. There was a one-day seminar on the Mycenaean hoard during its stopover in Washington, whose papers and panel discussion can be found in Howland, op. cit.

79. James Wright, in correspondence with author, 06.14.04.

80. Fitzpatrick, quoted in Patricia Failing, "Conflict of Interests," *ARTnews*, vol. 100, no. 1 (January 2001).

81. Stiebel, quoted in Failing, op. cit.

82. *United States vs. Schultz*, United States Court of Appeals for the Second Circuit, No. 02-1357, Brief for the United States of America, p. 64.

83. *Federal Register* Notice: January 23, 2001; 66(15): pp. 7399–7402. Import Restrictions Imposed on Archaeological Material Originating in Italy and Representing the Pre-Classical, Classical, and Imperial Roman Period. In a bow to numismatists, coins were excluded from the Italian agreement.

84. James Cuno, "The Whole World's Treasures," *Boston Globe*, March 11, 2001.

85. Ricardo Elia interview, 12.18.02.

86. Ricardo Elia, "Analysis of the Looting, Selling, and Collecting of Apulian Red-Figure Vases: A Quantitative Approach," *Trade in Illicit Antiquities*, ed. Brodie et. al.

87. Ibid. Elia calculated that, of the 13,361 Apulian red-figure vases known to exist in the world, 9,347 appeared between the years 1767 and 1979. The rest appeared in 1980 or later. Thus nearly one-third of all such pieces appeared in only the twelve years until 1980, a staggering amount considering that the remaining two-thirds were discovered over the previous two centuries. His figures would suggest that in the years before the Italian MOU, the traffic in these kinds of looted objects from Italy was accelerating rapidly. Most, however, may not have been reaching the United States. Of the total 13,361 vases, 40 percent were in Italy as of 1992 and 12 percent were on U.S. soil.

88. Ibid.

89. Elia, in Rowland, op. cit., p. 60.

90. *United States vs. Schultz*, p. 9.

91. Cited in Peter Watson, "The Investigation of Frederick Schultz," *Culture Without Context*, no. 10 (spring 2002).

92. *United States vs. Schultz*, p. 9.

93. Ibid., pp. 19–20.

94. Ibid., p. 16.

95. U.S. Attorney Peter Nieman, quoted in "Selling the Past: The Trial," *Archaeology*, online edition, February 2002.

96. Ibid.

97. *United States vs. Schultz*, p. 45.

98. See Patty Gerstenblith, "United States v. Schultz," *Culture Without Context*, no. 10 (spring 2002). The Schultz ruling was upheld on appeal, and the U.S. Supreme Court let that ruling stand.

99. Ibid. I am grateful also to Lawrence Kaye of Herrick, Feinstein in New York, who was retained by the Egyptian side in the Schultz case, for sharing his views on the significance of the case.

100. Elia, quoted in Alexi Shannon Baker, "Selling the Past: United States v. Frederick Schultz," *Archaeology*, online edition, April 22, 2002.

101. "Selling the Past: Details on the Trial," *Archaeology*, online edition, 2002.

102. Ibid.

103. MacGregor interview, 12.06.02.

104. Hawkins, quoted in David D'Arcy, "Legal group to fight 'retentionist' policies," *Art Newspaper*, October 25, 2002.

105. William Pearlstein interview, April 2003; Roger Atwood, "The Disappearing Treasure of Iraq," *Washington Post*, April 23, 2003.

106. Orlando Mendez interview, 11.05.02.

9: The Smugglers

1. Orlando Mendez interview, 09.26.02.

2. Ibid.

3. My account of this meeting is based on interviews with Orlando Mendez, 09.26.02 and 11.05.02, and with Robert Wittman, 03.04.02 and 12.18.02.

4. Ibid.

5. My account of the alleged actions of the Peruvian players in the backflap case is based on their testimony in the subsequent legal proceedings in Lima, interviews with Mendez, Wittman, and Goldman, and others, and U.S. court documents. United States District Court, Eastern District of Pennsylvania, *United States v. Garcia and Mendez* (October 1997); República del Perú, Poder Judicial, declaración instructiva de Jorge Modesto Ramos Ronceros, op. cit.

6. Salas recounts the plane anecdote in República del Perú, Poder Judicial, declaración instructiva de Juan Carlos Ignacio Salas Arnaiz, March 17, 1999, page numbers illegible; Garcia's wife said he had never been in a plane accident.

7. Mendez interview, 09.26.02; Ramos Ronceros repeatedly declined to be interviewed. In his testimony later to Peruvian prosecutors he confirmed the $100,000 payment but denied knowing that Mendez and Garcia would take the backflap outside of Peru. He said he regarded the sale as a simple business operation. República del Perú, Poder Judicial, declaración instructiva de Jorge Modesto Ramos Ronceros.

8. Mendez interviews, 09.26.02 and 11.05.02; República del Perú, Poder Judicial, declaración instructiva de Juan Carlos Ignacio Salas Arnaiz, March 11, 1999, page numbers illegible; Ramos Ronceros, in his testimony, op. cit., said the money was wired to him in Lima, as do the indictments of Garcia, Mendez, and Iglesias in U.S. court and some later Peruvian news reports. Mendez, however, told me he was certain he transferred the money to a bank account in New York, not Peru. Juan Carlos Salas agreed in his testimony. This would seem to make more sense because, with U.S. pressure on drug-money operations, a transfer of that size to Lima would unquestionably raise red flags and might even be refused. Salas testified that he understood the money was transferred to a branch office to a Peruvian bank that operated inside the offices of an American bank in New York and that Ramos Ronceros then called the bank to ensure the deposit had been made before releasing the backflap.

9. The figures of $175,000 for Ramos Ronceros and $100,000 for Salas were cited by Peruvian prosecutors in their questioning of the two men in 1999, in both cases attributing the accusation to statements by Garcia and Mendez in the United States. República del Perú, Poder Judicial, declaración instructiva de Juan Carlos Ignacio Salas Arnaiz.

10. Mendez interviews, 09.25.02 and 09.26.02.

11. Ibid.

12. Elías Huamán recounts Garcia's visit and his impressions of Mendez in República del Perú, Poder Judicial, declaración instructiva de Guillermo Antonio Elías Huamán.

13. Elías Huamán's role and the fee he charged were stated by Peruvian prosecutors again citing statements by Garcia in the United States. República del Perú, Poder Judicial, declaración instructiva de Guillermo Antonio Elías Huamán.

14. Ibid.

15. Ibid.

16. Mendez interviews, 09.25.02 and 09.26.02.

17. Interviews, in confidence, with Panamanian diplomats, 2002.

18. República del Perú, Poder Judicial, declaración instructiva de Guillermo Antonio Elías Huamán.

19. República del Perú, Poder Judicial, declaración instructiva de Juan Carlos Ignacio Salas Arnaiz. Mendez also knew Salas was there for the backflap deal. Mendez interview, 11.05.02.

20. Wittman interview, 03.04.02; Mendez interviews, 09.25.02 and 09.26.02.

21. Wittman interview, 03.04.02.

10: The Consul

1. Article 41 of the Vienna Convention on Consular Relations and Optional Protocols of 1963: "Consular officers shall not be liable to arrest or detention pending trial, except in the case of a grave crime and pursuant to a decision by the competent judicial authority. 2. Except in the case specified in paragraph 1 of this Article, consular officers shall not be committed to prison or liable to any other form of restriction on their personal freedom save in execution of a judicial decision of final effect." Consulates are quite different from embassies, which are the representation of a foreign government to the government of the host country. Consulates mainly provide services to the citizens of the sending country who happen to be in the host country. The privileges and immunities that apply to the employees of embassies and consulates are similar but not identical.

2. Robert Goldman interview, 07.10.02.

3. Clark Erickson interview, 09.20.02.

4. Robert Sonin interview, 02.02.04.

5. Ibid.

6. Elizabeth Benson interview, 07.18.02.

7. Wittman interviews, 12.18.02 and 03.04.02.

8. Goldman interview, 07.10.02.

9. Ibid.

10. Mendez interview, 09.26.02.

11. Betty Brannan Jaen, "Vinculan consulado con contrabando," *La Prensa* (Panama), November 3, 1997.

12. Gionela Jordán, "Renuncia consul en Nueva York," *La Prensa*, November 4, 1997.

13. Interviews, in confidence, with Panamanian diplomats, 2002.

14. Wilfredo Jordán Serrano and Vilma E. Figueroa, "Ex consul niega nexo con tráfico de valiosas piezas arqueológicas," *La Prensa*, November 5, 1997.

15. This and the following paragraph, Mendez interview, 09.26.02.

16. In an essay published in Britain, Alva attributed the recovery to "good intelligence and excellent work by the Philadelphia FBI." Walter Alva, "The Destruction, Looting and Traffic of the Archaeological Heritage of Peru," *Trade in Illicit Atiquities*, ed. Brodie et al., p. 93.

17. Walter Alva interview, 11.13.02.

18. Like the UNESCO convention that followed it by seven months, the Philadelphia Declaration was a farsighted document that set an ethical benchmark that few at the time could meet. It read in part, "Probably the only effective way to stop this wholesale destruction of archaeological sites is to regulate the trade in cultural objects within each country just as most countries in the world today regulate domestic trade in foodstuffs, drugs, securities, and other commodities." Meyer recounts that the Harvard University museums took a similar stand in 1971 and the Field Museum in Chicago the following year. See Renfrew, op cit., p. 72; Meyer, op. cit., p. 75.

19. Erickson interview, 09.20.02.

20. Walter Alva interview, 02.25.04. Complete chemical analysis on the backflap and its metal content has, at this writing, not been carried out.

21. Samuel Bernal interviews.

22. Wittman interview, 03.04.02.

23. Stille, op. cit., p. 83.

11: The Golden Rattle

1. Brian Midkiff interview, 02.22.02.

2. Chávez interview, 02.19.02.

3. Ibid.; Wittman interview, 03.04.02.

4. Chávez interview, 02.19.02.

5. Midkiff interview, 02.22.02; Chávez interview, 02.19.02.

6. Chávez interview, 02.19.02; also, see Hollis Walker, "FBI Seizes Gold from Museum," *Santa Fe New Mexican,* October 1, 1998, in which Chávez made similar statements.

7. Ibid.

8. Midkiff interview, 02.22.02.

9. Midkiff interviews, 02.22.02, 09.24.02; Wittman interview, 03.04.02.

10. My account of the meeting is based on interviews with Midkiff and Wittman, except the dollar figures for the value of the pieces, which are from museum documents later forwarded to the U.S. Attorney's Office, District of New Mexico, and obtained under the Freedom of Information Act. Chávez was quoted in news reports as estimating the pieces' value at $60,000 to $150,000. See *Albuquerque Journal,* October 2, 1998.

11. Chávez interview, 02.19.02.

12. Wittman interview, 03.04.02.

13. Chávez interview, 02.19.02.

14. Chávez, quoted by Walker, op. cit.

15. Thomas Chávez, unpublished letter to William Walters, editorial page editor, *Santa Fe New Mexican,* dated October 2, 1998, made available to the author.

16. República del Perú, Ministerio de Educación, Resolución Ministerial no. 628 98-ED, October 19, 1998.

17. Walter Alva interview, 12.12.01.

18. Ibid.

19. Chávez interview, 02.19.02.

20. Ibid.

21. John Bourne, letter to author, April 23, 2002.

22. Alva affidavit to FBI, Santa Fe, October 24, 1998 (FOIA).

23. Heather Lechtman, "Traditions and Styles in Central Andean Metalworking," *The Beginning of the Use of Metals and Alloys*, ed. Robert Maddin (Cambridge: MIT Press, 1988).

24. Such a furnace is described in Christopher Donnan, "A Precolumbian Smelter from Northern Peru," *Archaeology*, vol. 26, no. 4 (October 1973).

25. Wester interviews; Alva interview, 11.13.02.

26. Alva interview, 11.13.02.

27. Ibid.

28. Hollis Walker, "Archaeologist: Museum Items Were Stolen," *Santa Fe New Mexican*, October 25, 1998.

29. Heinz Plenge, "The Robber's Tale," *Connoisseur* (New York), February 1990.

30. Plenge, in an interview 04.12.02, stood by his story. At least one photograph in the article, the monkey's head, could not have been taken on the backseat of Bernal's car, as the article claimed, because it was not discovered at La Mina until 1988, a year after Bernal's death.

31. Gabriel Apesteguía interviews, op. cit.

32. Lavalle, *Oro del antiguo Perú*.

33. Alva affidavit to FBI Santa Fe, op. cit.

34. Hingston, in Messenger, op. cit., p. 135.

35. See Paul Ciotti, "Don't Call Him Indiana Jones," *Los Angeles Times*, September 22, 1988.

36. Christopher Donnan interview, 03.11.04.

37. Ibid.

38. Kirkpatrick, op. cit., p. 152; Nagin, op. cit.

39. Nagin, op. cit.; see also, Brian Alexander, "Archaeology and Looting Make a Volatile Mix," *Science*, vol. 250 (November 1990), and Donnan's subsequent letter in *Science*.

40. Chávez interview, 02.29.00. Documents obtained through the Freedom of Information Act did not contain any written opinion by Donnan, and, judging from U.S. Attorney Sasha Siemel's letter quoted below, officials at the U.S. Attorney's office may never have seen Donnan's opinion, although they were evidently aware of it.

41. Donnan interview, 03.11.04.

42. Alva interview, 05.06.02.

43. Ed Able, quoted in Walker, "Archaeologist: Museum Items Were Stolen."

44. Chávez, unpublished letter, op. cit.

45. My account of the dinner and its aftermath is based on accounts from Alva, Chávez, Midkiff, and Wittman.

46. Walker, "Archaeologist: Museum Items Were Stolen."

47. Midkiff interview, 02.22.02.

48. Chávez interview, 02.19.02.

49. Alva interview, 12.12.01.

50. Doubts about the authenticity of the crown prevented it from going on public exhibit from more than four years. During that period, it stayed in storage at the Brüning. There was no question the piece was made of real gold, but curators at the museum thought the incisions on the piece looked too recent. The museum later concluded it was real on the basis of expert opinion, although chemical tests that might ascertain its age have not been carried out at this writing.

51. Alva to Chávez, private correspondence, November 21, 1998 (FOIA). Author's translation.

52. Malavé to Alva, private correspondence, May 10, 1999 (FOIA). Assistant U.S. Attorney Paula Burnett was copied.

53. Eduardo Rivoldi, Counselor, Cultural Department, Embassy of Peru, to Burnett, private correspondence, December 29, 1998 (FOIA).

54. Burnett to Soller, private correspondence, November 3, 1998 (FOIA).

55. Soller to Burnett, private correspondence, March 26, 1999 (FOIA).

56. Ibid.

57. Ibid.

58. Siemel to Chávez, private correspondence, January 4, 2000 (FOIA). The note was copied to Wittman, Midkiff, Soller, Burnett, and an official at the Peruvian embassy in Washington.

59. Prosecutors declined to comment personally on the case in detail. Bob Gorence, acting U.S. Attorney at the time and now in private practice in Albuquerque, told me: "We tried to be aggressive on issues of stolen antiquities but there was an evidentiary problem here." Gorence interview, 06.17.02.

60. Chávez interview, 02.29.00.

61. Ibid.

62. Donnan interview, 03.11.04.

63. Lavalle, op. cit.

64. Midkiff interview, 02.22.02.

65. Wittman interview, 03.04.02.

66. María Elena Córdova interview, op. cit.

67. Bourne, letter to author, April 23, 2003.

68. Ed Able interview, 06.05.02.

12: The Jaguar's Head

1. Kathryn Zedde, of the Department of Canadian Heritage, quoted in Atwood, "Standing Up to the Smugglers."

2. Luis Repetto interview, 02.17.00.

3. Ibid.

4. República del Perú, Poder Judicial, Novena Fiscalía Provincial en lo Penal de Lima, Denuncia no. 754–98, January 6, 1999.

5. República del Perú, Poder Judicial, Declaración instructiva de Guillermo Antonio Elías Huamán, page number illegible.

6. Ibid.

7. República del Perú, Poder Judicial, Declaración instructiva de Juan Carlos Salas Arnaiz, p. 170. The name of the prosecutor in Salas's and Ramos's testimony is unclear from the transcript, but it is not Judge Piedra.

8. Ibid.

9. República del Perú, Poder Judicial, Declaración instructiva de Jorge Modesto Ramos Ronceros, page numbers illegible. The fourth person indicted was Luis Bacigalupo.

10. Goldman interview, 07.10.02.

11. *El Comercio*, February 5, 2000.

12. Walter Alva, "Problemática y puesta en valor del patrimonio arqueológico peruano," *Patrimonio cultural del Perú* (Lima: Fondo Editorial del Congreso del Perú, 2000). This two-volume set includes the texts of all speeches given at this important conference.

13. Ibid.

14. Ibid.

15. Adriana von Hagen, "Feathers for the King: Bird Trappers at the Laguna de los Cóndores," unpublished paper, Museo Leymebamba (Leymebamba, Peru, 2002).

16. Interviews with Adriana von Hagen, Sonia Guillén, and Miguel Huamán, July–August 2002; see also Sonia Guillén and Adriana von Hagen, "Tombs with a View," *Archaeology,* vol. 51, no. 2 (March/April 1998).

17. María Luz de Zyriek interview, 11.26.01.

18. Fernando Paniagua interview, 01.14.02. Roger Atwood, "Straight Outta Brooklyn," *Archaeology,* vol. 55, no.3 (May/June 2002).

19. The Honduran case was especially important because there was no bilateral treaty between the two countries. The pieces were seized and repatriated because of false statements in the customs declaration; the shippers said they had paid $11,000 in Honduras for the pieces but declared their value in Miami as only $37.

20. MFA officials admitted this to *The Boston Globe* in its series on the vases. "MFA officials said they are confident the pieces from Guatemala, which [collector and museum trustee Landon] Clay donated in 1988, entered the United States before the import restrictions took effect and before a 1983 law that bound the United States to the provisions of a 1970 UNESCO convention aimed at stopping the international trafficking in looted artifacts." John Yemma and Walter V. Robinson, "Questionable Collection," *Boston Globe,* December 4, 1997.

21. *American Indian Art,* vol. 28, no. 1 (November 2002); *Arizona Republic,* September 25, 2003; Wittman interview, 12.18.02.

22. Wittman interview, 03.04.02.

13: The Brigades

1. Portions of this chapter and Chapter 1 originally appeared in Roger Atwood, "Guardians of the Dead," *Archaeology,* vol. 58, no. 1 (January/February 2003).

2. I was not present at the ceremony. I am grateful to Alva's staff at the Museum of the Nation, Lima, for providing me with a videotape of it; see also "No más saqueos en zonas arqueológicas, juramentaron grupos de protección," *La Industria* (Chiclayo), July 1, 1995.

3. Alva's paper "The Úcupe Murals at the Valle de la Zaña, Northern Peru," was published in 1983 by the German Archaeological Institute, which also in part financed the excavation.

4. "Preso ex presidente de Cayaltí," *La Industria* (Chiclayo), May 5, 1996; "Policía decomisa piezas arqueológicas en Cayaltí," *La Industria* (Chiclayo), July 17, 1999.

5. "Huaqueros a la fiscalía," *La Industria* (Chiclayo), January 16, 1996.

6. Guillermo Cock, "Inca Rescue," *National Geographic*, May 2002; see also Roger Atwood, "Squeezing the Squatters," *Archaeology*, vol. 55, no. 4 (July/August 2002).

7. This particular land invasion was large enough to appear in the papers the next day. "Frustran invasión a reserva arqueológica de Mocupe; 80 familias quisieron apoderarse de área" *La Industria* (Chiclayo), December 14, 2001.

8. Gerardo Pérez Descalzi, "Trabajadores de la empresa azucarera y comuneros invasores se enfrentan en brutal batalla campal" *La República* (Lima), January 15, 2003; *New York Times*, January 15, 2003. The number of dead was never clarified; numbers given by press reports ranged from eight to thirteen.

9. Walter Alva, "The Destruction, Looting and Traffic of the Archaeological Heritage of Peru," in *Trade in Illicit Antiquities*, ed. Brodie et al.

10. Ibid.

14: Recovering the Past

1. Worldwide container shipping volumes doubled in the seven years up to 2003, according to the Shipping Statistics and Market Review. Growth has been concentrated in Asia, with Hong Kong, Singapore, and Busan now the busiest container shipping ports in the world.

2. Hugh Thomson, *The White Rock* (Woodstock, N.Y.: Overlook Press, 2001), p. 97; Guillen, communication with author, August 2004.

3. Internal Revenue Service, *The Art Advisory Panel of the Commissioner of Internal Revenue: Annual Summary Report for 1997, —1998*, and—*2002*; Grant, op. cit.

4. Marina Papa Sokal, "Stemming the Illegal Trade in Antiquities," *Culture Without Context*, no. 11 (fall 2002).

5. María Elena Córdova interview, op. cit.

15: Coming Home

1. Kirkpatrick relates the story, op. cit., p. 86.

2. I am grateful to many friends and associates of Susana Meneses de Alva, in particular Vania Távara Palacios, for their recollections.

3. Walter Alva interview, 12.11.01.

4. Ibid.

5. For a news account, see "Restos del Señor de Sipán ya están en el museo Tumbas Reales," *El Comercio,* October 11, 2002.

6. For a news account of Toledo's inauguration, see Reuters, "Peru's New President Replays Inauguration In Ancestral Andes," *New York Times,* July 30, 2001.

7. Donnan, *Moche Art of Peru,* pp. 100–01; Moseley, op. cit., pp. 262–64; Federico Kauffmann Doig, "Orfebrería lambayecana," *Oro del Antiguo Perú,* Lavalle, ed., op cit., pp. 258–59.

8. Moseley, op. cit., p. 262.

9. Cited in Kauffmann Doig, op. cit.

Epilogue

1. Ralph Blumenthal, "Spanish Police and F.B.I. Get Their Men and Stolen Art," *New York Times,* June 26, 2002; see also Daniel Woolls, "The Spanish Sting," *ARTnews,* vol. 101, no. 9 (September 2002).

2. Chávez interview, 02.29.00.

3. Frances Levine, letter to author, September 12, 2002.

4. Orlando Mendez interview, 09.25.02.

5. Dañan con maquinaria pesada mural en huaca Dos Cabezas," *El Comercio,* July 27, 2001; Colleen Popson, "Moche Mug Shots," *Archaeology,* vol. 27, no. 2 (March/April 2004).

6. José Rosales and Santiago Cubillas, "Sorprenden a huaqueros cuando empacaban restos arqueológicos," *El Comercio,* September 18, 2002.

7. D'Arcy, "Legal Group to Fight 'Retentionist' Polices," op. cit.

8. Ibid.

9. William Pearlstein interview, 04.17.03, in which Pearlstein said his comment, originally in *Science* magazine, was "the stupidest thing I ever said. It was very ill-considered on my part . . . There was no intention to relax Iraqi antiquities policy."

10. André Emmerich, "Let the Market Preserve Art," *Wall Street Journal,* April 24, 2003.

11. Edmund L. Andrews, "Iraqi Looters Tearing Up Archaeological Sites," *New York Times,* May 23, 2003.

12. See John Simpson, "Why I Fear for the Safety of Iraq's Monuments," *Daily Telegraph* (London), September 28, 2003.

13. Russell to author and others, private correspondence, October 1, 2003.

14. "Building Trust in Iraq," *Archaeology,* vol. 27, no. 1 (January/February 2004).

15. Ibid.

GLOSSARY

algarobo. A tree, genus *Pithecellobium,* that grows in arid areas of coastal Peru, prized for its hard wood and its sap, which is used to make traditional medicines and syrups.

backfill. The soil removed during mining, archaeology, or other excavation.

backflap. A piece of metal body armor worn in combat by male members of the Moche elite and covering the lower back and buttocks.

Chavín. Civilization centered in Peru's northern highlands around Cajamarca, from about 900 to 300 B.C., whose cultural influence was felt throughout the Andes.

chicha. A mildly alcoholic beverage drunk throughout the Andes, usually made with fermented corn, although drinks called *chicha* are made from various fruits and grains.

Chimú. A pre-Hispanic people who lived on the north coast of Peru, with its capital at Chan Chan near the present-day Trujillo, from about A.D. 1000 to 1470, when it was conquered by the Cuzco-based Incas.

chullpa. A funerary monument or tower in pre-Hispanic Peru, often found on a ledge, island, or other isolated locale.

coca. An evergreen shrub, genus *Erythroxylum,* of the Andes whose leaves, when chewed, have a mild anesthetic effect and are believed to ward off hunger; cocaine is made from it.

context. In archaeology, a description of the surroundings and position of an artifact in its original spot.

El Niño. A warm Pacific Ocean current that, when it shifts southward and reaches Peruvian coasts, causes heavy rains and flooding.

estelero. Guatemalan word for a professional looter; derived from *estela*, the Spanish word for stele (see below).

Grupa. Acronym for *grupo de protección arqueológica*, citizens' patrols formed in parts of northern Peru to combat looting.

huaca. In pre-Hispanic Peru, any sacred place or object but particularly any one of the thousands of burial mounds on the Peruvian coastal plain made of adobe bricks. Also spelled *waka*.

huaco. In Peru, any pre-Hispanic ceramic vessel or pot.

huaquero. One who digs for huacos; a looter. Has given rise to the verb *huaquear*, to dig for *huacos*.

Inca. A pre-Hispanic culture with its capital in Cuzco, noted for its sophisticated architecture and system of government, that ruled much of present-day Peru from about 1400 to the mid-16th century, when it was conquered by the Spaniards.

khipu. A knotted-string device used in Inca times for recordkeeping and accounting.

llonque. Liquor made from sugarcane.

Moche. A Peruvian pre-Hispanic culture, noted for its sophisticated art, metallurgy, and engineering. The Moche lived on the northern coast from about the year 100 B.C. to A.D. 700. Also known as Mochica.

provenance (or provenience). The precise place where an artifact is found and a description of its three-dimensional surroundings; more generally, the history of the location in physical space of an object once removed from its context, and its chain of ownership.

Quechua. The principal indigenous language of Peru, spoken today by about one-quarter of Peru's 25 million people.

San Pedro. A Peruvian coastal plant, genus *Trichocereus*, whose leaves and roots are boiled to produce a hallucinogenic drink.

Sicán. A pre-Hispanic culture of north-coast Peru centered on the Batán Grande *huaca* complex near Chiclayo, dating from roughly A.D. 800 to 1200. Also known as Lambayeque culture, and not to be confused with

Sipán, a Moche site about forty miles south of Batán Grande and dating from A.D. 100.

stele. An upright stone slab with an inscribed or sculpted surface.

tombarolo. Italian word for looter.

Wari. A pre-Hispanic civilization that flourished on the southern coast and highlands of present-day Peru, roughly A.D. 700–1100, whose cultural influence was felt throughout the Andes. Also spelled Huari.

ziggurat. In ancient Iraq, a temple tower built in the form of a terraced pyramid.

SELECT BIBLIOGRAPHY

Books

Alva, Walter. *Sipán*. Lima: Colección Cultura y Artes del Perú, 1994.

—— and Christopher B. Donnan. *Royal Tombs of Sipán*. Los Angeles: UCLA Fowler Museum of Natural History, 1993.

Aruz, Joan, ed. *Art of the First Cities*. New York: Metropolitan Museum of Art, 2003.

Beard, Mary. *The Parthenon*. London: Profile Books, 2002.

Boone, Elizabeth Hill. *Andean Art at Dumbarton Oaks*, vol. 1. Washington, D.C.: Dumbarton Oaks Research Library and Collection, 1996.

Borges, Jorge Luis. *Ficciones*. Buenos Aires: Emecé Editores, 1956.

Braudel, Fernand. *The Structures of Everyday Life*, trans. Siân Reynolds. New York: Harper & Row, 1979.

Brodie, Neil, Jennifer Doole, and Colin Renfrew, eds. *Trade in Illicit Antiquities: The Destruction of the World's Archaeological Heritage*. Cambridge, England: McDonald Institute for Archaeological Research, 2001.

Byron, Lord. *Complete Poetical Works*. London and New York: Oxford University Press, 1970.

Caroline, Queen of Great Britain. *Voyages and Travels*. London: Jones & Co., 1821.

Carter, Howard. *The Tomb of Tutankhamen*. London: Cassell, 1923–; Washington, D.C.: National Geographic Society, 2003.

Casas, Bartolemé de las. *Breve relación de la destrucción de las Indias Occidentales*. 1542. Reprint, Mexico: Libros Luciérnaga, 1957.

Chamberlin, Russell. *Loot! The Heritage of Plunder*. New York: Facts on File, 1983.

Denevan, William M. *Cultivated Landscapes of Native Amazonia and the Andes*. London and New York: Oxford University Press, 2001.

Diamond, Jared. *Guns, Germs, and Steel: The Fates of Human Societies*. New York: W. W. Norton, 1997.

Donnan, Christopher B. *Moche Art of Peru: Pre-Columbian Symbolic Communication*. Los Angeles: Museum of Cultural History, University of California, 1978.

—— and Donna McClelland. *Moche Fineline Painting: Its Evolution and Its Artists*. Los Angeles: UCLA Fowler Museum of Cultural History, 1999.

Emmerich, André. *Sweat of the Sun and Tears of the Moon: Gold and Silver in Pre-Columbian Art*. Seattle: University of Washington Press, 1965.

Fondo Editorial del Congreso del Perú. *Patrimonio cultural del Perú*. vols. 1 and 2. Lima: Fondo Editorial del Congresso del Perú, 2000.

Freeman, Michael, and Claude Jacques. *Ancient Angkor*. Bangkok: Asia Books, 1999.

Gibson, Charles. *Spain in America*. New York: Harper Colophon, 1966.

Gündüz, Réna. *El mundo ceremonial de los huaqueros*. Lima: Editorial Universitaria, 2001.

Hemming, John. *The Conquest of the Incas*. New York: Harcourt Brace Jovanovich, 1970.

Hoving, Thomas. *Making the Mummies Dance: Inside the Metropolitan Museum of Art*. New York: Simon & Schuster Touchstone, 1993.

ICOM [International Council of Museums]. *Cent objets disparus: pillage à Angkor*. Paris: ICOM, 1997.

Jenkins, Ian. *Cleaning and Controversy: The Parthenon Sculptures 1811–1939*. London: The British Museum, Occasional Paper, No. 146, 2001.

Jenkins, Myra Ellen, and Albert H. Schroeder. *A Brief History of New Mexico*. Albuquerque: University of New Mexico Press, 1974.

Jones, Julie, ed. *The Art of Precolumbian Gold: The Jan Mitchell Collection*. Boston: Little, Brown, 1985.

Keats, John. *Complete Poems and Selected Letters*. New York: Modern Library, 2001.

Kirkpatrick, Sidney D. *Lords of Sipán: A True Story of Pre-Inca Tombs, Archaeology, and Crime*. New York: William Morrow, 1992.

Lavalle, José Antonio de, ed. *Oro del antiguo Perú*. Lima: Banco de Crédito del Perú, 1992.

——. *Moche*. Lima: Banco de Crédito del Perú, 1985; 2d ed., 1989.

—— and Werner Lang, eds. *Paracas*. Lima: Banco de Crédito del Perú, 1983; 2d ed., 1990.

MacCarthy, Fiona. *Byron: Life and Legend*. London: John Murray, 2002.

Maddin, Robert, ed. *The Beginning of the Use of Metals and Alloys*. Cambridge: MIT Press, 1988.

Marcus, Amy Dockser. *The View from Nebo: How Archaeology Is Rewriting the Bible and Reshaping the Middle East*. Boston: Back Bay Books, 2000.

Mason, Alden J. *The Ancient Civilizations of Peru*. London and New York: Pelican, 1957; Revised Edition, 1968.

Messenger, Phyllis Mauch, ed. *The Ethics of Collecting Cultural Property*. Albuquerque: University of New Mexico Press, 1989; 2d edition, 1999.

Meyer, Karl E. *The Plundered Past: The Story of the Illegal International Traffic in Works of Art*. New York: Atheneum, 1973.

Moseley, Michael E. *The Incas and their Ancestors: The Archaeology of Peru*. London and New York: Thames and Hudson, 1992; rev. ed., 2001.

Murúa, Fray Martín de. *Historia general del Perú*. c. 1600. Reprint, Madrid: Dastin, 2001.

Oates, Joan. *Babylon*. London: Thames and Hudson, 1979; rev. ed., 1986.

Pillsbury, Joanne, ed. *Moche Art and Archaeology in Ancient Peru*. Washington, D.C.: National Gallery of Art, 2001.

Purdy, Barbara A. *How to Do Archaeology the Right Way*. Gainesville: University Press of Florida, 1996.

Ramírez, Susan Elizabeth. *The World Upside Down: Cross-Cultural Contact and Conflict in Sixteenth-Century Peru*. Palo Alto: Stanford University Press, 1996.

Renfrew, Colin. *Loot, Legitimacy and Ownership: The Ethical Crisis in Archaeology*. London: Duckworth, 2000.

Russell, John Malcolm. *The Final Sack of Nineveh*. New Haven: Yale University Press, 1998.

——. *From Nineveh to New York: The Strange Story of the Assyrian Reliefs in the Metropolitan Museum and the Hidden Masterpiece at Canford School*. New Haven: Yale University Press, 1997.

St. Clair, William. *Lord Elgin and the Marbles*. London and New York: Oxford University Press, 1967; 3d ed., 1998.

Salomon, Frank, and Stuart B. Schwartz. *The Cambridge History of the Native Peoples of the Americas: Volume III, South America*. Cambridge, U.K.: Cambridge University Press, 1999.

Shimada, Izumi. *Pampa Grande and the Mochica Culture*. Austin: University of Texas Press, 1994.

Someda, Hidefuji. *El imperio de los Incas: imágen del Tahuantinsuyu creada por los cronistas*. Lima: Fondo Editorial de la Pontificia Universidad Católica del Perú, 2001.

Stille, Alexander. *The Future of the Past*. New York: Farrar, Straus and Giroux, 2002.

Thomson, Hugh. *The White Rock: An Exploration of the Inca Heartland*. Woodstock, N.Y.: Overlook Press, 2001.

Tubb, Kathryn Walker. *Antiquities Trade or Betrayed: Legal, Ethical & Conservation Issues*. London: Archetype Publications, 1995.

Uceda, Santiago, and Elías Mujica, eds. *Moche: propuestas y perspectivas*. Trujillo, Peru: Universidad Nacional de La Libertad, 1994.

Valcárcel, Luis E. *Memorias*. Lima: Instituto de Estudios Peruanos, 1981.

Wearne, Phillip. *Return of the Indian: Conquest and Revival in the Americas*. Philadelphia: Temple University Press, 1996.

Articles and Periodicals

Alberge, Dalya. "Collector to Fight Iraq over 'Stolen' Sculpture," *The Times* (London), October 29, 1998.

Alexander, Brian. "Archaeology and Looting Make a Volatile Mix," *Science*, vol. 250 (November 1990).

Alva, Walter. "Discovering the New World's Richest Unlooted Tomb," *National Geographic*, vol. 174, no. 4 (October 1988).

——"New Moche Tomb: Royal Splendor in Peru," *National Geographic*, vol. 177, no. 6 (January 1990).

Atwood, Roger, "Standing Up to the Smugglers," *ARTnews*, vol. 99, no. 6 (June 2000).

——"Guardians of the Dead," *Archaeology*, vol. 56, no. 1 (January/February 2003).

——"A Public Disservice?" *ARTnews*, vol. 102. no. 2 (February 2003).

Bailey, Martin, "A New UK Law to Fight the Illicit Trade," *The Art Newspaper*, January 12, 2004.

Barreto, Mabel. "Panorama mortal." *Sí* (Lima), April 27, 1987.

Bator, Paul. "An Essay on the International Trade in Art." *Stanford Law Review*, vol. 34 (January 1982).

Bourget, Steve. "Politics of Oblivion: Looting and Destruction of Ancient Andean Sites in Peru." Unpublished paper, MacDonald Institute, University of Cambridge (Cambridge, U.K., 2000).

Cock, Guillermo. "Inca Rescue." *National Geographic*, vol. 201, no. 5 (May 2002).

D'Arcy, David. "Legal Group to Fight 'Retentionist' Policies." *Art Newspaper*, October 25, 2002.

Donnan, Christopher B. "Unraveling the Mystery of the Warrior-Priest." *National Geographic*, no. 174 (October 1988).

——. "A Precolumbian Smelter from Northern Peru." *Archaeology*, vol. 26, no. 4 (October 1973).

—— and Donna McClelland. "The Burial Theme in Moche Iconography." *Studies in Pre-Columbian Art & Archaeology*, no. 21, *Dumbarton Oaks* (1979).

Eakin, Hugh. "Debating 'Illegal Archaeology.'" *ARTnews*, vol. 102, no. 8 (September 2003).

——. "Looted Antiquities?" *ARTnews*, vol. 101, no. 9 (October 2002).

Elia, Ricardo J. "Chopping Away Culture." *Boston Globe* December 21, 1997.

Emmerich, André. "Let the Market Preserve Art." *Wall Street Journal*, April 24, 2003.

Fahim, Kareem. "The Whistle-Blower at the Art Party." *Village Voice*, August 6–12, 2003.

Failing, Barbara. "Conflict of Interests." *ARTnews*, vol. 100, no. 1 (January 2001).

Gerstenblith, Patty. "United States v. Schultz." *Culture Without Context*, no. 10 (spring 2002).

Gibson, McGuire. "The Loss of Archaeological Context and the Illegal Trade in Mesopotamian Antiquities." *Culture Without Context*, no. 1 (fall 1997).

——. "Cultural Tragedy in Iraq." *IFAR Journal*, vol. 6, nos. 1 and 2 (2003).

Gottlieb, Martin, and Barry Meier. "Of 2,000 Treasures Stolen in Gulf War of 1991, Only 12 Have Been Recovered." *New York Times*, May 1, 2003.

Grant, Daniel. "Appraising Appraisals." *ARTnews*, vol. 101, no. 5 (May 2002).

Gugliotta, Guy. "U.S., Italy Act to Halt Pillage of Antiquities." *Washington Post*, January 20, 2001.

Haner, Jim. "Career Criminal Faces Last Stand." *The Sun* (Baltimore), August 6, 1995.

Jenkins, Ian. "The Elgin Marbles: Questions of Accuracy and Reliability." *International Journal of Cultural Property*, vol. 10, no. 1 (2000).

Kaulicke, Peter. "Investigación y protección del patrimonio arqueológico: balance y perspectives." Unpublished paper, Pontificia Universidad Católica del Perú (Lima, 2000).

Kaye, Lawrence M. "The Future of the Past: Recovering Cultural Property." *Cardozo Journal of International and Comparative Law*, vol. 4, no. 1 (winter 1996).

Merryman, John Henry. "Thinking About the Elgin Marbles." *Michigan Law Review*, vol. 83, no. 8 (August 1985).

——. "Two Ways of Thinking About Cultural Property." *American Journal of International Law*, vol. 18, no. 4 (1986).

Nafziger, James A. R. "International Penal Aspects of Protecting Cultural Property." *International Lawyer*, vol. 19, no. 3 (summer 1985).

Nagin, Carl. "The Peruvian Gold Rush." *Art & Antiques* (May 1990).

Paley, Samuel M. "Nimrud, the War, and the Antiquities Markets." *IFAR Journal*, vol. 6, nos. 1 and 2 (2003).

Popson, Colleen. "Grim Rites of the Moche." *Archaeology*, vol. 55, no. 2 (March/April 2002).

Renfrew, Colin. "A Thieves' Kitchen." *Times Literary Supplement* (London), June 30, 2000.

Rose, Mark, and Ozgen Acar, "Turkey's War on Illicit Antiquities Trade." *Archaeology*, vol. 48, no. 2 (March/April 1995).

Toner, Mike. "The Objects of Their Desire." *Orange County Register*, November 28, 1999.

Verano, John. "Human Skeletal Remains from Tomb 1, Sipán (Lambayeque River Valley, Peru); and Their Social Implications." *Antiquity*, no. 71 (1997).

Watson, Peter. "The Investigation of Frederick Schultz." *Culture Without Context*, no. 10 (spring 2002).

Yemma, John, and Walter V. Robinson. "Questionable Collection; MFA Pre-Columbian Exhibit Faces Acquisition Queries." *Boston Globe*, December 4, 1997.

Zileri, Marco. "Ampay Sipán." *Caretas* (Lima), no. 1487 (1997).

Documents

Government of Peru vs. Benjamin Johnson, et al., United States Court of Appeals for the Ninth Circuit (Los Angeles), Docket No. 90-55521, 1990.

Peru vs. Peruvian Artifacts, et al., defendants, United States District Court, Central District of California, No. CV 88-6990-WPG (later *Government of Peru vs. Benjamin Johnson, et al.*, same case no.), 1989–90.

Report of the Cultural Property Advisory Committee on the Request from the Government of the Republic of Italy, Recommending U.S. Import Restrictions on Certain Categories of Archaeological Material, U.S. Department of State, 1999.

Report of the United States Delegation to the Special Committee of Governmental Experts to Examine the Draft Convention on the Means of Prohibiting and Preventing the Illicit Import, Export, and Transfer of Ownership of Cultural Property, Prepared by Mark B. Feldman and Ronald J. Bettauer, U.S. Department of State, 1970.

República del Perú, Poder Judicial, 31era Fiscalía Provincial en lo Penal de Lima, denuncia no. 754-98, declaración instructiva de Luis Eduardo Bacigalupo Remy, 1999

————— declaración instructiva de Jorge Modesto Ramos Ronceros, 1999

————— declaración instructiva de Guillermo Antonio Elías Huamán, 1999

————— declaración instructiva de Juan Carlos Ignacio Salas Arnaiz, 1999.

United States of America vs. Denis Garcia and Orlando Mendez, United States District Court for the Eastern District of Pennsylvania (Philadelphia), Indictment, 1997.

United States of America vs. Francisco Iglesias, aka "Frank," United States District Court for the Eastern District of Pennsylvania (Philadelphia), Indictment, 1998.

United States of America vs. Frederick Schultz, United States Court of Appeals for the Second Circuit (New York), Docket No. 02-1357, 2002.

INDEX

ABOUT THE AUTHOR

ROGER ATWOOD is a journalist whose articles on art, culture, and politics have appeared in *ARTnews, Archaeology, The New Republic, The Washington Post, Mother Jones,* and *The Sunday Telegraph* (London). He was a correspondent for the news agency Reuters in Latin America for ten years, serving as its bureau chief in Chile, and a fellow at the Alicia Patterson Foundation. He holds degrees from the University of Massachusetts and the School of Advanced International Studies at John Hopkins University. He lives in Washington, D.C., and in Maine, in a house built by his great-great-grandfather.